MINNESOTA AND THE MANIFEST DESTINY
OF THE CANADIAN NORTHWEST

MINNESOTA *and the* MANIFEST DESTINY *of the* CANADIAN NORTHWEST

A Study in
Canadian-American Relations

ALVIN C. GLUEK, JR.

University of Toronto Press

For Ellen

Preface

FROM THE LAKE OF THE WOODS TO THE ROCKY MOUNTAINS, ONLY A LINE separates Canada from the United States—the mute evidence of each nation's manifest destiny. As a boundary, the 49th parallel is entirely man-made and will never really divide the Northern Great Plains, for it is a region at once geographically and historically united. Certainly from 1821 to 1869–70, the years limiting this study, a unity was most evident; the history of the British Northwest was inextricably bound up with that of the American Northwest.

Within this half-century, there were three means of access to the Northern Great Plains and each of them played a significant part in the history of the area. The border lakes and rivers—presently dividing the Province of Ontario from the State of Minnesota—stretched westward, a watery chain linking the St. Lawrence and the Great Lakes to the Red River. This route carried first French-Canadian and then English-Canadian fur traders into the Northwest. It traversed magnificent canoe country, blessed with deep, clear lakes and breath-taking palisades but cursed with a terrain so rugged that many Manitobans motoring to eastern Canada still detour below the border in order to travel more rapidly and more comfortably. Hudson Bay provided the second entrance to these inland plains; from bayside a long line of rivers, lakes, and portages bore the "Adventurers of England" south to Lake Winnipeg and the mouth of the Red River.

The third and ultimately the best of all avenues into the Northwest was the Red River Valley. An oddly attenuated triangle, it lies with its apex at Lake Traverse and its base along Lake Winnipeg's southern shore. Approaching from afar, the traveller saw merely the promise of a river, a thin straggling line of poplars and cottonwood trees tracing the river's course over an incredibly flat stretch of grassland. When he came to the river side, his reactions must have been as varied as the moods of the Red itself. It was always a capricious stream, now a rivulet without depth and then a raging torrent; but regardless of temperament, it flowed forever northward—as one riverman characterized it—with "more twists than a Chinese puzzle."[1] Thus the river was usually disappointing. It was the valley, a broad, flat corridor more than 300 miles long, that gave mid-nineteenth–century man his most accessible highway to the British Northwest. The Red River Valley was the bridge between the American and British Northwests and upon it was built a regional economy of the broadest proportions. In crude, high-wheeled carts the men of the Red River Settlement transported the products of the chase and trapline down the valley to a Minnesota market where they exchanged them for goods of every description. If the cart created a common market, stage and steamboat companies enlarged it until the economies of both Northwests were intimately entwined. With the coming of the railroads in the 'fifties, the economic bonds grew tighter; and each year they grew somewhat stronger too, as the strands of society, blood, and culture were spliced into the whole.

Thus perhaps one can pardon the nineteenth-century Minnesotan for recognizing obvious regional relationships and concluding that the Hudson's Bay territories would some day become a part of the United States. His vision, however, was blurred by expansionist motes and beams, for this was neither the time nor the place for another "Oregon." In arresting Minnesota's commercial designs upon the Northwest, the Hudson's Bay Company played, till 1867, the primary role. It employed its competitive and charter-given powers both to check the growth of a free trade in furs within its territories and to control the resultant exchange of products between the Red River settlers and the fur traders of Minnesota. When these methods seemed to falter, first in the mid-'forties and then again in the following decade, the Company cleverly turned adversity to its own advantage. It magnified the apparent evidence of American manifest destiny—the chance manœuvres

[1]The *Nor'-Wester*, 28 Sept. 1860. This frontier paper was founded in the Red River Settlement in December, 1859, and was published for nearly a decade. The Provincial Library of Manitoba—hereafter cited as P.A.M.—possesses a nearly complete file of the newspaper.

of cavalry on the border—and convinced the Crown that it needed protection. The presence of Her Majesty's troops at Fort Garry (1846–48 and 1857–61) temporarily restrained the rampant growth of free trade, restored the political powers of the Company, and slowed down the development of the north-south trade. And when the Company found it could no longer compete with Minnesota's traders, whose transportation system became so startlingly efficient in the late 'fifties, it turned to the route of its rivals and, with its capital and managerial skills, re-established much of its old superiority in the fur trade.

Furthermore, till the close of the Civil War, Minnesota's ambitions regarding Rupert's Land were commercial, not annexationist. She wanted to engross the wealth of the region, dreaming of the day when her merchants could corner its trade and commerce, when all the Northwest's lines of communication and transportation led down to St. Paul. Such a dream seemed only the fulfilment of natural laws. Had not geography bound Minnesota to Rupert's Land and separated the latter from both Britain and Canada? The failure to enlarge and then to renew the Reciprocity Treaty of 1854 awakened fears that the dream might never be realized; Canada's efforts to obtain the Northwest confirmed them; and suddenly the mood of Minnesota became militantly expansionist. From 1866–67 until 1869, Minnesotans strove to annex all or part of the British Northwest. When the Riel Rebellion occurred in 1869, it seemed to these jingoists as if fate had presented them with a perfect opportunity to seize property that nature had already promised them. On this final occasion, however, they were frustrated by Sir John A. Macdonald's statecraft and by the dispatching of an imperial military expedition to Red River.

And yet neither Canada nor the Company ever exerted any deterrent influence upon the northwestward march of Minnesota's frontiersmen. For two decades, they followed a path that threatened to envelop the Hudson's Bay territories. It was a natural course, skirting the coniferous forests and swamplands of the northeastern part of the state and seeking out the flat, fertile valleys of the Sauk and Red rivers. By the 'fifties, pioneers were entering Minnesota by the tens of thousands; but theirs was no irresistible tide. The Panic of 1857 dammed its waters and ". . . times were hard and dull; the [Civil] War came, and the Indian War on top of that to make them harder and duller."[2] Its progress thrice interrupted, by 1865 the Minnesota frontier movement had stopped well short of the 49th parallel.

[2]The St. Paul *Press*, 1 Aug. 1869. All St. Paul papers cited in this study are located in the Minnesota Historical Society, St. Paul, Minnesota.

Not till the Civil War had ended, could Canada begin seriously to challenge Minnesota's expansionism. The American conflict had strengthened Canada by tending to force confederation upon her; and the new Dominion desperately needed the Northwest if she were to grow into nationhood and share the continent with the United States. The final struggle for the British Northwest started when Canada purchased the Hudson's Bay Company's lands in 1869 and culminated in the Riel Rebellion which quickly followed. Despite Minnesota's pleas for active intervention, President Ulysses S. Grant pursued a feckless, short-of-war policy that failed to accomplish any end. With distinctly superior diplomatic skills, Canada's first prime minister, Sir John A. Macdonald bested his American adversaries, won the Northwest for his young country, and assured it of a transcontinental greatness.

The taproot of this study was put down many years ago in graduate school at the University of Minnesota, where the author enjoyed the experience of working under Professor Alfred L. Burt. My obligations to him for constant encouragement, criticism, and friendship could never be repaid. I should also like to express my thanks to the personnel of the Minnesota Historical Society, the Provincial Archives of Manitoba, the National Archives, the Manuscript Division of the Library of Congress, and the Public Archives of Canada. Though the aid of all was freely and cordially given in the furtherance of my research, particular thanks are extended to Lucile M. Kane and Katherine A. Johnson of the Minnesota Historical Society and Wilfred Smith and William Ormsby of the Public Archives.

Many colleagues at Michigan State University helped with the manuscript, either by suggestion or by reading and criticizing portions of it. My thanks are given to Professors Marjorie Gesner, Stuart W. Bruchey, Harold B. Fields, Harry Brown, Paul Varg, and, above all, to Frederick D. Williams. Acknowledgement is also due the All-University Research Fund of Michigan State University for funds which were variously and most usefully employed in the research and writing of this book. I should also like to thank Miss. M. Jean Houston and Mrs. A. M. Magee of the University of Toronto Press for their aid and encouragement. To Mrs. Magee and her editorial skills, I give special thanks. To Major C. C. J. Bond, who drew the maps, I offer my gratitude; his cartographical talents have added an artistic and utilitarian dimension to my book.

To the Governor and Committee of the Hudson's Bay Company, I give thanks for their permission to use materials in the Company's archives which are on microfilm in the Public Archives of Canada. My gratitude to the Social Science Research Council of Canada is manifest, for this work has been published with the help of a grant from the Social Science Research Council of Canada using funds provided by the Canada Council.

A.C.G.

Contents

Maps

MINNESOTA AND THE MANIFEST DESTINY
OF THE CANADIAN NORTHWEST

Chapter 1. *The Red River Settlement*

I

FOR MORE THAN A CENTURY, ENGLAND AND FRANCE COMPETED FOR THE
Northwest and its wealth in furs. Two ingratiating rascals from New
France, Pierre Esprit Radisson and Médard Chouart, sieur des Groseilliers, were the first white men to learn of the Northwest's riches. What
was of greater importance, they were the first to discover that Hudson
Bay provided a cheaper and faster route to those furs than any highway leading out of the Great Lakes. However, as French Canadians,
they gained little satisfaction from their knowledge. Canada's trade in
furs, like that of all her important staples, was hedged about with
monopolistic practices and fenced in with regulations. The spirits of
the two traders were stifled and their purses pinched. Forced to share
their profits with others, they became disenchanted, shifted allegiance
from Versailles to the court of Charles II, and associated themselves
in business with certain of his countrymen.

The offspring of this union, a marriage of money and ideas, was the
Hudson's Bay Company, one of England's greatest and most powerful
joint stock companies. In 1670, Charles II handed over a charter to
"The Governor and Company of Adventurers of England trading into
Hudson's Bay." It was a munificent grant, conferring regal rights and
powers. In return for the symbolic fealty of two elks and two black
beavers, the king made less than twenty of his subjects the lords and
owners of Rupert's Land, a vague but vast region embracing the
drainage basin of Hudson Bay and Hudson Strait. In addition to

bestowing ownership, the charter vested the proprietors with the joint powers of governing the land and monopolizing its trade.

For many decades the Company's title to Rupert's Land was more apparent than real. The French refused to recognize its claims to any part of the Northwest until the events of Queen Anne's War forced such recognition upon them. In 1713, the Treaty of Utrecht sanctioned the territorial pretensions of the English; even then, recognition was qualified by the men along the St. Lawrence. So far as they were concerned, Utrecht had guaranteed the English a title only to the bayside and not to the hinterland where most of the furs were to be found. Before too long France's definition of Rupert's Land was reinforced by French possession of the interior. Beginning in the 1730's with La Vérendrye, Canadian fur traders pushed westward from Lake Superior through the border lakes and eventually encircled the posts of the Hudson's Bay Company. They forestalled fur-laden Indians en route to the bay, and in the process of constricting the Company's supply of furs, constructed a magnificent trading empire that reached all the way from Montreal to the Rockies. With the French entrenched in Rupert's Land, the English had either to compete against them in the back country or waste away on the bay. They began establishing inland trading posts to offset their rivals, but before the final issue could be joined between them, the Seven Years' War intervened. The conflict sapped the strength of the French voyageurs and the ultimate victory of the English ended French competition in Rupert's Land.

The Treaty of Paris did not eliminate interlopers from the St. Lawrence, however. Marching into Canada with the British armies, English, Scots, and American merchants and sutlers quickly recognized the commercial possibilities of the St. Lawrence. They allied themselves with the more experienced French Canadians and, victors and vanquished together, restored Montreal's old inland empire. For two decades thereafter, the Montrealers foolishly fought among themselves until the individual merchants resolved their differences and consolidated in the North West Company. Once again the St. Lawrence stood ready to challenge the right of Hudson Bay to the wealth of Rupert's Land. In the long, forty-year struggle between them, each company held its advantages. The English owed much to geography; the Canadians, almost everything to personnel and organization. With their system of profit-sharing, the Nor'Westers were more strongly motivated than the Company's salaried servants, and the independence gained thereby gave them an *esprit de corps* unseen in their rivals.

Moreover the shrewd Montreal merchants organized their company so efficiently and precisely that they could conduct a transcontinental business with a minimum of waste. These advantages made the North West Company such a strong antagonist that in 1810–11 the Hudson's Bay Company was forced to re-assess its position in the fur trade and make certain adjustments if it were to survive.

Two comparatively young men, Andrew Colvile and Thomas Douglas, Earl of Selkirk, were the guides who led the English concern to victory. Related by marriage and economic interests, they collaborated in bringing about great changes in the management and policy of the Hudson's Bay Company. Colvile swept away the cobwebs of ancient management and installed a more efficient organization, one that allowed some measure of local supervision over the fur trade and engaged the employees' loyalty by sharing the Company's profits with them. Together with Selkirk, he devised the scheme of establishing an agricultural colony in Rupert's Land to provide the trade with cheap food and sufficient servants. Colonization appealed to Selkirk as a philanthropist as well as a stockholder. He was deeply concerned with the plight of his fellow Scots, the crofters then being uprooted from their farms in the Highlands by the enclosure movement, and he longed to help them by establishing an asylum in North America. In 1811, the Hudson's Bay Company conveyed to Lord Selkirk an estate of approximately 116,000 square miles. This segment of Rupert's Land, known thereafter as Assiniboia, sprawled southward from Lake Winnipeg to cover much of the northern part of North Dakota and Minnesota. It was a huge estate, rivalling in size many of the old seventeenth-century proprietorships, and the Company did not simply give it away. Assiniboia was meant to be an investment and its returns to the Company would theoretically be measured in servants, wheat, and cattle. All the charity involved was Selkirk's. He agreed to underwrite the costs of colonization, and during the quarter century that Assiniboia remained in his and his family's hands, thousands of pounds were spent on its care and development.

One Scotsman's meat was another man's poison. So far as the Montrealers were concerned, the Selkirk grant imperilled their very existence. It not only blocked their entry to the fur country but also enclosed some of the best buffalo grounds in the Northwest. Moreover the region was already inhabited by people of a half-breed "nation," the semi-nomadic, semi-civilized children of countless marriages *en façon du nord* between white traders and Indian women. These half-breeds or *métis* had lived in Assiniboia long before it was so named and naturally resented the invasion of alien farmers into their buffalo grounds. Furthermore, the Selkirk settlers ignored the squatters' rights of the half-breeds and threatened their very livelihood. For the latter served the North West Company as purveyors of pemmican in addition to working as carters and voyageurs.

From the moment of its establishment in the summer of 1812, Selkirk's Red River Settlement seemed to have charted its course by an unlucky star. Situated at the confluence of the Red and Assiniboine rivers, the settlers found themselves boxed in between the half-breeds and the Nor'Westers. Initially suspicious of the colonists, the half-breeds soon became hostile when their masters from Montreal told them that Assiniboia was their land; and when the Montrealers laced this nationalist brew with bribes of money, the *métis* began to bully and harass the Red River settlers. No match for their assailants, the settlers fled from one Company post to another in order to avoid the *métis*. When a group of the settlers finally challenged the *métis* on Frog Plain in 1816, it was almost annihilated. Not till the following year, when Selkirk arrived on the scene with a troop of mercenary soldiers, was the settlement freed from the terror of the half-breeds.

Despite an uncertain infancy, the Red River Settlement played its part in wearing down the North West Company. It only remained for the force of geography to crush the Canadian concern. Though its trading empire was vast, its operating costs were almost as extraordinary as its extent. In the final accounting, the men of Hudson Bay had one advantage that the spirit and the system of the Montrealers could not overcome: they could lay down their trading goods in the heart of the Northwest. The Montrealers had to paddle and portage theirs halfway across a continent and more. They could not—as their chief, William McGillivray, confessed—compete forever "against a Chartered Company, who brought their goods to the Indian country at less than one half the Expence [sic] that ours cost us."[1] In 1821 the North West Company averted bankruptcy by merging with its rival, and once again the honourable company was mistress in her own home. The St. Lawrence had lost its commercial empire and would not regain it for another fifty years. To ensure that this rupture was permanent, the Hudson's Bay Company trapped out the beaver meadows between Rupert's Land and Canada and then allowed most of the canoe routes to recede into the wilderness.

[1]Quoted by Marjorie W. Campbell, *The North West Company* (New York, 1957), p. 275.

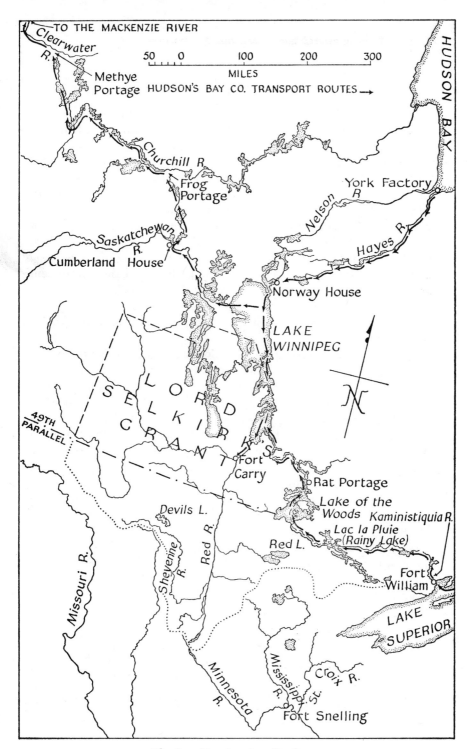

TO THE MACKENZIE RIVER

Clearwater R.

Methye Portage

50 0 100 200 300

MILES

HUDSON'S BAY CO. TRANSPORT ROUTES →

HUDSON BAY

Churchill R.

Frog Portage

York Factory

Nelson R.

Hayes R.

Saskatchewan R.

Cumberland House

Norway House

LAKE WINNIPEG

L O R D

S E L K I R K ' S

G R A N T

49TH PARALLEL

Fort Garry

Rat Portage

Devils L.

Lake of the Woods

Kaministiquia R.

Lac la Pluie (Rainy Lake)

Missouri R.

Sheyenne R.

Red R.

Red L.

Fort William

LAKE SUPERIOR

Minnesota R.

Mississippi R.

St. Croix R.

Fort Snelling

The Canadian-American Northwest

II

Eighteen hundred and twenty-one marked the beginning of a new era in the history of the Hudson's Bay Company. Amalgamation with the North West Company had ended competition. An act of parliament in the same year completely freed the Company from any other British competition. For it bestowed an exclusive, twenty-one-year trading monopoly over the rest of the Northwest, a region of historically varying dimensions known either as the North West Territory or simply as Indian country. Moreover when the British government subsequently neglected to establish law and order in the North West Territory—as it was empowered to do under the act—the Company offered to substitute its own governmental offices and the government straightway accepted the offer.[2] Save for the occasional American in Old Oregon, the Company was now (1821) the unquestioned arbiter of the entire Northwest—and its writ ran from Canada to the Pacific slope.

Having acquired an empire, the Company faced the problem of operating it. The Governor and Committee split their holdings, both chartered and licensed, into a Northern and a Southern Department. (The names are somewhat misleading. The departmental division, though lying roughly along the line of James Bay, cut the trading area into a western and an eastern section.) Each department was given a governor and council to determine policy and manage the trade within its geographic limits. Councils were composed of "wintering partners," the chief factors and chief traders who also controlled the day by day activities of the various districts or trading units within departments. As governor of the Northern Department, the Company selected George Simpson. It was an excellent choice. Within five years, the Company had given him both governorships, and in 1839 Simpson became Governor-in-Chief, a post he held until his death in 1860.[3]

With the administrative framework of the trade in hand, the Governor and Committee turned their attention to specific problems

[2]John H. Pelly to the Earl of Bathurst, 21 May 1822 and Bathurst to Pelly, 31 May 1822, Hudson's Bay Company's Archives on microfilm in the Public Archives of Canada, Series A.8/1. (Hereafter the Company's archives will be cited as H.B.C.) Pelly was Governor of the Company; Bathurst, the Colonial Secretary.

[3]See Arthur S. Morton, *Sir George Simpson* (Oregon Historical Society, 1944).

involved in business reorganization. While competing for the Northwest, both the Hudson's Bay and the North West companies had
dotted the map with posts and personnel; but after their merger such
coverage was senseless. In the interests of economy, the surviving
company scrapped countless posts and released hundreds of employees.
It was a simple matter to abandon a post but a most perplexing one
to discharge a small army of servants, particularly when they were
scattered throughout the wilderness. Left in the interior, the ex-
servants and their families might cluster about the remaining posts
and become a financial burden. Yet to allow them to shift for themselves would be imprudent and impolitic. Such a course of action
might either endanger the Company's trading monopoly in the Northwest or jeopardize its reputation—and its charter—in the United
Kingdom by exposing it to charges of inhumane conduct. There was
thus only one solution: to transport these people, at Company expense,
to the Red River Settlement, "where they . . . [could] maintain themselves and be civilized and instructed in religion."[4] Each head of a
family would receive a land grant; and with the added gifts of seed,
clothing, and other necessities, the Company trusted that they would
soon be useful and self-sustaining settlers.

How well the experiment would turn out remained to be seen; but
the odds against success appear, in retrospect, to have been formidable.
The Company was gathering up ex-servants all over the Northwest,
white and half-breed alike, bringing them to an unproven colony,
mixing them with men of a different cultural and ethnic background,
and then placing the whole group under two incompatible authorities.
According to the plan, all displaced persons were to be in the care of
Chief Factor John Clarke. Here was a man of middle age with a
chequered, flamboyant, often inglorious career in the service of the
North West Company, the Pacific Fur Company, and finally the
"honourable" Company. Though it is not known why a man of his
character should have been posted to Fort Garry, probably the lack
of other chief factors and his reputed skills in managing half-breeds
were the major reasons. More important to him, however, was his
fundamental job of directing the Company's trade in the Lower Red
River District. In this endeavour, the Governor and Council of the
Northern Department had specifically ordered him, as chief factor, to
suppress the free traders "who have for some time past been carrying

4Governor and Committee to Simpson, 27 Feb. and 2 March 1822, H.B.C.,
Series A.6/20.

on an unauthorized Traffic in Furs upon the Red River with the Indians and other persons within the Company's Territories. . . ."[5]

To complicate matters even more, Clarke, his men, and all the Company's ex-servants were under the general authority of Andrew Bulger. He was the Governor of Assiniboia, an officer appointed by the Company itself rather than the Northern Department; and had he and Clarke been the most placid and amenable souls, they would have been hard put to define their responsibilities. Not only did their offices overlap but they themselves were responsible to different authorities. If a working compromise would have been difficult for most men, it was impossible for these two. Bulger was an ex-military man whose personality too closely resembled Clarke's. Each was painfully proud, overly imperious; each, a petty aristocrat unwilling to share his authority with anyone. The Hudson's Bay Company had unwittingly put two fighting cocks in the same pit.

Clarke became aware of illicit trading in the district shortly after his arrival in the fall of 1822. In fact, he had barely settled into his quarters when he drew up a proclamation "prohibiting all trade with natives or others. . . ."[6] Copies were sent to three individuals strongly suspected of free trading and to all the principal settlers, including one addressed directly to Governor Bulger at Fort Douglas. There was no response from the governor, although Clarke and his men were made uneasily aware of his displeasure. The reaction of the three suspects was scarcely more satisfactory. The first did not reply at all. The second denied that he had violated the Company's monopoly. And the third, a petty trader named Régis Larente, answered to say that he could not understand English. Larente's language barrier did not keep Clarke out, when he learned that the trader had illegally acquired furs from the Indians. He broke into the man's house, uncovered a cache of furs, and seized them in the name and by the authority of the Hudson's Bay Company. With one free trader virtually in hand, Clarke then made plans to proceed against the others.

One night, as the second suspect, Charles Forrest, was guiding his river boat past Fort Garry, he was met by a canoeman bearing a message that Clarke wanted to see him. Forrest wisely declined. Not easily put off, Clarke repeated the invitation. From the river bank,

[5]Minutes of the Council of the Northern Department of Rupert's Land, 20 Aug. 1822, in E. H. Oliver, ed., *The Canadian North-West: Its Early Development and Legislative Records* (2 vols., Ottawa, 1914–15), I, 640–1.
[6]Winnipeg Post Journal, 20 Sept. 1822, H.B.C., Series B.235/a.

another Company man re-hailed Forrest, but the only reply he received was a shower of musket balls that "whistled around him in every direction."[7] Indeed the poor fellow must have felt like a bewildered boy whose bag of firecrackers suddenly exploded. For the cannon of Fort Douglas instantly supported the gunfire from Forrest's boat; and at that moment, many of the more nervous Hudson's Bay men in Fort Garry were sure that they were surrounded by armed invaders. Clarke ignored the spectres; behind the disturbance he could see the hand of Andrew Bulger.

That very night, Clarke wrote to Fort Douglas for an explanation and thereby touched off a war of words that lasted for several days. At first, each man merely felt out the other's position, exchanging commissions and seeking recognition. And then Bulger blasted his foe in a long and curious report.[8] He took exception to Clarke's original proclamation about fur trading because it categorized him as a "contraband Trader" and was obviously meant to debase the government. Though the entering of Larente's house had violated the man's basic rights and undercut the very authority of the governor, Bulger had let the affair slide by rather than disturb the public peace. But when Clarke made plans to apprehend Forrest, he had gone too far. Together with two armed servants, Bulger had gone along in the trader's boat, and it had been his men who fired into the air in order to let Clarke know that the governor was aboard and thus avoid a collision between the colony and the Company. "I did not come to this country, to submit to any indignity," concluded Bulger, "and I will bear none. . . ." With that, he announced his retirement.

It was a long and bitter winter, but despite the weather, Clarke managed to thaw out Bulger long before spring and, at the same time, to put down the free-trade movement. Two dinners at Fort Garry were enough to settle most of the misunderstandings between him and the governor. The leading free traders also pilgrimaged to the fort, but theirs was no social affair. They confessed their sins, gave up their furs, and promised not to trade again. Even the half-breeds clustered about Pembina, just below the 49th parallel and thus beyond the Company's realm—the "freemen" who had never served any company —seemed reconciled to Clarke's new order. "In short," as the clerk of Fort Garry proudly noted, "through the firmness and determination

[7]*Ibid.*, 30 Sept. 1822.
[8]Bulger to Clarke, 4 Oct. 1822, Winnipeg Correspondence Book, H.B.C., Series B.235/b.

on which Mr. Clarke acted, a complete and permanent stop has been put to all the illegal Traffic within the bounds of this District."[9]

Simpson was in complete agreement; but London's reaction was quite the opposite and, at first, rather hard to understand. As soon as the Clarke-Bulger wrangle reached the attention of the Governor and Committee, they sent Simpson a dispatch that was highly critical of Clarke's conduct.[10] For Clarke to have served notice upon the Governor of Assiniboia was a most preposterous act, ridiculing the Company and undermining its authority. To have broken into Larente's house was both improper and illegal. These were patently political matters, belonging to Governor Bulger, and only he could warn free traders and issue search warrants. Though Clarke's zeal as a chief factor was commendable, how could he ever have imagined that he was superior to the Governor of Assiniboia? "There was never such a mistake."

The quarrel between Clarke and Bulger had probably been inevitable, for it rested upon a fundamental difference in their attitudes toward the Red River Settlement. Bulger's primary interest was the colony and the welfare of its people. Clarke's concern with the colony was based on material grounds. Like most of the wintering partners, he thought that the colony's costs reduced the Company's profits, that its very existence jeopardized the future welfare of the fur trade. Such a difference in opinion was intolerable. In a long series of dispatches to Simpson, the Governor and Committee tried to remove the wintering partners' "narrow and erroneous view of the relative situation of the Colony and the Fur trade" and reorient them in the proper conduct to display towards the settlers.[11] In the eyes of the Governor and Committee, the Red River Settlement was meant to be much more than an asylum for retired servants, cast-offs, and nomadic half-breeds. They made it clear that, in supporting the colony, they had several objectives in mind. A primary one was to "furnish a more certain and less costly supply of Provisions than could be procured by the Provision Posts." Such a goal would be attainable only if the colony were properly managed; and if it were not, if the job were bungled, the colony would be a "constant source of trouble and vexation." Furthermore, the sheer force of circumstances demanded that the Company take a "just and honourable line of conduct" towards the settlers in order to avoid hostile criticism at home. Trading monopolies were not

[9]Winnipeg Post Journal, 2 Nov. 1822.

[10]Governor and Committee to Simpson, 21 May 1823, H.B.C., Series A.6/20.

[11]Governor and Committee to Simpson, 12 March 1824, 11 March 1825, and 26 March 1826, H.B.C., Series A.6/20 and A.6/21.

highly regarded in the mother country—"It is upon this account only that we have been so pointed in our instructions as to your conduct towards the Colony." Moreover, the receipt of the exclusive licence imposed certain obligations upon the Company, including the training of Indians; and with its schools and churches, the colony provided an ideal proving ground for this purpose. And finally, if the settlers could be loyally and sentimentally attached to the Company, they might serve both the Crown and the Company as a defensive body against Indian uprisings or Yankee filibusters.

Needless to say, London's arguments won the day. Thereafter the conduct of the wintering partners towards the settlers was governed by these precepts. John Clarke was removed from the Red River District and shifted to another, less important district on the way to ultimate separation from the service. He was replaced by the serene and sagacious Donald McKenzie. Andrew Bulger was permitted to retire, and a new man, Robert P. Pelly, came out from London in the fall of 1823 to assume the governor's office. In collaboration with McKenzie and Simpson, he intended to make a supreme effort to fit the Red River Settlement into the grand design projected for it by the Governor and Committee.

III

To fit the settlement into the Company's design demanded much more than the acquiescence of the wintering partners. Merely managing it was destined to tax the skill, patience, and health of a parade of governors. For the colony was a pot-pourri of races, religions, languages, and nationalities. There were half-breeds of French and English-Scottish blood blended with the Indian. Some of them were Protestant but most were Catholic. There were De Meurons, Selkirk's mercenaries from central Europe; and there were the Swiss, French-speaking and Protestant. And finally, there were the Scots, some of whom could speak nothing but Gaelic—all of whom were staunch Presbyterians.

The Swiss had arrived in the Red River Settlement during the fall of 1821, the latest and certainly the most disillusioned of all the settlers. Softened up by the salesmanship of Selkirk's agents and then sold by a typical new world prospectus, they had left their home canton of Bern to look for Utopia in Rupert's Land. Neither by nature nor by profession were they fitted for the rigorous life awaiting them.

The frontier had quickly converted cheerful watchmakers and mechanics into embittered, unhappy pioneers. Their first winter had been spent—as one of them later wrote—"in empty Houses, without Doors, Windows, or Roofs, their engagement not being fulfilled."[12] A few of the most discouraged had left for the United States almost immediately; the rest lived on from day to day.

The Swiss and De Meurons were knit together by marital ties and a common sense of grievance. The latter were members of the regiment whom Selkirk had induced to take up land in Red River and serve as soldier-settlers. They proved to be drones rather than workers or fighters and lived off the largesse of the earl and his colony store. Moreover, as mercenaries, they were typical specimens of the trade— unruly, quarrelsome, and undisciplined. Until their final departure from the settlement, scarcely a season passed without rumours of some uprising by these rogues.

In the opinion of most observers, the Scots (the original pioneers) were the most respected people in the whole colony. They were industrious farmers and the rich soil of the Red River Valley eventually repaid their efforts. And yet they also spoke of personal injustices. Until mid-century, they deplored the absence of a minister of their own faith. Like Scots the world around, they wanted to be able to distil their liquor; like frontiersmen everywhere in North America, they objected to the restrictions laid upon their title to the land. And in common with all their fellow settlers, they complained about the colony store, the general store established and maintained by the Douglas family until 1823. Prices seemed high; the selection, too slim. Such were the complaints about a store that extended credit for the sake of humanity and not profit; but everyone, Scots and all, regarded debts due the store much as modern-day North Americans eye their income tax.

The most numerous group in the settlement were the half-breeds, many of whom had lived here since the birth of their nation and re- garded the site as their homeland. After 1821, they were joined by other half-breeds: discharged servants and the freemen, the majority of whom had dwelt near the American border. Fearful that these people might fall under the influence of American traders, the Hudson's Bay Company, working through the half-breed leaders and their missionary priests, had persuaded most of them to migrate from the borderlands and settle on White Horse Plain, about fourteen miles west of Fort Garry. The Company employed some of the half-breeds

[12]See the journal of an anonymous Swiss, H.B.C., Series E.8.

as voyageurs or carters, but the great majority of them derived their living from the chase, selling pemmican to the Company and finery to the other Red River settlers. Consequently, they lived in a half-way house neither savage nor civilized, and in the long run they failed to adapt their economy to the changing needs and demands of Rupert's Land. An improvident people, most of them quickly spent their gains from the buffalo hunts and lived out the winter in uncertainty. Yet with their numbers, their economy, their spirited independence, and their semi-nomadic way of life, they added a most unsettling and volatile influence to Red River's society. From the very start, Simpson was aware that, for the settlement's sake, this powerful and unstable element in the colony would have to be well and wisely governed.

Managing Assiniboia was further complicated by the curious nature of its governorship. In Selkirk's original grant, he had secured the right to have and to hold Assiniboia forever, "saving and reserving . . . to the said Governor and Company . . . all rights of jurisdiction whatsoever granted to said Company by their Charter."[13] In other words, all the political powers of the Governor of Assiniboia derived from the Company; and every governor was a man in two persons: manager of the Selkirk property and governor of a Hudson's Bay colony. And he continued to serve two masters until 1836, when the Governor and Committee bought back the Selkirk grant, "being of the opinion that it would be better and with greater facility managed if entirely in the hands of the Company. . . ."[14]

However, the initial task awaiting Pelly and Simpson in the fall of 1823 was not the establishment of a government in Red River but the alleviation of discontent among its people, particularly the Swiss and the De Meurons. Throughout the summer they had been in a sullen and semi-rebellious state, agitated by rumours that the Selkirks planned to abandon them as slaves to the Company's system. Towards its end, they threatened to remove themselves and their families to the United States, even if it meant the reduction of all obstacles in their way, including Forts Douglas and Garry. In reality, the Selkirk executors had abandoned the colony store and not the settlers, and when the truth was known, the rumours were dispelled. But when Pelly and Simpson installed a new policy for the management of the store, the

---

[13]Oliver, ed., *The Canadian North-West*, I, 156.
[14]Governor and Committee to Simpson, 9 March 1836, H.B.C., Series A.6/24. When Pelly came out to Red River, he brought along two sets of instructions: a memorandum from the executors of the Selkirk estate and his commission and orders from the Company. Moreover each party paid one-half of Pelly's salary.

temper of these irritable folk flared up again. The Selkirk estate had directed Pelly to collect all debts owed to the old colony store, and the Hudson's Bay store, which fell heir to the latter, refused from its inception to give any credit. Civil disorder nearly resulted. The De Meurons had always lived off the store, and often in the past, only its credit given as a bribe had checked their insubordination. Governor Pelly readied Fort.Garry against assault and gave them the choice of conforming or emigrating. He won. The De Meurons gave way and promised to behave—and peace of a sort prevailed in the settlement. There still remained the other colonists. Their grievances, though less violently expressed, so ran the gamut that Simpson often thought it "quite lost labor to attempt pleasing" them.[15] Thus more time and effort had to be spent in reconciliation before he and Pelly could finally sit down to their fundamental task of creating a proper government for the colony itself.

All winter long the two men laboured. With his greater experience and knowledge, Simpson undoubtedly guided Pelly through the intricacies of the Company's business and the colony's politics; yet it was still a joint enterprise. They laid down rules for the operation and guidance of the Governor and Council of Assiniboia (Red River's appointed government), established courts of justice, and brought a primitive police force into being. Crude though it was, the political pattern cut out that winter was destined to last with but minor changes in form and policy—and practically all of them were Simpson's—until the end of the Company's rule over Rupert's Land in 1870.

Yet Assiniboia did not then, nor would it ever, possess a strong government. It was Simpson's opinion in 1824—and he never changed it—that nothing but the presence of soldiers would ensure a true respect for law and order among the settlers; and he firmly believed that, if the settlement ever became more than an agricultural colony, troops would not only be desirable but absolutely necessary. Till then, the Governor of Assiniboia might govern, but he could never rule, Red River. Even so, the successful governor would have to follow two guide lines: he would have to persuade those settlers amenable to reason to accept his administration; and somehow or other, he would have to remove the recalcitrant. His other—and the Company's—basic control over the colony lay in his economic influence, but even this authority would only endure as long as the settlement was effectually isolated from the rest of North America.

[15]Simpson to the Governor and Committee, 5 June 1824, H.B.C., Series D.4/87.

IV

By the time Pelly left for England in the fall of 1825, Red River's political atmosphere had grown amazingly calm. Pelly's successor was Chief Factor Donald McKenzie, a man who easily carried the double burden of overseeing the fur trade and governing the settlement. McKenzie was the sort of man whose judgment sent parties away "perfectly satisfied with each other and with his decision."[16] He was completely at home in Red River's heterogeneous society; a clever man, he always treated the settlers in an engaging fashion:

. . . with the Priests we will hold discussions . . . ever mindful of giving no kind of umbrage to their dearly beloved bigotry, else make our account to extenuate our offences by mortifications, fasting and watching, with the Scotch and Irish let us scour up our rusty Erse, and loudly extol that prince of heroes, old Fingal, with the French and the Swiss we will be frenchified, et vive la bagatelle, with the Canadians we can pass their voyages over again, with the Brules [half-breeds] listen to their feats against the Scioux, and with the indians you know we shall be indians still.[17]

For all his skill in the gentle and plastic art of politics, McKenzie was also shrewd enough to rattle the sabre when he found such a method useful. He had, for example, little trouble with the free traders. Confiscations promptly followed warnings, and in one case, a man was apprehended and threatened with deportation. Though McKenzie's actions were perfectly legal, they were also quite summary and reflected the power both of the man and of the Company.

Although McKenzie's long (1825–33) governorship was to give the colony some of its most tranquil years, it was a violent natural disaster that first brought serenity to the settlement. The winter of 1825–26 was marked by extraordinarily heavy snowfalls and extreme cold; and when the spring thaws began, the Red River could not carry away all the excess water, because its mouth (at Lake Winnipeg) was plugged with ice. Beneath a frozen skin, the river swelled ominously, rising until it was flush with the banks. Then, on a mild afternoon in early May, it "broke up with an awful rush; carrying away cattle, horses, trees and everything else that came in its way."[18] Within the

---

[16]Simpson to the Governor and Committee, 30 June 1829, H.B.C., Series D.4/96.
[17]Frederick Merk, *Fur Trade and Empire* (Cambridge, Mass., 1931), pp. 198–9.
[18]Extract from the Fort Garry Journal, enclosed in Simpson to the Governor and Committee, 14 June 1826, H.B.C., Series A.12/1.

first half hour, forty-seven houses had been swept away and the settlement turned into a vast lake. Miraculously, only one life was lost.
Working around the clock from their boats, McKenzie's Hudson's Bay
men snatched many a settler from drowning. To all in need, the
Company's magazines dealt out food and clothing.

By the time the flood reached its crest, a good many colonists had
reached the limit of their endurance. Certainly for the Swiss and
De Meurons, the great flood was the final act of an unkindly fate and
it drove them from the settlement. When Simpson came to Red River
in June, one of his first acts was to offer the victims either relief or
rehabilitation. To those who wished to go to Canada, he promised
passage; to those who preferred an American haven, he handed out
ammunition and fishing tackle; to the settlers made of sterner stuff,
the ones who wanted to try again, he gave cash or credit to rebuild
their lives. It was a policy that seemed to satisfy the people, especially
those who remained in Red River. For now—as one of them remarked—
"the dross had been purged away from our community."[19]

From that brief visit to the settlement, Simpson brought away little
but gloom. He was positive that the flood had ruined the colony. It
proved, however, to have quite the opposite effect, and Simpson's
black mood vanished when he began receiving reports of an incredible
recovery. Buffalo, driven so far afield by the winter storms, were
again grazing within 100 miles of the settlement; fishing nets were
being filled once again; and even the farm land, restored to production, was bringing forth better than average returns. Moreover, disaster
had given character to the colony. As it so often does in human
affairs, adversity, commonly shared, wrought a spirit of unity. Although
the dispersal of the hateful and hated De Meurons had something to
do with the growth of goodwill, it was the Company that brought it
to fruition. The settlers were genuinely grateful for the aid given them.
As Simpson himself related to London that fall, the Hudson's Bay
Company had "never [been] so popular in Red River before. . . ."[20]

The succeeding years of McKenzie's administration could almost be
called an "era of good feeling." The settlers were contented and
comfortable and no unseemly quarrels arose to disturb the peace.
Some of the credit for Red River's well-being should be given to
McKenzie's wise and careful management, but more has to be attributed to a change in climate. For the first time in its history, the

[19]Alexander Ross, *The Red River Settlement* (London, 1856), p. 109.
[20]Simpson to the Governor and Committee, 16 Oct. 1826, H.B.C., Series D.4/89.

colony was blessed, not cursed, by nature, and it responded in the way that Lord Selkirk and the Company had envisioned. After a visit in 1827, Simpson thought that, with one or two more good seasons, the settlers would be able not only to feed themselves but also "to furnish the Honble Company with any quantity [of provisions] that may be required for the Fur Trade."[21] The very next year he declared that the colony was no longer a burden to the Company; "on the contrary, it is becoming advantageous to its interests and if it continues to prosper . . . it will present a field . . . for other pursuits and branches of [the] Trade."[22] Time bore out his prognosis. By the 'thirties, the banks of the Red River were highly cultivated and returning ever increasing harvests, while numerous cattle and swine ranged the back plains. The orders of the Northern Department upon the settlement had lengthened with time and prosperity. Beef, pork, and ham had been added to earlier lists of wheat, barley, pease, and corn, and the quantity of every item mounted through the years.

A decade of good growing weather may have established the basic economy of the Red River Settlement, but it also brought the problem of overproduction. For the farmer and the plains hunter, there was only one market for their beef and their buffalo—the Hudson's Bay Company; and though Simpson promised to buy whatever provisions he needed from the colony, "in a short time all the wants of the Company were adequately supplied."[23] Unfortunately, the Company's demands were virtually static; it required just so much beef and no more. Thus as Red River's production rose, prices dropped, until London froze them at the 1834 level. The Company might have created a "provision post" that served its trading interests, but its satisfaction was scarcely matched by the farmers. By 1832, their market was saturated and their prices fixed.

The plains hunters were in the same position as the farmers. During this period of time, the buffalo herds were numerous and close at hand, and the number of half-breed hunters grew accordingly. They shot more buffalo; the farmers slaughtered more cattle; and consequently the pemmican market shrank. Here, too, the saturation point was reached in the fall of 1832. Indeed, even in the previous year Simpson had found the half-breeds "rather clamorous & dissatisfied because . . . [he had] declined purchasing all the pemican

[21]Simpson to the Governor and Committee, 25 July 1827, H.B.C., Series D.4/90.
[22]Simpson to the Governor and Committee, 10 July 1828, H.B.C., Series D.4/92.
[23]Ross, *Red River*, p. 115.

[*sic*] they presented for sale, although we [the Company] had no occasion for it."[24] Given his talent for frontier diplomacy, he quieted the half-breeds and the settlement remained tranquil; but its future would be most uncertain if the Company did not take steps to correct the colony's economic ills.

V

Regardless of the time or the place, man has always found it difficult to deal with the problems of over-production. The Hudson's Bay Company wrestled with them in the Red River Settlement for more than two decades and achieved only a limited success. For its surplus, whether beef or dried buffalo meat, the settlement needed a market bigger than the Company. And yet how could an external market be found for such bulky food products. The freightage alone would have precluded profit-taking. What the colony needed was some exportable staple other than food. Furthermore it needed some market other than the United States, which was ruled out by geography in the 'twenties and 'thirties and the Company's self-interest at any other time. In short, what Red River required was a staple of a relatively concentrated value which would find a ready market in the British Isles.

The need was painfully evident to Simpson. By 1830, as he himself well knew, cash sales in the Company's Red River shops ranged from £6,000 to £7,000 per year; and four years later, they exceeded £9,000.[25] Though the sum might seem small, it was much too large for the economic health of the colony, for it was greater than all the money disbursed by the Company to the settlers in Red River. The difference could only come from savings and the result of it all was an intolerable trading imbalance. The colonists were spending more than they were selling, and though they lived in a land of plenty, many were growing restive and discontented. Some thought of migrating to Canada or to the United States, "where they could find a market for the fruit of their industry."[26] Simpson feared that, if the Company did

---

[24]Simpson to the Governor and Committee, 10 Aug. 1832, H.B.C., Series A.12/1.

[25]Simpson to the Governor and Committee, 26 Aug. 1830 and 21 July 1834, H.B.C., Series D.4/97 and D.4/100. The Company had unwittingly aided in bringing about this unhealthy situation by endeavouring to carry goods of every price and description in its shops, lest the settler-customers grow dissatisfied and quarrelsome.

[26]Simpson to the Governor and Committee, 18 July 1831, H.B.C., Series A.12/1.

nothing to alleviate the situation, the settlement would "either break up, or the Settlers divert their attention to the Fur Trade, and under American protection they would be formidable opponents indeed."[27]

Therefore the Hudson's Bay Company followed a policy dedicated to the development of various staples within the Red River Settlement. To that end, markets were analysed, capital extended either directly or in the form of subsidies, skilled technicians sent out from England, and managerial talent supplied whenever necessary. Though business with a humanitarian cast, it was still business. Many of the projects conceived or actually carried out were under the direction of sub-sidiary companies; yet even these, while producing dividends for the parent (Hudson's Bay) company, if successful, would also have aided the average settler by creating new staples or building markets abroad. The Company's policies were always fashioned by both altruism and self-interest; and from this distance in time, no man can dissociate one motive from the other. The job of developing Red River's economy was given to Simpson. He handled it well. Indeed it would be hard to find a businessman with a more fertile and far-reaching imagination. He conjured up project after project. It is a credit to his intelligence that he never tried to establish a finished industry; all his trust was placed in agrarian operations or extractive industries where the unit cost depended almost entirely upon cheap and available natural resources.

In the late 'twenties, Simpson launched the first of several schemes to raise sheep within the settlement. He planned to import them from the United States and sell them to the settlers; for, if sheep could be reared successfully in Red River, the settlers could clothe them-selves in homespun instead of English woollens and perhaps have raw wool left over to export. Simpson accordingly contracted with a St. Louis merchant to arrange for the delivery of about 400 head during the summer. The American dutifully made all the arrange-ments, but the drovers never got beyond Big Stone Lake. A band of Sioux descended like wolves, slaughtered most of the sheep, and scattered the rest over the plains.[28] Although Simpson ordered again in the following winter, neither this nor any subsequent order materialized. Missouri's drovers never wanted to venture into Sioux country again.

At length Simpson acted for himself. At his suggestion, various

[27]Simpson to the Governor and Committee, 10 Aug. 1832, *ibid.*
[28]E. T. Langham to General William Clark, Fort Snelling, 14 and 18 Aug. 1828, Taliaferro Papers, Minnesota Historical Society (M.H.S.).

settlers pooled their resources in 1832 and actually oversubscribed to a fund for the purchase of sheep.[29] In effect, a joint stock company was created, composed of shareholders whose returns in sheep would match their investment in pounds. Led by a Hudson's Bay man, a group from Red River set out for Missouri. Disappointed by high prices there, they crossed into Kentucky and eventually acquired a large flock. Up to this point the journey had been pleasantly uneventful; however, the rest of the way was a nightmare. The long trail home was literally strewn with the carcasses of sheep which perished from disease and exhaustion. By the time the shepherds reached Red River, less than a fourth of their flock was alive. Simpson still managed to salvage something. After returning the individual subscriptions—and personally absorbing the loss—he placed the surviving sheep on the Company's experimental farm. There they thrived; their numbers soon doubled; and in succeeding years, their quality was enhanced by interbreeding with Merino and Leicestershire stock imported from England. Simpson's hopes for a staple grew brighter as more and more settlers, influenced by his example, turned to sheep-raising. Despite his expectations, the end result was a household industry instead of an export trade. By 1840 most of the Red River settlers were clothed in woollens of their own growth and manufacture, but no raw wool had been exported.

At first glance, it seemed to Simpson as if flax would make as good a staple as raw wool. Red River's climate and soil were ideal for the plant itself, and by 1828, the settlers were already growing enough for their own linen.[30] With its seeming abundance of cheap labour, all the colony appeared to lack was a mill to process the flax fibres for market. Simpson persuaded someone to erect a mill capable of processing one thousand tons of flax annually. Then to assure it of sufficient supplies, he held out the promise of generous premiums to the three farmers growing the largest and best crops and a similar reward to those who spun the best flax. The Governor and Committee added their support to the project. From the British Isles, they sent out a man skilled in the cultivation and production of flax, predetermined the state of London's market, and directed Simpson to buy all of Red River's marketable flax at a price that figured its transportation to London at cost. But once again paternalism failed to

[29]Simpson to the inhabitants of Red River, 25 Oct. 1832, H.B.C., Series F.30. See also Robert Campbell, "A Journey to Kentucky for Sheep," *North Dakota Historical Quarterly*, I (1926–27), 35–45.
[30]Simpson to the Governor and Committee, 10 July 1828, H.B.C., Series D.4/92.

beget a staple. Encouraged by the premiums, the settlers had eagerly set to work only to find that zeal was no match for ignorance. First they failed to cultivate their fields well enough and then they over-exposed the harvested flax fibres until part of the crop became too brittle for use, while the rest of it rotted "like dung" on the ground.[31] Eventually some flax was shipped to England, of fair quality but hardly able to compete with the superior Russian product; and ultimately, the mill stood idle. Though hemp, a plant whose production and growth bear close resemblance to flax, was also tried in the Red River Settlement, its sad history need not be told. It passed through the same experimental cycles and suffered the same fate.

In 1831, Simpson persuaded some Red River settlers to form the Red River Tallow Company, a joint stock company whose career began with several hundred cattle and wonderful prospects.[32] Simpson was positive that it would soon be exporting to Britain the hides and tallow of five thousand animals every year. The Governor and Committee never shared his optimism; and although the first shipments of tallow were sold, it was a product decidedly inferior to that of the Russian competition. None the less the Company supported the Red River Tallow Company, sending strychnine when wolves began preying upon the herds—and then wolf dogs and deer hounds when poison failed to work. Given protection, the herds waxed in number, but, ironically, the final result was not an export trade in hides and tallow to Britain but rather a brisk and growing (1839–40) trade in livestock with the United States.[33]

Much of the failure in the flax, hemp, and like projects could be attributed to the untutored mind of the Red River farmer, a not uncommon phenomenon in any frontier community. But to the Company and Simpson, such ignorance was intolerable so long as the colony lacked an export trade, "as without an export of some description it is impossible [that] a growing Settlement can prosper."[34] Therefore, at great cost to itself, the Company founded three experimental farms in order "to introduce a system of tillage and pastural [sic] agriculture previously unknown in the settlement, from which the inhabitants might, by pursuing the same, derive advantage."[35]

[31]Ross, *Red River*, p. 138.
[32]The Red River Tallow Company, H.B.C., Series F.31.
[33]Simpson to the Governor and Committee, 8 July 1839, H.B.C., Series D.4/106.
[34]Governor and Committee to Simpson, 7 March 1838, H.B.C., Series A.6/24.
[35]Governor and Committee to Duncan Finlayson, 4 March 1840, H.B.C., Series A.6/25. Finlayson was (1839–40) temporary Governor of Assiniboia.

The farms became known as the "three unfortunate sisters."[36] The manager of the first, really a Selkirk enterprise, soon exchanged his post for the greater economic opportunities of fur trading in the United States. The manager of the second, till then a highly respected chief factor in the service, stuck to the job, although in four years' time he produced little more than butter and pork for the Company's tables and taught nothing at all to the settlers. Of all the experiments, the third was the largest, most costly, and shortest lived. With a manager versed in the theory and practice of agriculture and twelve to fifteen indentured servants and their families, the farm was meant to be a showplace, demonstrating how to grow flax and hemp in the approved manner. Nothing worked according to expectations. The settlers disliked the farm, fearing that its output would further constrict an already limited market, and they learned little or nothing from its operations. The manager was wholly incapable of overseeing his servants, who were a second edition of the De Meurons—disorderly and indolent men who "could neither work nor eat without the beer pot at their lips."[37] In 1840, when merely a handful of them was left, the Company terminated the experiment.

Seen from afar, none of Simpson's designs seems to have really succeeded. Yet in some cases, a household industry was brought into being before its arrival in a frontier economy would have been expected; in others, a diminutive export industry was accidentally awakened, if in the wrong—that is, American—direction. These economic changes helped rectify Red River's trading imbalance. Of greater importance, they helped prevent the dissolution of the settlement and/or the diversion of its settlers into the fur trade—two events that Simpson had feared might come to pass during the 'thirties.

At any rate, Simpson managed to mix paternalism with statecraft, add a dash of diplomacy, and keep the people of Red River reasonably contented. Those English-speaking settlers for whom life held out neither hope nor happiness departed for other lands, and those who remained adjusted themselves philosophically to the slow pace of their bucolic economy. Even the half-breeds, who gave Simpson more than one anxious moment during the early and middle 'thirties, came to accept their lot. And it was not money alone that satisfied them, although the price of pemmican was raised in 1835. Simpson's diplomatic skills, coupled with the influence lent his cause by the

[36]Ross, *Red River*, p. 212.
[37]*Ibid.*, p. 215.

Roman Catholic Bishop of Juliopolis, played a great part in pacifying the *métis*.

Other adjustments, largely of a political nature, were also made during the 'thirties. Simpson enlarged and revitalized the council of Assiniboia in 1835, adding Anglican ministers, the Bishop of Julio- polis, and a French- and an English-speaking half-breed, as well as other men of worth and moment within the colony. With their blessing, he strengthened the colony's legal system, cutting a pattern that persisted till the 'fifties and was then altered only in minor ways. In the following year, the Company made the most significant change of all when it bought back the Selkirk grant and "put an end to separate interests" in Assiniboia.[38] Two years later, the Governor and Committee appointed Adam Thom, a Lower Canadian lawyer, to the new office of recorder of Rupert's Land in order to insure "a more regular and effectual administration of Justice."[39]

Thus, by 1840, the Red River colony was a most attractive sight in the eyes of its creators. To Simpson, it seemed another Arcadia, whose inhabitants lived with more comfort and ease than any other people in the world. The Governor and Committee were similarly gratified to learn that their plans to improve Red River had been so successful and it gave them "peculiar" satisfaction to know that the settlers were appreciative of everything that had been done for them.[40] The Company's sense of well-being was wholly spurious. In reality, the Red River settlers were complacent simply because there was little or no opportunity to be otherwise.

[38]Henry H. Berens to Lord Lytton, 8 Feb. 1859, H.B.C., Series A.8/9. Berens was Governor of the Company, 1858–63.
[39]Governor and Committee to Simpson, 7 March 1838, H.B.C., Series A.6/24.
[40]Governor and Committee to Finlayson, 4 March 1840, H.B.C., Series A.6/25.

Chapter 2. The American Approach

I

FOR MANY YEARS ASSINIBOIA REMAINED IN ISOLATION, HUNDREDS OF MILES
of grassland separating it from the American frontier to the south.
Although the valley of the upper Mississippi River belonged to the
United States long before the birth of the Selkirk settlement, it was
held in British, not American, hands until well after the War of 1812.
Till then, American penetration was shallow and short-lived. Till
then, local Indians draped medals of George III around their necks
and a scattering of fur-trading posts proudly flew the Union Jack. The
United States did not gain control over the area until the advent
of the army and the American Fur Company in the postwar era. But
once authority was extended, it was effective and complete. Treaties
were signed with the various Indian tribes acknowledging American sovereignty, and fortifications thrown up to sustain the new White
Father and protect his fur traders. In 1819, units from the 5th United
States Infantry assumed the strategic site at the confluence of the
Minnesota and Mississippi rivers and built an encampment that grew
gradually into Fort Snelling. In the following year, Major Lawrence
Taliaferro arrived to take up his duties as the Indian agent—and to
collect British medals. And thus American law, if not order, had
finally come to the Northwest.

Although chartered in 1808, the American Fur Company did not
assume its final form and character until nearly a decade later. In
its youth, the company (or more correctly, Astor himself) had been

forced to associate with the more powerful trading houses of Montreal, if it wanted to make money south and west of the Great Lakes. But in 1816, the tables were turned when the United States Congress— out of "revenge for the past and protection of the future"[1]—passed a law forbidding the issuance of fur-trading licences to foreigners. Astor was never one to overlook an obvious opportunity for self-gain. Within a year he had bought out his old foreign (Canadian) partners and taken up their trading heritage, a rich prize complete with posts and personnel. In 1822, by forcing his way into St. Louis, Astor virtually completed his trading empire. Then in the interests of more efficient management, he divided it into two giant satrapies: the Western and the Northern Departments. The first, with St. Louis as its headquarters, supplied the trading outfits of the upper Missouri River as well as those of the lower Mississippi. The second, centred at Michilimackinac, dispatched its trade goods to outfits surrounding the Great Lakes and penetrating as far as the upper Mississippi. Thus Minnesota was on a dividing line. The Northern Department worked westward from Fond du Lac at the foot of Lake Superior, while from the vicinity of Fort Snelling the Western Department reached out to the north and west.

With Astor and the army in Minnesota, it was inevitable that Assiniboia's isolation would end and that, as a consequence, some sort of commercial complex would arise between it and Minnesota. A regional trade was only natural, dictated as it was by geography and foreseen by Lord Selkirk as early as 1817.[2] Sage though he was, however, Selkirk could scarcely have predicted the first articles of trade or the accident that sent them on their way.

In late July, 1818, "a cloud of grasshoppers from the west darkened the air, and fell like a heavy shower of snow" upon the Red River Settlement.[3] The invaders consumed the crops and forced the colonists to forage off the plains. The following spring, when the settlers started to cultivate their fields, they found the ground already seeded with locust larvae. In fact, these loathsome little creatures blanketed the soil, devoured the young shoots of grain, and even polluted the wells into which they dropped. The reappearance of the locusts was the final misfortune. With their seed grain gone and its replenishment from Britain impossible, the Red River settlers

[1]Kenneth W. Porter, *John Jacob Astor Business Man* (2 vols., Cambridge, Mass., 1931), II, 695.

[2]John P. Pritchett, "A Letter by Lord Selkirk on Trade between Red River and the United States," *Canadian Historical Review*, XVII (Dec., 1936), 418–23.

[3]Alexander Ross, *The Red River Settlement* (London, 1856), p. 48.

turned to the United States for relief. In the early spring of 1820 a small party from Red River struck out through the snow for the nearest American settlement. Snowshoeing down the valleys of the Red and Minnesota rivers, the travellers pushed their way into Prairie du Chien, the site of Fort Crawford and a central station of Astor's American Fur Company on the lower Mississippi River. After buying the required seed grain and loading it into keel boats, they began the long voyage home. Poling and portaging their craft, they moved slowly up the Minnesota, struggled through the shallows of Big Stone and Traverse lakes, and twisted down the Red, to reach and revictual their fellow settlers in a little more than six weeks' time. In the minds of the men of Red River, it was a memorable voyage and "satisfactory to know, that the state of navigation between the two countries, during high water, was not only practicable, but offered every facility for future communication. . . ."[4]

In the summer of 1821 Alexis Bailly, an intelligent young half-breed working for the American Fur Company, drove a small herd of milk cows and oxen on speculation to the Red River Settlement. It was a hazardous but rewarding venture. He sold all his cattle at high prices, for the animals were among the first to be owned by the settlers since they had left their homeland. Thus the demand was great, the price, right; and, with the encouragement of the Hudson's Bay Company, a brisk trade soon developed. For the next few years, other Yankee drovers braved the terrors of the Sioux and brought cattle to Assiniboia from as far away as Missouri. But by 1825 the market had fallen off, and prices too, until profits were no longer attractive enough to gamble on the long drive up from the south. Within a decade, however, the dust of cattle drives rose again from the floor of the Red River Valley. This time, the drovers were men from Red River and their destination was the United States, where ready sales were made to Minnesota's Indian missionaries and fur traders.[5]

A second and much more important "article of export" from Red River to the United States consisted of people. The exodus came in two distinct waves. The first broke during the 'twenties, carrying down a great many Swiss and De Meurons. The force that set them in motion was a feeling of the utmost dissatisfaction with life in Red River, and when nature added the triple blows of famine, flood, and locusts, they had reached the limit of their long-suffering. The first

[4]*Ibid.*, p. 51.
[5]Simpson to the Governor and Committee, 8 July 1839, H.B.C., Series D.4/106.

of these unhappy folk left Red River in the fall of 1821 and a few of them settled down near Fort Snelling, where their success soon inspired imitators. Every year thereafter small parties groped their way southward, and in 1826—the year of the flood—the movement reached a climax, when approximately 250 people came to Minnesota. At Fort Snelling, where much of his time was taken up with giving advice and handing out passports, Major Taliaferro wrote in his journal: "The Red River Colony appears to be diminishing rapidly. . . . Since 1822 it appears that to the Number of 330 Swiss, Canadian & Irish Sett[l]ers, men, *women* & children have passed this Post for the interior of the United States."[6] Though the major did not know it, the migration was almost over; most of the Swiss and De Meurons had already left the Red River Settlement.

With only slight variations, the emigrants followed the same water-level route to Minnesota that had been traced out by fur traders and cattlemen before them. Whether by horse, cart, or canoe, it was a long and perilous journey passing through the very centre of Sioux country. These savages had never been known for their goodwill towards any white men. When they encountered the Red River emigrants during the 'twenties, they apparently had only theft or murder in mind, and on more than one occasion the arrival of survivors at Fort Snelling excited the pity of the commandant and the Indian agent. Although it might have been Taliaferro's duty to give out passports, nothing but humanitarianism prompted him to hand out provisions. As for Colonel Josiah Snelling, that middle-aged veteran of the War of 1812 treated the victims "in a truly philanthropic manner" and even took some of them into his own home.[7] Such kindness persuaded some of the immigrants to remain in the vicinity of Fort Snelling. Most of them continued on downstream, however, and ultimately settled in the river towns of Galena, St. Louis, and Vevay.[8]

The second wave of emigration began in 1835 and continued for the balance of the decade. The great majority of these people were Scottish Presbyterians. Their decision to leave Red River, though probably resting upon as many reasons as there were men, seems to have been brought about primarily by economic and religious distress. Perhaps for some of them the continued absence of a Presbyterian

[6]Taliaferro Journal, No. 4, 14 Sept. 1827, Taliaferro Papers, M.H.S.
[7]J. C. Beltrami, *A Pilgrimage in Europe and America, Leading to the Discovery of the Sources of the Mississippi and Bloody River; with a Description of the Whole Course of the Former, and of the Ohio* (2 vols., London, 1828), II, 353.
[8]Vevay is now the county seat of Switzerland, Indiana.

minister was enough to make life in the colony unbearable, but for most, the chief stimulus was economic. They left "because there was nobody there to purchase their produce, which had accumulated upon their hands."[9] Then by some malicious turn of events, Red River was struck by disastrous crop failures in 1836 and 1837. Seemingly entangled in a feast-or-famine economy, more and more Scots hearkened to the favourable reports of farm life in the United States and hastened to re-join old friends and neighbours who had already gone to Minnesota. Observing the departure of his fellows, one lifelong resident of Red River sadly wrote a friend in Minnesota that "few will remain here who can carry themselves away."[10]

Duncan Finlayson, temporary Governor of Assiniboia in 1840, looked upon the whole movement with mixed emotions. In a way, it seemed quite a good thing, for it helped solve the problem of Red River's surplus people and produce. But regarding it in another light, Finlayson was disturbed and wrote the Governor and Committee of his fears that the migrations had "lined out a road to the heart of your Territories, which, in the event of a war with the United States, would become exposed to depredations from the lawless hordes which are at all times to be found in the back States."[11]

II

There could be little doubt that the constant movements from Rupert's Land to the United States had lined out a road to the very heartland of the Hudson's Bay Company. Yet if one barrier to overland trade and traffic had been breached, there still remained the Company itself, an obstacle more unyielding than mere space. By vigorous competition with American traders along the international border and strong-armed tactics within its own territories, by diplomacy, and by guile—by all these means the Company managed to preserve the essential isolation of the Red River Settlement and protect its trading monopoly until the 'forties.

[9]G. W. Featherstonhaugh, *A Canoe Voyage up the Minnay Sotor* (2 vols., London, 1847), I, 217. A British traveller, Featherstonhaugh met and conversed with several Scottish emigrants from Red River, while he was staying at Prairie du Chien (Wisconsin) in September, 1835.

[10]Robert Logan to Martin McLeod, 4 May 1838, McLeod Papers, M.H.S. McLeod had migrated to Minnesota in 1837 and joined the American Fur Company.

[11]24 June 1840, H.B.C., Series A.11/95.

Shortly after the reorganization of the fur trade in 1821, the Hudson's Bay Company turned its attention to the business it conducted upon American soil. Though slight, this trade was significant. The Company's chief post was located at Pembina, near the present town of the same name in North Dakota. Here was a unique station that served a variety of purposes. As the rendezvous of Red River's buffalo-hunting half-breeds, it indirectly provided the settlement with most of its pemmican, in addition to substantial quantities of lumber, hay, and coal. However, its primary purpose was that of a fur-trading centre, procuring furs in the borderlands and supplying ancillary posts in Minnesota that stretched from Lake Traverse to Red Lake. Manifest though Pembina's virtues seemed, the Governor and Committee decided that it was neither wise nor expedient to continue trading within the United States; in March, 1821, they strongly suggested to Simpson that he cease all active operations on American soil.

The suggestion met with Simpson's ready compliance. Trading matters below the 49th parallel were not going well. During the summer of 1822, Joseph Renville, a Sioux half-breed and a minor clerk in charge of the sub-post at Lake Traverse, rebelled against his employer. Thinking himself safe in American territory, he refused to give up furs due the Company on the flimsy pretext that the latter was delinquent in some debt allegedly owed him. However, he foolishly agreed to meet Simpson at Pembina and settle the whole affair. But when Renville, accompanied by an armed body of Sioux warriors, reached the rendezvous, he found Simpson already there and with a more imposing retinue. He therefore "made a merit of necessity," delivered up the furs, took French leave, and traded thereafter for the Americans.[12]

Quite probably Renville was aware of the growing influence of the United States within the Northwest; undoubtedly he was conversant with Taliaferro's warnings to Company personnel against trading upon American soil. At any rate, Simpson himself knew of the agent's repeated remonstrations; and the agent's unyielding attitude, coupled with the fact that none of the Company's American enterprises was overly productive, convinced him that he should pull out of Minnesota.[13] In its late summer gathering at York Factory, the Council of

---

[12]Simpson to the Governor and Committee, 5 Aug. 1822, H.B.C., Series D.4/85.
[13]Taliaferro to "Mr. John Buck supposed agent for the Hudsons Bay Cpy.," 10 June 1821, Taliaferro Papers. John Burke was the Company clerk in charge of the Pembina post. In this letter, Taliaferro warned him against trading in the vicinity of Big Stone Lake, which lay just to the south of Traverse. Cf. Simpson to the Governor and Committee, 1 Sept. 1822, H.B.C., Series D.4/85.

the Northern Department resolved therefore to abandon Pembina, keystone of the Company's trading arch in northern Minnesota. In response, Chief Factor John Clarke ordered the clerk at Pembina to close down the post by the middle of October. It was too late to comply, however, for Pembina's runners had already been sent out. Moreover, the trade of the coming season appeared to be extraordinarily promising. Thus the decision to abandon the post was deferred until the following spring, when at last the Company officially withdrew from all its operations below the 49th parallel.

Because of Pembina's abandonment, at least three problems were presented to the Hudson's Bay Company. As a provision centre, it would have to be replaced by the Red River Settlement, and, as we have seen, this transition came about rather quickly. In the second place, Pembina had also been the home of a considerable number of half-breeds, who would have to be persuaded to move to Red River, there to be placed under the government of Assiniboia lest they be drawn into illicit fur trading with the Americans. And finally, the withdrawal necessitated a radical reorganization of the border trade which would have to be re-constituted in such a way as to continue the collection of furs along and above the line, meet the potential competition of Americans along the 49th parallel, and prevent the development of "free trade" within the Red River Settlement.

Although delayed for a time, the Company eventually enticed most of the Pembinese away from their American homes. In part, the delay was caused by the unexpected arrival at Pembina of an American expedition under the command of Major Stephen H. Long. With a fairly large party of soldiers and scientists, Long had left Fort St. Anthony (the later Snelling) in early June, 1823, and spent nearly a month progressing up the Minnesota River and down the Red until he reached Pembina on 5 August. The purpose of his expedition was to examine the Northwest, report upon its physical properties, and determine the true location of the 49th parallel. In the eyes of the major and his compatriots, Pembina was a wilderness settlement devoid of charm. Nearly 350 people lived there, crowded into log houses that were remarkable only for their state of ill repair; and, in Long's opinion, the character of the Pembinese, who were largely of mixed blood, was in harmony with their unkempt homes. Yet he treated them with kindness, and they, in turn, "appeared well pleased with . . . [his] visit, and the object of it."[14] When he had determined the 49th parallel

[14]Long's Journal, vol. 3, 6 Aug. 1823, M.H.S.

and driven stakes to mark it, it was clear to everyone that Pembina, save for a single house, was on American soil.

At first, the survey did not seem to dishearten the half-breeds. According to Long, they "appeared highly gratified . . . and steps were immediately taken to make a representation to Congress in respectful petition of their condition, views & wishes."[15] Only one member of the major's party, the self-invited Italian nobleman, J. C. Beltrami, scouted the petition and its authors, predicting that they "will be the partisans of whoever will pay them best . . . [and] will most probably desert to Fort Douglas. . . ."[16] He was right. Within a year, most of the half-breeds, yielding to the persuasions of George Simpson, had moved into Rupert's Land and settled down on White Horse Plain. And thereafter, to avoid disputes, Simpson moved the Company post well north of Long's line.

After Pembina's abandonment, the chief problem facing the Hudson's Bay Company was how to meet American competition along the international line. The competitors were—or would be—three in number. Two were partnerships associated with the American Fur Company, although in different departments; the third was the Columbia Fur Company, an independent concern. One of the partnerships was the Fond du Lac group, which sustained a number of posts stretching west along the British-American border lakes. The other partnership had its headquarters at Prairie du Chien—and later at Mendota, a hamlet just across the Minnesota River from Fort Snelling—and worked the river valleys to the north and west. In 1823 its northernmost post was situated at Big Stone Lake. The Columbia Fur Company scattered its posts along the axis of the Minnesota and Red rivers and, across the watershed, within the Mandan country of present-day North Dakota. These were the principal American concerns opposing the Hudson's Bay Company.

The circumstances surrounding the creation of the Columbia Fur Company are vague and uncertain. Among its principal agents were William Laidlaw, Kenneth McKenzie, Daniel Lamont, and Joseph Renville. They were birds of a feather. Save for Lamont, an American about whom we know little, they were Hudson's Bay men who had deserted the Company. Without exception, they were men of little principle, energetic and unscrupulous traders making their way in a lawless environment and giving to all fur traders an infamous reputation

[15]*Ibid.*, 7 Aug. 1823.
[16]Beltrami, *A Pilgrimage*, II, 356-7.

that is too often undeserved. Little is known of the early life of Kenneth McKenzie, though he was later regarded as "the sole [*sic*] of his concern."[17] A Hudson's Bay clerk in the summer of 1821, he had been assigned to a post on the Souris River, a branch of the Assiniboine that buttonhooks into North Dakota and then back into Manitoba. He was a thoroughly unsatisfactory servant who ignored orders, squandered Company property, and preferred the society of the Red River half-breeds to the isolation of the Souris. To cap his brief career, he committed the unpardonable sin of urging some of the half-breeds "to join with him in going over to the Americans."[18] But before the Company could discharge him, he "clandestinely left the Establishment and joined Mr. Laidlaw and others . . . who were at that time preparing to desert the Colony and in a few days afterward started for Prairie du Chien. . . ."[19] William Laidlaw had managed the colony's first experimental farm, and, as a leader of Red River's grain-gathering expedition of 1819–20, he was already familiar with the trails leading into the United States.

Moving southward in the fall of 1821 Laidlaw and McKenzie met Renville and Robert Dickson at Lake Traverse. Renville was still working, if half-heartedly, for the Hudson's Bay Company,[20] and Dickson, an ex-Nor'Wester and a former associate of the late Lord Selkirk, was also engaged in the fur trade, although at this time he was undoubtedly an independent trader.[21] Thus the meeting at Traverse brought together four disgruntled souls who, quite probably, made plans for the future Columbia Fur Company. It was a natural combination blending the background and talents of all men present. Through his experience trading on the Souris, McKenzie was familiar

[17]Ramsay Crooks to Astor, 24 May 1827. Quoted in Porter, *Astor*, II, 747–8. It has been commonly and erroneously supposed that both McKenzie and Renville lost their positions in the Hudson's Bay Company in the reduction of personnel taking place after 1821. See Porter, *Astor*, II, 745 and Hiram M. Chittenden, *The American Fur Trade of the Far West* (2nd edition; 2 vols., Stanford, 1954), I, 323.

[18]Simpson to the Governor and Committee, 1 Aug. 1823, H.B.C., Series A.12/1.

[19]*Ibid.*

[20]Gertrude W. Ackermann, "Joseph Renville of Lac Qui Parle," *Minnesota History*, XII (Sept., 1931), 231–46. Renville had been a protégé of Dickson's. Both men had ably served the British cause during the War of 1812 and both had been rewarded with commissions and, later, pensions. Dickson was a lieutenant-colonel; Renville, probably an interpreter holding the rank of lieutenant.

[21]Selkirk had apparently planned a "second" colony that would be planted in the United States and within the limits of his original grant. However, two events ended all planning: the unwillingness of American authorities to recognize his claim and Selkirk's own death in 1820. See Louis A. Tohill, *Robert Dickson, British Fur Trader on the Upper Mississippi* (Ann Arbor, 1927), chap. xi.

with the Mandan country, and both Renville and Dickson had laboured in the Red River Valley for many years.

There was only one serious drawback to their plans. All four were British subjects and, as such, excluded from trading within the United States. But to them the law was a formality. They proceeded to Prairie du Chien and stated (12 January 1822) in the presence of the Indian agent, Major Taliaferro, "that Josep[h] Rainville a halfbreed Sioux, who is established at Lake Traverse near Big Stone Lake—is not to be considered either hostile to the Americans nor disposed to defy the laws of the U States as has been verry [*sic*] industriously reported [,] he considers himself to be an American and wishes to be considered one—he has been generally hired by the Hudsons [*sic*] Bay Cpy to trade [,] it was not within the power of the AM. nation to furnish the Red River Country with merchandize for [the] Indian trade."[22] As added evidence of his altered allegiance, Renville renounced a military pension which he had gained fighting as a British army officer in the War of 1812; and despite a record that could scarcely have been more British, he got the licence and the Columbia Fur Company went ahead with its plans.

It was not until the following year (1823) that the company really got under way. The delay was probably occasioned by the search for a mercantile house which could provide the partners with articles for the Indian trade and serve as an outlet for the sale of their furs. It seems likely that Dickson personally investigated the possibility of an association with some eastern establishments. If so, nothing came of it, and the partners eventually made an agreement with Daniel Lamont of St. Louis and a firm of that city, Tilton and Company, with which the latter was undoubtedly associated.[23] It was an attractive agreement that not only provided the Company with trading goods on credit but also strengthened its "American" character. The Columbia Fur Company began its active trading life as a minute concern centred at Lake Traverse. When the members of Long's expedition stopped there in the summer of 1823, they were impressed neither with the company's primitive establishment nor with its trading prospects. However, they had overlooked the one intangible asset that would bring success to the company—the dynamic energy of its partners. The

[22]Taliaferro Journal, No. 2, 12 Jan. 1822. Renville's claim for American citizenship occurred several months before his final break with the Hudson's Bay Company.
[23]Chittenden, *The American Fur Trade*, I, 323–4. Dickson died on Drummond Island (Michigan) during the summer of 1823, while en route to the Minnesota country.

young company was already competing with the Hudson's Bay Company in the vicinity of Pembina, and during the winter of 1822–23 one of its partners had transported by dog sled a thousand pounds of trade goods to the Mandan villages on the upper Missouri River.[24] In 1824 the Columbia continued its Mandan operations and added three more posts to its string along the Minnesota and Red River valleys.[25] Overnight it had become a force for both the Hudson's Bay and the American Fur Company to reckon with.

In 1823 and 1824 George Simpson reorganized and reshuffled the trading districts of Rupert's Land. The once profitable Upper Red River District was discarded as a "superfluous and costly" department nearly barren of fur-bearing animals.[26] Its trading posts (including Pembina and Fort Garry) were abandoned as such; and the general administration of the area was entrusted to the Red River District, a new unit combining the old Upper and Lower Red River Districts, thereby saving the Company an estimated £2,000 per year. To meet the general trade of the settlement, the colony shop was regarded as more than adequate, but to secure the fur trade of Pembina and harass the American traders along the border, Simpson had to pull a new trick out of his bag. Simpson intended to make the border trade "as little profitable as possible to the American traders."[27] His was a simple plan of permitting individuals unconnected with the Company to trade directly with the Indians. Reliable Red River settlers were licensed and supplied with goods at moderate rates, and they, in turn, equipped small parties to trade with the border Indians both north and south of the international line. The furs were then brought to Fort Garry and sold to the Company at a price that yielded the traders a fair profit. The scheme worked almost to perfection. The Company secured the furs of the district without having to bear the expense of employing a large body of servants, and "the American Traders on the Lines . . . [had] active opponents in all directions, who . . . [could not] be identified with the Company."[28] There was one element of risk in the scheme. Might not the private traders be tempted by other Americans to serve two masters? In the future this would prove to be

[24]William H. Keating, *Narrative of an Expedition to the Sources of the Saint Peter's River* (2 vols., Philadelphia, 1824), I, 445–7 and II, 45 *et seq.* Keating accompanied Long's expedition.

[25]Joseph Brown to Henry Sibley, 3 Jan. 1855, Sibley Papers, M.H.S.

[26]Simpson to the Governor and Committee, 5 June 1824, H.B.C., Series D.4/87.

[27]Governor and Committee to Simpson, 12 March 1827, H.B.C., Series A.6/21.

[28]Simpson to the Governor and Committee, 20 Aug. 1826, H.B.C., Series A.12/1. As a district, Red River got more furs in 1825–26 than when it employed twenty servants just to protect the trade.

the case, but at the moment only a few men dared violate their agreement with the Company.

Though it is difficult to gauge the effect of Simpson's new policy upon the fortunes of the Columbia Fur Company, this much is certain: its posts in the Red River Valley could never have been too successful. They were situated in a region regarded by the Hudson's Bay Company as ruined and forced to compete for its meagre blessings with two strong foes: Simpson's runners from the Red River Settlement and the American Fur Company. It therefore seems likely that the profit-making ventures of the Columbia Fur Company were confined to the Mandan country, where McKenzie and his men held as strong a position as anyone in the trade—where Astor himself did not have a single post. Regardless of where it made money, the little company was soon doing Astor's concern "an annual injury of ten thousand dollars at least."[29] And in accordance with his policy of crushing weak rivals and absorbing the strong, Astor acquired the Columbia Fur Company in the summer of 1827 for an estimated $20,000, ending the life of the company but not the careers of its associates.[30] McKenzie, Lamont, and Laidlaw became partners in the American Fur Company, their Mandan establishment was transformed into the famous Upper Missouri Outfit, and McKenzie began his long and notorious reign as "King of the Upper Missouri."

A rare combination of events led to the revival of fierce competition for the furs of the Pembina area. Since 1823–24, the Hudson's Bay Company had allowed the Red River District and its environs, a region nearly destitute of fur-bearing animals, to recruit itself. When it came, recovery was startlingly swift. The flood of 1826 innundated the marshlands and built up extraordinary breeding grounds for muskrats. The aquatic rodents multiplied at a great rate and what was formerly a barren land began to bloom again.[31] At this precise moment the demand for rats, as for all furs, was strengthened. Prices that had languished in 1826 suddenly shot up, and the effect upon the Red River District was instantaneous and widespread. The Company's own collection of skins swelled; within the settlement free traders began to thrive again; and American traders moved north and threatened the entire line from Lake Superior to the Dakota plains.

To meet this new situation, the Company continued its policy of

[29]Chittenden, *The American Fur Trade*, I, 325.
[30]Porter, *Astor*, II, 748. It was more an amalgamation than an acquisition. Astor's price included only the value of the Columbia's trade goods, not its posts.
[31]Simpson to the Governor and Committee, 21 June 1827, H.B.C., D.4/90. Cf. Porter, *Astor*, II, 759–60.

licensing private individuals to trade in furs within the Red River District. Its own servants in the district were withdrawn from fur-gathering and concerned themselves only with the conduct of the Company's stores and the operation of Fort Garry. Though a good system, it was not without defects. In abandoning the trading field, the Company unwittingly created a corps of free traders who were soon to outnumber their own licensed brethren. Moreover the Company accelerated the progress of free trade by establishing a price policy which stipulated that a lesser sum was to be paid the Indians at Fort Garry than either to the half-breeds or to the white settlers.[32] The result was a price spread broad enough to encourage the latter to become middlemen, buying furs directly from the Indians and re-selling them to the Company. George Simpson was always aware of these faults. Almost from the inception of the licensing programme he knew that there had been petty trespasses, but he accepted them as minor failings in an otherwise satisfactory scheme.

Simpson did not retain this peace of mind for long. Once under way, free trade quickly developed into a movement in which it seemed as if every white man, half-breed, and Indian in the Red River District were involved. At first, the Company acted forthrightly, serving warrants upon free traders, confiscating their furs, and even threatening to deport one man whose illicit business had been less clandestine than his fellows.[33] But as the "rat boom" took a firm grip upon the economy of Red River in the fall of 1827 and attracted countless recruits into the ranks of the free traders, it became impolitic if not impossible for the Company to arrest the progress of free trade by the legal means at its command.

Inevitable with the increase in numbers of the free traders was the extension of their activities into the adjacent districts north and west of Red River. A primary stimulus for the continued growth of free trade was the ever rising cash price offered for furs at Fort Garry. This was an unfortunate but scarcely avoidable state of affairs; any other policy would encourage the free traders—and many were already yielding to temptation—to spirit their goods across the line and into the arms of the American Fur Company. George Simpson had to hold prices at a higher level than the Americans. At the same time

[32]Donald Gunn and Charles R. Tuttle, *History of Manitoba from the Earliest Settlement* (Ottawa, 1880), pp. 253–4.

[33]Simpson to the Governor and Committee, 25 July 1827, H.B.C., Series D.4/87. The unlucky man was Ferdinand Celo, who pleaded for mercy at York Factory, where he had been removed for deportation, and was ultimately permitted to return to his family.

he found it necessary to establish sub-posts staffed by his own men in Red River's hinterland in order to offset the expanded operations of free traders. To his dismay he found that these people, semi-nomadic half-breeds for the most part, were extremely difficult to control. As natives of Rupert's Land, they claimed the right to settle anywhere, trade with the Indians, and market their goods either in the Red River Settlement or in the United States.[34]

Simpson realized that the problem of dealing with free traders within Rupert's Land was bound up with the presence of American traders along the border. If he could best the latter, he might be able to manage the former. To checkmate American posts springing up below the line, he built new stations and strengthened existing ones lying above it. To fill in the gaps, he employed licensed half-breeds from Red River, mobile traders who ranged north and south of the border. Given time, the scheme worked well. It not only protected the Company's frontier but it also "drew large quantities of Furs from the other side . . . ,"[35] and it had the added attraction of achieving protection without drawing the Company into the delicate question of international rights. For the licensed half-breeds were only British citizens, not employees of the Company; and as half-breeds, they could be "either American or British subjects as suits their purpose, being natives of the soil."[36]

Simpson faced American opposition all along the frontier. From its vantage point in the Mandan Country, Kenneth McKenzie's Upper Missouri Outfit pushed northward to the line, drawing a good many furs from Rupert's Land and threatening to invade the northland itself. To the east, Simpson found himself opposed by William Aitkin of the Fond du Lac district, a division of the American Fur Company's Northern Department. Aitkin's chief post was on Rainy Lake, where he applied persistent pressure upon the Company's Lac la Pluie (Rainy Lake) District. Moreover, he had a line of auxiliary posts strung westward along the border, and in the winter of 1828–29 he added a final sub-post at Pembina in order to share in Red River's muskrat market.

---

[34]In a report to the Governor and Committee (30 June 1829) regarding this independent state of mind, Simpson claimed that "this feeling and opinion I am sorry to say is beginning to obtain among the Red River halfbreeds, particularly among those of European parentage . . . and may in due time become highly injurious to the Fur Trade." H.B.C., Series D.4/96.

[35]*Ibid.*

[36]Simpson to the Governor and Committee, 26 Aug. 1830, H.B.C., Series D.4/97.

In the early stages of the international contest, Simpson gave considerable attention to the western sector. He could not ignore rumours that McKenzie's men were planning to invade Rupert's Land. To prepare for that eventuality, Simpson had the 49th parallel secretly surveyed, but openly marked, westward from Pembina. But what should be his policy if this line were crossed? He himself favoured the use of force and intended to seize any American invaders and confiscate their property.[37] The Governor and Committee, with greater caution, overruled Simpson.[38] They instructed him to serve notice upon any American interlopers discovered in Rupert's Land and give the Company in London adequate proof of the invasion so that the Foreign Office could deal directly with Washington on the matter. Save in self-defence, Simpson was not to use force. In the final event there was no invasion. The problem of combating McKenzie became the relatively simple one of re-establishing old posts to the north of him and of employing vigorous half-breed traders from Red River to harass him south of the line. The tactics succeeded. By 1832, the temporary posts were abandoned and the border parties relaxed their efforts.

Pembina presented a far different and much stickier problem than that posed by McKenzie and his Missouri River runners. It was the gateway to the lower Red River Valley. If ever held in unfriendly hands, it would be a dagger pointed at the heart of Rupert's Land. Also, Pembina was still the home of quite a few half-breeds, both freemen and ex-servants; and twice annually, its population boomed when the buffalo hunters from Red River gathered there in preparation for their spring and fall expeditions to the plains. In short, Pembina was a potential weakness of which Simpson was always anxiously aware: ". . . should any difference hereafter arise . . . between Great Britain and the United States it [Pembina] is the point from whence the Hon'ble Company's trade is most likely to be disturbed, and which will therefore require to be most closely watched, as the [half-breed] Settlement would readily furnish the means necessary to overrun the Country. . . ."[39] Therefore the very moment that William Aitkin established a trading post at Pembina, he had created a situation that the Company could not tolerate.

Aitkin was a formidable opponent who had lived and traded in the Minnesota borderlands almost all of his life, and no sooner had he settled down in his new Pembina post than he began offering high

[37]Simpson to the Governor and Committee, 25 July 1827, H.B.C., Series D.4/90.
[38]Governor and Committee to Simpson, 16 Jan. 1828, H.B.C., Series A.6/21.
[39]Simpson to the Governor and Committee, 18 July 1831, H.B.C., Series A.12/1.

prices for all furs regardless of their origin. His prices had a magical effect upon Red River's free traders. Simpson and the Hudson's Bay Company soon learned that it was "a very difficult matter to prevent . . . [their] furs from being taken to" the competitor down the street.[40] They had to match Aitkin's offers. Consequently, during the American's first and second seasons on the border, prices skyrocketed. But the results were more pleasing to the Company than to Aitkin. In 1828–29 it collected more furs in the Red River District than it had over the past twenty years, and although the returns of the next season fell off, the net profit remained at an attractive height.[41] Of greater significance than mere profit, however, the men of Red River were less disposed in 1829–30 to trade across the line. In waging a price war with the Hudson's Bay Company, Aitkin was a little man in a big poker game, a game of high stakes in which he could never hope to match his rival in either capital or personnel. Aitkin never got more than a fraction of the furs being collected within his own bailiwick. Simpson's licensed half-breeds carted off most of them to Rupert's Land.

One of these men, a clever fellow named Augustin Nolin, proved to be Aitkin's *bête noire*. Wherever the American went, he found Nolin— at Pembina, Roseau, or at Red Lake, deep in American territory. Unable to shake his shadow, Aitkin complained to Simpson that a Company man was illegally operating within the United States. In rejoinder, Simpson said that Nolin was not a servant of the Company. Indeed, when Aitkin angrily ordered Nolin off American soil, the *métis* replied that he not only had a Hudson's Bay licence but that he was also a native American half-breed. Once again, Aitkin remonstrated to Simpson, but the only answer he got was that Nolin had a licence to trade in Rupert's Land and the Company was "unaccountable for his proceedings elsewhere."[42] Poor Aitkin—he was confused by the double-talk and helpless before intrigue. His position in the trade inevitably deteriorated. He could not cope with the competition from Red River, and to make matters worse, the supply of muskrats was fast approaching exhaustion. In the winter of 1830–31 he made Simpson a proposition. He agreed to abandon Pembina, if the latter would withdraw from the Lac la Pluie District. Simpson would not hear of it. It was an obvious bluff by a little man in a losing game. Aitkin

[40]Simpson to the Governor and Committee, 30 June 1829, H.B.C., Series D.4/96.
[41]Simpson to the Governor and Committee, 26 Aug. 1830, H.B.C., Series D.4/97.
[42]Simpson to the Governor and Committee, 18 July 1831, H.B.C., Series A.12/1.

lingered on at Pembina until Nolin crushed him with a diabolical *ruse de guerre*. In the winter of 1832–33, while North America trembled before a cholera epidemic sweeping westward across the continent, the cunning *métis* turned the disease to his own advantage. He warned Aitkin's Indians of the danger of infection at Pembina "and not a man . . . [would] venture near the American Post."[43] Aitkin had to throw in his cards.

Pembina may have perished but its mother post on Rainy Lake remained. The American Fur Company had established this station in the early 'twenties, and throughout the decade it provided the Hudson's Bay Company with the most formidable competition of all the border posts. Indeed, only in this district (Lac la Pluie) did the Hudson's Bay Company encounter a "uniform, well regulated opposition."[44] The long hard contest between them placed both companies under considerable strain. In such a highly competitive situation, demanding large expenditures in wages for personnel and liquor for the Indians, costs were higher than ordinary, while the margin of profit was uncomfortably thin. By exerting itself the Hudson's Bay Company held its own, even making money on the venture, but for Astor, there was little or no profit to be found. As the decade drew to a close he was faced with the choice of improving his position by some agreement with the Hudson's Bay Company or of withdrawing from the border with as much grace and money as possible.

At the same time that Aitkin was making his proposition to Simpson, Astor was trying to persuade the Hudson's Bay Company to eliminate liquor in the border trade.[45] He outlined a scheme whereby the Indian agent at Sault Ste. Marie would prohibit the introduction of spirits by all Americans into the contested area, if both the Hudson's Bay and the American Fur Companies would "take the pledge." To Astor's plan, both Simpson and the Governor and Committee agreed in principle, although they felt sure that prohibition would benefit Astor more than themselves. However, agreement in detail was another matter. Neither foe trusted the other; neither would disarm itself before the other; and, in the end, Astor wondered whether prohibition would work at all. Perhaps, he reasoned, the Hudson's Bay Company would be holding the head of the cow and his own company attending the other end, while the petty, fly-by-night traders would be helping

[43]Thomas Simpson to James Hargrave, 19 Dec. 1832, in G. P. deT. Glazebrook, ed., *The Hargrave Correspondence 1821–1843* (Toronto, 1938), pp. 95–7.

[44]Simpson to the Governor and Committee, 10 July 1828, H.B.C., Series D.4/92.

[45]The Secretary of the Company to William B. Astor, 3 March 1830, H.B.C., Series A.6/22.

themselves to all the milk.[46] In fact, the chief ill besetting both companies was not liquor, which was merely a symptom, but rather the expensive war being waged between them in a region that could support only one giant.

The Governor and Committee were distressed by the reports they received of the costly border struggle. It seemed bad business to hazard so much for so little. They urged Simpson to come to an agreement with the American Fur Company whereby each party would rule out the more expensive methods of competition yet allow complete freedom for the Indians along the border to seek the market of their choice.[47] This was merely another variation of Astor's prohibition scheme and doomed from the start. Simpson's thinking was far ahead of his London office. Before receiving the above advice, he had already reached an agreement with Aitkin and the American Fur Company that ended the contest. In March, 1833, Aitkin contracted to vacate the whole border, from Pembina to Lake Superior, for a period of three years. In return, Simpson agreed to pay him £300 per year "if that frontier remained unassailed by any opposition whatsoever."[48] Surprisingly enough, there had been little difficulty in coming to terms. It was a "quit-claim" arranged by two weary titans to suit their mutual interests. Surprisingly too, after the bitter struggle between them, was the friendship that arose between Simpson and Aitkin; undoubtedly, their cordial association had much to do with the contract's later success.

In the years to come, both parties lived up to the contract in letter as well as in spirit. Indeed, with but few alterations in its terms, it persisted until events beyond the control of either party brought it to an end in 1847. The Hudson's Bay Company gained much from the contract. Without Astor's competition, its border trade thrived. Operational costs were pared down—even the liquor allotment for the Lac la Pluie District was reduced—and the additional profit of the first year alone exceeded the contract's charges by five times.[49] The American Fur Company was similarly gratified. When their Indians visited Lac la Pluie, they were turned back by the Hudson's Bay men. Ramsay Crooks, President of the American Fur Company after Astor's retirement in 1834, went out of his way in the following year to assure Simpson of his company's goodwill by directing his associates in the

[46]Simpson to the Governor and Committee, 18 July 1831, H.B.C., Series A.12/1.
[47]Governor and Committee to Simpson, 1 March 1833, H.B.C., Series A.6/23.
[48]Simpson to Aitkin, 2 July 1834, H.B.C., Series D.4/100.
[49]Simpson to the Governor and Committee, 21 July 1834, *ibid.*

field to afford every facility to the British traders. The American Fur Company cheerfully forwarded drafts and trading goods for its erstwhile rival and supported the odd express that the British might dispatch through American territory. The two companies also managed to minimize invasions by private traders in their co-dominion; and despite the chances to cheat in such a vast and rugged country, each remained remarkably faithful to its pledge.

Of all the Americans in the vicinity, perhaps Henry H. Sibley was in the best position to violate the border agreement. He was within Crooks' Western Department and not connected in any way with Aitkin or the Northern Department. His main post was at Mendota; his sub-posts ranged northward and were anchored at their northernmost point by Lake Traverse. A natural extension of Sibley's system would be to add more trading stations between Traverse and the international line. In 1836, Joseph Brown, Sibley's associate at Lake Traverse, argued for the establishment of a post at Devils Lake (North Dakota), describing the virtues of the border trade in most persuasive prose:

The Half Breeds of Red River make a good portion of their hunts within a short distance of Devils Lake, and on our territory, This peltry swells the returns of the Hudson's Bay's [sic] Company. It is but reasonable that a portion of these furs could be brought to Devils Lake, and that they would look as well at New York, if they went by St. Peters, as if they went by London. You may ask why better returns were not made when there was a post there, In the first place [Joseph] Rock [sic] was the last man that could make returns any where, in the next place Aitkins [sic] at that time had a post at Pembina, which got the half breed hunts, and owing to that the Hudsons [sic] Bay Company traded liberally. At this time there is no other place for those people to get their necessaries, nor has [there] been for several years, this has caused that compy to change its conduct towards those people, and they are discontented, and would jump sky high at the chance of throwing off the yoke.[50]

His arguments were convincing: a permanent post either at Devils Lake or at Pembina would undoubtedly make large returns. Although his outfit was not then overly prosperous, Sibley could do nothing about Brown's suggestions. His association with Crooks prevented him even from considering them.

Crooks' willingness to co-operate with the Hudson's Bay Company was complete. Until 1838 the contract's fees had been paid to Aitkin. Thereafter, they were handed over to Crooks. While the reason for the change is unknown, one result of it was soon apparent. Aitkin

[50]Joseph Brown to Sibley, 23 Jan. 1836, Sibley Papers.

became a free agent who reportedly threatened to operate as an independent trader along the border. When apprised of the rumour, Crooks lost no time informing the Company. Furthermore, he sought and gained permission to oppose Aitkin on American soil. Thus Crooks became more than a party to a border lease. In later years he was almost an "employee" of the Company, performing common courtesies for a friend and underhanded dealings for an accomplice. So eager was he to aid Simpson's company that one wonders whether he did not receive a generous *douceur* in addition to the £300. At any rate Simpson kept renewing a contract "which has for many years been productive of much advantage to both concerns. . . ."[51] For he was safe from Henry Sibley and his fur-trading colleagues in Minnesota only as long as Crooks controlled the American Fur Company.

[51]Simpson to the Secretary, 14 May 1844, H.B.C., Series A.12/2.

Chapter 3. Norman W. Kittson and Free Trade in the Red River Settlement, 1843–1849

I

FOR ALL ITS CONTRACT WITH THE AMERICAN FUR COMPANY, THE HUDSON'S Bay Company never acquired an exclusive economic overlordship of the border region. Independent traders from either side of the line continued to operate within the corridor, while in the field of general trade, commerce between the half-breeds of Red River and the merchant traders of Minnesota stepped up its pace. Wandering widely in pursuit of the buffalo, the half-breeds touched and traded with American posts on the upper Red River and then were drawn by economic-geographic forces into a broader trade with the settlements farther to the south. The traffic had begun with a simple, irregular exchange of half-breed products for American goods. By 1835 the men of Red River "had already made several trips to the Mississippi, exporting horn cattle, horses, furs and some articles of colonial industry, and, on their return, bringing home cotton goods, groceries, ammunition, tobacco, &c., &c."[1] By the end of the decade, these same men were making "annual excursions to St. Paul and Mendota . . . [their] ox carts being laden with buffalo robes, furs, pemican [sic] and other articles which . . . [were] exchanged upon their arrival for merchandize suited to their wants."[2]

[1]Donald Gunn and Charles R. Tuttle, *History of Manitoba from the Earliest Settlement* (Ottawa, 1880), p. 286.
[2]Deposition of Joseph Bruce before Henry H. Sibley, Justice of the Peace, Clayton County, Iowa Territory, 13 July 1840, Sibley Papers, M.H.S.

Henry H. Sibley, a partner in the American Fur Company's Western Department, was dealing with these itinerant Red River traders soon after his arrival in Mendota in 1834. To a man with his business ability and vision, it must have been apparent from the start that the best way of exploiting this trade was to establish a post at Pembina, the gateway for all traffic between Red River and Minnesota. However there was nothing he could do about it at the time. He was held back not only by the terms of the American Fur Company's lease but also by the counsel of Ramsay Crooks, who instructed him to conduct himself in a gracious manner toward the Hudson's Bay Company.[3]

In 1842 Sibley was released at last from his obligations and given a free hand to pursue the border trade. In that year the venerable St. Louis firm, Pierre Choteau, Jr. & Company, purchased the Western Department from Crooks, and in the reorganization of the fur trade that followed, Sibley became a Choteau partner and was entrusted, as before, with the management of the Western or Upper Mississippi Outfit. Sibley's contract with the Choteaus created a "partnership" that was typical of the fur trade.[4] They promised to supply him with all necessary trade goods at 5 per cent over cost, plus any shipping charges involved; Sibley presumably assumed the transportation costs from St. Louis to his headquarters at Mendota. The goods were extended on credit, for which an annual interest charge of 7 per cent was paid. Sibley, in turn, promised either to let the Choteaus handle the sale of all his furs or give them 5 per cent of the sales, if he could find a better market. Invariably, however, he handed over the furs to his St. Louis partners, and any profits gained from their sale were then split on a predetermined ratio, the Choteaus getting the lion's share.

For Sibley, the last few years under the Crooks administration had been disappointingly lean. Expansion seemed the only possible cure, and, under the circumstances, he looked to the upper Red River Valley for his salvation. In May, 1843, he signed a contract with Norman W. Kittson, agreeing to supply him with whatever goods were needed to establish four trading posts within "... the country assigned by Agreement [with the Choteaus] to the Western or Upper Miss Outfit, which lies above Lac qui Parle. . . ." Sibley provided Kittson—on credit at 7 per cent—with trade goods at 10 per cent over cost, plus shipping

[3]Crooks to Sibley, 6 March 1835, *Calendar of the American Fur Company's Papers* (2 vols., Washington, D.C., 1945), I, 40.
[4]This pact and Sibley's subsequent contracts with Kittson may be found in the Sibley Papers.

charges; and the furs, in which the two would share equally, were to be sold by Sibley or the Choteaus.

By fall, Sibley and Kittson had selected Pembina as the head and front of their projected trading posts. According to their plans, Pembina would play three roles. In the first place, its very existence would jeopardize the economic and political welfare of the Hudson's Bay Company. Thus the hope would always remain that even if the trade itself failed, blackmail would not, and they could sell out to the Company in the manner of William Aitkin. In the second place, Pembina would be again the centre of a fur-trading operation extending along the 49th parallel. But the third role was the leading one, as daring as it was illegal: daring in the conception of Pembina as a trading warehouse serving the general wants of the Red River Settlement and illegal in the intention to use Pembina as a storehouse for furs smuggled out of Rupert's Land. To make a success of the proposed general trade, Kittson and Sibley had to ally themselves with the Red River Settlement's leading merchants, James Sinclair and Andrew McDermot. And, as Kittson knew, the same two were equally essential to any smuggling operation because they "were the only persons in the Settlement who . . . [made] any collection of furs."[5]

He might have added that it would have been difficult to find two more extraordinary businessmen in all North America. James Sinclair was a well-educated, English-speaking half-breed and a most enterprising if amoral businessman.[6] His neighbour and colleague, McDermot, was a fast-talking, hard-drinking, eel-like Irishman who had clerked for the Company for a dozen years before commencing an independent career in business.[7] Here were two men whom pride never prevented from stooping over to pick up a penny. For a long time

[5]Kittson to Sibley, 10 Sept. 1845, *ibid.*

[6]James Sinclair (c. 1806–1856) was the son of William Sinclair, chief factor in the Company. As a youth, James was educated in Edinburgh; as a father, he sent his own children to Knox College in Galesburg, Illinois. He was an articulate man who employed his oral and literary skills to further his own business affairs and to advance the cause of the free-trade movement in Rupert's Land. He served the Company for a single year before turning to an independent career, where he remained, despite George Simpson's efforts to get him back, until 1854. In that year, he returned to the service and led a party of Red River immigrants to the Columbia country, where he was killed in 1856 during an Indian uprising. See D. Geneva Lent, *West of the Mountains: James Sinclair and the Hudson's Bay Company* (Seattle, Washington, 1963).

[7]Andrew McDermot (1790–1881) was Red River's leading merchant and most prominent citizen. He served for many years as a member of the council of Assiniboia.

McDermot's business interests were wholly bound to the Company. He served for many years as a private, licensed trader in Simpson's system for operating the Red River District; and at the same time, he sold firewood, fencing, and beef to the Company. But his main source of income was probably derived from a long-standing contract which he and Sinclair held for the transportation of the Company's freight to and from York Factory. With capital amassed from this and other sources, the two men branched out into general trade, importing from abroad and retailing in the settlement. Their next step was, perhaps, inevitable. They extended their business to compete with the Company in the gathering and sale of furs.

During the winter of 1843–44, Kittson made the first of several trips to the Red River Settlement in search of an agreement with McDermot and Sinclair. His offer of the regular delivery of American commodities was irresistible and led to a long-lasting general trade between Sibley and McDermot. Sinclair, too, was "anxcious [*sic*] to make arrangements . . . for the Northern trade";[8] but neither he nor McDermot was willing at the time to sign any smugglers' pact. Although both men were undoubtedly smuggling furs, the greater part of their business, whether fur trading or freighting, was still legitimate. In the winter of 1844–45 Kittson once more pressed for an illicit alliance, and once again, he failed. Sinclair informed him that he had "rencwed his arrangements with the H.B. Compy. which debared him the previllage of undertaking any business, which might be injurious to them."[9]

When Kittson began the fur-trading season at Pembina in the fall of 1844, alone and with just enough goods to start the post, the country was as unpromising as McDermot and Sinclair. The local Indians were destitute, lacking even the traps to take furs. To make matters worse, autumnal fires had swept across the northern plains, consuming the grassland and driving the buffalo far to the south; and Kittson's other clients, the half-breed hunters, chose to stay home rather than risk their lives for a few robes. All in all, it was, as Kittson claimed, "a most discouraging year." His returns were meagre; the environment, cheerless; and by spring he had to confess to Sibley that the current outfit had been a losing venture.

Kittson was not, by nature, a pessimistic man. Attuned to the wilderness and its capricious moods, he had learned to accept adversity. Despite the winter's misfortunes and his rejection by Sinclair and

[8]Kittson to Sibley, 16 July 1844, Sibley Papers.
[9]Kittson to Sibley, 6 Feb. 1845, *ibid.*

McDermot, he was "certain that something . . . [could] be made in that quarter."[10] Although a third trip to Red River in the spring was again fruitless, his optimism remained; and as summer wore on, his spirits were rewarded by the improvement of the fur trade. Pembina proved to be a magnet, drawing half-breeds and their families to Kittson's side. With a flair for making friends and an open purse, he gained their sympathy and their support, and what was more, he was presently able to coax still other half-breeds into trading with him across the line. To cap a successful summer, when he returned to the settlement in late August, 1845, "every one . . . that had any means began to trade furs."[11]

The reason for Kittson's good fortune was clear. Apprehensive of the growing power of Red River's independent traders and of the free trade movement that accompanied it, the Hudson's Bay Company took the first of many steps to check this growth and thereby forestall a threat to their own commercial position in Rupert's Land. One of the first steps was to close Hudson Bay to importers like Sinclair and McDermot, the men who were suspected of using their businesses to further an illicit fur trade. But the result was not what the Company would have wished, for the action had an unexpected and unwelcome reaction. The closure of York Factory drove Sinclair, McDermot, and many lesser traders into Kittson's welcome arms. Not only did he secure "the promises and good wishes of most of the good hunters" but he also contracted with Sinclair and McDermot for the delivery of $2,000 to $2,500 of furs.[12] The terms were cash, and cash meant payment in gold and silver at a rate exceeding the Company's prices by 25 per cent.[13] It was a high price, elevated to better the competition and meet the risks of smuggling; but for the moment Kittson was king of the border, and the smugglers' road between Red River and his palace at Pembina became crowded.

The Hudson's Bay Company viewed the situation with obvious displeasure. To their way of thinking, Pembina was "a nursery and refuge for disaffection, and for the protection of those who may be employed in trading furs within the limits of the Company's Territories."[14] Kittson had to be eliminated; and the Company began its countermoves even before he had concluded his Red River arrange-

10Kittson to Sibley, 30 March 1845, *ibid.*

11McDermot to Alexander Christie, 30 Nov. 1845. "R.R. Correspondence, 1845–46–47," Christie's confidential letterbook, P.A.M.

12Kittson to Sibley, 10 Sept. 1845, Sibley Papers.

13McDermot to Christie, 30 Nov. 1845, "R.R. Correspondence, 1845–46–47."

14Christie to Simpson, 31 Dec. 1845, "R.R. Correspondence, 1845–46–47."

ments. Plans were made to guard Rupert's Land from further invasion by a line of posts stretching for miles along the border; and Pembina itself was to be directly offset by the existing post lying just north of the 49th parallel. This was meant to be the primary roadblock for the smugglers' carts from Red River. At the other end of the road and on American soil, there was to be a second station, planted right in Kittson's backyard. The Company's projected American post bore all the marks of Sir George Simpson's tactical genius. Through the good offices of Ramsay Crooks, he secured a standard American trading licence.[15] In form, the licence was legal; in practice, it was not. It was made out to Henry Fisher of Prairie du Chien, who was ostensibly an American, but actually an ex-Hudson's Bay man now brought secretly back into the service. The instructions given him for the operation of the post were short and simple: he was to compete with Kittson in cash or goods, wherever the latter traded.

Although rumours of his coming preceded him, Fisher's appearance in mid-February (1846) startled Kittson. Accompanied by a dozen or more rugged men, Fisher visited his intended victim, showed him the licence, and, in a neighbourly fashion, disclosed his plans for building a post in the vicinity.[16] Fisher's schemes immediately backfired. As he and his crew were erecting tents within yards of Kittson's post, the American repaid the visit. But on this occasion there was no pretence of neighbourliness. Kittson warned the invaders that if they did not leave in three hours, they would be arrested, fined, and sent to jail in Dubuque, Iowa Territory. The tactics worked perfectly. Fisher's men were so unnerved that "not one would cut a Piece of wood" and most of them hastily departed for Rupert's Land. Kittson's words were not all bluff. He had the solid backing of the Pembinese, and, in recounting the incident to Sibley, he added that "all praise . . . [was] due to the Half breeds of R. River for their promptness in coming forward and offering their services to us, for the protection of our laws, if required."[17]

Despite the initial setback, the Hudson's Bay Company persisted with its American design. With reinforcements from Red River, Fisher

[15]Charles Borup to Christie, 7 Aug. 1845 and Christie to Fisher, 13 Feb. 1846, Fisher Papers (on microfilm), M.H.S. Borup was a member of the American Fur Company's Northern Department and stationed at Lapointe, Wisconsin. Borup got the licence from the Lapointe Indian agent. Fisher was the perfect man for Simpson's ruse. He had been living at Prairie du Chien and had several relatives in the United States, including Kittson's own aide at Pembina, Joseph Rolette, Jr.

[16]Henry Fisher, "Journal of Occurrences at Pembina, and, for the year 1846," Fisher Papers.

[17]Kittson to Sibley, 2 March 1846, Sibley Papers.

finally succeeded in building a small house which he called Fort
Defiance. The name was ill chosen. During the winter of 1846 the
post did nothing more than defy Kittson. It certainly did little damage
to his position in the trade. For all its generous cash outlay for furs
and its well-equipped larder, Fort Defiance could not best Kittson,
although he began to look "very thin around the gills" and apparently
lacked trading goods as well as food.[18] He maintained the preference
of his American hunters, and when spring appeared it was evident
that he still enjoyed the favours of several Red River smugglers.
Cartloads of furs, some disguised and others openly displaying their
contents, rolled by Fort Defiance on their way to Kittson's establishment and returned to Rupert's Land bearing American goods of
every description.[19]

Fisher's immediate superior, Alexander Christie, knew that Fort
Defiance had never been a success. Indeed he had always doubted
that the post would succeed, but, facing failure he dared not abandon
it. As he confessed to Simpson, withdrawal would mean "paralysing our
authority as well in the [Red River] Settlement as out of it."[20]

In truth, nothing seemed to have worked in the Company's plans to
uproot Kittson. While Christie lamented the declining state of the
Company's affairs, Kittson jubilantly crowed to Sibley about Pembina's
present good fortune and its prosperous future:

For my part I think it should be kept up by all means, and it will
require to be extended considerably, for the Compy of H.B. can be brot
to terms, the shock they have received this year will be felt severely, eight
thousand dollars will not make up the difference in their trade, by the
means of our small opposition, but this is not the worst, we have created
quite a censation [sic] in our favour in their colony, which is working
strongly against them, and by a little exertion on our part, we must drive
them into terms before long; but this must be kept a secret from all, it
would not do to let [it] out, that we would accept any proposal coming
from them, as it might injure us with the Half breeds.[21]

The secret was well kept; but the "Kitson fever" of which Fisher
and his crew complained had already crossed the line and was
raging in the Red River Settlement.

[18]Joseph Braseau to Fisher, 7 and 8 April 1846, Fisher Papers. Braseau was
Fisher's subordinate.
[19]See Peter Garrioch's Journal, Part VI, "Seven Days' of the Pleasures of
Smuggling," George Gunn's MS, P.A.M.
[20]21 April 1846, "R.R. Correspondence, 1845–46–47."
[21]2 March 1846, Sibley Papers.

II

In 1843, the year marking Kittson's establishment at Pembina, Sir George Simpson had not been greatly concerned about either Kittson or the Red River Settlement. After the collapse of the muskrat boom in the early 'thirties, the Company's fur trade within the district had fallen to the point where it was at the very best upon "a very small scale."[22] Of course, Simpson knew about the free traders working in and around the settlement, but they seemed so few in number and slight in capital that the simple expedient of outbidding them apparently kept them under control. And although the settlement itself presented him with some political problems, nevertheless "by good management, without any other force than we at present possess, [the settlers] may be kept in order for a length of time, if proper means are taken, by encouraging emigration, to prevent any great increase of their numbers."[23]

Appearances were never more misleading. Before another year had passed, it was obvious that Simpson had misgauged the strength of the free traders, underestimated the opposition along the border, and failed to foresee an inevitable alliance between Kittson and the free traders. Indeed, during the winter of 1843–44 he foolishly gave a trading licence to Andrew McDermot so that the Company could compete more effectively on the American frontier. It was the last time that Simpson made that mistake. Throughout the winter, McDermot and Sinclair conducted their trading ventures in a free and easy way. With Simpson's licence, with goods—initially more English than American—and with liquor bootlegged from the United States, they supplied their subordinates with everything needed to carry on an illicit trade in furs. Though the cost of the American goods exceeded that of the English ones, it was less than one would imagine, for the two men simply smuggled them into Rupert's Land along with the liquor. Then, as if to cap their insolent behaviour, they used the Company's ships to sell their furs in England or sent them *via* their own carts to an American market.

In June, 1844, Chief Factor Alexander Christie assumed the governorship of Assiniboia. Six months in office and the continued presence of Kittson at Pembina convinced him that Red River's free

[22]Simpson to the Governor and Committee, 21 June 1843, H.B.C., Series A.12/2.
[23]Simpson to Pelly, 28 July 1843, *ibid.*

trade movement had exceeded the limits of toleration. But how was he to stop it? There was no police force in the settlement to uphold the Company's trading monopoly. The suggestion was made that he use certain "negative means" available to him: the Company's command of shipping into Hudson Bay, its court system, and its control over Red River's currency.[24] Perhaps these means, when combined with the positive policy of strenuous competition, could be employed to crush the free traders.

Christie's first attack was launched in December, when he issued a series of proclamations governing all importations into Hudson Bay. Hereafter, no man would be allowed to import any goods on the Company's ships without a licence; and no one could get a licence without swearing that he had neither traded in furs nor advanced goods or cash to another man suspected of trading. If the terms of the licence were later violated, the licensee's shipments would be either detained at York Factory for one year or confiscated outright. In either case, it was clear that the Company would no longer permit its vessels or its warehouses to serve any free-trading competitors in Red River. At first, Christie's "negative means" had little effect. The more prominent traders and smugglers, including McDermot and Sinclair, refused to obtain licences. Some of them, like Peter Garrioch, brazenly continued trading in Rupert's Land. He had nothing to fear from York's closure, for his entire stock in trade consisted of American goods.[25] Still others, like McDermot and his nephew, John McLaughlin, began shopping around for other American outlets in addition to Kittson's. If anything, Christie's proclamations only pushed the free traders into an informal businessmen's association of their own and strengthened their disregard for the Company and its authority.

Yet the Company was still a force to be reckoned with. Most of the free traders brought trade goods up from Mendota or St. Paul without paying any duties to the government of Assiniboia; and thus with cheap goods and cheaper liquor, they competed with the Company for the furs of Rupert's Land. But if Assiniboia's customs were ever collected, the free traders would lose their competitive advantage. Christie lost no time trying to seal the holes in Red River's tariff walls. His instrument of government, the Council of

[24]Thom to Christie, 7 Dec. 1844, enclosed in Christie to the Secretary, 31 Dec. 1844, H.B.C., Series A.11/95.
[25]Garrioch's Journal, Part V, 239.

Assiniboia, decreed in June, 1844, that any importer failing to pay the required duties would forfeit all his goods. It proved to be an empty gesture, for the customs collector could not collect the duties, let alone confiscate any goods. He posted public notices advising the importers to pay all duties then in arrears. He wrote personal letters to suspected smugglers such as Peter Garrioch. He even induced the latter's minister to plead with him to pay. It was all to no avail, for Garrioch, Sinclair, and all the rest of the smugglers' crew had made a pact not to pay any duties.

Garrioch and Sinclair were both educated men, able to articulate the sentiments of the other smugglers, and, in concert, they composed a petition to the Governor and Council of Assiniboia praying for relief from all impositions on American imports.[26] Not until the petition had been handed over to Governor Christie and that gentleman had made known his demands for payment of the delinquent duties before considering the petition—not till then, did Garrioch and his associates finally pay the customs collector. The Governor and Council, with Sir George Simpson presiding, received the petition on 16 June and responded to it in a curiously revealing way. "The said petition," declared the council, "abounds in imputations and opinions which are equally irrelevant and erroneous."[27] But the words were uttered out of pride and not strength, for the council prefaced them with generous customs allowances to the petitioners and the freedom to import certain goods from the United States without any duty at all. All this was done according to Simpson's usual political formula—to assert the Company's authority in one breath and then grant concessions in the next.

For all the vigour of his language, Simpson was worried. The past trading season had seen an alarming expansion of free trading; and for this growth, he blamed Sinclair and McDermot above all the others in the settlement. He recognized them as men of superior standing and influence whose example of lawlessness was "peculiarly pernicious." He fully approved of Christie's restrictive measures but doubted their efficacy. The day after the council had answered the

[26]Garrioch's Journal, Part V, 6, 7, and 9 May 1845. Every one of the men who signed the petition had carted goods up from Minnesota during the past season. They were experienced carters who knew every slough and sand hill between Red River and Mendota.

[27]Minutes of the Council of Assiniboia, in E. H. Oliver, ed., *The Canadian North-West: Its Early Development and Legislative Records* (Ottawa, 1914–15), I, 317–27.

free traders' memorial, he wrote the Governor and Committee that nothing except a military force would "permanently reconcile the enforcing of our rights with the preserving of the public tranquility."[28]

The free traders were not yet bent upon a lawless course. They still preferred to fight with their pens, and, on 29 August, they presented the governor with another petition, submitting a long list of questions regarding trade in Rupert's Land.[29] In their preface, the petitioners stated their belief that, as natives of the soil and as half-breeds, they had "the right to hunt furs in the Hudson's Bay Company's Territories, wherever . . . [they] thought proper, and again, sell those furs to the highest bidder. . . ."[30] The questions that followed were asked—as the authors stated in mock innocence—only because they did not want to violate the Company's charter. Christie was then called upon to interpret the law in a variety of hypothetical situations involving the direct or indirect acquisition of furs by the half-breeds. Though the petition posed a paradox which any answer given by the governor would merely exaggerate, yet he replied within a week, refuting every question that had been raised. Surely the free traders had not expected Christie to approve their petition and thereby bless their illicit activities. Yet they undoubtedly knew what they were doing and that as one result of this manoeuvre their ranks would be filled by more and more petty traders whose economy and numbers made them invulnerable to the Company's "negative" policy. And there was another result of equal if not greater significance. Kittson had arrived in the settlement the day before the petition was delivered; and when he left, after Christie's response, he carried off many contracts and more promises from some of the very men who had signed the petition.[31]

In the winter following Kittson's visit to Red River, Christie bore down on all the free traders. He refused to re-open the Hudson Bay route to Sinclair and McDermot and he replaced the Company's ordinary bills of exchange with non-negotiable currency theoretically fit only for circulation within the settlement. Such steps might have checked the men of property like McDermot, but they had no effect upon his followers, petty traders who were "beyond the reach of any indirect attack."[32] Although Christie dared not launch a frontal attack

---

[28]20 June 1845, H.B.C., Series A.12/2. He suggested that a garrison of two hundred soldiers would suffice "for all purposes, social, commercial and national."
[29]"R.R. Correspondence, 1845–46–47."
[30]Sinclair, et al. to Christie, in *ibid.*
[31]Kittson to Sibley, 10 Sept. 1845, Sibley Papers.
[32]Christie to Simpson, 31 Dec. 1845. "R.R. Correspondence, 1845–46–47."

against the petty traders, he made the occasional raid. He jailed one man, confiscated the trading goods of another, and even took the furs of the third. Beyond this, he was unwilling or unable to go, despite the provocations given him by Garrioch and his friends. In desperation, the Governor wondered about arresting and banishing the one "notorious offender"—whoever he might be—but doubted whether he could carry it off. Indeed, when he asked for the co-operation of Red River's magistrates in a plan to indict smugglers and impound their furs, most of them apparently "had wit enough to refuse having anything to do with the business."[33]

Goaded on by Christie and steered by the skilful hands of Sinclair and McDermot, the free-trade movement steadily gained momentum. By February it appeared as if the free traders and the Company were bent upon a collision course. But let Kittson from his vantage point at Pembina explain the situation:

Politics are running high in the Settlement at present more so than usual. The Half breeds held a meeting last thursday [26 February 1846], at which the Revd Mr Belcour [t] a catholic missionary precided, they are to petition the Queen, for, Freedom of trade, a Governor independent of the H.B.Co and an elective legislature, and if these are not granted, or if they do not recieve [sic] any releif [sic] from the B. Govt at home, I am certain it will end in a revolution, there seems to be a feeling of this Kind (and it is general) throughout the whole Colony, they are determined on some change and they cannot have any but for the better.[34]

In fact, the free traders had already convened many times and always in McDermot's home, passing resolutions which, if acted upon, might have undermined the government of Assiniboia.

Nearly one hundred men met that February evening. Presiding over them was the intense, idealistic though emotionally unstable priest, Father Georges-Antoine Belcourt. Till now, the leadership of the free-trade movement had been in the hands of Sinclair and McDermot. Why should this priest suddenly emerge as a champion of the free traders? Christie guessed that the Company's failure to license his trading with the Indians was responsible, but it seems unreasonable to attribute so gross a motive to a man who had unselfishly devoted his life to the Indians and the *métis*. Belcourt himself—and both

[33]Garrioch's Journal, Part V, 21 Jan. 1846. Writing Simpson at a later date (21 April), Christie admitted that "some" of the magistrates "have expressed a degree of reluctance amounting . . . to a fixed determination, not to adjudicate in cases arising out of illicit fur trafficking. . . ." "R.R. Correspondence, 1845–46–47."
[34]Kittson to Sibley, 2 March 1846, Sibley Papers.

Simpson and the Bishop of Juliopolis believed him—said that the free traders, disliking the drift towards anarchy, had asked him to "go among them for a time."[35] And he had accepted, "knowing that the influence . . . [he] had over them, generally speaking, would appease the trouble and cause them to proceed in an orderly manner."

But his actions that February night were scarcely those of a conciliatory priest. Although it was true that, as a priest, he had warned the half-breeds to "obey . . . your superiors even wicked"; yet he had also told them, as a political adviser, that they might obtain justice by addressing a petition to the Crown.[36] While waiting for a reply, they should restrain themselves. What if they received an unfavourable answer? Then to whom should they turn? In answer, Father Belcourt stole a leaf from Thomas Jefferson's book: "If the Government told them they could not relieve them, that they were under the Hudson's Bay Company, that they might if they choose declare themselves free and not be Governed by laws that was [*sic*] made by interested people, and in which they had no confidence, and to which they never gave their consent."[37]

Out of this meeting and in the weeks to come, emerged a petition to the Queen.[38] It complained of the Hudson's Bay Company, whose unrepresentative government had reduced the people of Rupert's Land to an "oppressed and injured race"; and it referred to the judge and councillors of Assiniboia as the "creatures of the Company." But the heart of the petition was a plea for commercial freedom:

That, feeling the utter inadequacy of the remuneration for their furs from the Company, many of the more enterprising of the natives have formed a resolution to export their own produce and import their own supplies, independently of the Company. They argue that, even supposing the charter to be still valid, and that it vests in the Company an exclusive right of trade to Hudson's Bay as against all other traders from Britain, none of its provisions are or can be binding on the natives to trade with the Company exclusively, or can prevent them from carrying their furs or other property out of the country, to the best market.

In conclusion, the petitioners, all of whom were either Indians or half-breeds, begged the Queen to examine and rectify this deplorable state of affairs.

[35]Vernice M. Aldrich, "Father George Antoine Belcourt, Red River Missionary," *North Dakota Historical Quarterly*, II (Oct., 1927), pp. 48–9.
[36]Belcourt to Christie, 15 June 1846, "R.R. Correspondence, 1845–46–47."
[37]McDermot to Christie, 18 March 1846, *ibid.*
[38]A copy of the petition may be found in "Correspondence Relative to the Complaints of the Inhabitants of the Red River Settlement," Great Britain, *Parliamentary Papers*, 1849, XXXV.

Christie fumed when he heard about the meeting and the petition. He upbraided McDermot as a councillor of Assiniboia for permitting a meeting in his house, whose sole purpose was the "subversion of all Government."[39] The Irishman merely submitted his resignation (later rejected) and went his own way. Christie complained to Belcourt's bishop and to the priest himself about the revolutionary doctrine that the latter had preached to the people of Red River. In reply, Belcourt denied any personal guilt but refused to elaborate upon the evening's activities. The bishop was more receptive, and Belcourt was eventually translated to eastern Canada for his part in the affair. Nothing, however, could be done to halt the progress of the petition. Garrioch and his friends carried it around the settlement, ultimately acquiring the amazing total of 977 signatures; and early in the summer they sent it off to London, where it was duly presented to the Crown.

Thus, in the early months of 1846, the Company's hold on trade and government in the Red River Settlement was steadily growing weaker. McDermot and Sinclair were offering more for illicit furs than the Company and getting their full share and more. They and Garrioch too were busily bearing the staple of the Company down to Kittson by the cartload, while the latter, no longer content with his American station, boldly crossed the line and began trading in Rupert's Land. It seemed to Christie as if the stage were set for the determination of "the grand question, whether law or lawlessness, the Hudson's Bay Co. or a conspiracy of smugglers . . . [were to] be paramount."[40]

Christie's present position seemed hopeless. The competitive practices he had employed to check the free traders and contain Kittson had not succeeded. Nor had his summary powers as governor enabled him to cope with the situation. Without police power, he dared not jeopardize the Company's interests by attempting directly to suppress the free traders. The recorder of Red River, Adam Thom, kept urging him to get a trial by jury of some notorious smuggler, but Christie knew that the local courts were dubious instruments for upholding the law. And if the verdict went against the Company, its position would only be worse; "while, from the inefficiency of our Executive, even a favorable [verdict] could hardly do much good."[41] In short, Christie was at the end of his rope, and had it not been for the arrival of British troops during the summer, 1846 would have equalled 1849.

---

[39]Christie to McDermot, 21 March 1846, "R.R. Correspondence, 1845–46–47."
[40]Christie to Simpson, 21 April 1846, *ibid.*   [41]*Ibid.*

III

The apparent reason for the dispatch of Her Majesty's 6th Regiment of Foot, Royal Warwickshires, to Rupert's Land in 1846 was to save British sovereignty from the American eagle, a rapacious bird then hovering over all the Oregon country.[42] In fact, the bird was a Democrat named James K. Polk, who had been elected President of the United States in the fall of 1844. Like a great many other presidential campaigns, this particular one was as remarkable for the slogans its protagonists generated as for the principles they ignored. In a campaign filled with Fourth-of-July oratory, the most memorable slogan of Polk's party had been "The reoccupation of Oregon and the reannexation of Texas." In a broader and more belligerent variation, the sentiment was expressed as "54° 40′ or Fight." The Whigs had countered weakly with "Who is James K. Polk?" By December, everybody knew the answer: Polk was President.

As every politician knows, victory, though sweet, presents problems. In Polk's case, there was the matter of his campaign promises. The slogan regarding Texas was stillborn, for Polk's predecessor had pushed through and signed a bill admitting Texas into the union just before the new administration took office. That left Oregon. In his inaugural address, Polk responded to the popular sentiment that had presumably elected him by re-stating his party's platform. He declared that he would "assert and maintain by all constitutional means the right of the United States to that portion of our territory which lies beyond the Rocky Mountains."[43] He referred, of course, to Oregon, then only a geographic expression; but to all of it, claimed the President, the American title was "clear and unquestionable."

When news of Polk's inaugural reached Whitehall, Sir George Simpson was in London, and at once he and Sir John Pelly, Governor of the Hudson's Bay Company, were closeted with the Prime Minister, Sir Robert Peel. Simpson and Pelly shrewdly saw in the British government's concern over Oregon a chance for them to garrison the Red River Settlement and thus preserve the Company's trading monopoly by overawing the free traders. Both men had come to

---

[42]C. P. Stacey, "The Hudson's Bay Company and Anglo-American Military Rivalries during the Oregon Dispute," *Canadian Historical Review*, XVIII (Sept., 1937), 281–300. See also W. E. Ingersoll, "Redcoats at Fort Garry," *Beaver*, outfit 276 (Dec., 1945).

[43]James D. Richardson, ed., *A Compilation of the Messages and Papers of the Presidents* (10 vols., Washington, 1897–99), IV, 381.

believe that the salvation of the Company's charter rights depended upon the stationing of troops at Fort Garry; now, they cleverly turned Manifest Destiny to their own advantage and, then and thereafter, brought all signs, real and fictitious, of Yankee expansionism to the attention of the Crown. Peel's government could not afford to disregard the warnings or question the motives of the Hudson's Bay Company. Nor did it dare ignore the seeming belligerence of Polk and the American press. An imperial responsibility demanded that certain precautionary measures be taken. Peel immediately ordered three warships from their South American station into north Pacific waters, and he dispatched two army lieutenants, Henry J. Warre and Mervin Vavasour, to assess secretly Britain's military position along the border from Lake Superior to the Pacific Ocean.

Upon his return to Canada and before his departure for Rupert's Land, Simpson assiduously—and deceitfully[44]—pursued the policy of awakening the Crown and its representatives to the need for troops in Red River as a makeweight to Manifest Destiny. He made sure that Canada's government was fully aware of the need for Red River's protection. Just before leaving for the interior, he visited the governor, Lord Metcalfe, and the commander-in-chief of British forces in North America, Sir Richard D. Jackson. They were ready converts to his gospel of preparedness. Only Warre and Vavasour remained as unknown quantities but Simpson was reasonably sure that he could also convince them.

En route to Red River, Simpson paused at an encampment long enough to write a report for their consideration.[45] Though of considerable length, it may be summarized as follows: The United States had built a chain of military posts along the northern frontier which gave them the upper hand in all border affairs. On the other hand, not one of the British settlements in the Northwest was fortified. He therefore recommended that posts be established at Pointe de Meuron (about seven miles north of Forth William) and at the Red

---

[44]Simpson himself was not greatly disturbed by Polk's attitude. En route from London to Lachine, he stopped off in New York City and Washington, D.C., and in both places acquaintances assured him that the President's words were meant for the ears of his more expansionist supporters and that the administration really meant to settle the whole affair in an amicable way. None of Simpson's informants, including "several influential members of Congress," feared war's possibility. In addition to congressmen, Simpson also consulted Ramsay Crooks and the British minister; and, on his way back to Lachine, he also sampled public opinion. All sources agreed that the Oregon affair would be peacefully settled. Simpson to the Governor and Committee, 4 May 1845, H.B.C., Series A.12/2.

[45]30 May 1845, *ibid*. Cf. Simpson to Pelly (confidential), 8 July 1845, *ibid*.

River Settlement—"the only two points where such protection appears, at present, necessary or desirable." Of the two, Simpson preferred Red River, which he endowed with all the salubrious qualities of a spa and populated with men of unquestionable loyalty. Here— he claimed—two hundred regulars could defend the heart of the Northwest; and with the addition of two to ten thousand native militia, they could even harass the American frontier. Only a little training would be needed to transform the militia into dashing cavalrymen in the summer and swift, snowshoeing marauders in the winter. It was a dramatic—and unrealistic—picture that Simpson painted. The population of Red River probably did not exceed 5,000 souls, and of that number, more than a few were in no mood to regard the Hudson's Bay Company with either loyalty or affection.

But when Simpson reached the settlement and learned at first hand of the unrest among the free traders during the past winter, he probably wondered if he had painted his canvas in bright enough colours. He was made more aware than ever before of the deterioration of the Company's authority that had accompanied the winter's growth of free trade. He was now absolutely positive that the Company needed troops at Fort Garry.[46] He wrote Metcalfe, underscoring the threat to British sovereignty posed by the American border posts and stressing the need to counterbalance them with a garrison at Red River. When he returned to Lachine in the late summer, he addressed the governor personally, stating that now was the time to urge Her Majesty's Government to protect the Northwest. Little did he realize how opportune the time really was.

In Pelly's and Simpson's efforts to get troops, time and again the United States would come conveniently to their aid with plausible evidence of expansionism. Superb businessmen, both Company men misrepresented the evidence to make their case look like a brief for the welfare of the empire. Indeed, they so adroitly blended the Company's commercial interests with Britain's sovereign interests that only the most astute servant of the Colonial Office could have separated them. Such evidence was given the Company in the summer of 1845 when Captain Edwin V. Sumner of the United States Army led his dragoons onto the Dakota plains.

Sumner's expedition was not jingoist in inspiration. Nor was it meant to detach the Red River half-breeds from the Crown or the Company. In no sense, then, were the manoeuvres a sign of Manifest Destiny. They were simply the response to a chronic frontier problem that had troubled the United States since the 1820's: the bi-annual

[46]Simpson to the Governor and Committee, 20 June 1845, *ibid.*

invasions of Red River's half-breeds, who had long been accustomed to hunt buffalo south of the line.[47] The American Sioux depended upon the same herds and the resulting economic competition between Sioux and half-breed led to friction and warfare. Scarcely a summer passed without bloodshed. Dealing with the Sioux was difficult enough for the Indian Bureau. They were testy, treatyless Indians who paid homage to no man. With the unsettling addition of the half-breeds, the problem of controlling them was almost insurmountable. For the Red River half-breeds slew an ever greater number of buffalo every year, threatening the food supply of the Sioux and making them annually more irritable. Moreover, the same half-breeds snatched countless buffalo robes out of the hands of American fur traders.

Ultimately, Washington was so plagued with complaints about these incursions that it had to take military action. In 1842 the Governor of Iowa Territory received disquieting reports from Henry Sibley and from the Indian agent at Fort Snelling. Sibley deplored the loss of American buffalo robes; the agent objected to the invasion of American soil by armed British subjects; and both men pleaded for a show of force to end the evils. The governor endorsed their reports and warned Washington: "In the event of hostilities between the British Government and ours, . . . [the half-breeds] would exercise a dangerous influence over all the Indians on our northwestern frontier . . . and from their numbers and hardy and daring character, would greatly endanger our border settlements. . . ."[48] At first these pleas were ignored. But, after the half-breeds had again clashed with the Sioux at Devils Lake in 1844, Iowa's officials repeated their request; and this time the Commissioner of Indian Affairs backed them up and persuaded the War Department to dispatch Sumner and his dragoons to the Dakota borderlands.[49]

[47]From his post at Fort Snelling, Lawrence Taliaferro, the Indian agent, complained to General William Clark, commander of the U.S. Army's western department, about the half-breed invasions and their unsettling effect upon the Sioux. It is interesting to note that Taliaferro feared the influence said to be possessed by the Hudson's Bay Company over the Sioux. He need not have. After its withdrawal from Pembina, the Company had little contact with the Sioux and desired less. See Taliaferro to Clark, 18 Aug. 1827 and 25 June 1834, Taliaferro Papers, M.H.S. Cf. Simpson to the Governor and Committee, 21 July 1834, H.B.C., Series D.4/100.

[48]John Chambers to the Commissioner of Indian Affairs, *Annual Report of the Commissioner of Indian Affairs, 1842, Senate Document No. 1*, 27th Cong., 3rd Sess., Serial 413, p. 423.

[49]Annual Report of the Commissioner of Indian Affairs, 1845, *House Document No. 2*, 29th Cong., 1st Sess., Serial 480, p. 454. See also Captain Edwin V. Sumner, "Report of Maneuvers Near Pembina," *Senate Document No. 1*, 29th Cong., 1st Sess., Serial 470, pp. 217–20.

The captain's orders were unmistakably clear and he carried them out to the letter. With two companies of the First Regiment of Dragoons, he was directed to proceed north from Fort Atkinson (Iowa Territory) and search out both Sioux and half-breed. He was to charm the Sioux with gifts and awe them with power, and he was to warn off any British half-breeds found hunting buffalo below the 49th parallel. In due course he met bands of Wahpeton and Sisseton Sioux, but there was little he could do with these savages either to conciliate or to impress them. He had better luck with a party of half-breeds whom he found hunting near Devils Lake. Towards them he acted in a straightforward, guileless way, telling them that their expeditions were "violations of our [American] soil" and could no longer be tolerated.

Sumner's warning posed a serious threat to the Red River half-breeds. To prevent them from running the buffalo would be denying them their livelihood. Late that fall a group of *métis* petitioned the Congress of the United States, "praying to be admitted as settlers within the Iowa territory, and to be allowed the priveledge [*sic*] of hunting. . . ."[50] To make sure of its delivery, the half-breeds entrusted the petition to John McLaughlin, who mailed it (in the United States) to the Secretary of State. Without comment, the secretary sent the petition on to the War Department, where it perished without eliciting any interest whatsoever.

Thus, from beginning to end, Washington's attitude was entirely correct. Indeed, no diplomat could have acted more decorously than Captain Sumner. Peter Garrioch was in that party of half-breeds at Devils Lake and his journal (11 July 1845) manifested a full and true understanding of Sumner's mission. There was no reason for anyone to misunderstand—unless, like Sir George Simpson, it served his purpose to do so.

Out of the material presented him by Sumner's manœuvres, Simpson quickly shot off a long and highly coloured account to the Governor and Committee so that they might use it to impress Peel's government. Then he turned his attention to Governor Metcalfe, describing the situation in Red River in a report that can best be characterized as a masterpiece of fact and fiction.[51] According to Simpson, the ostensible purpose of Sumner's expedition was to seize some Sioux braves for slaying American missionaries. However, the captain's real purpose

[50]Enclosed in McLaughlin to James Buchanan, Secretary of State, 22 Oct. 1845. See also McLaughlin to Buchanan, 14 Nov. 1845. Typewritten copies, M.H.S.
[51]6 Nov. 1845, H.B.C., Series A.12/2.

was quite different. He intended to meet the Red River half-breeds and induce them to migrate to Pembina. Evidently—Simpson continued —the United States was anxious to acquire influence over the half-breeds so that, in the event of war, the Red River Settlement could be easily overcome. Furthermore—he went on—the half-breeds had been delighted with the attention paid them and had sent a petition to Washington "praying Congress to assist & protect them in the formation of a Settlement at Pembina." The author of the petition was John McLaughlin; and regarding him, McDermot, and Sinclair, Simpson had "no doubt [they] have been employed by some of the United States authorities as secret emissaries among our half-breed settlers & the neighbouring Indians, with a view of sowing the seeds of disaffection as a preliminary measure to the overtures that have now been made, in which they appear to be highly successful. . . ." In conclusion, Simpson said that only with the establishment of a military garrison in Red River could the sentiment and loyalty of the half-breeds and border Indians be drawn again to the Queen.

Simpson's pursuit of military aid in Canada proved to be a task complicated by grim fate. Jackson died suddenly in June of 1845. By fall a fatal disease had forced Metcalfe into retirement. But if fate worked against Simpson in Canada, it once again collaborated with him in the United States.

On 2 December President Polk delivered his first annual message to Congress. In it he asked for authority to terminate the Convention of 1827, which had provided for Oregon's joint occupation by the United States and Great Britain. He also asked Congress to pass interim legislation for the well-being of Americans in or en route to Oregon, and, for their added protection, he recommended "that a suitable number of stockades and blockhouse forts be erected along the usual route." In summation, he restated the Monroe Doctrine and, in particular, that part of it which closed North America to future colonization by any foreign power.

As soon as Polk's message appeared in the Canadian press, Simpson was in attendance upon the Earl of Cathcart, the temporary administrator of Canada. He spoke to him at length upon the defenceless state of Rupert's Land and asked for protection. Obviously impressed, Cathcart wondered if Simpson would express his views more fully in a memorandum. He was delighted to oblige, and on 15 December he presented a richly embroidered report reminiscent of those already given to Metcalfe.[52] In it he stated that the president's message had induced him to draw Cathcart's attention to the vulnerable condition

[52]Enclosed in Simpson to the Governor and Committee, 24 Dec. 1845, *ibid.*

of the entire Northwest and pointed out that all that was required to protect the region was a garrison of two to three hundred men in Red River. Cathcart agreed to bring the matter before the home government. When dispatches from London arrived soon afterward inquiring whether troops could be supplied from Canada and what would be the best route for bringing them to Red River, he assented to the first query and turned to Simpson for his answer to the second. Before long, the earl and the "little emperor" were discussing details of a military expedition to which London had not yet agreed.

As if to try the Company's patience, the British government kept the matter of troops under consideration throughout the winter. Week after week, Sir John Pelly pleaded for men; and all the while Simpson kept dinning into his ears the same mournful tune: that if troops were not forthcoming, the Company's authority in Red River would "become a dead letter."[53] Though both the War Office and the Colonial Office sympathized with Pelly, yet the wheels of government turned ever so slowly. Even after the favourable reports from Simpson and from Warre and Vavasour had been received, the War Office still wanted additional information which only Cathcart could supply. Much therefore hinged upon the reply from Canada. But can it be doubted that the earl would favour the Company's cause, when Simpson was there to advise him? Cathcart's report reached London on 20 March and was immediately sent to Britain's ultimate military authority, the Duke of Wellington. In a most frustrating way, Wellington blew hot and cold. On 1 April, he apparently favoured sending troops. A fortnight later, he was opposed, believing it unwise to send men to Fort Garry before engineering officers had examined and approved its defensive works. Time was running out of the Company's glass. If troops did not leave the British Isles by the end of June, the ships carrying them could not get into and out of Hudson Bay before the freeze-up.

Out of desperation, Pelly sent another long memorandum to Wellington, restating his Company's needs for military protection.[54] He recalled Sumner's expedition to the duke's attention. Although he now admitted that, in itself, it had not been formidable, Pelly claimed that it had "had the effect of very much increasing the influence of some persons who had come to the Red River Country from St. Peters and St. Louis in the United States whose object seems to have been to detach the Half-breed population" from their allegiance to the Crown. Only

[53] (Confidential), 11 Nov. 1845, *ibid*. Cf. 24 Feb. 1846, *ibid*.
[54] Enclosed in Pelly to Lord Fitzroy Somerset, 22 April 1846, H.B.C., Series A.8/3. Somerset was Wellington's aide.

troops at Fort Garry could end this intrigue. If, however, they were
delayed for a year, Pelly "feared that the Emissaries from the South
side of the Boundary might succeed in permanently detaching these
[half-breed] people from their allegiance." Then to clinch his argument, he agreed "to do whatever any Officer whom the Government
may send may see necessary to render the Forts efficient."

It is not known whether the government believed Pelly's fairy tale
about Yankee emissaries, but it accepted his proposal. Details were
quickly worked out and a final bargain was struck. In return for the
troops, the Company promised to build and pay for military works at
Red River sufficient "to resist the attack of a Civilized Nation after
means shall have been found to bring up Artillery. . . ."[55] Under the
command of Major John f. Crofton, troops left Ireland on 26 June and
sailed off to York Factory and Fort Garry. It was a large, well-armed
contingent consisting of three infantry companies from the 6th Regiment of Foot, Royal Warwickshires, together with engineers and
artillerymen, and weighed down with cannon, mortars, and howitzers.
All in all, there were about 350 men—a force capable of creating
respect for law and order in the Red River Settlement.

IV

The 6th Regiment assured the Hudson's Bay Company of almost two
years of peace, order, and prosperity. Indeed, by the time Simpson
reached Fort Garry in June Red River's discordant voices had been
stilled, for news of the coming of the 6th had preceded the governor.
Gone too was the former truculence of Sinclair and McDermot. In a
letter to Simpson, Sinclair indicated a willingness to renounce free
trading—a decision that was encouraged by a gift of £100. McDermot
could also see the political weather vane, and presently he sold the
balance of his furs to the Company, arranged to leave the trade forever, placed his son in the service, and became "a jealous adherent to
the Company."[56] In return, Simpson forgave his sins and eased his
path with a note for £100.

In August Simpson was at York Factory to greet the men of the
6th and escort them to their new quarters. When Crofton's troops

[55]"Instructions to Colonel Holloway Commanding Royal Engineer in Canada
relative to the Employment of two Officers of Royal Engineers in the Hudson's
Bay Territory," enclosed in Sir John J. Burgoyne to Pelly, 29 April 1846, *ibid.*
Burgoyne was Britain's Inspector General of Fortifications.

[56]Simpson to the Governor and Committee, 24 July 1846, H.B.C., Series A.12/2.

reached their final destination in mid-September, they made a forceful impression on almost everyone they met. Simpson could scarcely
contain his delight: "Major Crofton, I am happy to say, shews every
disposition to support the Company's officers, and if any attempt be
made to infringe upon the charter, I am confident he will act with
promptitude. The presence of the troops, however, will, alone be
sufficient to restore tranquility and to check illicit trade."[57] Other
Company men were equally taken with Crofton's subordinates: they
all seemed such "a fine set of good looking young men."[58]

Once more peace reigned in Red River and the Company's writ
ran throughout the land. Within a year, the free-trade movement was
virtually suppressed, although the 6th was never called out to enforce
the Company's charter rights. There was no need for it. "While we
have the presence of the Troops," crowed Alexander Christie, "there
seems little or no ground for apprehending much interference with
the Fur Trade. . . ."[59] Only their presence, not their guns, was required.
The settlers "were deterred from trading with the Indians . . . by fear
of the strong measures that were likely to be resorted to on the part
of the authorities of Red River. . . ."[60]

Far fewer furs than before slipped out of Rupert's Land and into
Kittson's hands. Neither McDermot nor Sinclair outfitted petty traders
as of yore, and the old scenes of Red River carts and bull boats bearing
their smuggled cargoes down to Pembina were no longer evident. But
if Kittson's ties with these two men were weakened, they were not
cut. Sinclair continued to advance him gold in order to procure furs
from the half-breeds still working the southern tier of the Company's
districts. Although cognizant of the drain, Simpson believed it slight
enough to be ignored and almost impossible to prevent. He relied
upon the troops in the settlement and his own men along the border
to hold the American in check—and he achieved the desired effect.
Kittson's trade in furs declined sharply and would not be revitalized
for a couple of years. Indeed he might have been forced into bankruptcy, had it not been for an unforeseen consequence of the garrison-
ing of troops in Red River. For if the soldiers practically cut off his
supply of furs from the settlement, they also created a new market
for his general trade.

It has been estimated that £15,000 was spent merely to maintain

[57]Simpson to Pelly (confidential), 20 Aug. 1846, H.B.C., Series A.12/3.
[58]John F. Pruden to Henry Fisher, 13 Nov. 1846, Fisher Papers.
[59]Christie to Simpson, 30 July 1847, "R.R. Correspondence, 1845–46–47."
[60]Simpson to the Governor and Committee, 1 July 1847, H.B.C., Series A.12/3.

the 6th Regiment during its tour of duty.[61] Such a sum had a stupendous pump-priming effect upon the economy and benefited nearly everyone in the settlement. Ex-smugglers and free traders like McDermot forgot the pleasures of their former ways and turned to an honest and lucrative general trade. Indeed, sly old McDermot feted the officers and the 6th and the resident Hudson's Bay men at a "grand public dinner," complete with "champagne and a great variety of things for dessert . . . provided from the States."[62] He could certainly afford it. He and many others like him were making good money. Their orders upon Sibley and Kittson—and other commercial houses in the United States—mounted in volume and variety. Cart trains coming up from Minnesota and bound for Red River carried such diverse cargoes as tea and tea kettles, reapers and twine, medical supplies for the regimental doctor, sugar, candy, and tobacco, and mail for everybody.

Amidst this prosperity, the settlement's social life became quite gay. Resident members of the Hudson's Bay Company and Red River's "high society" delighted in the company of the officers of the 6th. And in these pleasant and serene circumstances, changes took place in Assiniboia that would probably not have been tolerated at any other time. So secure and carefree was the Council of Assiniboia that it suspended the exemptions hitherto allowed on exports from Red River.

The stationing of troops at Fort Garry bestowed many blessings upon the Hudson's Bay Company; had they been allowed to remain, much of the Company's later distress could have been avoided. But such was not to be. In May, 1847, the colonial secretary drew Pelly's attention to the probable withdrawal of the 6th Regiment. New to the office, he had just discovered that the Crown's original agreement with the Company stated that the latter would pay for the construction of substantial works at Fort Garry. This had not been done, because Simpson had "strongly pressed upon" the engineering officer attached to the 6th "the expediency of indefinitely delaying the erection of these works partly in consequence of the settlement of the Oregon Question . . . partly for other reasons. . . ."[63] "I find also," the secretary concluded, "that the Duke of Wellington has expressed a strong opinion in which I entirely concur that there is nothing in the ulterior state of our relations with the United States . . . which can justify our keeping a detachment of the regular Army at Fort Garry unless that post

[61]Alexander Ross, *The Red River Settlement* (London, 1856), p. 365.
[62]Letter of Robert Clouston, quoted in Ingersoll, "Red Coats at Fort Garry."
[63]Grey to Pelly (private), 24 May 1847, H.B.C., Series A.8/4.

is made defensible against a serious attack, by works on a very respectable scale."

At last Pelly had to face facts. If the works were not built, the troops would be removed; and since the Crown would contribute no money, his Company would have to bear all the costs. In the presumption that the Company would therefore not build the works, the colonial secretary suggested to Pelly that, if he still wished military protection, a small force of pensioners might be recruited. To all this Pelly's initial response was frank and agreeable. He explained that the Company had failed to fortify Fort Garry because the engineering officer's estimate of the costs had come to £120,000! Such a sum could not be considered under any circumstances, and, with the passing of the Oregon crisis, it seemed absurd. Pelly accordingly agreed that the troops should be withdrawn, provided pensioners could be sent to relieve them. But as to their immediate departure, that was impossible. The season was too far advanced to make the arrangements necessary to bring them back to the British Isles. The colonial secretary wisely concurred and left the regulars at Fort Garry till the following summer.

However, as the date for their removal drew nearer, Pelly grew less amenable. In December he wrote the Colonial Office of "the danger to which the Colony at Red River . . . [would] be exposed if it . . . [were] left entirely without the protection of regular Troops. . . ."[64] He admitted that the improvement of Anglo-American relations had removed one of the reasons for sending the troops. But he added: "the other reasons which led to that measure still subsist in full force, are likely to continue, and render the presence of a government force indispensable for the upholding of British interests in the Colony." Then came Pelly's "other reasons." He began this fanciful part of his tale by reminding the colonial secretary that, by tampering with the affections of Red River's half-breeds in 1845, some Americans had led fifty families away from their British connection and into the United States, "whence in conjunction with the lawless population of that district, they keep up a constant communication with the disaffected at Red River. . . ." Only with the coming of the 6th Regiment had the Company been able to halt the migration. But now—and here Pelly dipped into Simpson's most recent reports[65]—the same Yankee conspirators, aware that the 6th would soon leave, "have organized a plan of action which nothing but the unequivocal continuance of the Government, and the support of a military force will enable the Com-

[64]Pelly to Grey, 2 Dec. 1847, *ibid.*
[65]See the extracts, dated 12 Aug. and 4 Nov. 1847, enclosed in *supra.*

pany to defeat, but which if not defeated will assuredly effect the ruin of the Colony and ultimately increase in no small degree the facilities which the United States already possess of carrying out their well known designs on Canada." He did not elaborate upon either the "plan of action" or the "well known designs," perhaps for the reason that they, like so many of Simpson's other reports on American intrigue, would not stand close inspection.

The colonial secretary was unmoved. Not even a memorial from the Governor and Council of Assiniboia, pleading for protection lest their laws "be administered only by sufferance," had any effect upon him.[66] Early in the spring, he asked Pelly to make final arrangements for the withdrawal of the troops. They began to pull out of Fort Garry in August, and when the last of them had gone, a perceptive observer of the Red River scene saw in their departure "the signal for the recommencement of our troubles."[67]

V

Soon after Rupert's Land learned that the Company had recruited pensioners, Simpson wrote London that the Council of the Northern Department and the authorities at Red River agreed with him "that a pensioner corps . . . [was] not the description of protection required."[68] They would—he forecast with amazing accuracy—bring nothing to the Red River Settlement but difficulty and disorder.

At Pelly's request, the Crown had raised a body of ex-soldiers who pledged their arms to the Hudson's Bay Company for a price. They enlisted for seven years, promising to serve three days a week in the first year and six days a month thereafter "either on Public Works, or in drilling Militia, or such Military duty, as the Governor of the Settlement . . . [might] direct."[69] In return, the Company gave each pensioner the use of a plot of ground and promised him the title to it after his discharge. To command the corps the Crown selected a field officer, Major William B. Caldwell; and the Company subsequently made him Governor of Assiniboia so that he would possess a greater measure of authority within the settlement.

[66]Dated 18 Nov. 1847 and enclosed in Christie to the Governor and Committee, 30 Nov. 1847, H.B.C., Series A.11/95.
[67]Ross, *Red River*, p. 364.
[68]24 June 1848, H.B.C., Series A.12/4.
[69]Lord Grey to the Secretary of War, 31 March 1848, enclosed in Grey to Pelly, 6 June 1848, H.B.C., Series A.8/4.

Caldwell and his little force reached Red River in the fall of 1848 and began seven years of inglorious service. Despite their eye-catching uniforms, they were an unimpressive body of men; indeed the settlers took one look at them and recalled the De Meurons. They were mercenaries who would faithfully play the role that history has given hired soldiers throughout the ages; and as for the major, he was little better than his men. Although the Mutiny Act and the Articles of War gave Caldwell all the power needed for discipline, he could never adequately control the pensioners. They remained an intemperate, disorderly lot. They drank, riotously and defiantly within their barracks; and outside them, they and their mates lived in a sordid and squalid way—drinking, fighting, and philandering.[70]

As Governor of Assiniboia, Caldwell was equally inept. Though the eddies of Red River's politics may have been evident to him, its deep-running currents were always hidden. He held himself aloof from the half-breeds and free traders whom he regarded as "weak minded and ignorant."[71] He looked upon men like Peter Garrioch as tools of "the disaffected party" in the settlement, failing to recognize that the party contained a great many settlers and half-breeds who had long been engaged both in smuggling enterprises and in legitimate trade with Minnesota merchants. And now that the 6th had left, all control over their activities, legal and illegal, had been removed. They straightway returned to their old calling, procuring furs in Rupert's Land and spiriting them across the line to Pembina.

In 1848 Pembina was a greater threat to the Hudson's Bay Company than it had been in 1845 or 1846. It now harboured two men whose existence imperilled the Company's fur trade and its political command of Red River. One was Norman W. Kittson, stronger than ever before, and the other was Georges-A. Belcourt, who had recently returned to the Northwest in order to save souls and ruin the Company. By the spring of 1848 Kittson had a firm grip upon the border trade. In fact, he felt strong enough to blackmail the Company and submitted a proposal to Christie that was undoubtedly patterned after the Aitkin-Crooks contract—his removal from Pembina and the border trade for a price. Christie would give him no immediate satisfaction, and in the final event the Company gave him none at all. It believed in bidding up fur prices until he had been forced out of business.

---

[70]See, for example, Eden Colvile to the Secretary, 7 Feb. 1851, H.B.C., Series A.12/5.

[71]Caldwell's report to the Colonial Office, enclosed in Caldwell to the Governor and Committee, 28 March 1849, H.B.C., Series A.11/95.

Although Kittson thus received no answer from his proposition, he was not discouraged. He made arrangements to draw furs from Rupert's Land, spread his border net, and waited, confident that one more season would bring the Company to terms. "You can rest assured," he informed Sibley, "that I shall spare no trouble in giving them the 'Devil'."

The "devil" was present during the winter of 1848–49. John Ballenden, the chief factor who replaced Christie in the Red River District, had his hands full trying to offset Kittson and at the same time get his own returns. It was an exacting task that ultimately ruined his health. He pumped trading goods into border stations and jacked up prices throughout his district, but the results were not wholly gratifying. Though he gathered many furs, so did Kittson. In fact, both parties did better in 1848–49 than in the preceding season.

And since Ballenden had failed to knock out Kittson, Belcourt also remained, strong and inviolate. Here was a strange, vindictive man. After his departure from Red River as *persona non grata* to the Company, he had returned to Montreal. Then for reasons unknown, he was translated to the Dubuque (Iowa) diocese and permitted to establish a mission at Pembina. No other assignment could have pleased him more. As soon as he learned the good news, he exultantly —and somewhat satanically too—relayed it to Henry Sibley, remarking that his new arrangements would probably "play a trick [upon the Company] almost as serious as that of the [1846] petition. . . ."[72]

When he joined Kittson, Pembina's charms were twice enhanced. A chapel had been added to the trading counter. No sooner had the priest reached his destination than the *métis* began leaving Red River and flocking to Pembina. Observing their movements, Ballenden felt anxious and uneasy. He knew Belcourt hated the Hudson's Bay Company and feared he would convert Pembina into a hostile fortress, gathering free-trading refugees from Red River and cannonading the Company with propaganda. Moreover, he soon realized that the voice of Belcourt was not confined to his American parish. Before too long it was telling Red River's half-breeds that, despite its charter, the Company did not legally have an exclusive trading monopoly nor possess any political authority.

Unable to cope with either Kittson, Belcourt, or his own free traders, Ballenden grew desperate and more than a little frightened. He could see that the Company's powers and its position were deteriorating. To stave off their collapse, he brought suit against William Sayer and

[72] 15 June 1848, Sibley Papers.

three other half-breeds for trading illegally with the Indians. He hoped that their conviction in Assiniboia's courts "would remove the impression that had got abroad . . . that the chartered rights claimed by the Company could not be sustained in law."[73] No move could have been more foolish. Although the Company legally possessed an exclusive right to the fur trade of Rupert's Land, it had allowed the people of Red River to trade with the Indians for years, provided the furs were gathered for their own use or brought for sale to Fort Garry. Thus Ballenden was ill-advised to proceed against the "John Does" of the settlement. On the other hand, if he had brought suit against someone like Sinclair, a person manifestly guilty both of illicit trading and smuggling, the risks involved might have been worth considering. But to sue a petty trader like Sayer merely for trading was to hazard the Company's future for a mess of pottage.

As the date for Sayer's trial drew near, it became apparent that Red River's free traders, white and mixed blood alike, were thoroughly aroused. From his American sanctuary, Father Belcourt kept encouraging them to resist Ballenden, and within the settlement, Sinclair and others openly and repeatedly claimed that the Company possessed no trading monopoly, whether by charter or otherwise. Under these stimuli, the masses soon turned into "committees of the people," "delegates of the people," and other more menacing bodies. Two days before the trial, Ballenden was sure that armed partisans were going to attend the trial "either to intimidate the bench and jury by the mere demonstration, or else to prevent the execution of the law by actual violence."[74]

On the morning of the trial, crowds of armed and angry free traders gathered outside the court house. Where were the pensioners, the guardians of law and order? They stayed in their barracks that day and the Quarterly Court of Assiniboia was not even graced with its usual guard of honour. Caldwell dared not face a mob with a force he deemed barely large enough to protect Fort Garry. It was probably a wise decision, whatever the major's motivations, for the pensioners made better barroom brawlers than anything else. Since the pensioners were ruled out, Caldwell asked his recorder, Adam Thom, and the various magistrates whether Red River's "well disposed" citizens might be sworn in as special deputies; but they advised against it in the

[73]Simpson to the Governor and Committee, 30 June 1849, H.B.C., Series A.12/4.

[74]Thom to Ballenden, 5 June 1849, enclosed in Pelly to Grey, 13 Sept. 1849, H.B.C., Series A.8/4.

belief that the people would not risk life or property in the affair at hand.[75] Poor Caldwell had been placed in a quandary and he ultimately decided that he could do nothing but let events fashion their own course.

The court began its deliberations in the midst of a mob. After considering certain minor cases, it called Sayer to the bar. He did not appear. Considerable time went by as the sheriff and then a free trader (John McLaughlin) vainly tried to bring him before the court. At last, Sinclair, Garrioch, and a dozen of their free-trading compatriots presented themselves before the court as "Delegates of the people." The grim contest now started. Sinclair made a statement to the effect that the Hudson's Bay Company did not legally possess a trading monopoly. Thom, a man of courage, retorted that the question was a matter for the Queen and her parliament to decide. The recorder's colleagues on the bench then asked the "delegates" what they intended to do if the court proceeded with the case. Before a reply could be given, Thom intervened once again, asserting that whatever their intentions he meant to try Sayer. However he also said "all that he wished was a fair and impartial trial."[76] Accordingly, he offered Sinclair the opportunity to defend Sayer before a jury of his own choosing. After consulting at great length among themselves, the free traders returned to the court, Sayer in hand, and accepted Thom's offer. As a lawyer for the defence, Sinclair squeezed all that he could from the privileges of his office. He objected to five jurors already impanelled and to eleven alternates, until he had twelve men tried and true—a jury so well-packed with free traders that it included Kittson's father-in-law! Yet as the trial developed, it was revealed that Sayer was guilty as charged. His own son testified that he had taken presents "of a few skins" in return for blankets and "a dram of spirits." The facts were swiftly demonstrated; the law was explained; and the verdict rendered: "guilty of Trading Furs." No sentence was ever passed. If it had been, the court could never have executed it. The foreman of the jury pleaded with Ballenden to be merciful towards Sayer "as it appeared that he thought that he had a right to trade as he and others were under the impression that there was a free trade in furs."[77] Ballenden was caught in his own trap. To the plea for mercy, he answered that he was concerned with the principle of the case, not

[75]Caldwell to the Governor and Committee, 2 Aug. 1849, H.B.C., Series A.11/96.
[76]Records of the Quarterly Court of Assiniboia, 1844–51, P.A.M.
[77]*Ibid.*

just a few skins, and since the jury had handed down a verdict of guilty, he was satisfied. Therefore he returned Sayer's furs and dropped charges against the other three men.

Thursday, 17 May 1849, was beyond doubt the longest day in the history of the Quarterly Court of Assiniboia. At its closing, the elation of the free traders stood out in sharp contrast to the bitterness felt by the Company. "Had we had the day before us," Adam Thom unhappily reminisced, "I should rather have fought another battle with the insurgents, than have appeared to yield to the dictation of shot and ammunition."[78] To have tried Sayer or any other free trader without the means of enforcing a decision was a great mistake. Upon hearing of the trial, the Governor and Committee were horrified, questioning Ballenden's judgment in bringing suit in the first place—and the chief factor later acknowledged his error. Because of his stupidity, the Company had challenged a foe stronger than itself, had been defeated, and in defeat would have to make certain adjustments in its government and the management of its business.

Although the Company consequently made many wise changes, it did nothing about Kittson, who must be regarded as a mainspring in the whole free-trading movement. If the company had paid him blackmail money or had brought him into the service, it could have eliminated its greatest competitor. With his removal from the border, Red River's free traders would have lost their primary market. And without Kittson and his Minnesota associates, how long would Belcourt's mission have lasted? However Simpson elected to follow the unimaginative instead of the bold course of action. In a letter to London, he outlined a trading policy for the future that was couched in terms of the past: ". . . we . . . must trust alone to the Company's superior means in the way of trade to secure even a portion of the furs hunted in the disturbed parts of the country."[79]

Kittson and Belcourt remained in Pembina. The trader seemed invulnerable to all the Company's competitive tactics. Nor could the priest, with his persistent flow of propaganda to Red River's disaffected, be silenced. For they and their free-trading expatriates of Red River, who made up Pembina's population, were safe behind the 49th parallel.

[78]Thom to Ballenden, 5 June 1849, enclosed in Pelly to Grey, 13 Sept. 1849, H.B.C., Series A.8/4.
[79]Simpson to the Governor and Committee, 30 June 1849, H.B.C., Series A.12/4.

Pembina was an ineradicable, cancerous growth whose threat to the Company was demonstrated in May—and again in mid-summer—when American troops revisited the borderlands. As soon as the troops had arrived, the Red River Settlement was showered with rumours. Ballenden was sure that their presence portended the establishment of a military post at Pembina; and the possible consequences of that were almost too evil for him to contemplate. Surely American settlers would follow in the wake of the military; the habits of the Company's Red River subjects would change for the worse; "and even the quieter and most orderly class of our population, seeing the so called liberty of American citizens, [would] . . . imbibe the ideas of the latter & render it impossible without troops, to maintain any thing like tranquility in the colony."[80]

[80]Ballenden to the Secretary, 24 Aug. 1849, H.B.C., Series A.11/95.

Chapter 4. Minnesota's
Territorial Years, 1849–1857

THE YEARS, 1849 TO 1857, ENCLOSE AN ERA IN THE HISTORY OF THE BRITISH and American Northwests. Eighteen hundred and forty-nine was the first year in Minnesota's short life as a territory and the last in the Hudson's Bay Company's long career as the undisputed master of trade in Rupert's Land. It was also a period of significant decay and startling growth. The last of the large fur trading companies, Pierre Choteau, Jr. & Company, withdrew from Minnesota—to be replaced by a host of commercial houses centred at St. Paul. However, the retreat of the Choteaus was not brought about by competitors but by the advancing agricultural frontier. By 1857 a succession of Indian treaties had opened up for settlement almost all Minnesota Territory, and pioneer farmers were plunging into the newly ceded lands at a breath-taking rate.

As a territory in 1850, Minnesota had about 6,000 people; as a young state, ten years later, its population exceeded 172,000.[1] If the historian could have sorted Minnesotans into occupational groups, he would probably have discovered that land speculators were the most active if not the most numerous of them all. By 1857 the territory was dotted with town sites, both real and "paper." Even the Red River Valley, remote though it was from the heaviest influx of pioneers, gave evidence of the land boom. With the growth in towns, population, and

[1]Preliminary Report, 8th Census, *House Executive Document No. 116*, 37th Cong., 2nd Sess., Serial 1137, pp. 130–31.

transportation facilities, Minnesota's trade and commerce with Rupert's Land bulked larger every year; and, at the end of the era, the fortunes of Red River were intimately entwined with those of St. Paul.

I

For Norman W. Kittson and his business associate, Henry H. Sibley, 1848 had been a good year, the best that they had experienced since the initial launching of their Pembina experiment. The outfit had grossed better than $10,000 and netted for Kittson alone approximately $1,500.[2] Such returns were comforting and both men eyed the future with considerable optimism. If 1848 had been profitable, would not 1849 and all the succeeding years be even more rewarding? Surely the consequence of Sayer's trial would be an explosive expansion of free trade in Rupert's Land.

Always cautious, Kittson clung to his old trading patterns lest he lose a winning combination. Pembina remained the head and front of his business operation. It was a primitive trading depot consisting of about a dozen buildings, ranged in a square and situated on the bank of the Red River just south of its junction with the Pembina River. For much of the year Pembina was nearly deserted, but in the fall, and again in the spring, its grounds were crowded with Indians and half-breeds and its buildings gave back the confused echo of many tongues. Here Kittson bartered goods of every description for the furs and robes of the half-breed hunters of the plains and assembled outfits of trade goods which he extended, on credit, to the fur-trapping Indians of the eastern woodlands. To supplement these returns, he periodically visited the Red River Settlement and, with extensive cash outlays, procured the finest furs of the northland.

Despite the promise implicit in the Sayer trial, the trading season of 1849/50 brought nothing but ill luck to Kittson. In the winter, according to the mysterious cycles governing wilderness life, food became scarce in the forests east and southeast of Pembina. The rabbits vanished, victims of an unknown disease; and famine quickly followed. The lynx diminished in numbers until they too were no longer seen. But of greater significance than the decline in fur-bearing

[2]Sibley to Pierre Choteau, Jr. & Company, 25 July and 8 Aug. 1849, Sibley Papers, M.H.S. "Outfits," whether British or American, were usually based upon a fiscal year running from June to June. Thus the 1848 outfit was wound up on the last day of June, 1849.

animals was the condition of Kittson's Indians who were soon "in a state of Starvation" and remained so till spring.[3] They had begun the winter without their usual supply of dried corn, for that crop had inexplicably failed; and when the rabbits, the staff of forest life, disappeared, the Indians inevitably suffered. Whether motivated by hardheaded business principles or humanitarianism, Kittson had to feed them. It was a costly undertaking exceeding the mere expense of providing and dispensing food. Unused, his trading goods accumulated interest charges; but, most damaging of all, the Indians brought very few furs into his eastern posts at Roseau Lake, Lake of the Woods, and Rainy River, the very posts that had produced the bulk of his fine furs during the previous two seasons.

Unfortunately for Kittson, his troubles were not confined to natural disasters. The competition was stronger and more vigorous than in the past. His own territory was invaded by a great many whisky-laden scamps from the Red River Settlement, while the Company itself kept up a relentless pressure upon and above the border. After Sayer's trial the Company had strengthened its posts in the interior of Rupert's Land and multiplied the number of frontier stations. Thus its whole weight was brought to bear against Kittson and free trade: more personnel, more liberal outfits, more posts, and, above all, higher prices. The policy seemed extremely successful. Not only did the Company profit from its 1849 outfit, it also contained its free-trading opposition. "I think," Simpson wrote to London, "we have no reason to apprehend that the Company's affairs on the frontier will be in a worse condition than at present;—on the contrary, we believe we are gaining ground in that quarter, inasmuch as our opponents are evidently relaxing the hold they had obtained on the trade."[4]

When Kittson carted his returns to Mendota in June, 1850, his heart was heavier than his earnings. He had not enough fine furs from the forests and too many products from the plains, pemmican and buffalo robes. He needed more than five tons of pemmican and seven hundred robes to make money. At best, the plains were only a safety-valve; they could not provide him with a sufficient profit margin to make his business a success and he feared that the 1849 outfit would "come out a considerable loser."[5] His complete stock of furs was barely half that

---

[3]Kittson to William H. Forbes, 2 Jan. 1850, Sibley Papers.
[4]Simpson to the Governor and Committee, 26 June 1850, H.B.C., Series A.12/5.
[5]Frederick B. Sibley to Henry H. Sibley, 2 Aug. 1850, Sibley Papers. Frederick was Henry's brother and managed the business at Mendota while the latter was in Washington as Minnesota's territorial delegate, 1849–53.

of 1848. But for the only time in that dreary season, luck was with him. The fur market held high and he was able to minimize losses that might otherwise have been unbearable.

That summer he threw caution to the winds. Ignoring his heavy inventories in Indian goods and disregarding his own indebtedness, Kittson brought back to Pembina the biggest trading outfit to date. Perhaps he believed that the disasters of 1849/50 would not be repeated. Perhaps he hoped to recover his losses with one bold stroke. At any rate, he foolishly chose to expand rather than contract his business, although he made no basic changes in his trading patterns. The results were almost ruinous.

In the first place, Kittson found himself harassed by competition wherever he turned. Along the 49th parallel the Hudson's Bay Company maintained such an exhausting pressure that by mid-winter his spirits were flagging—and his hopes all but gone that the Company would ever buy him out. Moreover petty, unlicensed traders from Red River established themselves at nearly every one of his posts below the line. In the second place, the dreaded famine of 1849/50 reappeared. Throughout the winter, food was in short supply both on the plains and in the forest. Only in the plains country were Kittson's half-breed hunters able to tighten their belts and do fairly well. In the eastern posts, where Kittson's heavy expenses lay, nothing alleviated the situation. "I am," he confessed, "almost dèmontè [*sic*] and wish to God I was out [of] the infernal trade or rather that I had never embarked into it."[6] To give a final twist to his fate, fur-bearing animals were prevalent this season, waiting to be trapped, but with starving Indians, "the d——l . . . [was] to skin them."[7] Miraculously enough, Kittson escaped total ruin. The plains posts, with their wolves, foxes, and buffalo, saved him. He had some fine furs from the forest too, acquired in the late spring hunts; but despite their quality, there were not enough of them to matter. Although his returns exceeded $12,000, he lost money on the outfit.[8] With a large overhead, he had needed a big year in order to make money. Competition and a complicated tangle of misfortunes had made it a lean one instead.

It was now painfully apparent to Kittson that he had reached a critical point in his business life. If he continued in the trade, following the policies of the past, he would probably be bankrupt within a

[6]Kittson to Martin McLeod, 3 March 1851, McLeod Papers, M.H.S.

[7]Kittson to H. H. Sibley, 28 Feb. 1851, Sibley Papers.

[8]Joseph A. Sire to H. H. Sibley, 28 Aug. 1851, *ibid.* Sire was a partner in the St. Louis house of Pierre Choteau, Jr. & Company.

short time. But if he got out, what could he do? He had never known anything but the fur trade. He was now thirty-seven years old, married, and with a growing family. To launch a second career might be very difficult. He therefore decided to persevere; but, at the same time, he brought about a top-to-bottom reorganization of his business. For the next two seasons his guiding principle was conservatism in all things. He cut his requisitions for the fur trade almost to the bone; and having "unfortunately lernt that this credit business . . . [would] not succeed," he abandoned wherever possible the extension of credit to any hunters.[9] One by one, he eliminated the eastern posts until only Red Lake remained. These stations had demanded too much credit in the form of Indian goods and had proved too vulnerable to the capricious life cycles of the northern forests. To offset their loss, he expanded his practice of paying cash for the furs and robes secured by the men of Red River. What trading parties he still assembled at Pembina were sent off to the plains. The investment here, though small, was invariably productive. And finally, he broadened his general trade with the citizens and merchants of Red River.

A combination of good management and thorough reorganization of the business brought success, achieved despite heightened competition from Red River's petty traders and the Hudson's Bay Company. Indeed Kittson came to regard the Company almost with disdain and for a considerable part of the next four winters lived in St. Paul as a member of Minnesota's Territorial Council. However, it was not absence from Pembina that made his business grow more valuable. Both his business and economic circumstances had changed. Famine vanished from the forests as mysteriously as it had appeared; the supply of fur-bearing animals mounted and the price for buffalo robes doubled in three years on the American market. In these pleasant surroundings, Kittson began to make money. His outfit "clear[ed] something" in 1851 and, in the following year, "made splendid returns, his O. shewing a clear profit of nearly $10,000."[10] In both seasons he dispensed cash in the Red River Settlement with a lavish hand, often outbidding the Hudson's Bay Company. In the latter season his requisitions for trading goods climbed virtually by the month till it seemed to Kittson that his customers would "either smoke themselves dry or drown themselves in Tea."[11]

[9]Kittson to F. B. Sibley, 11 Oct. 1852, *ibid.*
[10]F. B. Sibley to Pierre Choteau, Jr. & Company, 26 July 1852; and H. H. Sibley to Pierre Choteau, Jr. & Co., 4 Aug. 1853, *ibid.*
[11]Kittson to F. B. Sibley, 29 March 1853, *ibid.*

The change in Kittson's fortunes came suddenly and as a surprise to the Company, which had been confident that it was checking his opposition. In June, 1853, the scales fell from Simpson's eyes when he learned that the American had grossed better than $30,000.[12] He had made a mighty breach in the Company's walls, and through it, along with the returns of his own district, he had extracted enough goods to fill more than sixty carts. The carts were crammed with furs and robes, pemmican, moccasins, and various "articles of dress worked with porcupine quills." Small wonder that Kittson was in high spirits when he reached Mendota. At last he was realizing the boom forecast by Sayer's trial.

Despite Kittson's gains, both Pierre Choteau, Jr. & Company and Henry Sibley had decided to withdraw from the fur trade. The profits from Pembina scarcely balanced the losses suffered by other men working for or with the Upper Mississippi Outfit. The general falling off of the entire outfit, coupled with Kittson's earlier decline, had awakened a chorus of protests from the Choteaus, who supplied Sibley with all his trade goods on credit. As early as 1849 the debts owed St. Louis by Sibley and his various partnerships had reached nearly ruinous levels, and, during the years immediately following, they grew larger and progressively more unstable because of the heavy inventories carried by the Mississippi Outfit. Letters from St. Louis to Mendota ran the scale of anger, fear, and anguish; all Sibley's efforts to mollify the Choteaus were in vain. His red-inked ledgers were simply too eloquent to be answered. "The sums standing on our Books to the debit of the several outfits up the Mississippi," roared one of the Choteau partners, "are really enormous—they exceed 400,000$! ! !"[13]

Moreover the Choteaus were realistic businessmen. They reasoned that the advancing agricultural frontier would wipe out the fur traders' wilderness and therefore had planned a systematic withdrawal from the upper Mississippi Valley. However, they knew that before Minnesota Territory could be legally opened to settlers, there would have to be a succession of Indian treaties ceding land to the federal government. They also knew that in the fashioning of these treaties, the fur traders would play the vital role of intermediaries between the tribes and the treaty commissioners. Here lay a last chance for the Choteaus to settle some of the debts owed them and their outfits. But it was a good one; for, as Sibley assured them, the Indians would treat "only as I may dictate . . . [and] no treaty can be made without our claims

[12]Simpson to the Governor and Committee, 2 July 1853, H.B.C., Series A.12/6.
[13]Sire to H. H. Sibley, 12 Oct. 1850, Sibley Papers.

being first secured."[14] According to this script, the Indians would receive an initial cash payment from the commissioners and give most of it to traders like Kittson, who, in turn, would use the money to meet obligations owed trading houses like the Choteaus.

During the summer of 1851 treaties were made with the Sioux, ceding to the United States all their lands in southern Minnesota except for a strip lying athwart the Minnesota River. The United States bought the "Suland" on the instalment plan, cash down and the balance in interest-bearing annuities. The cash was meant for the fur traders, without whom the treaties could never have been consummated. Only in this way could Sibley and the Choteaus hope to recover some of their debts before liquidating the Upper Mississippi Outfit. Their hopes were not immediately realized, however. Other traders and other companies also put forth claims, and, in the resulting confusion, the "down payment" was delayed for many months. Therefore it was not till June, 1853, that Sibley formally wrote Kittson of his plans "to make arrangements with you to take the business [of the lower Red River Valley] on your own a/c."[15]

During the summer and fall of 1853 Sibley was busy settling his own affairs and those of the Choteaus in the Minnesota fur trade. The various units of the Upper Mississippi Outfit were either sold to "partners" like Kittson or simply terminated. Kittson himself had decided to stay in the trade. Not only had the past season been rewarding, but the prospect of hauling all his stock back to Mendota seemed foolish as well as back-breaking. He acquired from Sibley all the trade goods on hand at Pembina, assumed his share of the partnership's remaining debts, and received cash for the credit remaining in his name on the accounts of the old outfit. For the forthcoming season only, Sibley agreed to furnish his ex-partner with whatever trade goods he might require and, in turn, was given the right to have first bid on all furs gathered by Kittson. Moreover, Sibley generously secured for his friend the authority to draw on London for any cash that might be needed for purchases in the Red River Settlement.

The 1853 outfit began its life in a most auspicious manner. When Kittson headed north in early August, 1853, his carts were "heavy loaded." Orders upon Sibley had been considerably larger than in previous years, and they would be greatly augmented before the year was out. Shortly after the Yankee trader reached his destination, he

[14]H. H. Sibley to Pierre Choteau, Jr. & Company, 3 Nov. 1850, *ibid.*
[15]4 June 1853, *ibid.* See Lucile Kane, "The Sioux Treaties and the Traders," *Minnesota History* XXXII (June, 1952), 65–80.

shifted his headquarters from the flats of Pembina to a site thirty miles to the east and at the base of Pembina Mountain. Here at St. Joseph, a newly fashioned parish town of half-breeds under Father Belcourt's care, he was not only near his hunters but also safe, like them, from the occasional flood waters of the Red River. The northward trek had been passed in near record time, and before the end of September Kittson had "no less than thirteen outfits out to the West and North."[16] Although his personal relations with the Hudson's Bay men grew steadily more sociable, competition with the Company stiffened as he pushed his operations deeper and deeper into the Northwest. None the less, there was an infectious optimism in the air that fall. "There [are] more minks in the country than you can shake a stick at," chortled one of Kittson's subordinates, "and good appearances for Robes—as also other Furs—we will have a good year."[17]

That winter, when Kittson once again deserted Pembina to attend the territorial council in St. Paul, he found time to discuss business as well as politics. Before the session was over, he and another councillor, William H. Forbes, had formed a partnership (known thereafter as Forbes & Kittson) in furs and general merchandise in northern Minnesota and Rupert's Land. Both partners were Canadian born and of an age; each had come to Minnesota as a young man to work for the American Fur Company. Forbes had clerked for Sibley at Mendota until 1847, when he assumed charge of the latter's St. Paul Outfit, which he managed till Sibley's retirement from the fur trade. According to the standards of a frontier community, Forbes and Kittson were men of property and prestige and apparently well suited for a mutual association in business. According to plan, Kittson would continue to manage affairs in the border country, while Forbes, situated in St. Paul, would stock trade goods and general merchandise for Kittson and his Red River clients and, in addition, handle all the fur sales.

Kittson was soon firmly entrenched in the border trade. Even in 1853, when facing a new Hudson's Bay Company policy and a new chief factor, he had airily commented to Sibley that "they have tried so many experiments to oust me that I do not think their present course will succeed any better than heretofore."[18] In the summer following his partnership with Forbes he brought down about 400 packs of furs and robes to St. Paul and probably cleared more than $7,000.[19] In the

[16]Kittson to H. H. Sibley, 16 Sept. 1853, Sibley Papers.
[17]Joseph Rolette to F. B. Sibley, 17 Nov. 1853, *ibid.*
[18]12 Nov. 1853, *ibid.*
[19]H. H. Sibley to F. B. Sibley, 3 July 1854, *ibid.*

next season, 1854/55, he accelerated his business campaign, buying furs in the Red River District—though his prices were lower than the Company's—and outfitting traders with American goods so that they could extend their operations beyond Red River. Emboldened by success, he set up a post in the spring of 1856 within sight of Fort Garry, openly buying furs and selling a wide variety of articles including such luxuries as champagne—an item scarcely to be found in the Company's Red River sales shops. But undoubtedly the height of his impudence was reached when he started to advance cash to his Red River traders so that they could buy goods from the Company's sales shops, trade with the Indians of Rupert's Land, and bring the furs back to him.

By 1856 Simpson regarded the Red River trading situation with unmitigated pessimism. He could see that his Company's charter was "almost a nullity . . . set at nought by the Americans and their Half-breed allies."[20] He knew Kittson was endeavouring "as far as [it] lies in his power, to divert the trade of the country from its present channel to the United States,"[21] but there was apparently nothing he could do about it. He dared not seize Kittson even though he was working in the shadow of Fort Garry, for to do so might provoke the free traders of Rupert's Land who were now much too numerous and strong to control.

II

Although Kittson was the chief agent in the awakening and subsequent development of trade between Rupert's Land and Minnesota, there were other elements combining to effect the explosive reaction of the mid-'fifties. The free-trading movement in Red River with its half-breed legions; the geographic bonds uniting the settlement and St. Paul; the rise of St. Paul as a commercial city of considerable stature; the American "revolution" in transportation—all these contributed to the expansion of commercial intercourse within the greater Northwest. But none was more forceful than the free-trading movement in Red River.

By 1849, the commercial relationship between Red River's free traders and Minnesota's merchants had so matured that they co-

[20]Simpson to the Governor and Committee (confidential), 2 Aug. 1856, H.B.C., Series A.12/7.
[21]Simpson to the Governor and Committee, 26 June 1856, H.B.C., Series A.12/8.

operated in the three fields of business, banking, and transportation. The men of Red River often asked Henry Sibley to fill their orders from his Mendota warehouse or order goods for them from some down-river city. At Pembina, Kittson frequently transmitted orders for all sorts of merchandise ranging from stoves to spy glasses. To expedite the international flow of business, merchants on either side of the line carried running accounts with one another, eventually settling their differences with cash or London and/or New York bills of exchange. The same merchants also used the cart trains operating between Red River and Mendota (or St. Paul) so much in common that the carters acted more like common carriers than private freighters. In fact, there were even men available for special trips across the plains, "tramp" carters who earned an uncertain livelihood before the advent of stage lines in the 'sixties.

The same commercial patterns persisted after 1849; only the parti-cipants were different. The older merchants of Red River had retired. McLaughlin had gone back to the British Isles; McDermot had renounced the pleasures of trafficking in furs in favour of a general trade and the friendship of Sir George Simpson; and Sinclair's career also came to an end in the 'fifties. Thus the way was clear for a new generation of free traders and general merchants. They were largely half-breeds, both French- and English-speaking; none the less, they were men of substantial property and political standing within the Red River Settlement.

After Sayer's trial, the free-trade movement remained in a sluggish state for three seasons. The free traders suffered from the same ills that beset Kittson—the inexplicable failure of fur-bearing animals and all the competitive pressures that the Company could exert. The Company tried to seal off Rupert's Land from the commercial world lying without and to eradicate free trade within its territories by well-staffed outfits, heavy inventories, and generous price scales. In addi-tion, it shifted its trading posts and districts around, seeking always the best defence against the free traders. Although it is difficult to locate exactly the districts adjacent to or near the Red River District, it is possible to give their approximate, mid-century position. Touching the international border, from Lake Superior to the Rockies, stretched the districts of Lac la Pluie, Red River, and Saskatchewan; along the western edge of Lake Manitoba was the Swan River District; and to its north lay Cumberland, whose worth was now reckoned by the site alone. It served as a buffer state between Swan River and the English (Churchill) River District. The latter was prized not only for its fur production but also for its possession of the famed Methye

Portage, which led to the Mackenzie District—"the most valuable fur district in the country."[22]

The containment policy seemed to work well for the Company. It was not bothered by free traders within the Red River District, where its returns mounted with every outfit, 1849–52. Nor was there any evidence of encroachments in Red River's neighbouring districts. Thus the Governor and Committee could be pardoned for their optimism in 1852 and their belief that the progress of free trade had finally been arrested. But it was circumstances, not the Company, which had conspired to retard the free-trade movement; and the circumstances changed. During the 1852/53 season the rabbits returned to the forests, heralding the reappearance of fur-bearing animals; high water on the prairies brought forth a rich crop of muskrats; and amidst all this abundance, the price of furs shot up. Suddenly and sharply, the Company began to feel again the true power of the free traders from Red River.

Simpson's annual report in 1853 to the Governor and Committee was a cheerless document.[23] The Red River District had gathered many more furs and robes than in the previous year, but they had all been collected at great cost, usually in cash, and many had been drained from the adjacent districts by far-travelling free traders. For this unforeseen calamity, Simpson blamed ". . . the high prices given by . . . [Kittson] and the traders on the Mississippi which have withdrawn the attention of the settlers from their ordinary pursuits to the less laborious but more profitable occupation of hunting and trading, the public mind being wrought up to a state of excitement almost equal to that which followed the discovery of the gold mines in California and Australia, particularly known as the 'gold fever.'" It seemed as if all Rupert's Land had been bewitched. In Swan River, the Company's trade was in a highly disorganized state because of the free traders who had overrun the district "in all directions & carried off a large proportion of the more valuable furs."[24] Chief Trader Henry Fisher, himself a half-breed and one with many dusky relatives, had provided a lot of the invaders—at Company expense—with food and lodging. Cumberland likewise felt the impact of free trade. Runners from Red River broke through its protective edge of

[22]Simpson to the Governor and Committee, 30 June 1854, H.B.C., Series A.12/7.
[23]2 June 1853, H.B.C., Series A.12/6.
[24]*Ibid.* Simpson claimed that Swan River had been overrun for the past two or three winters, but a careful examination of the Northern Department's annual reports failed to substantiate his contention.

posts and made off with many furs. Even Saskatchewan was not immune. Here were to be seen signs of disaffection and insubordination among the Company's servants, and it was discovered that one interpreter at a missionary post had been more active saving pelts for himself than souls for the Lord.

The following summer (1853) Kittson brought a handful of orders and a large company of Red River traders down to Mendota. Sibley's warehouse was overwhelmed. His brother filled what orders he could from his existing stock and that of the St. Paul Outfit. For the balance he sent off a lengthy list to merchants in Galena and St. Louis—together with the intriguing prophecy that "the day is not far off when the most of the Red River trade will be carried through this Country."[25] The prediction would come true, but it would be St. Paul, not Galena or St. Louis, which reaped the final and greater rewards from the trade. Downriver prices were no better than Minnesota's; and in 1854, the year he retired from the fur trade, Sibley directed all his old Red River customers to the vigorous young city of St. Paul across the Mississippi.

In the fall of 1853 the American customs collector at Pembina estimated that there were "at the Selkirk Settlement between on[e] hundred and fifty and one hundred and seventy-five traders who . . . [made] a practice of trading for themselves individually."[26] How many of them subsequently trekked down to Minnesota with their wares was unknown; but it was obvious that the Company had to check their growth and destroy their commercial bridge to the south, if it were to continue in business along the borderlands.

Yet how should the Company proceed? It was not facing isolated opponents whom it could put down one by one, but rather an amorphous, large, and lawless population. Although it was pleasant to dream of confiscations and seizures, Simpson knew that "it would be rash in the extreme to provoke a quarrel in which the strongest party must be successful, and which might result in the total ruin of the Company's trade in this [Northern] Department."[27] He toyed with the idea of tripling the duties on all imports into Rupert's Land, but

[25]F. B. Sibley to Pierre Choteau, Jr. & Company, 6 July 1853, Sibley Papers.

[26]Phillip Beauprie to the Secretary of the Treasury, 13 Sept. 1853, Letters from Collectors to the Treasury Department, National Archives and Records Service of the United States (N.A.).

[27]Simpson to the Governor and Committee, 2 July 1853, H.B.C., Series A.12/6. He had no intention of confiscating any furs. He remembered too well the Sayer fiasco and knew that any seizure, anywhere in the Northern Department, would be regarded "as a national affair by the Halfbreeds." To Governor John Shepherd (confidential), 15 Nov. 1856, H.B.C., Series A.12/8.

at the mere rumour of an increase ominous murmurs were heard throughout the settlement. From Fort Garry, the Company's chief factor bluntly warned Simpson: ". . . it can do no good . . . [and] it may hasten the object which . . . [we] are anxious to prevent—a more intimate connexion with the opposite frontier."[28] London wisely agreed, for even at the present duty level of 4 per cent, Assiniboia's collector could scarcely gather enough receipts to justify his existence.

Simpson had to rely solely upon the capital and organization of the Hudson's Bay Company. Accordingly he made considerable changes in personnel, bringing the "younger and more active men to . . . Red River" and exchanging one man for another in his search for a chief factor able to supervise this difficult district.[29] He abandoned the policy of advancing goods on credit, payable in furs—it had only served to arm the opposition—and instituted cash payments.

His schemes failed to achieve their desired results, for the free traders irresistibly extended their operations into one district after another. Only Swan River remained under the Company's control—a control gained by saturating it with trading goods and getting furs whatever the cost. Even so, the district was unable to fulfil its role as a barrier to the north. English River was invaded in the winter of 1853/54 and again in 1855/56 "by the Red River traders, who . . . [were] steadily pushing their way, step by step, towards the North."[30] In the west, there was no holding them back. During the season of 1855/56 between seventy and eighty traders, bearing cheap whisky, cloth, and tea, comfortably crossed the plains in over 300 carts and made off with large returns from Saskatchewan. Cumberland was also plundered, for it lay within easy reach by boat from Red River. And in both districts the petty traders were soon too numerous and too well organized to be expelled. If Simpson came to accept their presence somewhat philosophically, he must have choked a bit in the process, for they overbid the Company and carried off the lion's share of the furs and robes. Even more disquieting, by 1857/58 there was not a single district in the Northern Department, with the exception of York and Mackenzie, that had not been invaded.[31]

[28]Ballenden to Simpson, 16 Aug. 1854, H.B.C., Series A.11/96.
[29]Simpson to the Governor and Committee, 30 June 1854, H.B.C., Series A.12/7.
[30]Simpson to the Governor and Committee, 26 June 1856, H.B.C., Series A.12/8.
[31]Simpson to the Governor and Committee, 24 June 1858, H.B.C., Series A.12/9.

Desperate though the Company's position was in the interior districts, it was worse in Red River. Here, although the returns rose every year, it was painfully evident that they were drained from all the neighbouring districts because of the Company's high prices. High prices drew more and more furs into Fort Garry—and more and more men into the guild of free trade. In the season of 1855/56 the Company spent over £8,000 in cash within the settlement and still failed to eliminate competition, although prices had now reached such a height that it was doubtful whether the Company was making any money. Yet, paradoxically, the Company's annual indents (or orders) for Red River grew at a faster rate than its cash expenditures. Moreover, indents no longer consisted of trading goods for primitive people, but presented a large and varied assortment fit to tempt customers who had been to St. Paul and whose tastes were "more fastidious than formerly."[32]

The Hudson's Bay Company had been caught in its own toils. Unable to eradicate free trade by force, it had fallen back upon a price war whose results proved to be most unfortunate. Free trade spread uncontrollably throughout the Northern Department. The Company's trading patterns were torn apart. Its transportation system was subjected to dangerous new pressures. For although indents from some of the interior districts declined, those from Red River sales shops soared, thereby overtaxing the Company's trunk line from York Factory to Red River.

And always there was St. Paul, whose influence upon the Company, its settlement, and its trade was incalculably great. Whatever index the historian selects to measure the trade between St. Paul and Red River in the 'fifties, it is clear that it was already large and growing rapidly. In 1855 Simpson reckoned that 400 carts (each with a capacity of 500 to 800 pounds) had been required to carry off the furs exported by private traders from Red River to Minnesota;[33] and a St. Paul editor estimated their value at $40,000.[34] In the following year the estimate was doubled; in 1857 it was doubled again. By then there were at least three firms in St. Paul, each of which (Forbes &

[32]Simpson to the Governor and Committee, 26 June 1856, H.B.C., Series A.12/8.

[33]Simpson to the Governor and Committee, 29 June 1855, H.B.C., Series A.12/7.

[34]Trade statistics may be found in the St. Paul *Advertiser* (21 Nov. 1857), the St. Paul *Pioneer and Democrat* (28 April 1859), and the St. Paul *Press* (29 Aug. 1863).

Kittson, Culver & Farrington, and Myrick & Company) was annually importing $50,000 of furs and robes from the north.[35]

Although the volume and value of Red River's imports from Minnesota are more difficult to figure than its exports, nevertheless the Governor of Assiniboia asserted in 1856 that the goods imported from St. Paul could not "now be less than half, and in a few years will probably exceed in value the whole of the Company's [trade] to Red River by way of York Factory."[36] He admittedly possessed no positive data to support his statement; the inability of his government to collect import duties effectively precluded any statistics. Nor did the American customhouse at Pembina provide accurate figures, although letters and reports from its collectors amply testified to the commercial boom. A sure index to Red River's import trade was the importation of liquor. The source was invariably St. Paul, where merchants were "as thick as blackberries" and liquor dealers dispensed whisky crudely camouflaged as red lions, white lions, and cobblers or sold it by the bottle or the keg. In 1857 approximately 5,000 gallons entered Assiniboia—and Kittson's own father-in-law personally brought in several hundred gallons.[37]

Simpson himself never knew the exact dimensions of the free-trade movement or the volume of the trade with St. Paul, but he knew that both were beyond his control and much too large for comfort. True, the Company was still making money in the Northern Department. But how long could that last? So far as Simpson could see, it could "continue one, two or more years, although at all times liable to be suddenly interrupted."[38] John Shepherd, Governor of the Company, disagreed with him, cheerfully claiming that it would be many years before—under existing conditions and circumstances—the free traders could vitally damage the Company. But, in his eagerness to view the siatuation in an optimistic light, Shepherd overlooked two facts: The Company's present competition was the most difficult and dangerous it had ever faced in Red River; and at no time in history have "conditions and circumstances" remained unchanged.

[35]In the late summer of 1857, Culver & Farrington absorbed Forbes & Kittson and thereby became St. Paul's principal trading house. See the agreement between Charles Cavilier, Forbes & Kittson, and Culver & Farrington, dated 8 Aug. 1857, Cavilier Papers, M.H.S.

[36]Francis G. Johnson to the Secretary, [1] June 1856, H.B.C., A.11/96.

[37]Governor and Committee to Simpson, 16 April 1858, H.B.C., Series A.6/33. Simpson to the Governor and Committee, 30 June 1857, H.B.C., Series A.12/8.

[38]Simpson to Shepherd (confidential), 2 Aug. 1856, H.B.C., Series A.12/7.

III

Among the changing circumstances in the mid-nineteenth century of which the Governor and Committee of the Hudson's Bay Company seemed unaware was the transportation "revolution" occurring within North America. Though it was a worldwide phenomenon, this change in locomotion from horse- and wind-driven vehicles to steampower, Rupert's Land remained for some time in the older and more primitive age. While it languished, Minnesota thrived; and during the 'fifties, the Minnesota route to Red River threatened to supplant the Company's transportation system serving the southern districts of the Northern Department.

After the merger of the Hudson's Bay and the Northwest companies in 1821, the surviving concern had re-fashioned the Northern Department's transportation system. The canoe route from Lake Superior to the Red River Settlement was allowed virtually to slip back into the arms of the wilderness, and thereafter that picturesque waterway seldom saw any vessels from Canada. A new pattern was evolved, built upon Hudson Bay and the various rivers and lakes that drained into it from the south and west. Created in 1821, the pattern persisted almost without change until the late 'fifties.

The Northern Department's transportation system was an awesome triumph of man over nature. Each summer two ships sailed from England into Hudson Bay, bound for York Factory and bearing all the indents ordered by the various districts within the department. With good luck, a ship could make the 3,500-mile voyage from London to York in thirty days. But such speed was rare. Too often a ship made a fast crossing only to find Hudson Strait and the Bay beyond so choked with ice that the last leg of the journey required another month or more. At York the turnabout had to be swiftly executed, for the Bay had an inhospitably brief season of only six to eight weeks. Moreover unloading was complicated because the Hayes River was too shallow to accommodate sizable, sea-going vessels. All goods had to be lightered a considerable distance upriver before they could finally be put ashore and stored within the factory.

York Factory was the Northern Department's central depot. All its furs and robes were collected at this point for the outward voyage to London. Here too were stored all the trading goods of the inbound voyage for later distribution. Transportation beyond York rested upon an involved network of rivers and lakes. The trunk line ran from the Bay southwest to Norway House, a sub-depot at the foot of Lake Winnipeg; a gigantic spur line twisted westward along the Saskatchewan River as far as Edmonton, 1,000 miles away; and joined to this line by portages were two other huge spurs: the Mackenzie and Churchill river systems, serving the great northern districts.

Like an armada of water beetles, the Company's inland fleet sculled about the waters of the Northern Department; but unlike those aimless insects, it moved with purpose and precision. The capital ships were York boats, keel boats whose size and seaworthiness enabled them to navigate the large lakes and rivers. Although slower and less manageable than the conventional freighter canoes which they had largely replaced, York boats were safer and far more commodious. They operated in brigades of four to eight boats, carrying furs, provisions, and trading goods from one trading district to another; and beyond the reach of these boats, the Company used carts, pack horses, and canoes.

Perhaps the most famous of all brigades was that run by the "rough & terrible fellows" of Portage la Loche. Originating in the Red River Settlement as soon as the ice went out in early June, the brigade followed a back-breaking schedule until the freeze-up ended its labours.[39] From Red River, it carried provisions to Norway House, where it turned over its cargo for one of trading goods brought in the previous season from York. Then westward along the Saskatchewan swept the Portage la Loche "boys" till they reached their namesake, a twelve-mile carrying place more commonly known as Methye Portage. Here they exchanged goods for the furs borne to that rendezvous by the Mackenzie River brigade. That mission completed, the Portage la Loche brigade returned to Norway and headed for the Bay to deliver the furs to York Factory. After a final exchange of furs for goods, the brigade turned homeward; and some time in October, the sweat and strain of a long summer's voyaging (approximately 2,300 miles) were ended.

Such in brief was the transportation system of the Northern Department. Although extraordinary in so many ways, it was not without defects. Weather and climate were constant ills. While the inland waterways enjoyed four months of navigation, Hudson Bay, the key to the entire system, was usually closed for more than ten and, even in its open weeks, was plagued by floating ice. Some captains made "32 successful voyages to Hudsons [sic] Bay. . . . [without a]

[39]Joseph J. Hargrave, *Red River* (Montreal, 1871), pp. 160–2.

casualty worth speaking of . . . ";[40] others like the master of the *Kitty*, a vessel chartered to carry an "over-load" to York in 1859, failed to complete their maiden voyage. Despite the perils evident in these waters, the miracle was that freight rates from London to York were not unreasonable (£5 per ton) and that they stayed relatively constant through the years.[41]

Freightage from York Factory to Fort Garry, some 700 miles and thirty-four portages to the south, was in 1857 approximately four times that of the transatlantic passage, although the distance was only one-fifth as long. The difference in costs lay in the nature of the land and water to be traversed. The labour involved in working the York boats bore close resemblance to existence on a French galley. But the exertion required to pull the long oars probably seemed like child's play compared with the effort demanded to "track" the massive boats upstream whenever the water level dropped. Even the most ordinary portages were strenuous affairs. All the cargo had to be unloaded and carried, piece by piece, while the boats themselves were pushed or rolled upon logs across the carrying places. Good, reliable men were hard to find at any price to work the York boats. Conditions were so distasteful that few of the Company's own servants would undergo them, and after 1836, most of the freighting was done by private contractors. They too had difficulty getting recruits. Men in the Red River Settlement were loath to leave other more rewarding jobs for the toil and danger of the boats. As a result, brigades were often composed of "poor weak sapless fellows, a dozen of whom by themselves . . . [were] not able to manage a loaded boat in the rapids"[42]— or of the Portage la Loche "boys," who cared little for their cargo and banged and bumped their way over the portages.

Although the Company's transportation system had some ills, many of them as inconvenient as they were incurable, nevertheless it was superior to Kittson's when he first began freighting goods up to

[40]Oliver Warner, "Voyaging to York Factory," *Beaver*, outfit 288 (winter, 1957), 22. See also Donald Gunn's article, "How We Commenced Business," *Nor'-Wester*, 28 Feb. 1860.

[41]Great Britain, House of Commons, *Report from the Select Committee on the Hudson's Bay Company: Together with the Proceedings of the Committee, Minutes of Evidence, Appendix and Index* (London, 1857), p. 71, testimony of Sir George Simpson. Cf. James W. Taylor, special agent of the Treasury, to Salmon P. Chase, 15 Nov. 1860, Letters and Reports to the Treasury Department, N. A. Taylor stated that the freight per ton, London to York Factory, was $30; that from York to Red River was $125. Since the pound was then worth between $4.80 and $5, Taylor's figures do not vary much from Simpson's, *supra*.

[42]Donald Ross to James Hargrave, 21 Dec. 1843, in G. P. de T. Glazebrook, ed., *The Hargrave Correspondence 1821–1843* (Toronto, 1938), pp. 455–61.

Pembina in the early 'forties. His system consisted of a rather complicated interlocking of three means of transportation: railroads as far
as the westward-moving head of steel; steamboats and keel boats
wherever rivers would accommodate them; and beyond the river
banks—the Red River cart. Steam and rail services were destined to
improve, but the carts remained unchanged and the Red River trails
they used grew only in the sense that their ruts went deeper every
year. From a point of origin in the Mendota-Fort Snelling-St. Paul
complex the trails swept northward until they reached their destination within the Red River Settlement. Ultimately, there were three
trails: Kittson's, the Plains or Sauk Valley, and the Woods or Crow
Wing Trail. Though none followed a precise path, all were well
enough known to be named and the course of each can be roughly
outlined.[43]

Kittson's Trail was the natural, water-level route, bending along the
Minnesota River and rolling down the Valley of the Red. It was also
the oldest trail, having been picked out as early as 1820 by the Selkirk
pioneers and popularized during the next two decades by various fur
companies. However by mid-century it had become so closely associated with Kittson and his business that it bore his name. In fact,
it tied together the cardinal points of his trunk line: Mendota, Traverse des Sioux, and Pembina. From some downriver port, usually
St. Louis, steamboats brought trading goods to Mendota, where they
were transshipped to keel or barge-like Durham boats for a seventy-
mile jaunt up the Minnesota River to its head of navigation at Traverse
des Sioux. Here was Kittson's rendezvous—the site where he exchanged
the furs of the past season for the goods of the next, enjoyed a few
hours of conversation with his Mendota partners, and then turned his
cart train back along the 500-mile trail to Pembina.

To make the most efficient use of this trail required both good luck
and good management. If everything went according to schedule,
Kittson left Pembina in the middle of June and reached the Traverse
about thirty days later, averaging some twenty miles a day. But
averages are always deceiving. Kittson's travel time varied with the
condition of the trail. Even with the highest of heavens and the
driest ground, the trail was never an expressway, and when heavy
spring rains fell, they invariably converted the trail into gumbo and
transformed shallow streams into unfordable rivers. And yet the
Red River cart remained the plains' most perfect vehicle, rolling

[43]Grace L. Nute, "The Red River Trails," *Minnesota History*, VI (Sept., 1925),
279–87.

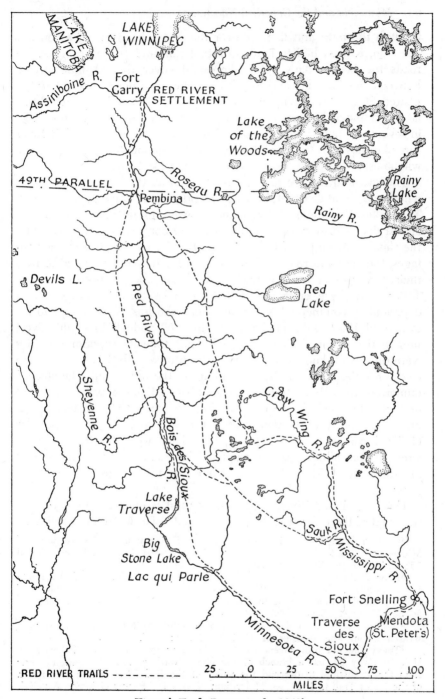

LAKE MANITOBA

LAKE WINNIPEG

Assiniboine R. Fort Garry

RED RIVER SETTLEMENT

Lake of the Woods

Roseau R.

49TH PARALLEL

Pembina

Rainy Lake

Rainy R.

Devils L.

Red Lake

Red River

Crow Wing R.

Sheyenne R.

Bois des Sioux R.

Lake Traverse

Sauk R.

Mississippi R.

Big Stone Lake

Lac qui Parle

Fort Snelling

Minnesota R.

Traverse des Sioux

Mendota (St. Peter's)

RED RIVER TRAILS - - - - - -

25   0   25   50   75   100

MILES

Kittson's Trade Routes in the 1840's

through the mud and floating over the water barriers. If, as on one occasion, Kittson had to battle constant rain and virtually impassable roads for twenty days before he could cover the 200-mile stretch between the Traverse and Big Stone Lake, consider the plight of the United States Army with its wagons: In 1849, a military expedition laboured under the same miserable conditions and made sixty-one miles in seventeen days.[44] The greaseless, screeching axles of the Red River cart may have grated upon the ears of the neophyte, but to the man who knew it, the cart always "discoursed most sweetly."[45]

The great drawback to Kittson's Trail was the uncertain passage, whether by land or water, between Mendota and Traverse des Sioux.[46] The fickle Minnesota River seemed always to be either flooded or almost dry; and even with high water, keel boats seldom went beyond the shoals and rapids of the Traverse. But for all the river's disadvantages, the overland route was worse, and fur traders continued to pole their way upriver until a small fleet of steamboats appeared in the 'fifties. But these craft also failed to make the Minnesota into a dependable, commercial waterway. None the less, Kittson kept to his trail until 1855. Only flood waters (in 1850 and 1851) could divert him to the Plains Trail, although by this time its superior qualities were quite well known. It was more than mere habit that bound him to the Minnesota River. By continuing on the older route, he steered numerous Red River traders past Sibley's Mendota warehouse and undoubtedly persuaded many of them to shop there instead of at St. Paul. And yet Mendota was not meant to be the *entrepôt* for civilized commerce within the greater Northwest, for its sustaining strength was Sibley, not geographical location; and when he closed his doors in 1854 and retired from the trade, Mendota stopped growing.

The second Red River Trail and the most famous and most heavily travelled of the three was the Plains Trail.[47] Like Kittson's, it followed

[44]Captain John Pope, "The Report of an Exploration of the Territory of Minnesota," *Senate Executive Document No. 42*, 31st Cong., 1st Sess., Serial 558, p. 18. See also Kittson to Sibley, 22 Aug. 1844, Sibley Papers.
[45]Isaac J. Stevens, "Narrative and Final Report of Explorations for a Route for a Pacific Railroad, near the Forty-Seventh and Forty-Ninth Parallels of North Latitude, from St. Paul to Puget Sound," *House Executive Document No. 56*, 36th Cong., 1st Sess., Serial 1054, p. 43.
[46]"Camp Notes," an unfinished draft of a letter to "Mr. Editor," apparently written during the summer of 1852 by Martin McLeod, McLeod Papers.
[47]Today the old trail covers virtually the same ground as that followed by U.S. Highway 52 and a branch of the Great Northern Railroad, bending over from the Mississippi to descend the valley of the Red River. For a description of the Plains Trail in 1849, see Major Samuel Woods, "Report of Major Wood[s],

the Red River Valley but, unlike that trader's path, it branched off
at the Bois des Sioux River and led east and then south to St. Paul,
via the valleys of the Sauk and the Mississippi rivers. The trail was
shorter (probably 100 miles or more) and faster (seven to ten days)
than Kittson's, and it terminated in a city, St. Paul, whose commercial
charms far outnumbered Mendota's. According to one disinterested
British observer, St. Paul in the middle 'fifties was "perhaps the best
specimen to be found in the States, of a town still in its infancy with a
great destiny before it."[48] It was handsomely situated, rising from the
Mississippi in two stages and possessing thereby an upper and a lower
town. Though the latter lacked the beauty of its scenic sister, it
allowed for easy access to the river banks and permitted the construction of the best port facilities on the upper Mississippi.

There were still other and stronger reasons fixing St. Paul's future
as the Northwest's commercial metropolis. Most obvious of all was its
location at the Mississippi River's head of navigation, the natural
terminus for all the upriver steamboat traffic. However, two other
advantages are now less apparent, though they were clear enough
to travellers one hundred years ago. In the first place, St. Paul
possessed a good, man-made road that ran northward along the river
to Sauk Rapids and Crow Wing and easily surpassed—with its high
dry bed—the overland route between Mendota and Traverse des
Sioux. By 1852 the odd wayfarer could find "daily opportunities" along
this river road; and, two years later, he could take a stage, then
running twice a week between St. Paul and Sauk Rapids.[49] And in the
second place, the Mississippi offered a more certain and direct
waterway to the north than the whimsical and undulating Minnesota.
Above the Falls of St. Anthony, boats could ascend a deep channel
for more than seventy-five miles to Sauk rapids. In the summer of
1850 a light steamboat began operating between these points; within
a year, it was running on a regular weekly schedule.

Long before steamboats sliced their way up to Sauk Rapids, Red
River carters were driving their oxen along the river road north of
St. Paul. This was the final leg of two trails—the Plains and the

relative to his expedition to Pembina Settlement, and the condition of affairs on
the North-Western frontier of the Territory of Minnesota," *House Executive
Document No. 51*, 31st Cong., 1st Sess., Serial 577. (Cited hereafter as Woods'
Report.)

[48]Laurence Oliphant, *Minnesota and the Far West* (Edinburgh and London,
1855), p. 252.

[49]Hercules Dousman to Henry Fisher, 8 Sept. 1852, Fisher Papers, M.H.S.
Oliphant, *Minnesota*, p. 236.

Woods trail—and it carried a lot of traffic. Most of its travellers came from the former route, however. For the Woods trail was far and away the worst of the three Red River trails. It was cut out of the wilderness in 1844 by a party of traders hurrying overland from the mouth of the Crow Wing River to the Red River Valley and their homes in the Settlement.[50] It was the wettest and roughest of the trails and Kittson limited its use to the winter months when his dog sleds could pass over is frozen sloughs and marshes with comparative ease.

Although Kittson had made no significant changes in the above methods of freighting northward from St. Paul, he had achieved a very strong competitive position within the Red River Settlement by the middle 'fifties. Not only was he underselling the Hudson's Bay Company but he was also providing his customers with a greater variety and abundance of merchandise. Since most American goods were fundamentally dearer than British goods and since there had been no meaningful cost-cutting improvements in Kittson's route between St. Paul and Red River, the explanation for his commercial success must lie elsewhere. In all likelihood, it lay in the radically— and recently—improved service, by both steam and rail, between St. Paul and the eastern seaboard.

Although the steamboat had been a vital link in Minnesota's chain of communications since 1823, it was not until the 'forties that the service was attained that would make St. Paul flourish. Till then, steamboats operated as "tramps," capriciously pursuing the most irregular of schedules. But by 1847 service had been greatly improved. Four or five boats were then running regularly between Prairie du Chien and Mendota. The same year saw the first "weekly" boat up from Galena; and within three years Galena's steamers were racing up to St. Paul three times a week. "Through" lines from St. Louis to St. Paul were inaugurated in 1851; "daily" lines from Prairie du Chien came into being a year later; and in the summer of 1853, an awed resident of that Wisconsin city wrote to an old friend in Rupert's Land that "we now see People from Red River almost every week."[51] As the traffic increased, so did competition—and freightage consequently fell; at the same time, with the helpful hand of marine science, the speed of steamboats inevitably increased.[52]

[50]See the excerpt from the Belfast *Whig* in the *Nor'-Wester*, 28 June 1860.
[51]Hercules Dousman to Henry Fisher, 6 Aug. 1853, Fisher Papers.
[52]The number of steamboat "arrivals" at St. Paul's levees rose at an incredible rate during the late 'forties and early 'fifties—from forty-five in 1845 to 563 in 1855. (For a detailed list of arrivals, see J. Wesley Bond, *Minnesota and its Resources*, 10th ed.; Chicago, 1856, pp. 192–3.) In 1850 the *Nominee*

Fantastic though they were, the developments in steamboat transportation were overshadowed by the tremendous growth of America's railroads during the 'fifties. The Michigan Southern, with the Michigan Central right on its heels, arrived at Chicago in the summer of 1852. The Galena and Chicago had already reached Rockford, Illinois, in the same year and would extend as far as Freeport (125 miles west of Chicago) by 1853. And, as if called into being by some sorcerer's wand, stage service was immediately made available between the end of the rail line and the banks of the Mississippi River. The most exciting year of all was 1854, the first year in which a railroad, the Chicago and Rock Island, ran to the river's edge. The significance of this "first" was not lost. In that uniquely Yankee way, the citizens of Rock Island had a grand celebration honouring the "nuptials of the Atlantic with the Father of the Waters."[53] Following the ceremony St. Paul held a "reception," to which was invited a long list of distinguished guests from the East who had already taken the train all the way to Rock Island and thence steamed upriver to St. Paul. It was a memorable June day filled with orations, excursions, feasts, and dancing. For all the falderal, it was a great event: In open season, St. Paul now lay only four days and nights from the nation's capital.[54]

In that same year, 1854, John Ballenden, the Company's chief factor in the Red River District, advised Sir George Simpson that the Minnesota route would soon afford the only practicable means for importing goods from either Canada or England. At first Simpson was somewhat sceptical, thinking that "the evil, if it be one . . . [was] in prospective only & need not occupy [our] attention."[55] But within six months' time the perspective had changed—and with it, Simpson's opinion. "I have reason to believe," he informed the Governor and Committee in June, 1855, "supplies will, in the course of another year or two, be imported from England via that [Minnesota] route at less cost than by the Company's vessels via York Factory."[56] Indeed

---

steamed up from St. Louis to St. Paul in thirty-six hours and back in twenty-four. The first steamboat, the *Virginia* (though it had stopped here and there en route) had required a fortnight to cover the same distance. See the letter from Alexander Ramsey, dated 28 April 1850, and printed in the Harrisburgh Telegraph, Ramsey Papers, M.H.S.

[53]"Rails West The Rock Island Excursion of 1854", as reported by Charles F. Babcock, *Minnesota History*, XXXIV (winter, 1954), 133–43.

[54]William Watts Folwell, *A History of Minnesota* (4 vols., St. Paul, Minnesota Historical Society, 1921–30), I, 358–9.

[55]Simpson to the Governor and Committee, 30 Dec. 1854, H.B.C., Series A.12/7.

[56]29 June 1855, *ibid.*

it already seemed to him as if the Company had reached a commercial crossroads. It could either let business take the most convenient (American) channel and allow New York City eventually to replace London as the fur capital, or it could attempt to maintain the present ascendancy of the York route.

For the moment, however, the Company had little choice in the matter. Though the Minnesota route would have to be investigated in the near future, York had to be preserved for the present, and even strengthened if possible. For not only was the highway of Hudson Bay and its tributaries threatened by a naturally superior rival, but in meeting this adversary, the York route also had to carry an ever mounting volume of goods at an ever increasing freightage. With the explosive expansion of business within the Red River and all the other districts touched by free trade and with the invasion of cheap and varied goods from Minnesota, the Company was forced to bring in larger and larger indents *via* York Factory. As a result, indents soared;[57] the York route began to labour under its unaccustomed load; and at last it seemed about to collapse. As Hudson Bay had supplanted the St. Lawrence in the 'twenties, so too would the Mississippi evidently replace the Bay as the most efficient supplier to Rupert's Land.

The Minnesota route held certain advantages that York could never hope to possess. The Mississippi River was open three times as long as the Bay and usually twice as long as the inland lakes and rivers of Rupert's Land; and it must always be remembered that the railroad system underpinning the Minnesota route provided year-around service. While it was true that the Red River trails remained in general use only from June to October, or roughly the same length of time as the waterways between York Factory and Red River, the time (three weeks or so) spent in transit over the plains was only one-third as long. Obviously, then, the Red River carts could make more trips in any given season than the Company's brigades. Furthermore, freight from New York City to St. Paul took only five to seven days; that from London to York rarely required less than thirty. In addition, to guard against breakdowns in its precarious transportation system, the Company had to order its trading goods two or even three years in advance of delivery and customarily kept a year's supply in reserve at York. By contrast, Kittson could order his goods and

57The indent for the Red River District rocketed from £8,000 in 1855 to £22,000 in 1857. Governor and Committee to Simpson, 9 April 1855, H.B.C., Series A.6/31; and the Secretary to Francis G. Johnson, 13 Nov. 1857, H.B.C., Series A.6/33.

get them within three months. Thus the Company not only paid heavily for invisible interest charges but also warehoused goods that too often deteriorated or simply went out of style before they could be used.

Unfortunately for the Company, Minnesota's superiority in meeting the commercial needs of Red River continued to grow vigorously as the 'fifties waned. The number of steamboats plying upriver to St. Paul and the frequency of their arrivals increased annually. Of equal if not greater importance, the western railroads more than matched the progress of these riverboats. In 1856 the Illinois Central reached Galena; the Milwaukee and Mississippi struck Prairie du Chien in 1857; and in the following year the Chicago and Milwaukee Railroad was running to La Crosse. By 1858 there were at least four railroads running to the very banks of the river; and in that year alone, sixty-two steamboats made over 1,000 voyages up to the city of St. Paul.[58]

In comparison with its lusty southern rival, the York system seemed caught in a straitjacket. The Company was hard pressed to recruit enough men for the York boats, suffered from mutinies and other breakdowns in its brigades, and was forced to meet a continuing demand for higher wages from the tripmen.[59] From all these difficulties, there was no northern escape. Auxiliary roads had been tried long ago and found wanting, and, in the 'fifties, no Company man thought seriously about steam navigation. In itself, York's inflexibility gave a decided advantage to the Minnesota route. But there was another and much more critical one—lower costs—an advantage not fully and positively revealed to the Hudson's Bay Company, however, until it began to experiment with the Minnesota route during the summer of 1858.

IV

In that flourishing era in Minnesota's history between territorial status and statehood, Pembina played a leading role. Though separated from the southern part of the territory by a vast stretch of grassland, the little settlement was always of significance, for it was the natural gateway for all traffic between Rupert's Land and the United States.

[58]See Arthur J. Larsen, "Early Transportation," *Minnesota History,* XIV (June, 1933), 149–55.

[59]Alvin C. Gluek, Jr. "The Fading Glory," *Beaver,* outfit 288 (winter, 1957), 50–5.

Through it passed countless travellers: British army officers en route to Fort Garry, Sisters of Charity going to Red River, American scientists seeking such things as a favourable site to observe an eclipse, explorers on their way to the Arctic, a host of English gentlemen bound for sport and adventure, and always the itinerant traders of St. Paul and the Red River Settlement. Pembina was a busy place; and since it was the gateway to the British Northwest, might not its proprietors also hold the "key" to the whole region?

During Minnesota's territorial days there was a keen interest in the commerce and lands of the Hudson's Bay Company and much of it revolved around the trading post and half-breed colony at Pembina. The trader, of course, was Kittson, but the moving spirit behind the colony itself was Father Belcourt, who had returned to the Northwest in 1848 in order to establish a chain of missionary stations below the 49th parallel. He planned to continue his efforts to transform the semi-nomadic, buffalo-hunting *métis* into settled, agrarian folk. He hoped to attract them from both sides of the line to his missions and eventually to convert missions and *métis* into colonies.

Belcourt selected Pembina as the centre of his missionary complex, a site that in 1849 was neither crowded nor charming. According to his tally, Pembina had a population of about 1,000; but if his census was not exaggerated, it was certainly misleading. In the eyes of one detached observer, Pembina did not even possess "a collection of huts, with the appearance of a village . . . ," merely a few rustic dwellings scattered whimsically along the river banks and the lodges and shanties of Pembina's floating population, the half-breeds and the Indians.[60] With the exception of Kittson, his handful of assistants, and Belcourt, these nomads made up the colony's entire population. With his little cluster of log huts at the forks, Kittson had the most prepossessing demesne. Belcourt resided farther upstream in a comfortable two-storey house, flanked by a crude chapel and several outbuildings. To the south of these solitary evidences of civilization, there was nothing for hundreds of miles—"No houses, no cattle, no sheep, all wild as nature made it."[61]

Despite Pembina's unpromising appearance, Father Belcourt predicted a great future for it. All that was needed to make it flourish was Washington's "green thumb"; and, to secure the support of

[60]Woods's Report, p. 19.
[61]Speech given by Charles Cavilier, 10 Dec. 1891, to a gathering of old settlers at Grand Forks. Cavilier was describing his impressions of Pembina when he first arrived there as its customs collector in 1851, Cavilier Papers.

the federal government, the priest composed a most alluring prospectus.[62] In it he claimed that since Pembina was the ancestral home of the *métis* it would inevitably entice them away from Rupert's Land. Furthermore, it was a place possessing material as well as spiritual charms: rich and arable land; a gateway to the buffalo grounds; salt springs, wood lots, and probably coal and iron too; thick grasslands ideal for cattle ranching; and a mild and salubrious climate. If the United States would only re-draw the 49th parallel to make it "incontestably American," keep out the British and their whisky, open up and sell the land, establish governmental institutions, and provide military protection, then Pembina's destiny would undoubtedly be assured. "Before three years shall have elapsed," the priest concluded, "if the Government of the United States . . . will extend its protecting hand to us, more than four thousand souls will soon embrace and enjoy the sweets of liberty. . . ."[63]

In his pursuit of federal aid, Belcourt was supported by many prominent Minnesotans. They favoured his design because it seemingly served so many of their territory's geopolitical interests. One of them suggested that, in the event of conflict with Britain, Belcourt's half-breeds "would form an invaluable defence to that exposed frontier. . . ."[64] Should war occur—asserted another—"a force would ever be found ready and sufficiently strong to carry the stars and stripes to York factory and supplant the cross of St. George between the 49° and Hudson's [*sic*] Bay."[65] And a third asked whether, without war's excuse, the people of Pembina "and the region they live in, [did not] present a case similar to that of Oregon Territory, in which the free gift of a quarter section of land to each person would be a judicious policy. . . ?"[66] These were heady speculations and the three men who made them (Henry H. Sibley, Henry M. Rice, and Alexander Ramsey)

[62]Belcourt to Major Samuel Woods, 20 Aug. 1849 (translated by H. H. Sibley), Sibley Papers.
[63]*Ibid.* If Belcourt's fanciful prediction had come true, Red River would have been virtually depopulated.
[64]Henry H. Sibley, "Description of Minnesota," *Minnesota Historical Society Collections*, I, 42. Sibley was Minnesota Territory's first delegate to Congress, 1849–53, and his state's first governor, 1858–60.
[65]Henry M. Rice to J. E. Fletcher, 30 Nov. 1848, quoted in Woods's Report, p. 9. Rice succeeded Sibley as territorial delegate and served in that office until he was elected to the United States Senate in 1858.
[66]Alexander Ramsey to A. H. H. Stuart, 7 Nov. 1851, Annual Report of the Commissioner of Indian Affairs, 1851, *Senate Executive Document No. 1*, 32nd Cong., 1st Sess., Serial 613, pp. 284–8. Ramsey was Minnesota's first territorial governor, 1849–53; the state's second governor, 1860–63; and a United States senator, 1863–75.

were destined to lead Minnesota through her territorial days, into statehood, and far beyond.

For these and other more personal and practical reasons, Minnesotans favoured the Pembina design. Its successful establishment and growth would strengthen Kittson's hand in his contest with the Hudson's Bay Company. As a nucleated settlement, it possessed attractions for Sibley, who was then just launching his political career as Minnesota's first territorial delegate. From Pembina's inception, he bestowed favours upon Father Belcourt and wooed him as if he were a precinct boss instead of a priest.[67] Sibley, in turn, drew Governor Ramsey's attention to the Pembina project, transforming this ex-Pennsylvanian into an ardent booster of the Northwest and one of Minnesota Territory's most zealous expansionists. If Sibley was Belcourt's most constant supporter in Washington, then Ramsey was the priest's best lobbyist at St. Paul. In his first message (1 September 1849) to the territorial legislature, Ramsey urged his listeners to petition for federal aid to develop and improve the transportation routes to Pembina. Two months later he signed a memorial from Minnesota Territory to Congress, pleading for a military post at Pembina and a treaty to extinguish the Indian titles to the Red River Valley.

In Belcourt's first year on the border, all seemed well with his little world and not the least of his signs of good fortune was the midsummer (1849) appearance of American troops. The military expedition itself bore no direct relationship either to the priest or his mission, however. It was the troubled state of the borderlands over the past four years that had brought about the army's reappearance. Captain Sumner's mission in 1845 had not solved any of the basic border problems. The *métis* had continued to invade the Dakota plains; and in 1848 alone Kittson estimated that their spring hunts had resulted in the illegal exportation from the United States of more than $50,000 of buffalo hides.[68] To him, as a fur trader, the loss in hides was painful. To the local Indian agent, the greater evil lay in the destruction of game, for he feared that the slaughter would seriously diminish the herds and lead either to intertribal warfare among the Indians or to a general uprising. His and Kittson's complaints mingled with others, old and new; and Washington listened and once again took action.

In the spring of 1849, the War Department ordered Major Samuel Woods, Fort Snelling's commandant, to lead a company of Dragoons into the lower Red River Valley and gather information "in regard to

[67]Sibley to Belcourt, 11 Aug. 1849, Sibley Papers.
[68]Kittson to Sibley, 16 Sept. 1848, *ibid*.

the best location of a military post in that region."[69] He was also directed to learn about the local Indians and discover what influence, if any, the Hudson's Bay Company had over them. Woods dutifully led his troopers up to Pembina, surveyed the valley, examined and interviewed its inhabitants, and wrote his report. With a few strokes of his pen, Woods ended the dream of a Pembina fortress almost before it had begun. Although the major considered Pembina the most suitable locality for a post, he did not "think at the present time it . . . [was] called for on any score." In his opinion, the best prescription for the border's ills would be to open up the land for settlement, attract Red River's half-breeds into the United States, and then control their actions by making citizens out of them. Thus there would be no fort. Nor would there be any troops available for manoeuvres on the plains. When Sibley and several other sympathetic Congressmen importuned the Secretary of War for additional military strength on the northwestern frontier, he refused their application on the grounds that, given the present limited state of the army, such a shift in personnel would be impossible.

After plans for military protection had been scotched, Sibley and Ramsey struggled for the last great gift of the federal government: a treaty with the Chippewa Indians for the cession of the lower Red River Valley. Ultimate success here depended upon the mood of the United States Senate and the political talents of Henry Sibley. Rarely has any new member of Congress, and a voteless territorial delegate at that, found himself in less promising surroundings than Sibley during the session of 1850. Sectionalism was consuming Congress. Not till September would it be able to pass the Compromise of 1850 and bank these dangerous fires. And amidst the conflagration, there were other unsettling events: President Taylor's sudden death, the uneasy accession of Millard Fillmore, and the subsequent "revolution" in the Whig party. As a result, there was a complete turnover in the cabinet and considerable changes elsewhere in the administration. Sibley had to deal with two secretaries of the interior and two commissioners of Indian affairs and it is a wonder that he accomplished anything at all.

To his credit, Sibley shepherded through Congress a bill appropriating $10,000 for carrying out a treaty of cession for the Red River Valley. Though the money came too late in the session to permit negotiations that year, there was time enough for interested Minnesotans to present their views upon the treaty. Belcourt, for one, made his

[69]Adjutant General's Office to Woods, Woods's Report, p. 2.

position clear. He wanted every half-breed to receive a free grant of
land; but few other men agreed with him. Neither Congress nor the
Indian Bureau nor most Minnesotans would accredit the half-breeds
with any rightful claims to the land. "The claim," said Kittson, "was
never thought of by the Halfbreeds before the arrival of Mr Belcourt
who has stuffed their heads with so many expectations which can
never be realized. . . ."[70] True to his trade, Kittson identified his
interests with those of the Indians. He wanted a large cession, sufficient in size and price to satisfy their needs and meet some of the
debts due to him.

In the end, it was Sibley who fixed the terms for negotiation with the
Chippewas. He took the middle ground between Kittson and the
priest, a compromising position—and yet high enough so that he had
regard for the welfare of the territory and himself. Though he probably
had something to say about the choice of Ramsey as treaty commissioner, it was an obvious choice; and in May, 1851, the governor
joined the territorial delegate in Washington, where they prepared the
instructions to be given to the commission by the Department of
Interior. By the middle of the month Ramsey received his "official"
instructions, picked up his expense money, and returned to Minnesota
for a summer filled with treaty-making. After spending a month
successfully negotiating with the Sioux for some of their lands (the
"Suland") in the southern part of the territory, Governor Ramsey and
his party left for Pembina. The funds given by Congress to underwrite
the Chippewa treaty were generous—and they were generously spent.
The trip to the borderlands resembled a festive outing of *bon vivant*
businessmen. Game was killed for sport and without regard for need;
campfires were convivial affairs—"uncle [Sam] being very liberal in
his supply of *spirits*"[71]—and by the time Ramsey and his retinue
reached Pembina (12 September) they were well rested and in the
best of spirits.

Throughout the negotiations, Kittson's hand was always apparent.
It was he who had gathered the Chippewas together, found the
interpreters (missionaries for the most part), and furnished (at a
profit) provisions to the entire assembly of Indians and whites. Moreover he was the vital intermediary between Ramsey and the
Indians. The relative ease with which the commissioner accomplished
his work can be credited more to Kittson's manoeuvres than to
Ramsey's diplomacy. Belcourt, on the other hand, conducted himself in a strange way. Not once did he appear on the treaty grounds,

70Kittson to Sibley, 4 Feb. 1851, Sibley Papers.
71Bond, *Minnesota*, pp. 307–8.

though he was only at St. Joseph, some thirty miles away. The excuse offered to Ramsey was that he could not attend because he was absent. Whatever his real reason Belcourt, by removing himself, jettisoned any influence he might have brought to bear on the treaty. Yet would his presence have mattered? Quite probably he realized that his *métis* would get very little from the treaty and assuredly not the large land grants he had so openly sought for them. Since many of the half-breeds had originally been drawn to the priest's side in the illusion that the United States would recognize their rights to the land and since Belcourt had created that illusion, how could he personally aid in breaking it at the treaty grounds? It was better to absent himself. But in any event, he became thereafter a frontier Savonarola, a prophet bearing neither arms nor gifts to his people.

The negotiations at Pembina had a delightfully informal air about them.[72] To the assembled Chippewas, Ramsey grandly and somewhat slyly announced that the President of the United States merely wanted to help them, as poor Indians dwelling in a land without game, by purchasing "such portions [of it] as may be comparatively useless." In return, he offered them a substantial down payment in cash ("to arrange your affairs and provide for your half breed relatives") and the balance in instalments over a period of twenty years. The Indians were unimpressed. One of them bluntly told Ramsey to omit the sweet words. Another, who bore the name of Moose Dung, said sweetly that he liked the land Ramsey wanted: "I love it, I love it, for I live by and on it." Only gradually were the dissenting voices silenced and the assembly won over. Gifts of tobacco and beef cattle, the arguments of the missionaries, Ramsey's threat to end the proceedings—these manoeuvres, when coupled with Kittson's politicking and the promise of more money, induced the Chippewas to sign away their lands on 20 September.

There is no doubt that the Indians gave up too much land for too little money. The grant itself was shaped like a huge, notched rectangle whose sides swept south from the 49th parallel to cut almost a sixty-mile swath through the heart of the Red River Valley.[73] Ramsey had bought this magnificent cession for $230,000—pennies per acre for

[72]Dr. Thomas Foster, "Journal (from August 18 to November 27, 1851) of the United States Commission to Treat with the Chippeway Indians of Pembina & Red Lake; with the Proceedings of the Council held at Pembina on the Red River of the North, Minnesota Territory," Sibley Papers. Foster was secretary of the commission. All quotations regarding the negotiations were drawn from his journal.

[73]See Ramsey to Stuart, 7 Nov. 1851, Annual Report of the Commissioner of Indian Affairs, 1851, *Senate Executive Document No. 1*, 32nd Cong., 1st Sess., Serial 613, pp. 284–8.

between five and seven million acres of the finest farm land in North America. Of the purchase price, $30,000 represented the down payment. None of the Chippewas received a penny of this money. Shortly after signing the treaty, they endorsed a traders' agreement binding themselves to hand over the down payment to various fur traders and half-breeds "to repay the kindness and liberality manifested heretofore." [74] This contract served two purposes, each as illegal as it was necessary. It permitted Kittson and a colleague to recover $4,200 from debts owed them by the Chippewas. It also allowed Ramsey, *sub rosa*, to give $25,800 to 141 half-breeds and thus substantiate at least some of Belcourt's promises.

The Pembina treaty received Minnesota's enthusiastic backing when it was transmitted to the White House, and President Fillmore, in turn, sent it and the other (Sioux) treaties on to the Senate with his blessing. Here they encountered immediate opposition, apparently on purely political grounds, and in the end Sibley considered himself lucky to get any of them ratified. But for a limited success, he had to pay a price. The Pembina treaty had to be sacrificed—as one of Sibley's friends remarked—"for the sake of the others."[75] Though Sibley could philosophically accept the verdict, to Belcourt it must have seemed like the work of the devil. Gone, swallowed up in the inscrutable depths of American politics, was his dream of a *métis* colony.

Ramsey's trip to Pembina in 1851 produced a lasting effect upon the man. After the negotiations, he accepted the invitation of the Governor of Assiniboia to visit the Red River Settlement. It was a pleasant as well as instructive experience. Indeed it was like giving Commodore Perry a peek at Japan. Thereafter, whenever Ramsey viewed Minnesota in all its destined proportions, he visualized a state in which would be centred a gigantic transportation and trading system stretching from New Orleans to "the plains of distant Athabaska."[76]

Ramsey's head might be caught up in the clouds, but his feet were always on the ground. As a working politician, he looked at life in the same practical way as his friend Sibley. They had a perfect understanding about the usefulness of Pembina. By 1851–52 it was a county, possessing a local government complete with a municipal council and a justice of the peace. It enjoyed generous representation in both

[74]This agreement, dated 20 Sept. 1851, may be found in the Ramsey Papers.
[75]Hugh Tyler to Ramsey, 27 June 1852, Sibley Papers. Tyler had been a member of the Pembina treaty commission.
[76]Annual message of the governor, 27 Jan. 1853, Minnesota, *Journal of Council, 1853.*

houses of the territorial legislature and it had a postmaster and a customs collector. Despite its outward appearance, Pembina possessed few governmental forms that did not serve the self-interest of Sibley and Ramsey better than the welfare of the Pembinese. The post office, the position of justice of the peace, and the customhouse—all were meant to preserve or promote Sibley's economic interests. As for Kittson, he was turned into an "unholy trinity": magistrate, postmaster, and Pembina's sole representative on the territorial council. As justice of the peace, he was much stronger than the ordinary citizen in dealing with unlicensed traders, American or British; and as postmaster, he could cultivate the good will of his and Sibley's business friends in Red River. But of all the offices created in their own self-interest, none was more flagrant than the customhouse. It was conceived by Sibley in 1850, staffed then and thereafter by his political associates, and intended solely to prevent British traders from poaching on American soil. Not till the 'sixties did it serve any real public purpose.[77]

Other governmental forms, such as county machinery and legislative representation, were extended to Pembina by Ramsey and Sibley in order to fabricate their own "pocket borough." Belcourt and Kittson were the political bosses and electioneers. In return for countless favours, the priest co-operated with the reluctant but efficient fur trader; and, together, they made sure that the winter carryalls bore "good & true" men down to the legislature at St. Paul from 1851 to 1855.[78] For all its geographic size, Pembina had a small, comfortably manageable electorate. Kittson always had an uncanny knack of forecasting every election and kept the area under control until 1858.

The only governmental service that really catered to the populace was Pembina's post office. Much of the Red River's mail had always gone, if ever so informally, *via* Pembina, and after the formal establishment of an office there in 1850, the volume and then the service increased. Most of the mail merely passed through Pembina, however. From the "barrel full of mail matter" that ordinarily came into his hands, the postmaster "would take out . . . [his] little portion . . . and then forward the balance to Fort Garey [*sic*] Selkirk Settlement Hudson Bay Territory."[79] Though the American postal service was faster than the Company's Bay route and safer as well as quicker than

[77]See James McFetridge to James Guthrie, 15 Sept. 1856, Letters from Collectors, and Daniel H. Hunt's Diary, 21 April 1858, Hunt Papers, M.H.S.
[78]See Sibley to Kittson, 15 Sept. 1851, Sibley Papers, and Ramsey's Diary, 5 March 1851, Ramsey Papers.
[79]Cavilier's speech to the old settlers at Grand Forks, 10 Dec. 1891, Cavilier Papers.

the Canadian, it left much to be desired.[80] When Captain John Palliser, director of a British expedition to the Northwest, halted at Pembina in 1857 in order to determine the 49th parallel and, incidentally, post some mail to London, his remarks were hardly flattering.[81] Within the "wretched" office, he discovered no one but the postmaster's assistant, an Indian woman who spoke nothing but Indian. Palliser dared not entrust his mail to her care until his half-breed guide informed him that the post office was "a very lucky one." In fact, handling was not only informal but the mishandling was outrageous. Till the advent of "through" mail, British periodicals addressed to the Red River Settlement often fell into American hands and never reached their destination.

Sibley, his business friends, and political associates had shaped the Pembina design to suit themselves, but what about Father Belcourt? How did his plans for a half-breed colony fare? Soon after spring floods had engulfed the Pembina settlement in 1850, he abandoned his mission, moved it further westward, and relocated it at St. Joseph; and in the next summer a new colony could be seen slowly rising from the plains. Despite the frustration and subsequent failure of the Pembina treaty, both the mother mission and its little colony thrived during their early years. A substantial number of half-breeds migrated from Rupert's Land, if only to squat upon land which would serve them as a base for their buffalo hunts, and by 1856–57 St. Joseph could boast of "from eighty to one hundred buildings" and from 1,000 to 1,500 inhabitants.[82] Yet though its population grew, St. Joseph never became more than an outpost of half-breed hunters precariously situated in Sioux country; and as the buffalo herds were

[80]Jacob W. Bass to Sibley, 24 Dec. 1850, Sibley Papers. According to Bass, St. Paul's postmaster, 1849–53, "by this [Minnesota] route the Hudson Bay Co. can get their mail from Europe to Fort Gary [sic] in thirty-five or forty days instead of one year by the Hudson Bay."

[81]Palliser to Her Majesty's Principal Secretary of State for the Colonies, 27 July 1857, enclosed in a letter from the Colonial Office to the Governor of the Hudson's Bay Company, 16 Jan. 1858, H.B.C., Series A.8/8. However, as Palliser pointed out in his final report, letters from the United Kingdom to Red River required from four to six weeks, and Pembina processed the great bulk of mail directed to the Settlement. *Papers Relative to the Exploration by Captain Palliser of that Portion of British North America which Lies between the Northern Branch of the River Saskatchewan and the Frontier of the United States; and between the Red River and the Rocky Mountains* (London, 1859), p. 56.

[82]Lieutenant-Colonel C. F. Smith, "Report of an expedition of Companies B and F, 10th regiment of infantry, to the Red River of the North, in 1856," *Senate Executive Document No. 1*, 35th Cong., 2nd Sess., Serial 975, p. 427 (cited hereafter as Smith's Report).

gradually reduced, the quarrels between Sioux and half-breed mounted. During the 'fifties, scarcely a summer passed without bloodshed—open battles fought far out on the plains or the murdering of St. Joseph's settlers within sight of their own homes.

After two leading citizens of St. Joseph had been slain in successive summers, the movement to establish a military post on the border revived. By this time (1853–54) both Sibley and Ramsey had been temporarily removed from office by the ballot box and replaced by Democrats: Territorial Delegate Henry Rice and Governor Willis Gorman. But political change did not mean any alteration in the territory's attitude toward the borderlands. In the same spirit as Ramsey, then new governor enthusiastically endorsed memorials to Congress calling for protection, while in Washington, Rice topped Gorman's most extravagant prose. Speaking in support of a bill to establish a garrison on the border, Rice claimed that 4,000 defenceless Minnesotans were shivering in fear of the Sioux. "All that we ask now," he pleaded (29 January 1855) in the House, "is a small force there; a company of infantry would form a nucleus, a sort of depot for arms and ammunition, which would enable the citizens [of St. Joseph] to protect themselves."[83] He won the support of Congress and the blessings of Jefferson Davis, the Secretary of War. Consequently Congress quickly passed a bill appropriating $5,000 to establish a fort on the Red River near the international line.

At last the wheels of the War Department began to turn but as they slowly revolved, the results were most strange. In May, 1856, almost a year after the bill's passage, Lieutenant-Colonel C. F. Smith received specific orders to build a post. Yet within a month, he got others, countermanding the first and directing him to lead a military expedition into the Red River Valley. Like his predecessors, Sumner and Woods, Colonel Smith was given the same general instructions: to determine the best location in the valley for a fort, attempt to check the Sioux, and warn off any British half-breeds found hunting south of the line. Smith faithfully carried out his orders during the summer and wrote up his report. In his opinion, Pembina, with its low ground, would not do as a site for a fort. St. Joseph on the other hand provided an excellent location, having all the natural resources needed for construction and strategically so situated as to arrest Sioux depredations and intercept any *métis* trespassing on American soil. In addition, the colonel was "assured"—undoubtedly by Belcourt—that a garrison at St. Joseph "would cause the immediate immigration of about 2,500

[83]*Congressional Globe*, 33rd Cong., 2nd Sess., p. 454.

of the Red River people, who are desirous and anxious to live under the protection of our laws."[84] However he saw one flaw in the scheme. In the event of trouble, a garrison at St. Joseph might be too remote to be relieved or reinforced, and therefore he also recommended the creation of an intermediary post, suggesting Graham's Point on Lake Travers as the best site.

Now it was up to the Secretary of War. At first, he commented somewhat cryptically that the knowledge derived from Smith's expedition would enable him to pick a site, if it should hereafter be thought advisable to build a fort.[85] Then, he found his "hereafter" in June of the following year (1857) and straightway decided to put up Fort Abercrombie on Graham's Point. To the dismay and disgust of the original Minnesota promoters, the army proceeded to spend $20,000 erecting a fort which never served a useful purpose. Not only was it a singularly unimposing structure but it was much too far from the 49th parallel to frighten the Sioux or control the Red River half-breeds.

With the building of Abercrombie, Belcourt's hopes for a fort at St. Joseph were dashed. Equally futile were his efforts to bring about another Pembina treaty, though every annual report of the Indian Office supported him. His half-breed charges had originally been persuaded to exchange their lot in Rupert's Land for land and protection within the United States; and some of them probably feared that if they did not migrate, they would not be allowed to hunt American buffalo. In the final event, all these motives for migration vanished. St. Joseph had neither a fort nor a land office. And, despite occasional manoeuvres by the United States Army, even the dullest British half-breed soon realized that he and his buffalo-hunting comrades had nothing to fear from American soldiers. St. Joseph inevitably declined—and with it, the power and influence of Father Belcourt. In 1858 he was dealt another crushing blow when Minnesota became a state exclusive of Pembina and St. Joseph. Lying beyond the Red River, Minnesota's new western boundary, these hamlets were consigned to unorganized Indian country. The *coup de grâce* came in the following year. Minnesota's Roman Catholic hierarchy summarily removed the priest from the Northwest forever and handed over his flock to the Bishop of St. Boniface.[86] When Belcourt left St. Joseph, one-third of

[84]Smith's Report, p. 431.
[85]Annual Report of the Secretary of War, 1856, *House Executive Document No. 1*, 34th Cong., 3rd Sess., Serial 894, p. 3.
[86]The Bishop of St. Paul to the Bishop of St. Boniface, 6 Oct. 1860 and 3 July 1861, Fisher Papers.

his parishioners returned to Rupert's Land; before too long there were only 300 left—and St. Joseph was fast settling back into the Dakota dust.

V

When most Minnesota promoters of the Pembina design thought about its future growth, they generally talked in terms of a British migration instead of an American one. They were also keenly aware of their own frontier moving up from the south. Ramsey, for one, regarded Minnesota's frontier as an irresistible force destined to spread, Oregon-like, over all the British Northwest. He liked to talk about "these hardy pioneers, who at the sacrifice of many of the comforts of life, have passed the frontiers of the Union, and with us, are moving steadily to the waters of Hudson's [*sic*] Bay. . . ."[87] As the years passed and he watched Minnesota grow, it probably seemed to him as if all his expansionist dreams would come true.

In 1851 the Sioux treaties opened up a large block of land in the southern and central part of the territory. Before the Senate could ratify them, quite a few settlers began staking out claims; and once ratification occurred a great many men broke out of the net which had hitherto confined them, rushed into the new cession, and started one of the most exciting land booms in the history of the West. Minnesota literally grew up overnight. Her land sales leaped from a paltry 1,000 acres to more than 850,000 within the next six years; and by 1857 over a million had been sold.[88] Moreover, the territory's spectacular growth could be measured in men as well as acreage. It was, in sum, a combination of available land, land-hungry pioneers, and a nation-wide prosperity that brought Minnesota to maturity. It must have been a thrilling phenomenon to observe. Writing a friend in 1854, Sibley could scarcely express his amazement at the volume of immigration. It went far beyond his "most sanguine expectations," with steamers docking daily at St. Paul "loaded to their utmost capacity with passengers."[89] And once the discovery was made that Minnesota's real

---

[87]Minnesota, *Journal of the Council, 1851*, p. 18.

[88]For statements of public lands sold, see the annual reports of the Commissioner of the General Land Office for the years 1851, 1856, and 1857: *Senate Document No. 1*, 32nd Cong., 1st Sess., Serial 613; *Senate Executive Document No. 5*, 34th Cong., 3rd Sess., Serial 875; and *Senate Document No. 11*, 35th Cong., 1st Sess., Serial 919.

[89]Sibley to Isaac J. Stevens, 6 June 1854, Sibley Papers.

estate values could be doubled in six months' time, eastern speculators lavishly poured risk capital into the territory. Taken with the fever, Ramsey invested heavily in real estate and figured his holdings in 1853 to be worth about $50,000—an impressive portfolio for a man who had been in Minnesota less than four years.[90]

According to the law governing all frontiers, Minnesota's rivers and roads determined the movements and fixed the locations of most immigrants. During the 'fifties the greater tide flowed into the south, where land was more accessible; but to the north, and reaching for the Red River Valley, there could be seen a faint line of settlement. Town after town was laid out along the banks of the upper Mississippi north of the Falls of St. Anthony. By 1853 Sauk Rapids had a land office whose mounting sales soon justified its existence. In 1856 Congress granted funds to extend the federal land surveys, permitting them to run west of the Mississippi and into the valley of the Crow Wing River and even further westward as far as the Red. Within two years all surveys had been completed and the land commissioner confidently predicted that all the land would soon be sold.

The valley of the Sauk River was an alluring highway to northwestern Minnesota and during the 'fifties it greeted an ever growing number of German immigrants. By 1857 and 1858 the traveller bound for the Red River Valley passed by hamlet after hamlet and farm after farm—a frontier salient recently thrust westward into the valley. Behind our traveller, St. Cloud had already risen, a town of some 500 people and, with its stores and taverns, the economic mainspring of the frontier beyond.[91]

Even the Red River Valley had its share of men who were infected with land fever. In 1855 claim jumpers could be seen all the way from Otter Tail Lake to Pembina and, as the fever went its course, more and more land prospectors entered the valley. Town sites—paper, to be sure—were laid out on every hand. Joseph Rolette, Jr., had at least two claims and several St. Paul speculators vied with him in the contest for sites. When Captain Palliser visited Pembina in the summer of 1857, he met a Mr. Iddings, a civil engineer who was busily surveying lots southward from the 49th parallel on land that had been "bought" by some American land company. It did not matter that this was really unceded Indian country. All these men optimistically awaited tomorrow's settlement and the profit that would be theirs on the day after that.

[90]Ramsey's Diary, March, 1853, *passim*, Ramsey Papers.
[91]See Daniel H. Hunt's Diary, 1 and 3 July, 9 Nov. 1857, and 12 March 1858, Hunt Papers.

Unfortunately, for most of them that golden day never dawned. The Panic of 1857 came instead, smashing their dreams and folding up their purses. By the spring of 1858 Rolette was almost penniless, forced to rely upon the charity of relatives in Red River; and he remained in that uncomfortable state till 1861. The only consolation for him and his fellows was that—as one pioneer later put it—"we all went down together."[92] The speculative mania in St. Paul had reached a dizzy height in the spring and summer of 1857. It was a gaudy era of "fast horses, fast women, wine and cards," a season when realtors paced the streets, their arms jammed with map rolls and deeds, frenetically peddling lots both real and imaginary. Fall brought a day of reckoning. In October St. Paul's banks closed their doors and money was soon so tight that the territory had to issue script. The real estate bubble had burst and the evaluation of Minnesota's taxable property fell about 30 per cent.[93]

Though the Panic of 1857 had been begotten in the East, it had raced westward, relentlessly running along the lines of credit. In its wake came a long and hard depression, the first of several blows to stunt Minnesota's material growth. Within the territory and elsewhere in the United States, prospective railroad lines watched their fancies take flight. In St. Paul, merchants who had grown rich on the Red River trade watched their businesses crumble. And the whole frontier movement within the territory received an immediate, definite, and readily ascertainable check to its progress.[94]

[92]Rebecca M. Cathcart, "A Sheaf of Remembrances," *Minnesota Historical Society Collections*, XV, 535.

[93]Rasmus S. Saby, "Railroad Legislation in Minnesota, 1849 to 1875," *Minnesota Historical Society Collections*, XV, 31.

[94]The records of Minnesota's land sales reveal a sharp and steep fall, 1858–60. Sales at the Brownsville-Chatfield land office, one of the busiest in the territory, plunged from a height of 238,323.26 acres in 1856 to 43,930.26 in 1857 to 12,138.30 in 1858 to 3,357 in 1859 and 1,212.82 in 1860. In 1860 Minnesota's land offices only sold slightly more than 7,000 acres in all. Thereafter sales slowly began to climb. (See the detailed statements accompanying the annual reports of the Commissioner of the General Land Office.) Another index to the growth and decay of the Minnesota frontier may be found in John H. Lowe, "The Post Office on the Minnesota Frontier," unpublished M.A. thesis, University of Minnesota, 1950. In a series of painstakingly drawn maps, Lowe outlined the developing frontier by plotting the biennial changes in its post offices. The frontier that he thus marked grew rapidly until 1859, but from that date until 1865 it grew imperceptively, if at all. Unfortunately his maps, which were based wholly upon biennial changes in the number and position of post offices, failed to record the impact of the Panic of 1857 in the year of its origin. Its effects were therefore not made evident to him until 1859.

Chapter 5. Challenge and Response: Between the Panic and the War

IN THE HISTORICAL RELATIONSHIP BETWEEN MINNESOTA AND THE HUDSON'S Bay Company, the years from 1857 to 1861 possess a certain distinctiveness. For the Hudson's Bay Company they were a combination of triumphant and tragic events. Though it recaptured much of its former position in the Red River trade, its ancient rights and privileges throughout the British Northwest were questioned—and in part revoked—by the Crown. For Minnesota, the age seemed at first to be a gap between two gigantic milestones, the Panic of 1857 and the Civil War, but in fact this was not so. Though the years were few and lean, they were also challenging. Impelled by new visions of wealth and empire, Minnesota renewed her movement into the Northwest, extended her frontier, and rebuilt her trade.

I

In the history of the Hudson's Bay Company, Sayer's trial and its aftermath were of the greatest significance. The trial "proved the Company's inability to enforce the law and gave the people [of Red River] a consciousness of their strength."[1] Within a fortnight the *métis* had made known their demands to the Council of Assiniboia: the

[1]Simpson to John Shepherd (confidential), 27 Sept. 1856, H.B.C., Series A.12/8.

"rescinding of the existing law respecting all imports from the United States of America"; the removal of the recorder, Adam Thom; the inauguration of judicial proceedings in both French and English; equality of representation on the council itself; and a "free trade in furs."[2] Such, in brief, was the platform that they informally nailed together just after the trial; and, with one or two added planks, it remained unchanged throughout the next decade.

By 1856 the *métis* had achieved most, if not all, of their demands. The duty schedule, re-set in July, 1849, remained thereafter at its slight 4 per cent level. Thom had departed in 1854 and had been replaced by Francis G. Johnson. The new recorder, a competent, conscientious, and charming lawyer, continued the practice begun in 1850 of conducting the proceedings of the Quarterly Court in both English and French; and after Caldwell's retirement in 1855, he succeeded him first (July) as deputy governor and finally (February, 1856) as governor. True, the half-breeds had not yet gained equal representation on the Council of Assiniboia, despite their memorials and Simpson's strong supporting endorsements. They had secured appointments to new magisterial posts created by Simpson, and one of them had even been selected as the customs collector. However they still did not have political equality. Aside from one priest (Louis Laflèche) and the new Bishop of St. Boniface (Alexandre A. Taché), no one represented the *métis* on the council.

Had a handful of magisterial appointments satisfied their political appetite? Such would seem at first to be the case, for after 1851 the *métis* no longer importuned the Company or the Crown for political changes. Or had they simply grown somewhat indifferent? This explanation is really the more logical one. The half-breeds were politically dormant from 1852 to 1856 because all their energies were being consumed in the free-trade movement. Why bother with politics when your purses are full? Furthermore, by 1856 the principal plank in their platform—a "free trade in furs"—had, though the Company never publicly admitted it, been fully realized.

The *métis* lost their interest in politics in 1852, the first year in which the free trade movement explosively broke out of the Red River District and invaded the rest of Rupert's Land. Every year thereafter Simpson's annual reports to the Governor and Committee grew more pessimistic as he recited the penetrations and conquests of the free

2Minutes of the Council of Assiniboia, 31 May 1849, in E. H. Oliver, ed., *The Canadian North-West: Its Early Development and Legislative Records* (2 vols., Ottawa, 1914–15), I, 351–3.

traders. There was no way he could check or combat their movements. Neither trading restrictions nor seizures were feasible without the power to back them up. Only as a competitor, not as the governor of Rupert's Land, could he oppose free trade; thus there were no clashes with the *métis*, and Red River remained outwardly serene. Yet, with each season's passing, Simpson's anxiety mounted. Although the times were prosperous and the Company was making money, its profit margin was declining; and Simpson wondered how well it would do in more normal, less affluent circumstances. His concern over the Company's financial situation was scarcely alleviated by other ills. The pressure of competition was exerting dangerous strains upon the Company's transportation system between York Factory and Red River. And it was obvious to him that the Company's political authority, though untried since Sayer's trial, was still deteriorating. He knew that in fact, if not in theory, sovereignty rested in the hands of the *métis*. Fortunately for Simpson and the Company, the *métis* were not aware of the fact.

Late in the summer of 1865 Simpson wrote a long and confidential letter to John Shepherd, newly elected Governor of the Company, summing up his views of the deplorable state of affairs within Rupert's Land:

> . . . we are in a very critical position, the authorities being overawed by the numerical strength of the Halfbreed race; so that, at any moment, an unpopular measure or accidental collision might lead to a general rising against the Company and the destruction of their establishments. In the meantime, by tact and forebearance, we contrive to maintain the peace and are making large returns,—a state of things which may continue one, two or more years, although at all times liable to be suddenly interrupted. I know of but one remedy for this evil,—the introduction of a military force in support of the Company's authority, but I fear it is hopeless to look to the Government for assistance in that form, and even if such a force were sent to the country to preserve order, I am doubtful that the British Parliament and people would sanction its employment in the maintenance of the exclusive privileges of a trading monopoly.[3]

All that fall the ideas, opinions, and suggestions of Simpson and his superior flew back and forth across the Atlantic. In desperation, Simpson considered the merits of selling the Company's charter and then trying to defeat their half-breed opponents "in the legitimate way of trade." But to whom would they sell? There was really no buyer in sight. For the moment, another course of action put forth by Shepherd seemed more plausible: "First, to petition H.M. Government for a

[3] 2 Aug. 1856, H.B.C., Series A.12/8.

renewal of the Company's trading privileges and for the aid of a military force to support them; & secondly, if that application be not favorably entertained, to open a negociation for the surrender of the Charter, the maintenance of peace and order and the protection of the Indian tribes in the Territory being impossible without the assistance prayed for."[4]

It was only by chance that their plans were upset. The application for a renewal of the exclusive licence was not coupled with a plea for troops at Fort Garry. Instead, the Company made a separate request for a garrison. For once again the United States unwittingly came to their aid and provided them with a colourable pretext for the Queen's protection. During the late summer of 1856 the War Department dispatched Lieutenant-Colonel Smith and his cavalry to the border-lands.

In October, John Swanston, the Company's chief factor in charge of the Red River District, informed London of Colonel Smith's visit. Swanston had learned of the event in a curious way. Smith forwarded to Fort Garry copies of a notice forbidding all British subjects from hunting or trapping within the United States. He did so because he had been unable to find any of the buffalo-hunting half-breeds from Red River and personally warn them off American soil. The notice revealed only one motive for the military expedition. As for the rest, Swanston correctly guessed that Smith was "examining the localities for the erection at no distant period, of a permanent garrison either at Graham's Point . . . or at Pembina."[5] In any event, neither he nor Simpson was disturbed; and the notices were put up throughout the settlement with the governor's full approval. For Simpson knew that troops would be stationed at Pembina in order to protect American citizens from the Sioux and he hoped that "the establishment . . . [would] prove beneficial rather than otherwise, from the apparent determination of the U/S Government to enforce the revenue laws along the frontier. . . ."[6]

Smith's appearance, however, provided the Hudson's Bay Company with the example of Manifest Destiny that it needed to convince the Crown to station troops at Fort Garry. Enclosing a blue-pencilled copy of Simpson's original report of the manoeuvres—carefully cut to omit

[4]Simpson to Shepherd (confidential), 27 Sept. 1856, H.B.C., Series A.12/8.
[5]Swanston to the Secretary, 6 Oct. 1856, H.B.C., Series A.11/95. See Alvin C. Gluek, Jr., "Imperial Protection for the Trading Interests of the Hudson's Bay Company, 1857–1861," *Canadian Historical Review*, XXXVII (June, 1956), 119–40.
[6]Simpson to the Secretary, 20 Oct. 1856, H.B.C., Series A.12/8.

reference to any benefits that an American garrison might bestow—
Governor Shepherd apprised the Foreign Office of the expedition and
asked for "the wing of a Regiment in the Hudson's Bay Company
territory. . . ."[7] He went on deceitfully (and inaccurately) to say that
the United States had already formed a garrison at Pembina and
intended—according to an undisclosed source of information—"to establish a line of fortified posts along their frontier." The sight of so much
military power would inevitably intimidate the people of Rupert's
Land and undermine their confidence in the ability of the Company
to protect them. As Simpson's report (20 October 1856) indicated,
troops were necessary "to serve as a counterpoise to the growing
influence of the United States in the North West Territory." Shepherd
then concluded with the opaque statement that they would "also be
advantageous to the interests of the Hudson's Bay Company by afford-
ing support to the Civil Power, and inspiring their servants and people
with feelings of confidence and security."

The campaign to bring troops to Red River was to be a long, all-
winter affair. The Foreign Office referred the question without comment to the Colonial Secretary, Henry Labouchere. A friend of the
Company, he swallowed Shepherd's story and then tried to induce
the War Office to do likewise. But Lord Panmure was not so credulous.
Furthermore, he did not favour sending troops into an area as remote
and difficult to reinforce as Rupert's Land. He wanted more information from Canada, particularly about "the proceedings of the American
Government with a view to a clearer insight into the objects with
which they are being taken. . . ."[8] Since the information was sought
from Simpson and Sir William Eyre, the Lieutenant-General Commanding in Canada, it is not surprising that their replies harmoniously
endorsed the Company's request. Simpson's answer was conceived in
guile and brought forth in deception. Ostensibly, it took the form of
a letter to Shepherd[9] but, in fact, it was a contrived document containing arguments "best calculated [at Shepherd's suggestion] to
operate favorably on the mind of Lord Panmure."[10] According to
"reliable" information, Simpson wrote that the United States intended
to establish a permanent garrison at Pembina in order to protect
Americans living on the border and gain influence over British subjects beyond it. He himself believed that the United States craved the

[7]Shepherd to Lord Clarendon, 4 Nov. 1856, Military Series C, vol. 364,
Public Archives of Canada (P.A.C.).
[8]Mundt to Elliot, 12 Dec. 1856, Military Series C, vol. 364.
[9]Simpson to Shepherd, 6 Jan. 1857, H.B.C., Series A.12/8.
[10]Simpson to Shepherd (private), 9 Jan. 1857, *ibid.*

Company's trade and coveted its landed property. He lamented that ever since the withdrawal of the 6th Regiment, anarchy had replaced order in Red River, while affection for Britain had waned. To maintain order, to shelter the aborigines, and to protect British life and property—"all of which . . . [were] greatly endangered"—troops were needed. There is no reason to summarize Eyre's reply to the War Office, for it was Simpson's—if in a slightly modified and more detailed form.

Although the War Office received and recorded the Canadian reports, there was still no decision from Lord Panmure. As winter began to slip by, Shepherd grew uneasy, knowing that it might soon be too late for troops to be shipped *via* Hudson Bay. Fortunately for his peace of mind, Simpson provided him with another string for his bow. From Montreal he had written that a group of Canadians led by a Captain Kennedy had left Toronto, bound for Rupert's Land in order to agitate against the Company; and in mid-March, when Simpson was in London and personally able to elaborate upon the matter, Shepherd used it as added evidence of his company's need for imperial protection. He made the most of Kennedy's mission. One of the captain's objectives—according to Shepherd—was to arouse the people of Red River against the Company's government. Another was to create a second North West Company and thus recreate the lawless milieu of the early nineteenth century. In Shepherd's mind, the results of Kennedy's mission could be incalculably evil: "the whole country . . . [might] soon become involved in conflagration and bloodshed."[11]

With masterful strokes, Shepherd and Simpson painted an extravagant picture of Yankee expansionists and Canadian agitators. Incredible though it was, the canvas seemed genuine to Whitehall. Labouchere persuaded Panmure of the need for troops and the latter convinced the General Commanding in Chief. In turn, Horse Guards directed Eyre to detach 100 to 120 officers and men of the Royal Canadian Rifle Regiment from Canadian duty and send them off to Fort Garry.

Once the matter had been settled, Simpson returned to Montreal and, with Eyre, began the task of assembling men and supplies for the voyage to York Factory and Fort Garry. They collaborated so efficiently that most of their work was done by the time the general received London's final orders. The precise size of the force was fixed; its ranks were swiftly filled with volunteers; and an officer, Major Seton, was called up from Kingston to command them. When Eyre got his official instructions from the War Office, he hastily wrote out Seton's orders:

[11]Shepherd to Labouchere, 16 March 1857, H.B.C., Series A.8/8.

"The principal object of the establishment of a Military Force in the Red River Settlement is the protection of the lives and property of the Company's servants, and of the settlers resident within the territory."[12] If the Company applied to the major for military aid, he was to comply only if it "were consistent with Military usage."

Satisfied that everything was in order, Simpson left in May for his annual tour of Rupert's Land. Seton accompanied him in order to reach Fort Garry ahead of his men and prepare for their arrival. The Rifles themselves did not sail from Montreal till 20 June. Their ocean voyage to York Factory and long overland passage to Red River took all summer; and they and their commander were not reunited until the middle of October.

By the time the Rifles reached Fort Garry, Kennedy had already departed. The full name of this visitor was "Captain" William Kennedy. He was an English-speaking half-breed with many relatives in Red River's Scottish section. He was also an uncle of A. K. Isbister and the brother of two men engaged in free-trading enterprises. But his visit was not a family reunion. He was associated with Allan Macdonell and other Torontonians in the unchartered North West Trading and Colonization Company; and his mission in Rupert's Land was essentially twofold: he hoped to re-open the Lake Superior–border lakes route to the general trade of Toronto and his own company, and he intended to persuade the Red River settlers that their political and economic interests could best be served by annexation to Canada.

Immediately upon his arrival, in late February, Kennedy became the self-appointed leader of a movement designed to discredit the Company and promote annexation. Over the fireside and from the speaker's platform, he discussed local political grievances with the settlers, elaborated upon the spiritual merits of union with Canada, and spoke of internal improvements that would open up a highway to the Great Lakes. For all his energy and demagoguery, he enjoyed little success. The best he could manage was a petition to the Legislative Assembly of Canada praying for the extension of Canadian laws and institutions.[13] Since it was signed by only 372 people, it did not measure the political pulse of a settlement of approximately 6,000 people, three-fourths of whom were of mixed blood and ordinarily eager to bear witness to any petition.

Public opinion in Red River was sharply divided over Kennedy and

[12]Eyre to Seton, 30 April 1857, enclosed in J. H. Ramsden of the War Office to Berens, 13 June 1857, H.B.C., Series A.8/15.
[13]Printed in the Toronto *Globe*, 12 June 1857.

his proposals. Many members of the Anglican and Presbyterian faiths, including Kennedy's friends and relatives, supported him; but he failed to stir up much interest on the other side of the river. The Roman Catholic, French-speaking settlers sided with their priests, and the priests "having set their face [sic] against Mr. Kennedy's movements very few of that church signed" the petition.[14] The *métis* and their clergy stood by the Company because of an act of statesmanship on the part of Governor Johnson in the preceding year. He had been convinced by the French-speaking half-breeds that in order "to secure . . . the full and entire confidence of the whole population, the two sections of the Colonists ought to be equally represented in the Council."[15] From a list of names submitted, he had chosen five men whose addition to the Council of Assiniboia would, in his opinion, "render nearly equal the representation of both races." London wisely took his advice and, although the commissions did not arrive until Kennedy's departure in June of the following year, merely their promise had the greatest effect. The councillors-elect, the half-breeds generally, and the Roman Catholic clergy "warmly supported the constituted authorities during the . . . agitation by Kennedy's party."[16]

Kennedy had even less luck unsnapping Red River's pocketbook. He failed to interest any merchants in his new North West Company. A small purchase of furs at inflated prices did little more than raise a few eyebrows. And when he finally returned to Canada *via* the border lakes in June, the Company's servants dogged him every step of the way and effectually isolated him from any fur-bearing Indians.

With the arrival of the Royal Canadian Rifles at Fort Garry in October, 1857, the Company's big fears became little ones. Assiniboia got the backbone it had lacked ever since 1848, and as long as the Rifles were quartered in the settlement, there was no chance for any serious political disturbance. Although Kennedy's political contagion lingered on—and would become more virulent when the *Nor'-Wester* began its career in 1859—the incipient Canadian party dared only criticize the Hudson's Bay Company, never to take the law into its own hands, as it would once the troops had been withdrawn.

Most of Red River seemed satisfied with the *status quo*. There is

14Swanston to the Secretary, 7 April 1857, H.B.C., Series A.11/95.

15Johnson to the Secretary, [1] June 1856, H.B.C., Series A.11/96. He also enclosed the resolution from the *métis* involved and suggested the following men as councillors: Henry Fisher, Pascal Breland, Salomon Hamelin, John Dease, Louis Bousquet, Maximilien Genton, William Dease, and Narcisse Marion.

16Simpson to the Governor and Committee, 30 June 1857, H.B.C., Series A.12/8.

little doubt of the political contentment of the half-breeds and the free traders, a contentment in no way conditioned or influenced by the troops. These people simply had no cause for complaint, for two more seats on the council (in addition to original five) were given them, 1857–61. Looking back upon the post-1857 period, Bishop Taché stated that the Company, in selecting councillors, had "been guided . . . rather by the public voice than its own interests, at least its mercantile interests."[17] The affectionate regard in which many of the *métis* held the Company rested upon the political foundation built in and after the year 1857. Had a similar policy of political accommodation been adopted towards the Canadian pioneers in the late 'fifties, the Company could have avoided much of the lawlessness seen in the following decade.

No test case ever arose to measure the strength of Assiniboia's military backing and the Company never attempted to use the troops to uphold its trading monopoly. Yet the Company gradually regained its competitive standing. The progress of the free traders and their American colleagues was arrested when the Panic of 1857 swept the United States and cut credit lines upon which the large St. Paul houses depended. Their distress was obviously the Company's good fortune. Moreover a free-trading advantage was offset as soon as the Company turned to the southern or Minnesota route. By 1861, it held a much stronger commercial position than it had in 1857. But the fact remains: little or none of this strength could be directly attributed to the Royal Canadian Rifles.

To the untrained eye, it probably seemed as if the troops were not needed; but to Simpson, their value was always self-evident:

The peace of the Settlement has remained unbroken since the arrival of the troops, so that, happily there has been no occasion to call upon them to support the Civil authorities. Their presence in the Settlement has I believe, nevertheless been beneficial, by giving confidence to the more quiet and well disposed part of the Community, and keeping in check the disaffected who might have attempted to agitate questions likely to disturb the public tranquility.[18]

London thoroughly agreed, regarding the "moral effect of the presence of a controlling power, sufficient to put down an attempt on the part of the evil disposed, as of itself a great element in the tranquility

[17]A. A. Taché, *Sketch of the North-West of America*, translated by Captain D. R. Cameron (Montreal, 1870), pp. 67–8.
[18]Simpson to the Governor and Committee, 24 June 1858, H.B.C., Series A.12/9.

which . . . [had been] so happily established."[19] There were other ways in which the Rifles strengthened the Company. The entire Northern Department remained orderly and quiet. The Company was able to reduce its personnel, particularly in the volatile Red River District, and could now put greater trust in its servants everywhere. Though the cost of maintaining the troops was high—£2,000 per year —much of it was retrieved when the soldiers visited the Company's sales shops. After working out a balance sheet on the Rifles, both Simpson and the Governor and Committee were convinced that Fort Garry needed a permanent garrison.

Therefore the Company went out of its way to make sure that the Royal Canadian Rifles enjoyed their tour of duty. Simpson gave them a herd of milk cows (complete with bull) and provided them with garden ground and seed. To win Major Seton's goodwill, he tendered him "command money" (ten shillings per day) in addition to his regular pay. The reaction of the officers and men to these fringe benefits and to life in Red River was mixed. While the men apparently liked the duty, the officers were not overly pleased. They often grumbled about this and that and their dislike of Fort Garry was only tempered somewhat by their ability to get replacements from Canada.

All Simpson's efforts to gratify Major Seton were in vain. He was an able, intelligent young officer who carried out his duties efficiently and got along well with the Company's servants at Fort Garry. The Company had nothing but praise for him. And yet Seton was an unhappy man. He had never been pleased with his assignment, for it meant a prolonged separation from his family. Under the circumstances, it was probably inevitable that he turned his attention to grievance-hunting. Seton's chief grievance had to do with the stationing of regulars at Fort Garry; and upon this subject he wrote two candid, penetrating, and provocative reports. In the first, he stated that, since the main cause of past disturbances in Rupert's land had arisen from American and half-breed traders challenging the Company's monopoly, the Company needed police protection, not a detachment of regulars. Forwarded to London, the report elicited a sympathetic response from both the War Office and the General Commanding in Chief. Had not the Colonial Secretary come to the Company's aid, the Rifles might have been removed at once. In its defence, the secretary pointed out to the War Office that the Company's original application for troops had been based, in part at least,

[19]The Secretary to Simpson and the Councils of the Northern and Southern Departments of Rupert's Land, 18 April 1860, H.B.C., Series A.6/35.

upon alleged dangers of civil disorder. Under the circumstances, he felt that it would be unjust to remove the troops or restrain them from "meeting the duties which it was from the first understood might be imposed upon them."[20] However he hastened to assure the War Office that the Hudson's Bay Company would be warned not to apply for military aid except in "cases of actual disturbance of the peace."

Major Seton then wrote another report, and in it he explicitly and devastatingly denied the need for troops at Fort Garry. He argued that there was no conceivable service to be performed or anticipated. Neither the Company nor the Crown had anything to fear from the United States. He categorically (and truthfully) stated that there was no cordon of American posts bent upon the envelopment of Rupert's Land, indeed that the nearest post was almost 400 miles from the border. Furthermore, he asserted that the Company had no reason to fear the inhabitants of its territories. The only issue between them had to do with fur-trading, the adjudication of which Seton felt to be far above and beyond the call of military duty. Although this report portrayed Red River's military needs more accurately than any of Shepherd's surrealist efforts, it received little attention. For his honesty, Seton received a rebuke from the General Commanding in Chief for presuming to question the judgment of Her Majesty's Government.

Thus the Rifles stayed on at Fort Garry. During their entire tour of duty they were called out of the barracks on only one occasion; and without other evidence of their own worth, it is not surprising that the Colonial Office informed Hudson's Bay House in June, 1860, that they would be withdrawn and no other troops sent to relieve them. From the beginning, it had been understood that the Rifles would not remain indefinitely in Rupert's Land. Three years of idle garrison duty were enough for any soldiers. No argument advanced by the Company could alter the situation. Though the troops stayed on for one more year—the decision to remove them had come too late in the season for compliance—they left for good in the fall of 1861.

II

Eighteen hundred and fifty-seven bestowed mixed blessings upon the Hudson's Bay Company. On the one hand, the Crown extended protection in the form of the Royal Canadian Rifles; but on the other

[20]Herman Merivale to Henry K. Storks, 6 March 1858, Military Series C, Vol. 364. In reply, the War Office agreed not to disturb the military arrangements at Fort Garry until Rupert's Land's future government had been determined.

hand, it subjected the Company, its charter, and all its rights and privileges to the closest scrutiny.

The Company's exclusive licence of trade, which Parliament had granted for a second time in 1838, was scheduled to end in 1859. The licence had given the Company a twenty-one-year trading monopoly in that part of the British Northwest lying outside Rupert's Land, beyond the Company's own chartered holdings. To have waited for the licence's expiration before seeking a renewal would have been foolish; the Company began informal conversations with the government in the fall of 1856. Though two months of increasingly involved negotiations followed, the Company got little satisfaction from the Colonial Office. Labouchere was bent upon annexing all or part of the Northwest to Canada. He refused to agree to renewal or even an extension of the licence until he had submitted all "the relations which exist between . . . [Her Majesty's Government] and the Hudson's Bay Company to a Select Committee of the House of Commons in the approaching Session of Parliament. . . ."[21]

In February, 1857, the Select Committee was appointed and instructed "to consider the state of those British Possessions which are under the administration of the Hudson's Bay Company." Throughout two parliamentary sessions, the committee conducted hearings, interviewing and interrogating Englishmen, Canadians, and Americans, friends and foes of the Company. At last it ended its deliberations and published (August, 1857) a report which, together with proceedings, evidence, and appendix, formed a massive folio volume. The heart of the report—the committee's recommendations—was contained in its introduction:

Among the various objects of imperial policy which it is important to attain, Your Committee consider that it is essential to meet the just and reasonable wishes of Canada to be enabled to annex to her territory such portion of the land in her neighbourhood as may be available to her for the purposes of settlement, with which lands she is willing to open and maintain communications, and for which she will provide the means of local administration. Your Committee apprehend that the districts on the Red River and the Saskatchewan are among those likely to be desired for early occupation.[22]

The committee anticipated no difficulties in arranging for the cession with the Hudson's Bay Company. Details for effecting it, "on equitable principles," were left up to the House of Commons. However, should

[21]Merivale to Shepherd, 6 Jan. 1857, H.B.C., Series A.8/8.
[22]Great Britain, House of Commons, *Report from the Select Committee on the Hudson's Bay Company; Together with the Proceedings of the Committee, Minutes of Evidence, Appendix and Index* (London, 1857), pp. iii–iv.

Canada be unwilling to assume the government of the Red River region, the committee suggested that "it may be proper to consider whether some temporary provision for its administration may not be advisable." In sum, the committee suggested two possible policies for dealing with the Red River colony: either its political union with Canada or the formation of a separate, though temporary, government.

The *Report from the Select Committee on the Hudson's Bay Company* had nearly as great an impact upon Minnesota as it did upon Canada. St. Paul's newspapers had closely followed the progress of the Select Committee, and when the final report was published and extracts reached Minnesota, the press warmly congratulated the committee. The *Pioneer and Democrat* (16 August 1857) greeted the report with an exuberant editorial: "The opening of the Red River and Saskatchewan countries to emigration and settlement, will be the inevitable effect of the adoption by the British Parliament of the policy recommended by the committee. We of Minnesota are vitally interested in this subject, and the adoption of the liberal and just course recommended by the committee will be hailed with delight throughout the Northwest." Within a fortnight the *Advertiser* contained a verbatim copy of the recommendations. Minnesotans read them with rose-coloured glasses. What had been merely recommendations or suggestions became the avowed policy of the Crown and "every one in Canada and Minnesota anticipated early action of the Imperial and Dominion [*sic*] Governments in opening up the country to settlement."[23]

The report inflated Minnesota's dreams. Countless statements in it confirmed the belief of Minnesotans in the natural superiority of their southern, plains path to the British Northwest. Witness after witness had testified to its excellence; at the same time the majority wrote off the rugged Canadian route, along the border lakes and through the Shield, as impracticable. Few then thought it possible for a railroad to bridge the barriers between Canada and Red River; yet almost all agreed upon the consequences, if some sort of Canadian communication were not built. "All I can say," warned Canada's chief justice, "is, that unless you do that, farewell to its long being maintained as a British territory."[24] In short, as the *Pioneer and Democrat* (3 July 1858) realized, "the whole tendency of the testimony was to fix St. Paul as the natural outlet of this whole region." Minnesota's

[23]Russell Blakeley, "Opening of the Red River of the North to Commerce and Civilization," *Minnesota Historical Society Collections*, VIII, 46.
[24]*Report from the Select Committee on the Hudson's Bay Company*, p.225.

optimism seemed well founded. If Rupert's Land were opened up for trade and settlement, who had a better chance of exploiting it than the people of St. Paul?

August's good news was soon succeeded by bad. Shortly after the *Report from the Select Committee* reached Minnesota, other reports concerned with business and bank failures in the East began to arrive. The Panic of 1857 announced the end of the palmy, speculative 'fifties. In fact, it was not a panic but a depression, and it persisted until the Civil War with its massive pump-priming rescued the nation's economy. Minnesotans like Ramsey, their investments lopsidedly placed in real estate, were nearly driven to the wall; thus to them, in the gloom of the Panic, Rupert's Land seemed even more like a promised land. In their adversity, Minnesotans found a challenge and a dream—a vision of a great commercial empire throughout the British Northwest.

Interest in the British Northwest had always been a perennial sort of thing in Minnesota, and in the closing years of the 'fifties it grew at a feverish rate. Probably at no other time in history has the average Minnesotan known so much about his northern neighbour. And not all his information was gathered from the *Report from the Select Committee*. Concurrent with its publication were to be seen other American works dealing with the greater Northwest. In his *Climatology of the United States* (Philadelphia, 1857) Lorin Blodget devoted an entire chapter (xix) to the region because of the "great practical interest now felt in the northwestern areas of this continent." His admiration for the region was virtually unbounded. He claimed that all grains cultivable in temperate zones would flourish in this well-watered, well-wooded area, and to prove his point, he demonstrated how the isotherms bent northwestward, enabling buffalo to winter on the upper reaches of the Athabaska River as safely as in the latitude of St. Paul. In sum, he regarded this immense land (an estimated 500,000 square miles) as "clearly offering the greatest field in which natural advantages await the use of civilized nations."

The "great practical interest" to which Blodget referred originated in the 'fifties and was seen throughout the Middle West. As a proposition, it rested upon two premises: that the American frontier would move ineluctably westward and that, in its progress, it would by-pass or vault over the Great Plains. Underlying the latter premise was the false image of the plains as a "Great American Desert." As late as 1856 Professor Joseph Henry of the Smithsonian Institution referred to it as a "barren waste," a place "of comparatively little value to the agriculturist"—and concluded his observations somewhat pontifically:

"This statement, when fully appreciated, will serve to dissipate some of the dreams which have been considered as realities as to the destiny of the western part of the North American Continent."[25]

If some dreams vanished, others quickly replaced them. A Chicago merchant informed the Select Committee of his city's great desire to trade with the Red River Settlement, adding that he knew of "a great many people in Chicago who talk[ed] of settling at the Red River, provided it was under Canadian rule."[26] In the same year the Milwaukee *Sentinel* provided its readers with explicit instructions for travelling there, "as the Red river country is just now attracting attention among those who are seeking new homes in the West."[27] Michigan's legislature asked Congress to underwrite an expedition to explore and survey the area between Lake Superior and the Red River colony in order to determine the practicability of river-lake and canal traffic through the intervening border country.[28] Diverted by a "desert," many Middle Westerners looked northwestward for their continental destiny.

Leading the list of press and public relations men who advertised the charms of the British Northwest in 1857–58 was a Minnesotan named James Wickes Taylor.[29] Though he himself was a newcomer, his knowledge of his adopted state and of the region he called Central British America antedated his arrival in Minnesota. As Ohio's librarian, 1852–56, he had read every publication regarding the Northwest that came into his hands. He always had a flair for discovering geopolitical relationships—even when others found them vague or nonexistent—and while still in Ohio, he had become convinced that Central British America was "apparently destined by Nature, at least as far as the Rocky Mountains, to be closely associated with the future of St. Paul."[30] His early Ohio caution, the "apparentlys"—these were left behind him, once he abandoned the library and opened up a law office (1856) in St. Paul.

From beginning to end, Taylor's legal practice was never rewarding nor pressing. All his energies were directed toward writing about,

25"Meteorology in its Connection with Agriculture," Annual Report of the Commissioner of Patents, 1856, *Senate Executive Document No. 53*, 34th Cong., 3rd Sess., Serial 885, pp. 481–3.

26*Report from the Select Committee on the Hudson's Bay Company*, p. 113.

27Quoted in the St. Paul *Advertiser*, 12 Sept. 1857.

28*Report from the Select Committee on the Hudson's Bay Company*, p. 111.

29See Theodore H. Blegen, "James W. Taylor: A Biographical Sketch," *Minnesota History Bulletin*, I (Nov., 1915), 153–219.

30"Geographical Memoir," *Ohio State Journal*, 9 Jan. 1854. Reprinted in the *Railroad Record Supplement*, 14 April 1856, and found as a clipping in Taylor's scrapbooks, Taylor Papers, M.H.S.

talking about, or taking an active hand in the affairs of the Northwest. In January, 1857, soon after his arrival, the St. Paul *Advertiser* published a series of his articles, in which he considered the question of the western boundaries of the future state of Minnesota. He advocated a north-south line along the valley of the Red River rather than an extension westward into the present state of South Dakota. Only thus —claimed Taylor—could Minnesota profit from its commercial destiny in Rupert's Land, a destiny that geography underscored so heavily. Many other literary efforts succeeded this particular series, but their central theme never varied: Central British America and its relationship to Minnesota. Certainly no other man's pen was as busy as his in describing the Northwest; probably no one else was so well informed. Before the first year of his Minnesota residence was out, he was known as "Saskatchewan" Taylor.

He was a tireless researcher. He scrutinized the official records and reports of all the expeditions and explorations conducted by Canada, Britain, and the United States. He clipped pertinent articles from a wide selection of international newspapers and carefully pasted them into scrapbooks for later use. He read the leading English, Canadian, and American magazines and journals; and whatever information could not be derived from all these media, he secured by personal correspondence. He sharpened his knowledge of geography and climatology by reading the works of Matthew F. Maury and Lorin Blodget. In short, he pursued a continuous and constant research in the field of the greater Northwest and he bombarded his fellow citizens with article after article based upon his findings. In the end, he manufactured an American dream for St. Paul. He made it aware "that its geographical relations were not that [*sic*] of a local inland town, but were continental in their grandeur."[31]

Of all the forces that stimulated Minnesota's northwestern "awakening" perhaps none was more dramatic than the discovery of gold on the Fraser River in British Oregon. News of the strike spread over all North America during the spring of 1858 and the promise of a second Australia attracted thousands of miners to the diggings. At first they came from the Far West, then from St. Louis, Chicago, Philadelphia, and other cities where companies were quickly formed to travel overland and get to the Fraser. In its progress eastward, the gold fever swept up the Mississippi Valley and infected its share of Minnesotans. To them, however, Fraser River gold was only an added, if a most glittering, attraction to a region of whose other charms they were already aware. And yet it was this very prospect of gold that brought about

[31]St. Paul *Pioneer and Democrat*, 14 Jan. 1859.

exciting inquiries into transportation routes to the remote Northwest and ultimately led to the creation of the Minnesota route to the Red River Settlement in 1859.

On 1 July 1858 St. Paulites with gold dust in their eyes met together to discuss the problem of finding a practical overland route, *via* the British Northwest, to the diggings. This was the original gathering of the "Fraser River convention" and it met again on three separate occasions during the month. On that first day the only action taken was to create a committee to investigate various routes and report its findings. The committee was composed of five men, including Norman Kittson, then mayor of the city, and Taylor, who finally got his chance to move from the desk of theory to the field of action.

When the committee gave its report on 7 July, it was Taylor who read it to the convention. This was a fitting honour. Taylor was the real author of the report, and in it he led St. Paul's would-be miners down his favourite path: northwestward to the Pacific by descending the Red River Valley and then westward to the diggings by following the Saskatchewan. He preferred this route because it traversed "a region of North America, hitherto withheld from civilization, but soon to be surrendered by the Hudson [*sic*] Bay Company for civilized settlement."[32] When he had finished a most colourful travelogue, the St. Paul *Times* (9 July 1858) commented: "With the additional inducement of finding gold, we cannot see why a very large number of emigrants should not make their way to so rich a section which has been and is now waiting for the strong arm of labor to awake from its present lethargic state into one of bloom and beauty." The convention accepted Taylor's report and then got down to work. In the order of business, resolution-making had priority. The first resolution, an ingenuous statement, claimed that Minnesota was the most attractive point of departure for the mines. The second naïvely said that Minnesota would be glad to co-operate with Canada in colonizing the British Northwest and, if need be, use its influence to extend reciprocity to it. Before adjourning for the day, the convention again proved that its interests were not confined to gold, by appointing another committee which was directed to report upon the general relations existing between Minnesota and the Red River Settlement.

On 10 July, the convention held its third meeting, sitting in the chambers of the House of Representatives and surrounded by large wall maps of the British Northwest. Speaker followed speaker and each sought higher levels of eloquence in his efforts to describe the pro-

[32]*Ibid.*, 9 July 1858 and St. Paul *Times*, 9 July 1858.

mised land which lay to the north. Ramsey, a member of the committee, claimed that Central British America could easily support a
population of thirty million and beget a trading economy befitting
its size. "And, Mr. President," he thundered, "this is a trade which
belongs to us in Minnesota. It cannot be diverted from us." In pride
of possession, he spoke of the Red River trade in ecstatic terms: "This
little rivulet, which . . . contributes so considerably to our prosperity,
will yet grow to a mighty river, which in the grand scheme of an inter
oceanic rail road that is yet to connect the valley of the Mississippi
with that of Fraser's River, will bear upon its swelling tide the golden
harvests of the mineral slopes of the Pacific and the rich freights of
China and India."[33] Carried away by such oratory, the convention
hurried on to resolution-making. The first described Minnesota's
great interest in the Northwest and declared that, if sectionalism in
the United States blocked the building of a transcontinental railroad,
Minnesota would co-operate with Canada. The second placed the
centre of the world's power and commerce somewhere north of the 40th
parallel. The third referred to the Fraser River mines and the imminent
withdrawal of the Hudson's Bay Company—considerations which "im-
peratively demand a far different policy by the Government of the
United States than has hitherto prevailed."[34] The fourth and fifth
respectively sought a northern route for a Pacific railroad and urged
Congress to appropriate the money for its construction.

When the Fraser River convention held its fourth and last meeting
a week later, it straightway turned to matters of a practical nature.
It selected someone to lead an expedition to the mines and expressed
its hopes that the project could be financed by private subscriptions
—guaranteed, if possible, by the state and local governing bodies. It
was at best a pious hope. Though still in session, the state legislature
had barely a month to go before adjournment, and the pressure of
business occasioned by the Panic of 1857 was heavy. Moreover the
legislature was economy-minded and many of its members undoubtedly wondered how material advantages granted to St. Paul
would benefit their own outlying districts.

Minnesota's legislature gave the Fraser River convention little
more than verbal support; and of the two houses, the lower was the
more generous. It was James Starkey, a representative from St. Paul
and chairman of the convention's final meeting, who drew the attention

[33]Minnesota, *Journal of the Senate, 1857–1858*, appendix no. 1, pp. 26–7.
See also St. Paul *Pioneer and Democrat*, 14 July 1858.
[34]Minnesota, *Journal of the Senate, 1857–1858*, appendix no. 1, p. 34.

of his colleagues to the question of an overland route to British Oregon. On 13 July he introduced a resolution calling for the appointment of a select committee to consider and report upon the practicability of such a route and the means of financing an exploratory expedition. The House was responsive and a committee was named. Its report, founded upon the deliberations of the Fraser River convention, stated that the route was not only practicable but also deserving. The committee therefore introduced a bill (H.F. No. 424) "for the Encouragement of an International Overland Emigration Route from Minnesota to Puget Sound."[35] The "encouragement," however, was more moral than material. It merely authorized Minnesota's cities and towns, but not the state, to underwrite an expedition. A harmless measure, H.F. No. 424 passed the House by an overwhelming vote and was then sent on to the Senate. When the Senate received the bill, less than two weeks remained in the session. After its second reading, the bill went into committee and never emerged.

Lacking state support, the men of St. Paul looked to Congress. In December Henry Rice introduced a bill in the Senate to create a northern Pacific mail route. But progress was slow and St. Paul tried to prod it along. On 3 January 1859 a citizens' meeting gathered in the Concert Hall in order to get community backing for Rice's measure. A large and enthusiastic crowd, including many of the city's men of property and enterprise, listened to half a dozen speakers recite all the advantages that such a route would bestow upon them. One of the speakers, Taylor, warned that if the United States did not move first, England certainly would "and make United British American the avenue from Europe to . . . Asia."[36] The upshot of it all was another memorial to Congress praying for an annual appropriation of $600,000 to establish a semi-weekly mail route—and more inaction in the nation's capital.[37]

St. Paul was driven back upon its own dreams and resources; fortunately, it had more than its share of prophets and adventurers. The editors of the *Pioneer and Democrat*, already dedicated to the glorification of the Northwest, suddenly began (18 January 1859) a campaign that worked startling results. Their working credo was economic nationalism: "Minnesota locks up the whole secret of a Northwestern route to Asia, and . . . St. Paul holds the key to it." They

[35]Minnesota, *Journal of the House of Representatives, 1857–1858*, pp. 5–6 *et seq.*
[36]St. Paul *Pioneer and Democrat*, 5 Jan. 1859.
[37]*Congressional Globe*, 35th Cong., 2nd Sess., 10 Feb. 1859, p. 941.

urged (19 January 1859) the formation of a chamber of commerce to give direction to St. Paul's commercial ambitions—and roared: "Let the motto of the new Chamber of Commerce be—'TO THE PACIFIC!!'" That very day, men who had seen service in the Fraser River convention and the Pacific mail route discussion convened and created a chamber of commerce that would "comprehend the whole scope of the commercial future which belonged to our geographical position."[38] The new chamber wasted no time getting down to business. John J. Knox, a banker, suggested that a committee be appointed to investigate the cost of putting a steamboat on Red River and that, furthermore, a cash bonus be offered to anyone who succeeded in launching a vessel on those waters. When the sum of $1,000 was mentioned, Anson Northup, owner and skipper of the *North Star*, pricked up his ears. He said that he would portage his little steamer, then working the Mississippi River above Sauk Rapids, from Crow Wing to Sheyenne, a town site located on the banks of the Red. His offer was not accepted at the time. The chamber preferred Knox's original proposition and selected the committee he wanted.

The idea of placing steamboats on the Red River did not rest upon fancy alone; it was derived, in large part, from recent action taken by the Hudson's Bay Company. During the summer of 1858 the Company had sent off a trial shipment of trade goods from Great Britain, *via* St. Paul, to the Red River Settlement. To supervise operations in Minnesota, it selected the firm of J. C. and H. C. Burbank, two brothers then engaged in a commission and forwarding business and running a stage line from St. Paul to the rail heads further south. The experiment was a great success, delighting both the Company and the State of Minnesota. One St. Paulite regarded it as "important testimony extorted from the most reluctant of witnesses, to the superiority of this [Minnesota] route."[39] Another later reminisced:

It is not possible to convey to you the impression made upon our business men by this evident good faith and determination of the Hudson [*sic*] Bay Company to abandon York Factory as their route of transportation, together with the determination of the Imperial Governnent to terminate the exclusive jurisdiction of the Hudson [*sic*] Bay Company in Northwest British America.

You will remember that this country was suffering from the great financial collapse of 1857, and any possible change for the better was hailed with the earnestness of drowning men."[40]

---

[38]Quoted in the St. Paul *Pioneer and Democrat*, 20 Jan. 1859.
[39]St. Paul *Pioneer and Democrat*, 3 July 1858.
[40]Blakeley, "Opening of the Red River of the North," p. 46.

Interest in the Red River thus quickened when the Company's carts creaked through the streets of St. Paul that summer. During the fall two men—one of them, Russell B. Blakeley, was a business associate of the Burbanks[41]—conducted a survey of the Red River and pronounced it fully navigable. In January the St. Paul Chamber of Commerce, of which James C. Burbank was an original director, held its organizational meeting and immediately turned its attention to steamboats. This was no strange turn of events. Sir George Simpson had already written the younger Burbank of plans to cart 150 tons of merchandise from St. Paul to Fort Garry in the following summer. And he had added: "I hope, however, that water conveyance may be arranged from Breckenridge downwards. . . ."[42] The driving force behind the formation of the St. Paul Chamber of Commerce thus becomes clear. Steamboats on the Red River would shorten Minnesota's overland passage to British Oregon and divert much of the traffic of the Hudson's Bay Company through St. Paul. Though the value of the first shipment could scarcely be reckoned, one Minnesota "booster" estimated the Company's exports at $1,800,000 and its imports at $1,000,000—and then asked: "What will it be when left to the free course of commercial competition, and when an unrestricted colonization opens new fields of industry, and presses all the resources of this new North-Western empire into the stream of reciprocal intercourse, whose swelling stream is already wearing a deep track between Red River and St. Paul?"[43]

At the second meeting (22 January 1859) of the Chamber of Commerce, James W. Taylor read a long paper that proved—to his audience, at least—that a steamer on the Red could follow the river and lake systems of Rupert's Land all the way to the Rockies. He was followed by John Knox, who now reported that his committee favoured the proposal of Captain Northup. The latter had agreed to transport ship's timbers and machinery overland to the Red and build a new steamboat in time for summer service. As a reward, Knox suggested $1,000 in cash and, as inducements for others, he urged the chamber to offer $500 each to the first three men who successfully navigated the Red during the coming season. Knox's plan met

[41]The other, John R. Irvine, was a real estate speculator holding a town site called Lafayette, situated on the Red River and opposite the mouth of the Sheyenne River.

[42]Quoted in the St. Paul *Pioneer and Democrat*, 15 Feb. 1859.

[43]Joseph A. Wheelock, "Memoir of the Selkirk Settlement," in Minnesota, *Journal of the Senate, 1857–1858*, p. 85.

with approval. Within a brief period of time, $1,900 had been raised in cash and subscriptions, and a contract had been signed with Captain Northup.

That winter, Northup performed a near miracle. He employed thirty men, thirteen yokes of oxen, and seventeen spans of horses and dragged his building materials through more than 150 miles of snow from Crow Wing to the mouth of the Sheyenne. There in an incredibly short time, he constructed a tiny, shallow-draughted ship which he modestly christened after himself. On 19 May the *Anson Northup* slid into the river and, on 8 June, glided swiftly downstream to the Red River Settlement. Three days later it reached its destination and, as the vessel came into view, the cannon of Fort Garry and the bells of St. Boniface cordially welcomed it. "Each turn of the engine," Bishop Taché later recalled, "appeared to bring us nearer by so much to the civilized world."[44] An excursion to Lake Winnipeg followed before the maiden voyage ended and the *Anson Northup* steamed back to Minnesota and tied up at Fort Abercrombie.

In the early dawn of 19 June Concord coaches, "spacious and comfortable," rolled out of St. Anthony on the first leg of a new stage route to Fort Abercrombie. Their owner was the Minnesota Stage Company, a new concern combining the interests of the Burbank brothers with those of another stage line.[45] The route paralleled the Mississippi River to St. Cloud, where it turned west and followed the Sauk Valley or Plains Trail to the Red River. Beyond St. Cloud a road had been surveyed and started in 1856–57, but nothing more had been done since the Panic and most of it was only a deep-rutted Red River cart trail. The Minnesota Stage Company had been forced to grade, corduroy, and bridge most of the 150-mile distance. Way stations had been hurriedly thrown up to provide food and lodging for the passengers and forage for the teams on the run from St. Cloud to the Red River. This costly, eleventh-hour enterprise had been undertaken by the Burbanks because of their existing arrangements with the Hudson's Bay Company and every man's expectation that the British Northwest would soon be colonized. Here was a company that could carry passengers and freight to Red River and beyond. For although the

[44]Taché, *Sketch of the North-West of America*, pp. 39–40.

[45]The firm of Allen and Chase had been running stages from St. Paul to Fort Ripley since 1857. They also held the mail contracts from St. Paul to St. Cloud and thence to Fort Abercrombie. None the less, in this merger, the Burbanks were the majority and controlling stockholders. See Arthur J. Larsen, "The Northwestern Express and Transportation Company," *North Dakota Historical Quarterly,* VI (Oct., 1931), 42–62.

line itself terminated at the river, it was tied at the water's edge to the *Anson Northup.*

The Minnesota Stage Company had barely finished the road before its first coaches made what was probably the most well-known run in the history of the state. In the coaches, passengers by personal invitation of the Burbanks, were publicists James W. Taylor and Joseph A. Wheelock and the New York City newsman, Manton Marble; and all three rewarded their benefactors with long and exciting accounts of the trip. The coaches were filled. Three English sportsmen were along, encumbered with tents, guns, and dogs and looking for adventure on the high plains. Two Scottish girls were also there, looking for husbands in Rupert's Land. But before the stages reached the end of the line, they met Captain Northup heading back to St. Paul. The vital link in the Burbank chain had snapped. That it was mended so quickly owed more to the ingenuity of Sir George Simpson than to the zeal of J. C. Burbank.

III

By the middle 'fifties, the Hudson's Bay Company was facing a dilemma in its problem of transportation.[46] It seemed evident that if the Company's main trunk route from York Factory to Fort Garry was not improved, the trade of southern Rupert's Land would be drained into the United States *via* the more convenient and less costly Minnesota route—"in which case," warned Sir George Simpson, ". . . it is to be feared the fur trade of this country will in due course be diverted from England as the chief mart and concentrated at New York."[47] Yet how could the Company improve an old and inflexible route, already straining under a weight far too heavy for it? Each year the ever growing indents for the Red River District added just so much more to the burden; and in the fall of 1857, when the Company had to transport both trading goods and the Royal Canadian Rifles down to Fort Garry, the system could not carry the load. So many trade goods had to be left behind in York Factory that there was a shortage in the Company's sales shops, while the shelves of its competitors were jammed with attractive American imports.

46See Alvin C. Gluek, Jr., "The Minnesota Route," *Beaver*, outfit 286 (spring, 1956), 44–50.

47Simpson to the Governor and Committee, 29 June 1855, H.B.C., Series A.12/7.

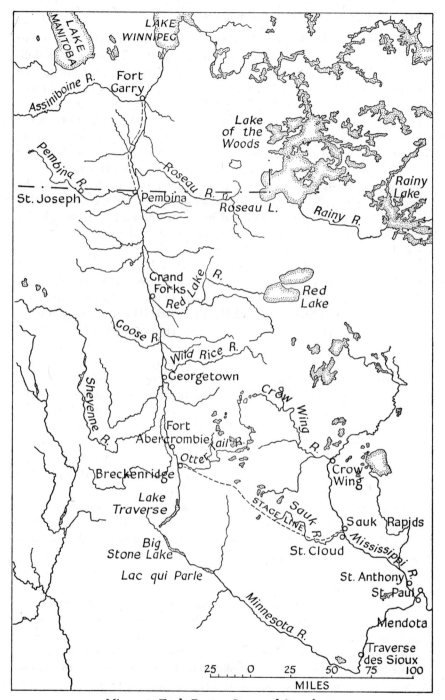

Minnesota Trade Routes—Stage and Steamboat

William Mactavish, the chief factor in charge of the Red River District, found himself in a hopeless situation. It had always been difficult for him to keep the York route going, let alone expand it. The route was so laborious and distasteful that only Indians and half-breeds would work in the brigades. Yet he dared not substitute his own men for the unreliable regulars, lest they, demoralized by the duty, jump both ship and the Company's service. Facing the present crisis, Mactavish discovered that he could not even get enough crews from the usual source of supply, and those who would work the boats demanded and got wage increases of 25 per cent and more. In desperation, he even tried and failed to get volunteers from the Royal Canadian Rifles. He fretted throughout the fall and by winter he had had enough. He drew up and submitted a small indent for his district to be imported *via* the United States during the coming summer.

After some consideration, the Governor and Committee authorized a trial shipment of about forty tons to be sent from England to Rupert's Land, *via* New York and St. Paul. Once the decision had been reached, detailed planning quickly followed. The first step was to secure a man in New York City to receive and forward the goods. Simpson's choice there was Ramsay Crooks and he could not have made a better one. Crooks not only arranged with the Treasury Department to bond the Company's shipments through the United States but also managed, with the aid of Senator Rice, to get a St. Paul agency—the Burbank brothers—to receive and warehouse the merchandise. By early spring all arrangements had been made for the shipment: by sea to New York, by train and steamboat to St. Paul, and by the Company's own carts to Fort Garry. As it turned out, the shipments were staggered over the summer, but by mid-September the last of them had come safely into Mactavish's hands.

This success called for a further evaluation in the fall by Simpson of all the transportation routes from England to the Red River Settlement.[48] In making his assessment, he realized that York required relief in the form of another route; it was "no longer a question of relative costs, but of necessity." He made a comparison of the character and the cost (per hundredweight) of four different itineraries and came up with startling results: *via* York Factory, $8.67; *via* New York City and St. Paul, $5.85; *via* New Orleans and St. Paul, $4.00; and *via* Montreal and St. Paul, $5.25. Despite its cheapness, Simpson ruled out New Orleans because it was the least known and, with its transshipments, the most complicated. There was little to choose

[48]Simpson to the Secretary, 20 Oct. 1858, H.B.C., Series A.12/9.

between Montreal and New York. Freightage by either was approximately 35–40 per cent—or about $3,000 per year—less than the Hudson Bay–York Factory system. Montreal promised to be somewhat simpler in operation as well as being a bit less in cost. British shipping lines could act in concert with Canadian railways (the Grand Trunk and its rail and water connections) and thus eliminate agencies. But whatever the coastal point selected, St. Paul remained the linch-pin in the southern or Minnesota route.

Simpson's report convinced the Governor and Committee that the York route could not be materially enlarged and that the Minnesota route offered the only practical alternative. Therefore the Hudson's Bay Company went ahead with its plans for the coming (1859) season, cutting a transportation pattern that, with few variations, persisted for the next decade. The trading goods from England—about 120 tons in all—were shipped to Montreal, whence the Grand Trunk transported them by rail and water to St. Paul, *via* Collingwood, Milwaukee, and La Crosse.[49] The balance of the indent—approximately thirty tons—was composed of American goods and sent from New York City to St. Paul. There, the Burbank brothers, now officially named as "temporary" agents, were to transmit all the goods (English and American) to the Company's cart trains for the final overland journey to Fort Garry. There was a slight chance that the pattern might be altered and the long passage across the plains from St. Paul to Fort Garry cut in half. During the fall and winter, 1858–59, Simpson heard of several schemes for putting steamboats on the Red River, but he did not believe that a boat could be built and launched before the water dropped too low for navigation. If he were to use the river at all, he intended to build bateaux and float the merchandise downstream. But if a steamer were constructed in time and if it proved a success, Simpson meant to patronize it. With steam transportation on the Red, his cart trains would have to carry only half the distance, or from St. Paul to the Red River's head of navigation, and thus the capacity of the Minnesota route would be greatly increased while its costs declined.

To check the "ifs" in the new route and make final arrangements for the coming season, Simpson visited Minnesota in the spring and in the early summer of 1859. Each was a whirlwind visit, typical

[49]In later years, both Canadian and American systems (rail and water) were employed to carry English trade goods to St. Paul. However the Company was wedded to neither system, shifting back and forth according to its financial advantage.

of the man, but each was filled with decision-packed days. On the first occasion, he met with the Burbank brothers and came away, more convinced than ever that their work was being done more satisfactorily than the Company itself could do it. At the same time he learned that the *Anson Northup* was scheduled for a June launching, a date he thought much too late to insure a full season's navigation. None the less the reported tariff of 50 cents per hundredweight kept his interests alive. His work done in St. Paul, Simpson took the Woods Trail to Fort Garry and thence travelled to Norway House, where he met the Council of the Northern Department. By late June he was back again in Fort Garry and making last-minute changes in the Minnesota route. Now, the carts were to shuttle back and forth between St. Paul and Fort Abercrombie only; between Abercrombie and Fort Garry, bateaux (to be constructed on the spot) would carry the shipments on their last, one-way passage downstream. Nothing was decided about steam navigation, although Simpson knew by now of the *Anson Northup's* successful maiden voyage. He merely remarked upon its speed and cargo—and kept his mind open for further developments.

On his return through Minnesota in July, Simpson made another change—the most important to date—in the Company's new route, when he added the *Anson Northup* to the system. The addition was quite unplanned. When Simpson reached Fort Abercrombie, he found the vessel, but not her owner. The latter had just departed for St. Paul in order "to secure the freight of the Company's goods and any others he could obtain."[50] Northup had suddenly became a captain without any cargo. Believing that he held an invulnerable monopoly, the foolish fellow demanded freight rates ranging from $1.50 to $2.00 per hundredweight. The heroic figure of the winter had become summer's clown. He had not even enough money to run the ship. The little game ended when Simpson refused to pay and threatened to go ahead with his bateaux. The captain had to come to terms with the Company; without its patronage, his venture could never succeed. Simpson "induced" him to sell the *Anson Northup* to a secret partnership composed of himself (acting for the Hudson's Bay Company) and the Burbank brothers. The Company was and remained a secret, silent partner whose interests were best served by the fiction of American ownership. As the registered owners of the *Anson Northup*, the Burbanks allowed the Company to get around an American statute

[50]Simpson to the Governor and Committee, 18 July 1859, H.B.C., Series A.12/10.

that prohibited it from owning property in the United States. As operators of the line, they contracted to carry the Company's goods from Breckenridge to Fort Garry at not over 75 cents per hundred-weight. To all the world, the vessel was Burbank property, not another ship of the odious monopoly. The *Anson Northup* would carry freight for all the world too, but the scheduled and public rates (as revealed in the press of the time) were almost twice as great as those paid by the Company. All this, Simpson managed to do on the vague authority vested in him by London to expend "a moderate outlay toward the establishment of Steam navigation on [the] Red River."[51]

Before returning to Lachine, Sir George completed the final details of the Company's Minnesota system. One thousand acres of land were indirectly acquired on the east bank of the Red River and a post was established there ("Sheyenne"), which eventually bore the name of Georgetown. In the years to come, the operations of this station grew until it possessed dormitories, warehouses, and a saw and grist mill. It was meant to serve several purposes. With its grassland, Georgetown could supply the Company with forage for its cart teams. It was also the vital point of transshipment between overland and water carriage. In addition, the post permitted the Company to trade, without a licence, on American soil, reaching out for the casual Indian trader and forestalling Red River merchants en route to St. Paul. At the last minute, Simpson made one further change: the utilization of steamboat transportation from St. Anthony to Sauk Rapids. Now only the shortest length of the Minnesota route was overland. All the rest was either by rail or by water.

For its 1859 performance, the Minnesota route received high praise from its greatest critics, the Governor and Committee of the Hudson's Bay Company. All shipments reached Fort Garry within scheduled time and without damage. In London's opinion, the route was a "complete success" and would "to a certain extent" supersede Hudson Bay.[52] All arrangements, despite their seeming complications, had been more than satisfactory; the costs (per ton) from England to St. Paul had been £1/4/6 less than from England to York Factory.[53] London's satisfaction did not rest upon freightage alone. The Minnesota route saved time as well as money. With fewer days wasted in Transit the Company saved some 5 per cent in invisible interest

[51]*Ibid.*
[52]The Secretary to Simpson and the Councils of the Northern and Southern Departments, 18 April 1860, H.B.C., Series A.6/35.
[53]The Secretary to William Mactavish, 19 Aug. 1859, H.B.C., Series A.6/34.

charges and could, moreover, alter its indents in accordance with last-minute changes in fashion and style. The route trimmed costs all along the line and greatly improved the Company's competitive position in the fur trade. Furthermore, it allowed the Company to import a greater volume and variety of general merchandise to the Red River Settlement. As a result, its sales shops were well stocked and attracted crowds, while those of independent merchants were comparatively deserted, unable to compete in price, quality, or quantity. And there was one other advantage that particularly appealed to Simpson. With the opening of the Minnesota route, the Company could shut down the canoe route from Montreal to Fort Garry at a considerable saving; and once the forests reclaimed the portage trails, prospective interlopers from Canada would be deterred from attempting to reach Rupert's Land.

In the original planning of the transportation system between St. Paul and Fort Garry, the Hudson's Bay Company had wisely intended to have it both manned and managed by their own servants. Simpson distrusted Americans "whose desire to push business frequently exceeds their means to fulfill their engagements" and the Governor and Committee wished no outside group to learn of their intimate business affairs. But the Burbank brothers soon changed Simpson's mind and he, in turn, overrode London's objections to a different system. Temporary agents in 1858, the Burbanks had become secret partners in the following year, and as the summer of 1859 began to fade away J. C. Burbank suggested to Simpson that his firm and the Company could profitably expand their economic alliance. Many letters from St. Paul to Lachine kept the subject alive until Burbank could follow up his correspondence with a personal visit to Simpson in November. It was a short trip that paid off for the American, if not the Company. With speed and skill, the adroit Yankee sold the old gentleman on the merits of an all-American line from St. Paul to Fort Garry.

Burbank surprised Simpson with a proposition calling for an answer in three days. Unable to write London for advice, the latter bound the Company to a fateful, four-year (1860–1863) contract in which the American firm agreed to ship about 250 tons (or 5,000 pieces) of trade goods annually from St. Paul to Fort Garry at the rate of $4 per hundredweight.[54] Although this was a greater rate than the Company now paid, Simpson argued that "the contract price of $4 per 100 lbs. differ[ed] little from the estimate of $3 per 'piece' of 90 @ 100 lbs."[55]

---

[54]Dated 3 Nov. 1859 and enclosed in Simpson to the Secretary, 11 Nov. 1859, H.B.C., Series A.12/10.

[55]Simpson to the Secretary, 11 Nov. 1859, *ibid.*

In the scheme of things, the *Anson Northup* remained the joint property of both parties. The Minnesota Stage Company would be the exclusive owner of the projected overland service but, to aid in its establishment, Simpson generously advanced $5,000 at a low rate of interest. These and other terms made up a contract that was primarily conceived and drawn up in the interests of the Burbank brothers. It is strange that Simpson did not see this. He was convinced that, without such an arrangement, the Company would have to construct and maintain its own wagon road between Sauk Rapids and the Red River —that, with it, all such costs would be assumed by the Burbanks, who, in turn, could shift them to the state or federal government. For the moment, he did not intend to make any further reductions in the Company's share of the Minnesota system; but, for the future, he urged London to limit its transport activities to Rupert's Land as soon as it could "safely entrust the whole of our [American] transport to contractors."[56]

London confirmed Simpson's contract with the greatest reluctance. The Governor and Committee sagely questioned the good sense of binding the Company to the shipment of a fixed volume of goods over a definite period of time when the Minnesota route was so new and in such a state of flux. However the chief flaw in the contract escaped the notice of both Simpson and the Company. Although heavily subsidized by the Company and given access to its business affairs, the Burbanks had not been bound from dealing with the Company's competitors. There was no fine print restricting or governing their activities in any way. This was a serious omission; without such a clause the contract created an incompatible alliance leading to mutual incriminations and the eventual end of the partnership.

The once amicable relations between the Burbanks and the Hudson's Bay Company slowly corroded. Also left undefined in the contract had been that fundamental difference between them—a difference that was well explained by an ex-stockholder of the Minnesota Stage Company: "We wanted immigration and trade; they did not want immigration nor mails nor any one to trade in the Hudson Bay Company's territory but themselves. The expectation that the country would be opened proved a delusion."[57] Though agents of the Company, the Burbanks continued their own forwarding and commission business. They catered to many private citizens in the Red River Settlement; their fleet of common carriers was patronized by many free traders of Rupert's Land. Under the circumstances, the Hudson's Bay Company was not

[56]*Ibid.*
[57]Blakeley, "Opening of the Red River of the North," p. 61.

only annoyed but often felt that it was not as well treated as its competitors; and all its suspicions were confirmed in 1861, when a Burbank captain accepted the shipment of a free trader but had no room for the Company. On the other hand, the Burbanks also had a justifiable grievance. When the Company failed to ship the stipulated 250 tons in 1860, J. C. Burbank filed a claim against the Company and was rewarded with the dishonest reply that the Company had intended the tonnage to be only a maximum, not a minimum load! Another and constant irritation was the steamboat. When one partner wished to keep it running, the other wanted it laid up. The sum of it all was that the Burbanks grew bitter and dissatisfied in dealing with a giant who broke promises, while the Company was convinced that its partners were "acting more with a view to the interests of the Minnesota Stage Company than of the Steamboat Company."[58] Both parties were glad to sever relations in 1863.

Despite the troubles between them, the Minnesota route developed by the Burbank brothers and the Hudson's Bay Company was completely established within its first three years and remained unchanged until the railroads began to eat into its structure after the Civil War. Though not a simple system, it worked surprisingly well. Trade goods were brought upriver by the Burbanks from St. Paul/St. Anthony to St. Cloud and then transferred to overload carriers bound for Georgetown. The Burbanks' fleet of covered wagons coursed from water's edge to water's edge, tying together the traffic of both rivers. Travelling in trains, each with its own captain, cook, and crew, the wagons rolled westward to the Red River at the rate of fifteen miles per day. At this junction, the cargo was shifted from land to water and borne to Fort Garry by the *Anson Northup* and her two successors: the *Pioneer*, merely the *Anson Northup* refurbished and re-named in 1861, and the *International*, a new vessel launched in the spring of 1862.

The Minnesota route completely altered the transportation system of the Hudson's Bay Company. Once in use, the route improved annually, and with improvements, its use expanded. Time wasted in transit through North America was reduced. Freightage during the formative years, 1859–62, was cut to within one-third of its original basis. Long before statistics could lend him factual support, Sir George Simpson was convinced that the route would change his Company's way of life. "Fort Garry," he prophesied in 1860, "must become the Depot for all the Districts in the Southern part of the Territory, the

[58]William Mactavish to the Secretary, 22 Aug. 1862, H.B.C., Series A.11/97.

outfit to York Factory being limited to the supply of the posts in the Bay and the country north of the Saskatchewan."[59] In 1860 the indent for the Saskatchewan District was sent over the Minnesota route and in the following year, Swan River's was added to the list. Thus began the inevitable process by which Fort Garry displaced York Factory.[60] As the southern route improved—when, for example, the Hudson's Bay Company extended the use of steam navigation to Lake Winnipeg and the Saskatchewan River—the northern deteriorated. By 1862 Rupert's Land had two trunk lines and two central depots. By 1875 there was really only one: Fort Garry and the southern or Minnesota route. By then, Fort Garry received the outfits for all the interior districts of Rupert's Land and managed all their returns; to York was left itself— and a highly uncertain suzerainty over the bayside posts. Fort Garry had become what York was, the "capital" of Rupert's Land.

Although shipments over the Minnesota route consisted largely of Hudson's Bay Company indents and returns, there was always plenty of room for the goods of independent traders and merchants of St. Paul and the Red River Settlement. The *Anson Northup* (and the *Pioneer*) carried up to forty tons of cargo and the *International* nearly sixty; of this tonnage, the Company usually had well over half, with the balance divided among various private individuals. While the squeal of the Red River cart was never drowned out—silence awaited the coming of the railroads—none the less the proportionate volume carried by this humble conveyance declined. If the Burbanks freighted merchandise at a cost exceeding the cart, they did so with greater dispatch and regularity. For orders in excess of 2,000 pounds from St. Paul to Fort Garry, their published rates (in 1862) were $4.80 per hundredweight; for lesser amounts approximately $5.[61] Of that sum, about one-third paid for the river carriage from Georgetown to Fort Garry. As a consignment and commission house, the Burbanks also transported British goods, bringing them all the way from Liverpool in forty to fifty days for $8.50 per hundredweight.[62] With these services, the Burbank brothers conducted a considerable business in the Red River Settlement.

The Burbank line catered as eagerly to passengers as it did to merchants. Twice a week, their stages left St. Paul in the dawn for a

[59]Simpson to Edward Ellice, 26 Jan. 1860, Ellice Papers (microfilm), P.A.C.
[60]See Alvin C. Gluek, Jr., "The Fading Glory," *Beaver*, outfit 288 (winter, 1957), 50–5.
[61]In 1860 the Burbanks charged $6, regardless of the weight involved. See rates published in the *Nor'-Wester*, 28 June and 28 Sept. 1860 and 5 March 1862.
[62]*Nor'-Wester*, 17 March 1863.

jolting, four-day run to Fort Abercrombie, where all passengers going through to Fort Garry had to change—and as often wait—for the steamboat. Accommodations on the early boats were scarcely regal. One captain of the *Anson Northup* characterized his craft as "nothing better than a lumbering old pine basket . . . which you have to handle as gingerly as a hamper of eggs."[63] Even when the ship was re-built and re-cast as the *Pioneer*, the most she had to offer as quarters were four small staterooms and the ordinary open berths in the main saloon. However the *International* afforded a more glamorous passage. On her maiden voyage to Fort Garry in the summer of 1862, she was crowded with Americans bound for the Cariboo diggings in British Columbia. A reporter from the *Nor'-Wester* claimed (25 June 1862) that, had it not been for the exciting talk about the new gold discoveries, "Why, some of our old stagers on board would be fairly killed off with ennui and high-feeding. . . . Sleeping and eating and sleeping—the hours glide quietly by."

One thing seems certain from this point in time: the passengers riding the Burbank line probably got their money's worth—if they figured their fares on a mile-per-hour basis. Passenger rates were more reasonable than the length of the voyage. A one-way fare, cabin class, was originally advertised at $35, but after 1861, it had slipped to $30, while a round trip cost about $50. The Minnesota Stage Company nearly always maintained a regular schedule from St. Paul to Fort Abercrombie. Yet it must be remembered that they possessed no super-highways; a heavy rainfall could convert clay roads into muck within hours and delay the stages for days. Rain was always a controlling factor, governing both overland and water transportation. Although the Burbanks advertised fortnightly trips between Fort Abercrombie and Fort Garry, a round trip could be made in a week if the water were high—or the vessel might be five weeks late. Eighty miles below Georgetown lay the Goose River rapids, a constant worry to every captain. Despite a wing dam built to raise the water level, the depth never seemed great enough to guarantee passage. Throughout its length, the Red River wandered like a snake; and once a vessel was under way, there were few places where it could turn around. Indeed, normal navigation was so difficult that the *Pioneer* employed a stern sweep in addition to its rudder.[64] The amazing thing is that, with all its natural obstructions, service was maintained on the Red River until the beginning of the Indian Wars in the fall of 1862.

[63]*Ibid.*, 28 Sept. 1860.
[64]Joseph J. Hargrave, *Red River* (Montreal, 1871), p. 57.

IV

The effect of the Minnesota route upon the fortunes of the Hudson's Bay Company is very clear. Less apparent is the effect upon Minnesota-Assiniboia relations. It is possible only to make certain generalizations, none of which rests upon a solid foundation. Certainly the new route gave a decided fillip to Minnesota's "nationalist" spirit; and it aroused Canada's nationalist feelings in proportion to the fears awakened there by stories of American penetration into Rupert's Land. Undoubtedly, trade between St. Paul and the Red River Settlement was stimulated; and, with its growth, other more intimate relationships developed. Also, the route re-awakened Minnesota's frontier movement, encouraging the pioneer and the speculator to take up land along the north-south axis.

There was a very close relation between Minnesota's "Manifest Destiny" and Canada's nationalist spirit. It was somewhat like psalm-reading: whenever one voiced an expansionist sentiment regarding Rupert's Land, there would be an echoing response from the other. Many were the comments in Canada upon the *Anson Northup* and the Americanization of Rupert's Land. When the Toronto *Globe* printed an article on the subject, the St. Paul *Pioneer and Democrat* (19 July 1859) hastened to point out that Minnesota's designs were commercial only: ". . . instead of Sharpe's rifles, Bowies, and Colts, our filibusters will go armed with the steam engine, printing press, and patent reapers and mowers. With these formidable implements . . . and a complete commercial reciprocity, we will make British Canada as much tributary to Minnesota as if the Star Spangled banner floated from the flag staff of Fort Garry instead of the red cross of St. George." Editorializing like this did little to quiet Canadian fears.

The *Nor'-Wester*, a newspaper run by Canadians in Red River to enlighten their countrymen back East, remarked time and again upon the dangers of Americanization. Article after article referred to the development of trade and transportation between Minnesota and Assiniboia, "producing sympathies which ere long might result in a demand for annexation to the United States."[65] Many were reprinted in Canadian journals, thereby quickening an interest in the Northwest, but in Minnesota they produced the same old response. Minnesota was interested in British trade, not land. As James W. Taylor wrote a

[65]28 Sept. 1860.

Canadian acquaintance, Thomas D'Arcy McGee, "We exclude altogether the idea or term of 'Annexation'—we have learned a better word 'Reciprocity.' "[66] He also reminded his friend, however, that if Britain failed to colonize Rupert's Land Minnesotans could not be expected "to imitate such neglect."

It is easier to measure the volume of trade than to record the exact degree of nationalist temper. In the commercial exchange between Minnesota and Assiniboia after the opening of the southern route by the Hudson's Bay Company, it is evident that the quantity of goods and/or money conveyed in either direction grew. The increase is measurable in many ways: customs reports and receipts (or complaints about the lack of receipts); fur sales in St. Paul and purchases in Red River; investigations conducted by special agents of the United States Treasury; and innumerable statements from current periodicals. No one index is complete; none gives a thorough accounting; but taken altogether they show a large and undeniable growth in the Red River trade.

St. Paul became the centre of commerce for the Red River Settlement. Recorded fur sales, after a dip occasioned by the Panic of 1857, climbed higher than ever.[67] It is true that such sales included furs of both British and American origin, but by far the greater proportion of them came from the British Northwest. Moreover the Red River traders carried down cash as well as furs and eagerly emptied their pockets in the stores of St. Paul. The pages of the *Nor'-Wester*, 1859–62, were peppered with advertisements of St. Paul bankers, jewellers, druggists, hotel men, clothiers, grocers, and hardware men—all in addition to the furriers. In the fall of 1859 two carts alone hauled over $1,200 worth of clothing away from one store and forced the delighted proprietor to make a second and unexpected fall order.[68] As the 1860's drew near Red River traders were reportedly spending well over $100,000 in St. Paul every season.

[66]6 June 1862, Taylor Papers.
[67]St. Paul *Press*, 29 Aug. 1863, presented the following statistics:

Year	Sales ($)	Year	Sales ($)
1844	1,400	1858	161,022
1845	3,000	1859	150,000
1846	5,000	1860	185,165
1850	15,000	1861	198,000
1855	40,000	1862	200,000
1856	97,253	1863	250,000
1857	182,491		

[68]St. Paul *Pioneer and Democrat*, 4 Oct. 1859.

The structural nature of the trade between Minnesota and Assiniboia changed with new developments in transportation and mounting traffic on the old Red River trails. The role once played by large wholesale and retail houses was diminished and their place gradually assumed by other forms of business. Culver & Farrington and Kittson too, "the leading names engaged in this overland trade,"[69] continued to fill orders, large and small, for the Red River businessman. Indeed, Kittson's general trade did not differ substantially from the early days when he had supplied Sinclair and McDermot with American manufactures. But by the late 'fifties it had become pleasant as well as profitable for the small buyer from Red River to cross the plains to St. Paul and make his own selections in the specialty shops there. Once regular lines of communication had been established—both for postal and transport purposes—forwarding and commission merchants came into existence, serving Rupert's Land and stealing away a lot of trade that formerly had gone to firms like Culver & Farrington. The foremost of these concerns was J. C. Burbank and Company, which specialized in forwarding British and Canadian goods to a large Red River clientele; and in another decade, James J. Hill would begin his climb to economic prominence by pursuing the same line of business.

At the other end, in the Red River Settlement, Americans opened up retail outlets. Kittson's establishment, a typical Yankee store, had pioneered in this field, having been in existence since the middle 'fifties. When he retired in the spring of 1862 and entered the service of the Hudson's Bay Company, his position as the primary American storekeeper was taken over by St. Paul's Alexander Paul, "the princely merchant of St. Boniface."[70] Paul and his countrymen were initially regarded as hard-dealing, fast-talking Yankees, but in time they were accepted and their stores freely patronized. Alongside these general stores were the places of an increasing number of St. Paul furriers who either operated their businesses through local agents or personally visited the settlement at regular buying intervals. As the years passed by, the American population in Red River grew, eventually to rival in size the Canadians who began migrating to Rupert's Land in the late 'fifties. In the nature of things, the American outlet grew increasingly important to the Red River Settlement. The variety of imports carried up from St. Paul was astounding. Though the old lines persisted—

[69]James W. Taylor to H. Cobb, Secretary of the Treasury, 29 March 1860, Letters and Reports to the Treasury Department, N.A.

[70]*Nor'-Wester*, 11 Sept. 1862. In his first (1861) season, Paul's business reached a reported height between $20,000 and $30,000, *ibid.*, 28 May 1862.

groceries, clothing, hardware, and the like—new items appeared every year. When Robert Tait married and built a new home for his bride in the settlement, "All the oak and walnut woodwork for the house, and the sashes and the doors and the walnut furniture . . . were brought across the plains from St. Paul. . . ."[71] Andrew McDermot imported a steam mill in 1860, having already acquired the mill stones in the previous year; a newfangled pump, one of the settlement's "seven wonders," was imported; and fancy cutters were introduced to rival the carioles. In short, Red River began to taste the fruits of the industrial world.

One citizen of Red River credited the agricultural advance which had recently taken place in Assiniboia to the importation of American farm machinery. Orders for agricultural implements poured into St. Paul. In 1860, J. C. Burbank and Company sent a shipment valued at nearly $5,000.[72] Even the *Nor'Wester*, which feared the American connection, was forced to remark (15 October 1860) upon this feat: "For full thirty years, they [the farmers of Red River] sat in darkness; but at last a ray of light, like the feeble beams of a distant star came struggling through the gloom. . . ." In 1856, Henry Yule Hind, the Canadian explorer, had recorded only two reapers and eight threshers in the entire settlement;[73] in 1860, the *Anson Northup* alone freighted to Fort Garry twelve power threshers, twelve reapers, fourteen fanning mills, and sixty-one plows.[74] It will never be known exactly how many implements were conveyed northward by other means; but this much seems certain: by 1861, St. Paul had revolutionized agriculture in the Red River Settlement.

The development in trade and transportation revived Minnesota's northwestern frontier movement; the speculator and the pioneer were but a step or two behind the merchant and the freighter. That settlement should be thus stimulated was not unexpected. In 1859 St. Paul's "boosters" had prophesied the pioneering powers of Burbank's stage coach and Northup's steamboat and their predictions quickly came to pass. During the next two or three years proprietors and speculators, possessing sites adjacent to the stage route or located on the banks of the Red, energetically advertised their landed wares; independent pioneers pre-empted more modest holdings; and both classes of men

[71]W. J. Healy, *Women of Red River* (Winnipeg, 1923), 91–2.

[72]*Nor'-Wester*, 28 July 1860, quoting from the St. Paul *Pioneer and Democrat*, 29 June 1860.

[73]Canada, Provincial Secretary's Office, *Report on the Exploration between Lake Superior and the Red River Settlement* (Toronto, 1858), pp. 348–9.

[74]*Nor'-Wester*, 15 Oct. 1860.

were sustained by the belief that the dynamic interest in all the Anglo-American Northwest would trigger another real estate boom.

The Breckenridge proprietors were more enthusiastic than most, for their site possessed great promise. It was situated at the head of steam navigation on the Red River; power was provided by the tumbling waters of the Otter Tail River, which flowed into the Red near Breckenridge; and the town site itself lay astride the Burbank-Hudson's Bay Company route. But above all, it was the opening of the stage-and-steam line that inspired Breckenridge. Its chief promoter was George F. Brott, a "professional" town-builder whose successes included St. Cloud and Sauk Rapids. Early in 1859 he gathered his business associates together—among whom was Governor Sibley—to consider the best means of developing their property. Their plans were cast on a grand scale. During the following summer a hotel was raised, a costly structure of impressive proportions. A saw mill, its machinery freighted all the way from Connecticut, was even more expensive and said to be "one of the largest and best in the State."[75] In these and numerous other ways the proprietors fitted out Breckenridge for the boom to come.

Other men were similarly stricken with "town site fever," drawing the frontier closer and closer to the last remaining Indian territory in Minnesota. County after county was carved out of the northwestern plains. Otter Tail County was organized in 1858 and, within a year, claimed five settlements within its borders. South of it and along the stage line, tiny hamlets appeared wherever the Burbanks put up way stations or speculators stacked up their dreams. One such town was Alexandria, a half-way house on the road from St. Cloud to Breckenridge. It came into existence in the late 'fifties, stimulated by the stage line and inspired by proprietors. The spring of 1859 saw the beginnings of a hotel and a saw mill, the harbingers of civilization; and by mid-summer nearly 150 people had settled there—"the extreme outpost of settlement on the new road this side of the Red River Valley."[76]

Pioneers of German-American extraction, the "lager-whisky" mixture, moved steadily westward from St. Cloud and wound their way up the valley of the Sauk River. These migrants were drawn by the promise of future transportation and led on in pursuit of the arable land lying below Minnesota's tangle of swamps, rocks, and conifers in the north and northeast. Throughout this latest "garden spot" of the Minnesota frontier were to be seen claim stakes and shanties. Wagonloads of families pushed forward, literally by the hundreds, and "settled along

[75]St. Paul *Pioneer and Democrat*, 24 Sept. 1859. [76]*Ibid.*, 8 July 1859.

the road from St. Cloud to Breckenridge, while many of more than ordinary enterprise have planted themselves on the banks of the Red River."[77] By 1861 Minnesota's agricultural frontier extended nearly to Alexandria.

Federal surveyors tried to match the movements of the immigrants. By 1858 surveying parties had reached the Red River Valley, and by this time St. Paul's surveyor general was convinced that some of the land should be subdivided as soon as possible, for much of it was already being pre-empted. In his opinion, the entire block of townships, from the Mississippi to the Red, would be quickly filled because of "the immediate opening up of the Red River country and the trade with the British possessions."[78] For the most part, his pleas and those of his successors had little effect. Year after year, the St. Paul office importuned the federal land commissioner to enlarge its field work, but although the land commissioner generally supported the requests, an economy-minded Congress was never generous during the depression years. Furthermore it could always be shown that there was plenty of vacant land in southern Minnesota, surveyed and subdivided, which had not been taken up. Nevertheless, by the fall of 1859 the southern half of the Red River Valley had been surveyed, with parts in townships and some subdivided; and two years later a surveyor's map of the valley showed a tier of townships stretching all the way north to the Wild Rice River.[79] A land office was established at Otter Tail City in 1858 but no sales were reported until two years later, when the office began to render very small returns. These records did not mirror the process of settlement, however. They failed to show transactions in scrip; nor did they, quite obviously, take into account land assumed by squatters. There were pioneers like Wright, who squatted down on the banks of the Otter Tail River at "Dayton," farmed forty acres, and lived with his family in an "unfinished log house."[80] Behind him, the central frontier cut out a salient along the valley of the Sauk River. Ahead, to the north and down the Red River Valley, lay nothing but a few more outposts, other "Daytons" manned by the other "Wrights" who had dared to outdistance their contemporaries and risk their lives in Indian country.

[77]*Ibid.*, 5 Jan. 1860.
[78]Annual Report of the General Land Office, 1858, Report from the Surveyor General, St. Paul, 11 Oct. 1858, *Senate Document No. 1*, 35th Cong., 2nd Sess., Serial 974, pp. 160–76.
[79]Alfred J. Hill's geographical notebook number 16, Hill Papers, M.H.S.
[80]St. Paul *Pioneer and Democrat*, 8 Sept. 1859.

By 1861 Minnesota apparently stood on the threshold of her destiny. Trade with the British Northwest had grown in accordance with the "recognized law of western growth, that the extension of facilities of transportation creates commerce."[81] And as the concomitant of developments in both trade and transportation, Minnesota's agricultural frontier had moved out along the Sauk River and started to edge down the Red River Valley. A new era seemed at hand, promising either a commercial empire or, perhaps, even another Oregon.

[81]*Ibid.*, 15 Feb. 1859.

Chapter 6. The Stagnant Civil War Years, 1861–1865

THE WAR YEARS ENCLOSED AN ERA OF RELATIVE STAGNATION IN MINNESOTA'S history, a period within which men accomplished far more in their dreams than in reality. From the fall of Fort Sumter until Appomattox, Minnesotans fought in two wars, the Civil and the Sioux. Although the Sioux uprising of 1862 spent itself within a month or so, memories of those bloody August days prolonged the evacuation of farms and homes everywhere on the frontier. And unlike many of her sisters in the Union, Minnesota realized little economic gain from the Civil War.

Despite the wars and the bad temper of Anglo-American relations, Minnesota's trade with the British Northwest grew. Commerce was infinitely more important to Minnesotans than the *Trent* affair or the St. Albans raid. Led by James W. Taylor, the state sought to extend the Reciprocity Treaty to the British Northwest and then to save its life. Led by Taylor and others, the state tried to expand the existing means of communication with Rupert's Land and create other channels. Neither effort really succeeded. None the less, trade and commerce with Rupert's Land mounted and the lines of transportation were improved. But in the broad, international relation between Minnesota and Rupert's Land, it was the Hudson's Bay Company and the people of the Red River Settlement who lent it strength, not the prophets of Minnesota's manifest destiny.

I

In the late summer of 1862, the Sioux of the Minnesota Agency left their reservations without warning and began a month's blood-letting that suspended the movement of the Minnesota frontier. Death stopped frontiersmen and their families by the hundreds, and fear drove thousands more into retreat. Everywhere, advance outposts and isolated farms came to the end of a short and precarious life. "The panic was general," wrote the Sioux agent in describing to Washington the work of his former charges, "a belt of country nearly, if not quite, two hundred miles in length, and, on an average, fifty miles wide, was *entirely abandoned. . . .* What were, a few days before, prosperous frontier settlements, were now scenes of disturbance, desolation, ruin, and death."[1]

Though the Sioux concentrated their efforts upon the Minnesota River Valley, they lifted enough scalps in the valley of the Sauk to induce mass hysteria. In the unreasoning panic that followed the first murders, settlers believed the rumours that even the Chippewas were about to join their old enemies against a common white foe. Within three weeks of the first raid, the frontier salient in the northwest had shrunk to within a morning's ride of St. Cloud. Men's hearts remained filled with terror long after danger had passed. They were not comforted when the military expeditions, 1862–64, either captured the majority of the Sioux warriors or drove them into exile far out on the Dakota plains. They felt little security in the presence of volunteer scouts who roamed the Big Woods in pursuit of the bounties given out for Sioux scalps or bodies. The average Minnesota frontiersman was not a man of unlimited courage. The memory of 1862 persisted. During the summer of 1863 some Sioux returned to the Sauk Valley, killing a few people and inspiring fearful rumours. Fields continued to lie untended and cattle roamed at will throughout the region. A wide swath had been abandoned along the valley, over which fear had "fallen . . . like the cold shadow of an eclipse."[2] Westward from St. Cloud were to be found only "deserted houses or wrecks of houses . . . that had been noisy taverns and stage stations a year ago. . . ."[3]

[1]Annual Report of the Commissioner of Indian Affairs, 1863, *Senate Executive Document No. 1*, 38th Cong., 1st Sess., Serial 1182, p. 405.
[2]St. Paul *Pioneer and Democrat*, 12 Sept. 1863.
[3]*Ibid.*, 22 Sept. 1863.

In making his annual estimate, the Surveyor General of St. Paul informed the federal Land Commissioner in 1862 that it seemed useless to extend his work beyond the western lines already established, "as no demand for land can be looked for in that section, or hardly, indeed, in any part of the State. . . ," until the Sioux had been controlled.[4] The mood was pessimistic but the forecast was accurate. A correspondent for the *Nor'-Wester*, traversing the Sauk Valley in 1864, found the region still morbidly scarred. Mile after mile of his progress was marked by signs of death, destruction, or panic: ruined homes, abandoned fields, and once comfortable hostelries that now housed soldiers instead of settlers. Here and there, he noted that a few men had returned to their homes, but though the valley was slowly being repopulated, it was done so "in a great measure in fear and trembling, and only by those who . . . [were] well armed, for there . . . [was] yet considerable danger of another Sioux raid."[5]

Although physical danger from the Sioux was slight by 1865, a strange, irrational "Sioux-phobia" still haunted Minnesotans. In June the St. Paul *Press* started a statewide campaign for a "Blood-hound Fund," asking its readers to send contributions to the governor; and enough money was collected to send some one into the South and bring back half a dozen dogs. Though the Sioux had already been driven out of the state, the effects of their uprising could never be told by merely counting dead men. It was fear, more than death or danger, that checked Minnesota's march towards the Red River Valley.

Fear was not the only impediment in the northwestward advance of the Minnesota frontier. Throughout the era, 1861–65, Minnesotans waged two wars—against the Sioux brave and Johnny Reb—and the resultant drain on the state's manpower was staggering. It was estimated that about 20,000 men enlisted or were drafted to serve in the Union Army.[6] Put such statistics into their context and the numbers become meaningful. According to the federal census, Minnesota had scarcely more than 172,000 people in 1860; and according to the Adjutant General, there were approximately 24,000 men in the state who were liable for military service, that is, counting all white, able-

[4]Report from Surveyor General, St. Paul, 10 Oct. 1862, Annual Report of the General Land Office, 1862, *House Executive Document No. 1*, 37th Cong., 3rd Sess., Serial 1157, p. 84.

[5]"Wayside Jottings" (St. Cloud, 20 June 1864) published in the *Nor'-Wester*, 18 Aug. 1864.

[6]Annual message of the Governor of Minnesota, Stephen Miller, 4 Jan. 1865. Reprinted in full by the St. Paul *Press*, 5 Jan. 1865.

bodied males between the ages of eighteen and forty-five.[7] How could George Brott's Breckenridge project have succeeded when most of his men enlisted in 1861 and the few that were left were killed by the Sioux in the following year?[8] St. Cloud and Stearns County, which formed the economic mainspring of the Sauk Valley, furnished more than their quota of men for the Union Army in 1862 and were left with idle farm machinery and unharvested wheat fields.[9] In addition to these recruits, many hundreds of other Minnesotans either fought under Generals Sibley and Sully in their long campaigns against the Sioux or served locally as volunteer scouts.

The Panic of 1857, the Civil War, and the Sioux uprising had effectively braked the northwestward movement of Minnesota's frontier; and in the wreckage strewn about by these disasters could be found many a personal fortune. Not all men were as lucky or perceiving as George Brott, who "went east before the end of the Civil War, loaded a steamer with supplies for the South, steamed around to New Orleans, and there patched up his shattered fortunes."[10] When Henry McKenty, a well-known St. Paul realtor, committed suicide in 1869, he died penniless. He had never recovered from the Panic of 1857. The sympathy extended to his mourners by the St. Paul *Press* (11 August 1869) was based upon an understanding of the times: ". . . times were hard and dull; the war came, and the Indian War on top of that, to make them harder and duller. He could not even make a living at the business."

Although the Sioux had no quarrel with the British, they injured or inconvenienced both the Red River Settlement and the Hudson's Bay Company. With terror and death as their tools, they temporarily "derailed" the Minnesota route and isolated the settlement. American stage drivers were slain and their way stations burned out or deserted; the white population throughout the American half of the Red River Valley retreated. In the southern end of the valley, those fortunate enough to escape the initial onslaught were holed up in Fort Abercrombie; in the north, the people of Pembina either fled to Fort Garry or took the longer path to safety at St. Paul. It was mid-October before communication lines could be partially and informally resumed, and no regular mail delivery existed between Fort Garry and St. Paul for more than two months.

[7]Minnesota, *Journal of the House of Representatives, 1859–1860*, pp. 793–4.

[8]D. S. B. Johnston, "A Red River Townsite Speculation in 1857," *Minnesota Historical Society Collections*, XV, 433–4.

[9]St. Paul *Pioneer and Democrat*, 28 Aug. 1862.

[10]Johnston, "A Red River Townsite Speculation in 1857," pp. 433–4.

And yet both time and good fortune came to the aid of the Hudson's Bay Company in 1862. They lost no men and suffered relatively little property damage because of the Sioux uprising. The transportation season was nearly at an end when the Sioux struck and most of the Company's indents (for the districts of Saskatchewan, Swan River, and Lac la Pluie) arrived safely at Fort Garry. Had the Indians attacked in June, they might have closed the Minnesota route for the entire summer and seriously injured the Company. As it turned out, although the Company's chief traders had to abandon Georgetown, they were able to carry off most of the movable property. The *International,* however, was of no use to them. The water below Georgetown had fallen too low for navigation, and the steamer had to be unloaded, turned about, and brought back to Fort Abercrombie, where it was berthed throughout the following season. Escape, for the traders and their goods, was made in a barge and whatever wagons were available.

The barge floated uneventfully down to Fort Garry but the wagon train ran into opposition as soon as it reached Grand Forks. At first glance, it would appear that the characters in this minor melodrama were strangely confused. The Indians were Chippewas and the leader of the Hudson's Bay train was Norman W. Kittson. The latter had been recently hired by the Governor of Rupert's Land and miraculously transformed from the Company's worst gadfly into one of its honoured chief traders. The role of the Chippewas is less clear. They had gathered in the vicinity in order to treat with American commissioners for the cession of their lands in the Red River Valley. The meeting never took place, for when the commissioners reached St. Cloud on August en route to the treaty grounds, the Sioux rising had already occurred and further progress was out of the question. The longer the Chippewas waited, the more disgruntled they became; but it was only pure chance that when they finally broke camp, Kittson's train crossed their path. The irate Indians pillaged his wagons of approximately $10,000 worth of goods (or about one-tenth of the cargo) and then confiscated and ate a good proportion of his cattle.

The news of these disturbances puzzled the Hudson's Bay Company. Had they avoided the Sioux only to clash with the Chippewas? Ought they to consider opening an alternate route or should they try to increase the capacity of the Hudson Bay line? An interview with Kittson only deepened William Mactavish's despair. "I fear," he wrote London, "that the St. Paul route for some time to come will not be safe for the transport of goods."[11] Kittson disagreed. He believed that

[11] 30 Sept. 1862, H.B.C., Series A.11/97.

the Sioux would be quickly expelled from Minnesota and that the Chippewas, the chief danger to the Company's welfare, would soon be mollified by getting the cession they wanted. Both men were partially right. Kittson's predictions came true and, in theory, the Minnesota route was soon as safe as it had ever been. But fear, not theories, governed the actions of J. C. Burbank and Company. In their opinion, the route was not safe and, as a consequence, it was not utilized in its usual way until 1865.

Much of the blame for the subsequent damage done the Minnesota route could be laid at the doorstep of the Burbanks. In March of 1863 an advertisement appeared in the *Nor'-Wester* announcing that, beginning in May, they would again carry both passengers and freight from St. Paul to Fort Garry. Notice was also given that American troops would be stationed at Georgetown, Grand Forks, and Pembina. In late April the editors of the *Nor'-Wester* said they were ready and asked why the Burbanks had not started. Part of the answer was presented in a second (23 May 1863) advertisement. Because General Sibley could not spare troops either to man the wayside posts or provide an escort, they now planned to run their lines no further than the Red River. But the rest of the answer had already been revealed to the Hudson's Bay Company. The Burbanks did not want to risk men, horses, and wagons on the road between St. Cloud and Georgetown and had asked the Company to regard the Sioux war as an act of God which released them from all contractual obligations.

For the Company, the whole arrangement with the Burbanks had become a "nightmare . . . without any morning in prospect."[12] The season of 1863 must have been very trying. A considerable amount of the outgoing 1862 shipment still lay in the customs sheds at Milwaukee; and although the brothers themselves were unable to clear it, they blamed the Company for failing to meet the tonnage requirements stipulated in the original contract. Clearly enough, Sioux Indians might release the Burbanks from their obligations, but contrary customs officers in the United States could not free the Company. This, however, was a minor irritation. The Company's chief objection to Simpson's "blind bargain" with the brothers was that they provided indirect competition and were aided thereby because of their knowledge of the Company's business. To cap their record of double-dealing and mismanagement, the Burbanks had ordered the *International* to be laid up at Fort Abercrombie at the end of the 1862 season. In the following spring, the Red River reverted to normal; its water level

[12]Dallas to Edward Ellice, 10 March 1863, Ellice Papers (microfilm), P.A.C.

dropped and the vessel was trapped in the shallows above Goose Rapids for the entire summer. Nothing remained for the Company but to manage the Minnesota route by itself. After getting promises from the Sioux not to interfere, the Company fell back upon summer cart trains and winter sledges. It was a slow, cumbersome, and costly process, but eventually all the goods were brought up to Fort Garry.

Needless to say, when the Burbank contract ran out in the fall of 1863, it was not renewed by the Hudson's Bay Company. The Company acquired the brothers' half-share of the enterprise; but instead of operating the Minnesota line by themselves as they had intended to do, the Company turned right around and signed another contract with a group of St. Cloud and St. Paul businessmen.[13] This agreement differed only in detail from the Burbank partnership. The new partners, headed by Henry Gager of St. Cloud, paid handsomely for their half, bonded themselves as a guarantee of their performance, and agreed to transport goods from St. Paul to Fort Garry for approximately $4.60 per hundredweight. Viewed from most sides, it seemed like a good deal for the Company. Gager and his partners were responsible men, well supported and heavily bonded, and they promised to carry the Company's freight for a sum much less than that demanded by the private carters of Red River. Put to the test, Gager and his associates were as unsuccessful as their predecessors. But though they were not the most efficient businessmen, much of their undoing could be blamed upon circumstances. The fickle Red River remained at a low and largely unnavigable level in 1864 and 1865. Certainly it did not fit the *International*, a vessel too long and too deep for that shallow, meandering stream. Only May's high waters accommodated the steamer; as a result, it made but one voyage in 1864 and only a few more in the following year. And if water impeded the passage between Georgetown and Fort Garry, the Sioux scare encumbered the overland stretch between the Red and St. Cloud. In the midst of the Southern and Sioux wars, Gager & Company had trouble getting enough recruits to man their wagons, and the teamsters they did hire were not the heroic sort. Imaginary Sioux Indians frightened some of them; Red River carters bullied the rest. By July of 1864 the Gager group had freighted no better than five tons of goods and by the season's end they had not carried enough cargo to make a profit. Wartime's prices and high wages added to their difficulties. At their request and to the delight of the Company, the contract was dissolved

[13]Dallas to the Secretary, 5 May 1864, H.B.C., Series A.12/43.

in the spring of 1865. Once again the Red River carts filled the breach, freighting all the way to Fort Garry.

It was a bad era for the Minnesota route, but for the York route it was even worse.[14]Although the former suffered from growing pains and the ills of circumstance, the latter was beset by a terminal illness. The chief fault in the Bay route was its absolute dependence upon York boats and the brigade system. Until the introduction of steam navigation, the Company could do little but curse the workings of the York route. In 1863 a Red River brigade bound for York Factory broke down, a victim of both a chance epidemic and chronic mismanagement. Two years later, all four of the Mackenzie River brigades failed. Of the four, one got lost and the others mutinied at Norway House. Faced with a similar situation in 1853, the Company's officer at Norway had seized the ringleaders and dispatched them to Red River—and "some weeks" in prison. But 1853 was not 1865, when none but the riff-raff of Red River would work the boats and there were not even enough of them to go around. Because of the brigade system, the York route declined, and the Minnesota route grew in spite of its shortcomings.

However, the Company was not satisfied with the Minnesota route merely because it was better than York. There was no assurance that its ills would clear up overnight. Thus Simpson's successor as the governor of Rupert's Land, Alexander G. Dallas, became intrigued with the possibility of an overland route from Superior City, Wisconsin to Fort Garry. The matter came to his attention in the spring of 1863, when several parties offered to carry the Company's freight between those terminals at a rate equal to that of the Burbanks. The advantage of Superior City seemed obvious to Dallas: an all-water passage *via* the Great Lakes and an Indian-free road *via* Crow Wing. With the revelation of each added defect in the Minnesota system, the charms of Superior City grew more apparent. After the summer's disorder, Dallas's mind was made up; he was "inclined to favor the adoption of the route via Superior and Crowwing, for the Red River, McKenzie river and Athabaska Outfits. . . ."[15] For the next four years the Company and various public officials of Superior City considered ways in which to finance and operate a wagon road on a basis that would fit the interests and needs of both parties. At least two agreements

[14]See Alvin C. Gluek, Jr., "The Fading Glory," *Beaver*, outfit 288 (winter, 1957), 50–5.
[15]Dallas to the Secretary, 16 Oct. 1863, H.B.C., Series A.12/43.

were proposed. Both were fund-matching schemes nearly identical in their nature. The Hudson's Bay Company would agree to construct and use the road and, in return, the citizens of Superior City would promise to hand over $25,000 upon completion of the project.[16] No contract was ever signed, however. When the Company, caught up in the troubles of the Minnesota route, was convinced that Superior City was fated to be the commercial depot of the Northwest and eagerly sought to bargain, the absentee property owners of Superior City could not be reached. When the owners were finally reached and agreed to terms, the Company's enthusiasm had vanished. Further study had revealed that the Superior road could never be as good as the Minnesota route, and events soon proved that the ills of the Minnesota system were only temporary. For when the railroad line reached St. Cloud in 1867, that centre straightway possessed an advantage that the best wagon road from Superior City could never enjoy.

Although at first glance the Minnesota route (1862–65) looked more like an obstacle course than a commercial highway, quite the opposite held true. Called out of semi-retirement, the Red River carts operated in larger numbers and with greater efficiency than ever before, and the volume of trade between Fort Garry and St. Paul moved up to new heights. Customs reports from the Port of Pembina demonstrated a progressive growth in the importation of goods from the Red River Settlement, both in terms of duties collected and the declared value of the goods themselves. Moreover Pembina's records showed that the trade matured as it grew, for the dollar value of all foreign (entering under bond) and domestic importations into the United States rose from approximately $74,000 in 1861 to $325,000 and $314,000 in 1864 and 1865 respectively.[17] Unfortunately for the historian, these records did not cover exportations from the United States. Even the data for incoming commerce were unreliable. Smuggling, first seen in Kittson's heydey in the 'forties, was still an honourable profession during the 'sixties. How much trade was conducted through this irregular extension of the Reciprocity Treaty is unknown.

[16]Dallas to the Secretary, 30 Dec. 1863, *ibid.* Kittson to Mactavish, 26 Dec. 1865, enclosed in Mactavish to the Secretary, 22 Jan. 1866, H.B.C., Series A.12/44.
[17]Enos Stutsman, Special Agent of the Treasury, to the Treasury Department, 10 Aug. 1866, Reports and Correspondence from Special Agent Enos Stutsman, 1866–1869, N.A. See also letters from Joseph Lemay, *et al.*, to the Treasury Department, Letters from Collectors, N.A.

Neither the Sioux nor the Civil War gave more than a slight check to trade within the greater Northwest. Even as American soldiers headed north and west in the spring of 1863 searching for Indians, they passed Red River carts moving south to St. Paul. Quite probably there was more noise on the Red River trails that summer—more carts squealing in greaseless agony—than in the previous season. The reasons for the traffic are not hard to find. The Company had to use "monster brigades" to fill the gap left by the boat and the Burbanks. Private traders turned to St. Paul as much from necessity as from desire, for the Company had refused them cargo space on the ship to York Factory that summer. For security, they too travelled in large numbers. Neither they nor the Company were troubled by Indians. In early July the St. Paul *Pioneer* (3 July 1863) claimed that the Red River traders had bought up "nearly every pound of crushed sugar and cheap tobacco in the city. . . ." Two months later, the *Press* (18 September) remarked that "if the proper policy is continued, [we shall] have the entire monopoly of their business."

The next season, 1864, was like the last. Red River cart trains operated from June till November. The Burbanks might have been bothered about "border troubles" but the men of Red River lost little sleep worrying about their scalps. They suffered more from St. Paul's prices and its money changers than from any Sioux met along the trail. Market conditions were particularly muddled. Since the beginning of summer, gold in the United States had been skyrocketing while greenbacks had fallen as low as 35 cents. Thus to a steadily rising price structure had been added the volatile element of diverse and madly fluctuating moneys: greenbacks, gold, and Hudson's Bay notes. And when the Red River traders reached St. Paul, prices shot up 20 to 40 per cent in a day. In fact, values often changed so quickly that some traders claimed they could have made a profit before leaving the store. Nevertheless, Red River men and Minnesota jobbers carried on a brisk and bulky business that summer. As St. Paul's business houses hummed with activity, the vicinity of Fort Garry really came alive—"which, as store after store . . . [was] run up, . . . [was] fast assuming the appearance of a town. . . ."[18] That town would soon be called Winnipeg; its creator was the city of St. Paul.

To the historian, it might appear that but for the intervention of the Civil and Sioux wars, the Minnesota frontier would have overlapped and overwhelmed Rupert's Land. It is true that this frontier, or at least its northwesternmost extension, was checked by the Civil War

[18]*Nor'-Wester*, 9 Nov. 1864.

and smashed by the Sioux, and it is equally true that there would be
no recovery till Appomattox and later. But the historian should also
remember that this frontier rested upon a weak foundation. There
certainly had been more paper than proper townships between St.
Cloud and Pembina and there probably had been more speculators
than farmers between Georgetown and Pembina. Those whom the
Panic of 1857 had not blown down were weakened by the Civil War
and toppled over by the Sioux. Despite the disruption of the Minnesota frontier, despite the breakdown of American freighters like the
Burbanks and the Gager group, the bonds between St. Paul and
Fort Garry were tighter in 1865 than they had been in 1861. In the
main, the bonds were commercial and the hand that had drawn them
tighter was British. By 1857, by 1861, and by 1865—crucial milestones
in the history of the international Northwest—the chief contact between Rupert's Land and Minnesota was mercantile rather than
personal; from 1861 to 1865 it was the British not the Americans who
developed this commercial relation. Perhaps the historian concerned
with what-might-have-been should conclude that the Sioux and Civil
wars built up the commercial frontier more than they tore down an
already unsteady agricultural frontier.

II

Neither the private traders of Rupert's Land nor the Hudson's Bay
Company had much to fear from the Sioux. These Indians had always
lived on friendly if not sociable terms with the Company, and
although they loathed the Red River *métis* for his ancestry (often
Chippewa but rarely Sioux) and his buffalo-hunting economy, they
had the greatest respect for the military strength of a Red River caravan, whether it was bent upon a buffalo hunt in the Dakota plains or
a trading jaunt to St. Paul. On the other hand, the Minnesota Chippewas, particularly those of the Red Lake and Pembina bands, were
neither fearful nor fond of British subjects, Company men or free
traders, white-skinned men or those of a "burnt-wood" complexion.
   Though they were neither numerous nor especially warlike, the
Chippewas were uniquely powerful. Their strength depended upon
their claim to the better part of the American Red River Valley, a
wide corridor of approximately eleven million acres extending from
the Wild Rice River northward to the 49th parallel. Ever since the
failure of Congress to ratify the Pembina Treaty of 1851, the Red

Lake and Pembina bands of the Chippewa nation had been moody and disgruntled. They wanted to sell their property and they feared that, without a sale, the United States would simply usurp the land. As time passed, their bitterness broadened; and it helped not at all to know that they were the only annuity-less Indians in Minnesota and that theirs was the last bit of aboriginal land in the state. Throughout the 'fifties, Indian superintendents and commissioners were aware of the Chippewa problem and applied almost annually to Congress for a cession, but not till Minnesota's "great awakening" in 1857–58 did the state show any real interest in the cession. Not till then did it exert any political pressure for a treaty and cite urgent reasons for acquiring the valley. New developments in transportation and an expanding commercial relationship with Rupert's Land had made the valley in fact what it already was in nature—the gateway to the north; and some Minnesotans wanted to control it. Furthermore, the valley was recognizably rich and coveted for its farm lands which many men believed would be taken up almost as soon as the Indians had ceded them. Still other Minnesotans concealed their motives. These were the fur traders like Sibley, Kittson, and Rice, who wanted a treaty in order to liquidate old Indian debts with an up-to-date interest.

By 1860 nearly all the parties for a cession were present: the seller, the broker, and the buyer. Absent, however, was the banker; and before any treaty could be consummated, the approval of and appropriations by Congress were necessary. Minnesota began to prod Washington. In February, 1860, the state legislature dispatched a memorial praying for the desired cession, and at the nation's capital Senator Rice made the expected responses. When the Senate considered appropriations for Indian treaties in late March and again in May, he tried repeatedly to amend the Indian Appropriations Bill to include funds ($10,000) just to treat with, not to buy from, the Chippewas. In explanation of his amendment, Rice said that the eventual treaty would be "for the purpose of extinguishing the title to the small strip they [the Chippewas] own, or to so much as will permit the free navigation of the [Red] river. . . ."[19] He was not asking for a great deal of money. Moreover he enjoyed the official support of the administration and the vigorous *ex tempore* aid of Senator Jefferson Davis. But he got no help from the rest of Davis' Southern colleagues: every amendment proposed by the Democratic gentleman from Minnesota was killed by his Democratic fellows from the South.

[19]*Congressional Globe*, 36th Cong., 1st Sess., 20 March 1860, pp. 1245–8. Cf. *ibid.*, 26 May 1860, pp. 2365–71.

Sectionalism, not nationalism, ruled Congress. There would be no banker until the Civil War.

The Red Lake and Pembina bands began to bargain more forcefully. The steamboat, they asserted, frightened game away from the valley and kept fish away from the hook. Furthermore this noisy invader ate up trees at an alarming rate. The Indians became more sullen until, exasperated by federal inaction, they demanded tolls from all white traffic crossing their lands. Mail contractors were stopped, and at Pembina the Indians gathered near the American customhouse so that they could conveniently take their tolls whenever the collector went aboard the river boats. In the fall of 1861 they stopped the *Pioneer*, demanding $40,000 or an interest in the profits—or else: the destruction of the boat and its cargo.[20] On this occasion, they were bought off with $300 in goods and supplies, but during the following summer the *International* was stopped time and again. The distraught collector did not know how to handle these highwaymen and anxiously warned Washington: "Unless a treaty is soon made or we have soldiers stationed here, there is no telling what may happen."[21]

When it was finally taken, Congressional action was almost too late. Appropriations were made in 1862 "for the purpose of treating with . . . [the Chippewas] for their lands and the right of navigation on the Red River of the North."[22] Everything seemed in order that summer. The Chippewas assembled at Grand Forks and the Indian Commissioner, William P. Dole was en route to the treaty grounds. But he never got beyond St. Cloud, for when he reached that point the Sioux uprising had already begun. Dole and his party had to return without a treaty. At the rendezvous, the Chippewas waited until their provisions ran out and then broke camp and vented their wrath upon Kittson's passing caravan. Here was the gauntlet, the final challenge— and the Indian Office knew it: "If there is no treaty made with these Indians at once, it will be necessary to abandon the lines of transportation, mail routes, &c., between the United States and the northeastern portion of Dakota Territory and the Hudson's Bay Settlement, or to establish *this winter* forts along the line for protection."[23]

[20]*Nor'-Wester*, 19 Feb. 1862.

[21]Joseph Lemay to the Secretary of the Treasury, 13 June 1862, Letters from Collectors, 1862.

[22]Clark Thompson to William P. Dole, 14 Nov. 1862, Annual Report of the Commissioner of Indian Affairs, 1862, *House Executive Document No. 1*, 37th Cong., 3rd Sess., Serial 1157, p. 202. Thompson was chief of the Northern Superintendency, with his headquarters located in St. Paul.

[23]*Ibid.*, p. 202.

Washington wasted no time in arranging for negotiations with the Chippewas the following summer. Alexander Ramsey was selected to head the commission, to re-accomplish what he had already achieved a dozen years before. It was an intensely busy year for him. Given the blessings of the Minnesota legislature in January, he succeeded Henry M. Rice as Senator; yet he held on to his former office as governor until summer, when, at an extra session of Congress, he was sworn into his new office. Thus it was as Senator rather than Governor Ramsey, that he received his instructions from the Secretary of the Interior. The Chippewas got their instructions from the fur traders.

Ramsey's party left St. Paul on 2 September. Neither in size nor conviviality did it resemble the 1851 outing. This was a small party bent upon business and without funds for pleasure, and Ramsey took the most direct route, following the well-grooved wagon and cart trail that led right to the treaty grounds. On the nineteenth he crossed the Sandhill River and reached his destination (Grand Forks) later that day, setting up camp where Red Lake River flowed into the Red itself.

Ramsey lost no time in getting to the business at hand. In addressing the assembled chiefs on 23 September he stressed the Great Father's interest in a right-of-way rather than a cession: "He has no special desire to get possession of their lands. . . . He simply wishes that his people should enjoy the privilege of travelling through their country on steamboats and wagons, unmolested."[24] He then offered $20,000 for an easement but as he had expected, and undoubtedly hoped, the Indians refused. Fortunately for the Chippewas—and for Ramsey— the latter had been given authority to treat as he saw fit, either for a right-of-way or a cession. Although Minnesota's immediate requirement was for the easement only, Ramsey, always a true apostle of his state's manifest destiny, did not bother to press the Indians on this point.

St. Paul clearly expected the "extinction of the Indian title to the country bordering on the Red River"[25] and Ramsey had no intention of going against the wishes of his constituents. He offered the Chippewas $510,000 for their entire claim, payable in instalments, and the Indians accepted at once. Handed over was an immense block of land, the most fertile and flat farm land in the whole state. Of the total sum paid the Chippewas, approximately one-fifth was put aside

[24]Joseph A. Wheelock's reporting of Ramsey's speech in the St. Paul *Press*, 4 Oct. 1863.
[25]*Ibid.*, 1 Sept. 1863.

to meet the damages done by them in the previous year and to liquidate debts owed by them to various American fur traders. Such payments were a regular part of Indian treaties and Ramsey did not bother to elaborate upon the subject in his official report.[26] However, he felt a need to justify buying some eleven million acres rather than a thin corridor:

Though the original motive to the treaty was the pacification of the Indians occupying the Red River valley, and the removal of the obstructions . . . placed in the way of travel and trade through that region, you will perceive that it was really demanded by considerations of far wider scope, and that its ratification would not only promote the local interests of the communities concerned in the commerce of the valley, but advance the general develop-ment of the Northwest and strengthen the bonds of international comity.

This time, in a Republican and Northern Senate, there was no problem of sectionalism. The treaty was duly ratified and then proclaimed by the President in May of 1864.

As Ramsey had reported, the very position of the tract made the extinction of the Indian title "a matter of the first consequence to the people of the State, and essential, indeed, to the development of the Northwest." Without the Red River Valley, St. Paul's dreams of a commercial empire in the greater Northwest could never be realized. Without the valley as a highway, Minnesota's frontiersmen could never approach Rupert's Land. With it, St. Paul might convert Rupert's Land into an economic outpost and change a British colony into an American state.

III

During the Civil War years, the Sioux rather than the British caused the greater disharmony in Minnesota-Assiniboia relations.[27] When the Sioux were forcibly dislodged from the state, they fled by the hundreds to seek sanctuary in the Red River Settlement. Here they were unwelcome guests who placed their host, the Hudson's Bay Company, in a compromising position. The presence of Sioux plagued the Company, which did not know what to do with them. The absence

[26]Ramsey to Dole, Oct. 1863, Annual Report of the Commissioner of Indian Affairs, 1863, *Senate Executive Document No. 1*, 38th Cong., 1st Sess., Serial 1182, pp. 547–54.
[27]See Alvin C. Gluek, Jr., "The Sioux Uprising: A Problem in International Relations," *Minnesota History*, XXXIV (winter, 1955), 317–24.

of the Sioux vexed the state of Minnesota, which knew what it would like to do with them but was prevented from carrying out its plans by the international line.

When news of the Sioux uprising reached Fort Garry in September, 1862, the officers of the Hudson's Bay Company realized they would soon suffer the consequences. William Mactavish, governor of Assiniboia, could see that American military pressure would squeeze the Sioux out of Minnesota and either force them onto the Dakota plains or into Rupert's Land. In the latter event, the exodus could end only in the Red River Settlement, a defenceless outpost lacking even an ordinary police force. It was apparent both to him and to Alexander G. Dallas that the Company needed troops and the latter wasted no time in acquainting the Governor and Committee in London of this fact. Indeed, Dallas claimed that some of the settlers, recalling the Sepoy Mutiny in India, feared that the Sioux insurrection would trigger a general Indian rising resulting in the massacre of all the whites in the British Northwest.

The chances of getting troops were very slight. Ever since the departure of the Royal Canadian Rifles, the Company had been seeking their return. After the *Trent* affair, an event following upon the heels of other Anglo-American differences during the first year of the Civil War, Governor Henry H. Berens called the Crown's attention to the "defenceless state of the [Red River] settlement."[28] Although the Colonial Secretary, the Duke of Newcastle, expressed his awareness of the gravity of the situation, nothing could be done about it, because it was winter and Hudson Bay was ice-locked; when summer came, the clouds of war had momentarily rolled away. Thereafter Newcastle was rigidly unsympathetic to all pleas for protection, for he was more interested in ending the Company's rule over Rupert's Land than in perpetuating it. Unaware of Newcastle's opposition, the people of Rupert's Land determined upon a policy designed to get military aid from England. In late October Dallas convened the Council of Assiniboia to discuss the apprehended arrival of the Sioux and consider the best course of action. He advised the councillors, if they wished troops, to memorialize the Crown for protection. Such a step—he quite candidly told them—would strengthen the hand of the Company in its own pursuit of troops, for it would show that the Company's officers were "the exponents of the wishes of the people

[28]Governor and Committee to Alexander Dallas and the Councils of the Northern and Southern Departments of Rupert's Land, 16 April 1862, H.B.C., Series A.6/37.

and not of their own interests."[29] The council agreed and drew up a petition to the Queen, explaining the danger facing Red River and asking for troops to meet it.

Fall and winter passed without word from London, and by spring the inhabitants of Red River grew worried as the Sioux drifted northward and began to gather in large bands just below the border. In March they petitioned the Governor and Council of Assiniboia to enrol from 200 to 400 men into cavalry companies in order to give the settlement some protection until the hoped-for troops reached Fort Garry. The response to the petition seems strange: the council deferred the matter to "some future day."[30] But the reasons it gave seem even stranger. The council claimed that, since danger from the Sioux was not imminent, it would be "somewhat premature" to establish a home guard. It also pointed out that the costs would certainly exceed what the petitioners would be willing or able to pay and that, if the application for imperial aid were honoured, Victoria's regulars might arrive in time to avert any danger.

In truth, the Company did not want a local militia whose loyalty to the Company might not be as great as its devotion to the public welfare. The Company wanted disciplined soldiers whose attachment to the Crown, and to itself, would be unquestioned. Ironically enough, at almost the very moment that the Governor and Council of Assiniboia set aside the petition from the people of Assiniboia, the Colonial Office rejected the petition of the Hudson's Bay Company. Throughout the month of February the Governor and Committee had directed Newcastle's attention to the defenceless state of Rupert's Land, but no plea advanced ever moved the duke. The suggestion that the Crown should protect Rupert's Land because the Company had no funds for public expenditure was disdainfully scouted: "His Grace cannot for a moment admit that the Company is not responsible for providing funds for the protection of a Territory of which they claim to be the sole and absolute proprietors."[31] Self-defence was a matter for militia, and Newcastle absolutely refused to recommend troops unless the Company would defray all their expenses.

The Hudson's Bay Company either could not or would not pay Newcastle's price. And for this refusal to pay the piper, the Company discovered that the Sioux were soon calling the tune. The first occasion arose in December when a small party of Sioux visited Fort Garry,

[29]Minutes of the Council of Assiniboia, 30 Oct. 1862, in E. H. Oliver, ed., *The Canadian North-West: Its Early Development and Legislative Records* (2 vols., Ottawa, 1914–15), I, 511–13.
[30]Minutes of the Council of Assiniboia, 11 March 1863, *ibid.*, I, 515–17.
[31]Chichester Fortescue to Berens, 12 March 1863, H.B.C., Series A.8/10.

but for the moment the American State Department seemed more concerned about these visitors than the British. Secretary of State Seward wanted assurances that no weapons would be given them. Whitehall consequently suggested that the Company use its "authority and influence to prevent the hostile Indians on either side of the frontier from being supplied with Arms, Ammunition, or Military Stores to be used against the peaceable inhabitants of the United States."[32] Berens complied, dispatching circulars to all the border posts, and from Fort Garry Dallas confidently advised the Governor-in-Chief of British North America to tell Seward there was no probability of the Sioux getting either arms or ammunition in Rupert's Land.

Dallas soon discovered that it was easier to make promises regarding the Sioux than to keep them. During the last weekend in May, 1863, Little Crow, alleged leader of the Sioux uprising, arrived in the Red River Settlement with about eighty members of his band. They came, not as humble suppliants, but as desperate men led by one who knew he was fighting with a rope around his neck. His visit with Governor Dallas seems, in retrospect, more like an audience than a conference. After reminding the governor that his people had been promised a sanctuary by the British during the War of 1812, Little Crow demanded both food and ammunition. He got the food, for Dallas had little choice in the matter. Indeed it was with the greatest difficulty that he was able to withhold the ammunition. Fortunately for the hapless governor and his settlement, Little Crow remained in Rupert's Land for only a few days before he returned to Minnesota.

During the following summer, while the armies of Generals Sibley and Sully were playing hares and hounds with the Sioux on the plains, isolated bands of these savages continued to harass the Minnesota frontier. Thus the conviction of certain men was apparently borne out: what Minnesota needed was a mobile cavalry outfit. The same men brought pressure to bear upon Washington with the result that the War Department commissioned Edwin A. C. Hatch, an ex-Indian agent, as a major and ordered him to raise an independent battalion of volunteers for service against the Sioux. Late in the summer, Hatch's Battalion came into being, eventually to consist of four cavalry companies, three of which were mustered in at Fort Snelling.[33] The fourth, composed for the most part of Red River settlers, was

[32]Berens to Newcastle, 20 April 1863, *ibid.*
[33]See Charles W. Nash, "Narrative of Hatch's Independent Battalion of Cavalry," *Minnesota in the Civil and Indian Wars, 1861–1865* (2 vols., St. Paul, 1890–93), I, 595–601; W. W. Folwell, *A History of Minnesota* (4 vols., St. Paul, Minnesota Historical Society, 1921–30), I, 289–94; and Hatch's papers and diary, M.H.S.

recruited in the early autumn by Captain Hugh S. Donaldson and not enrolled until November. The total force numbered approximately 350 to 400 men. As soon as the Minnesota companies had been enrolled, Sibley sent them to Pembina. The usual delays in procuring horses and arms put off the departure until late in the season, however. When Hatch finally left his encampment, it was the eighth of October and Minnesota was approaching that time of the year when anything could happen to the weather—one day, the balm of Indian summer, and the next, the horror of a Great Plains blizzard. Hatch was damned by fate. He and his men had to struggle through rain, snow, and wind, leaving a trail that was marked by the carcasses of their livestock. Just getting to Pembina was a heroic feat. And when the troops arrived in mid-November, they found, instead of shelter, only four or five crude buildings which Captain Donaldson had described to likely volunteers in Red River as "a sort of fort."[34] It was not until the first of the year, a day when the thermometer stood at sixty degrees below zero, that all Hatch's men were quartered.

When news of the formation of Hatch's Battalion first reached the Red River Settlement, it was well received. During the summer nearly thirty-five settlers had enlisted as "Mounted Rangers"; and when the battalion finally arrived at Pembina, its needs provided farmers of Rupert's Land with "an abundant market and high prices."[35] But when the troops made a show of their military strength, many a Red River man began to eye them as somewhat of a mixed blessing. Their arrival at Pembina had an immediate and most undesirable effect: fugitive Sioux came "flocking in upon [Fort Garry] by hundreds."[36] After a slight skirmish with the Americans in mid-December, more Indians joined their brethren north of the line. Before the year was out, about 500 Sioux, all of them involved in the Minnesota massacres, had gathered at Fort Garry. Even though the Sioux were destitute, they got little sympathy from the people of Red River. That they were also starving aroused little compassion, for there was not enough food in the settlement to feed them for any length of time. Furthermore Red River could never forget that the Sioux, for all their appearance, were still well-armed, defiant, and desperate savages. Regardless of their hosts' feelings, the Indians poured into the settlement—"men, women, and children—'bag and baggage'—without any special object apparently beyond getting something to eat and escaping the hated 'long-knives.'"[37]

[34]*Nor'-Wester*, 11 Nov. 1863.
[36]*Ibid.*, 7 Dec. 1863.
[35]*Ibid.*, 25 Nov. 1863.
[37]*Ibid.*, 17 Dec. 1863.

When the problem of the Sioux was handed over to Governor Dallas and his subordinates, they were stretched to "their wits end as to the course to be pursued to get rid of them."[38] The Company could afford neither to quarrel with the Sioux nor indefinitely to maintain them. Dallas was in a quandary. He offered them food and ammunition, provided they used the latter only for hunting and straightway left the settlement. Lacking transportation for their sick and aged, the Sioux refused. Dallas then raised his offer, adding more food and spicing the bribe with the gift of transportation. On this occasion his strategy worked, for on Christmas day they finally got under way. The Sioux travelled only as far as White Horse Plain, however, where they seemed likely to spend the winter. With each tightening of the screw, Dallas's imagination was strained just a bit more. He believed that the Indians would eventually run out of food and be "reduced to straits from which . . . the latter would have little scruple in relieving themselves by killing the Settlers' Cattle and committing other depredations naturally leading to consequences of a serious character."[39] Indeed he feared they might permanently reside in Rupert's Land.

Dallas had always hoped to settle the problem without American aid, but now he had reached the end of his wits. From every side he was continually and ever more urgently pressured to act. Minnesotans began piously to complain that by refusing to let them pursue the Sioux, he was protecting the Indians. And by feeding Indians who would otherwise starve or surrender, he was allowing them to recruit their strength and resume their murderous course. The upshot of such complaints was a callous note from the State Department to the British minister " . . . those Indians should either be restrained from making hostile incursions into United States territory, or United States troops should be allowed to pursue, subdue and disperse them. . . ."[40] In the Red River Settlement, citizens voiced much the same sentiment when they pleaded for American intervention. Once again Dallas took his dilemma to the council, and both now agreed to invite Hatch and his men into Rupert's Land "with the view of inducing . . . [the Sioux] to surrender themselves to their authority."[41]

[38]Henry H. Sibley to Ramsey, 30 Dec. 1863, Ramsey Papers, M.H.S. Sibley was recounting an excerpt in a letter from William Mactavish to Norman Kittson.
[39]Minutes of the Council of Assiniboia, 7 Jan. 1864, in Oliver, ed., *The Canadian North-West*, I, 532–5.
[40]William H. Seward to Lord Lyons, 21 Jan. 1864, *Senate Executive Document No. 13*, 38th Cong., 1st Sess., Serial 1176, p. 2.
[41]Minutes of the Council of Assiniboia, 7 Jan. 1864, in Oliver, ed., *The Canadian North-West*, I, 532–5.

Hatch proved strangely unco-operative. He foolishly insisted upon an unconditional surrender, an unimaginative doctrine that has generally had but one effect—to prolong the conflict. Most of the Sioux, including Chiefs Little Six, Little Leaf, and Medicine Bottle, refused Hatch's term-less offer. None of them wished to exchange a sanctuary for the hangman's noose. Thus the bulk of the Sioux stayed across the line, as sticky as ever; and thus the pressure upon Dallas grew daily more ponderous until virtually all the settlers were urging him to call in the American troops. Indeed some of them had already sounded out Hatch, and he had intimated that, if Dallas gave him permission, he would enter Rupert's Land and resolve the Indian problem.

In the middle of January, and without Dallas's permission, there occurred a unique bit of Canadian-American co-operation: the kidnapping of Little Six and Medicine Bottle. Here was a deed demanding close collaboration on either side of the line. Since Hatch's arrival there had been a great deal of coming and going between Pembina and the Red River settlement. By January every American officer save Hatch had visited the settlement. That a Masonic lodge sprang up in the settlement shortly after the Americans came to Pembina was no coincidence, for there were many fervent freemasons among Hatch's men. But above all, the mortar bonding together men north and south of the line was a mutual fear of the Sioux. Fear, fellowship, and money accounted for this shanghaiing. Acting in concert with the Americans, certain Red River settlers, led by A. G. B. Bannatyne, trapped the two chiefs. They were invited to Bannatyne's house and offered liquor liberally spiked with laudanum. Both Indians drank till they fell to the floor, where their sleep was deepened by an application of chloroform. In that stupefied state, they were manacled to a toboggan and dragged over the line. When they awoke, they were in Hatch's hands; and when they had been brought back to civilization, they were hanged. Some of the Red River settlers, including Dallas, deplored the deed. Some Canadians, like the editors of the Montreal *Telegraph*, regarded it as an invasion of British sovereignty. But most men of Red River, like the editors of the *Nor'-Wester*, believed that the end justified the means and replied (20 May 1864) to their Canadian critics that people in the British Northwest did not pay much attention to the "niceties" and "sacred right" of international law.

To deal with the rest of the Sioux would not be so simple and Major Hatch knew it. He intimated to Dallas that, although official orders forbade his crossing the line, he would do so if the governor sought his aid. He was even willing to let his troops serve under British command and he promised that they would not shoot any Indians save in self-defence. Though the *Nor-Wester* (18 January 1864) regarded this invitation as "an extremely liberal offer," Dallas turned it down. In the face of the shifting winds blowing down from Fort Garry, Hatch tried another tack. He knew that when spring came the Sioux would be off to the plains and beyond his reach. Therefore he plotted with certain Red River settlers to aid him in getting hold of these rascals. But the scheme was doomed from the start. The settlers could never have drugged the rest of the Sioux and they were not strong enough to dislodge them. Having gained no ground in this direction, Hatch came about again. "I shall make one more effort," he informed his wife on 3 March, "but the case is nearly hopeless—I feel very badly when I think of the matter, and know that these Indians never expect to make peace and that they were so near and I could not be permitted to reach them."

On the next day, Hatch formally asked Dallas if he could "pursue and capture these savages, with an armed force, wherever they may be found."[42] The governor quickly accepted, declaring "that a powerful tribe of Indians, inhabiting the borders of an undefined and unprotected frontier of large extent, should be disabused of the belief that they can with impunity commit their depredations and murders in one territory and take refuge in the other. . . ."[43] In fact, Dallas changed his mind for two good reasons: pressures in the settlement seeking American aid had become too strong to resist; and he was really afraid that the Sioux might not leave Rupert's Land. Hatch's unusual request, however, is a mystery. He knew that General Sibley had forbidden him to cross the 49th parallel; he also knew that long before diplomacy could resolve this Indian problem, the Sioux would have flown the coop. Presumably too he felt that despite diplomacy and army orders, neither Minnesota nor Assiniboia could be offended if he took the advice of the St. Paul *Press*, lost his way, and managed to "kill or bag the whole lot."[44] After writing Dallas for permission to cross the line, Hatch must have wrestled with his conscience. In the end he proved that he was no Andrew Jackson; he dared not cross the international line in pursuit of the Indians.

[42]E. A. C. Hatch, Major Commanding, to His Excellency A. G. Dallas, 4 March 1864, Appended to the Minutes of the Council of Assiniboia, 12 March 1864, in *ibid.*, I, 536–7.

[43]Dallas to Hatch (no place, no date), Appended to the Minutes of the Council of Assiniboia, 12 March 1864, in *ibid.*, I, 537.

[44]Quoted in the *Nor'-Wester*, 26 April 1864.

On 3 April Hatch received orders to withdraw to Fort Abercrombie. He waited until the ice went out of the Red River and then took the *International* back to Fort Abercrombie in May. Pembina had been abandoned. But surely Hatch's Battalion could have served no military purpose that spring. Three-quarters of their horses were dead; the mobility of a cavalry outfit had been ruined by negligence and a miserable Dakota winter. By June there was little left to commemorate a long, cold winter except the bleaching skeletons of the troopers' horses and "dozens of unfinished houses" outside the walls of the fort.

The Sioux continued to nettle Minnesota-Assiniboia relations for some years to come. Minnesotans resented the existence of a British asylum and distrusted the Hudson's Bay Company. Many of them apparently believed that the "commercial gentlemen . . . under the protection of the Union Jack, at Fort Garry . . . [were] supplying the hostile Sioux of the adjacent American territory, with powder and ball wherewith to shoot American citizens. . . ."[45] In his annual messages of 1865 and 1866, the governor of the state suggested that the British government either station troops at Fort Garry and control the Indians or allow American soldiers to cross the border and catch them. What could the people of Red River do? In 1864, nearly 3,500 Sioux returned to Assiniboia and sauntered truculently about the settlement. Again the settlers petitioned for a home guard; again their petition was rejected. In 1866, another large band of Sioux visited them. Again the request for a local volunteer force was made and once again the Hudson's Bay Company turned it down. The Governor and Committee saw too many difficulties in the way. The settlers would look to the Company for the needed expenses; the Company could not depend upon the militia for unquestioned loyalty. And there the problem of the Sioux remained—insoluble until Canada acquired the Hudson's Bay territories and brought law and order to the Northwest.

With the exception of the Sioux irritation, Minnesota's wartime attitude toward the British in North America was surprisingly even tempered. There was little of that ill feeling evidenced elsewhere in Anglo-American relations. As always, James W. Taylor was a good weathervane for the state, seeking out the winds that seemed most promising for Minnesota's progress. Before and during the Civil War he rarely equated Anglophobia with anti-Canadianism. On the contrary, he strove for the advancement of Canadian interests. Believing that Canadian federation would, if realized, embrace Rupert's Land, he collaborated with Canadians working to open up the British North-

[45]St. Paul *Press*, 29 March 1865.

west. To his way of thinking, the two Northwests (Minnesota's and the British) were a geographic unit possessing unlimited capabilities for settlement and growth. It did not matter which nation, Canada or the United States, owned the northern half; of importance only was its development by the Anglo-Saxon race.[46] Taylor's association with Thomas D'Arcy McGee, whom he had met in Quebec, illustrates the point. Taylor tried to support McGee's schemes in the Canadian parliament for promoting Canadian migration to the Northwest by mailing him Minnesota's official immigration pamphlets and by lending his own advice. The Canadian was appreciative and agreed with Taylor's "wide and generous views of the harmony of interests which ought to prevail between *our common* 'North-West'. . . ."[47]

This gentle harmony was not without discordant moments. Fourth-of-July speeches by American politicians occasionally injected a sour note. Yet more disruptive than oratory was the uncertainty of Anglo-American relations because of the Civil War. Incidents arose which created ill feeling and, at times, a fleeting belligerence in the American Northwest. When, for example, news of the *Trent* affair reached St. Paul, Taylor instantly reminded the Secretary of the Treasury that "in case of a collision with England, Minnesota . . . [was] competent to 'hold, occupy, and possess' the valley of Red River to Lake Winnipeg."[48] He added, significantly, that there were no troops at Fort Garry—a fact of which the Red River Settlement was uneasily aware. Citizens of that settlement were cognizant of the growing Anglophobia manifest in the American press and realized, fully as well as Taylor, their vulnerability to invasion from the United States.

Although the anxious days of the *Trent* crisis soon passed, a latent antagonism towards Britain remained in Minnesota throughout the war. It must be made clear, however, that a distinction seems always to have been made between Britain and Canada—or between the Hudson's Bay Company and the Crown. Whatever the origin of a given incident, only Britain was censured, never the member states of her empire. When Canada freed the St. Albans raiders in December, 1864, many Americans were intensely irritated; and belligerent statements

[46]See the "Relations between the United States and Northwest British America," *House Executive Document No. 146*, 37th Cong., 2nd Sess., Serial 1138. This document is an 85-page report submitted by the Secretary of the Treasury to the House in answer to its resolution of 20 May 1862. It consists for the most part of the letters and reports of the Special Agent of the Treasury, James W. Taylor.

[47]The italics are mine. McGee to Taylor, 6 July 1862, Taylor Papers, M.H.S.

[48]17 Dec. 1861, in "Relations between the United States and Northwest British America," p. 40. The news of the *Trent*, received by Taylor that very morning, provoked this martial outburst.

appeared in paper after paper throughout the country. In the United States Senate, Zachariah Chandler (Michigan) and James Rood Doolittle (Wisconsin) responded with angry words and bellicose resolutions.[49] Minnesota's response was not nearly so threatening. Her senators were silent. The St. Paul *Pioneer and Democrat* (21 December 1864), a Democratic paper, categorized Chandler's outbursts as "political buncombe." The *Press* (15 December 1864), a Republican organ, though more warlike in tone, blamed the British. The Canadians were wholly absolved, for "they . . . [were] known to sympathize warmly with the Union."

Thus the war, for all its emotionally charged incidents, did not awaken a hostility in Minnesota towards Rupert's Land. No known schemes of territorial aggrandizement were spun by Minnesotans during the war. The state might have been anti-British, but it was not anti-Selkirk. From 1861 to 1865 it was the Sioux, not the British, who brought the greater disharmony into Minnesota's relationship with the Hudson's Bay territories. And even this discord was of short duration. Minnesota was soon more interested in revitalizing her trade with the Red River merchants than in worrying about any red-skinned mavericks north of the 49th parallel.

IV

Until Lee's armies had been defeated, Minnesota could do little more than wait and wonder about the future. But dreams are always cheap and many Minnesotans dreamt night and day about the commercial destiny awaiting them within the greater Northwest. Only in this economic sense were they motivated by imperialist visions. They needed trade, not land; and throughout the Civil War, strenuous efforts were made by individuals, commercial organizations, and the state herself to promote better trade relations with the Red River Settlement.

Overshadowing all men and organizations, and the undoubted chief of Minnesota's boosters, was James W. Taylor. A man of prodigious energy and a scholar obsessed with his subject, he had continued to speak wherever and whenever he could. After a visit to Red River in

---

[49]*Congressional Globe*, 38th Cong., 2nd Sess., 14 Dec. 1864, pp. 33–4. Jacob Howard, Michigan's junior senator, supported (19 December) the above action taken against "those who have been harboring these rebel vipers at their bosoms. . . ." *Ibid.*, p. 57.

the summer of 1859, he toured the state, giving lectures on Rupert's Land which were "well calculated to inspire enthusiasm and confidence in respect to the future prospects of Minnesota. . . ."[50] That winter he addressed a St. Paul audience on "the importance of our relations to the Selkirk Settlement." And so it went, throughout this and other busy years, until by 1861 he had made "the Red River and Saskatchewan valleys as familiar to . . . [the] people [of Minnesota] as the fertile regions they inhabit[ed]."[51]

Taylor's pen was even more active than his tongue and won him greater acclaim. In 1859 alone, he wrote article after article for the St. Paul *Pioneer and Democrat*, contributed to a pamphlet entitled "Overland Emigration to British Columbia," and personally compiled a report called *Northwest British America and Its Relations to the State of Minnesota*. At the end of the year, he got his reward: an appointment as Special Agent of the United States Treasury "to examine and report (among other enumerated duties) upon the trade and communications between Minnesota and Northwest British America, and the interests of the public revenue connected therewith."[52] Put into office by Democrats Rice and Sibley, he was kept there till 1869 by Republicans Ramsey and Wilkinson.

Working for the Treasury Department gave Taylor a magnificent opportunity to speak out for the Northwest. In letters to the department and in various governmental publications, he always pushed policies that would benefit Minnesota: the construction of overland routes to the Pacific, a northern transcontinental railroad, the enlargement of the Reciprocity Treaty of 1854, and a host of other less significant matters. As an agent, he served at least two masters: the federal government and the State of Minnesota; and of the two, he gave better and more loyal service to his state. Proof of this greater loyalty was demonstrated in his struggle to broaden, then to preserve, and finally to revive the Reciprocity Treaty of 1854.

In 1854 the United States and the various British North American provinces consummated a trade agreement known as the Reciprocity Treaty.[53] It permitted the free entry into both countries of a great many natural products. Canadians hoped that the treaty would open

[50]Letters from St. Cloud, 7 and 8 Nov. 1859, to the editors of the St. Paul *Pioneer and Democrat*, 10 and 13 Nov. 1859.
[51]St. Paul *Pioneer and Democrat*, 15 Feb. 1861.
[52]Taylor to the Secretary, 20 Dec. 1859, Letters from Special Agents of the Treasury Department, N.A.
[53]See Lester B. Shippee, *Canadian-American Relations 1849–1874* (New Haven, 1939), chaps. ii–v.

up a new market to replace the British Isles, whose preferential comforts had faded away when Britain embarked upon free trade. Americans agreed to it because of certain provisions that had nothing to do with reciprocity itself: their freedom to exploit the inshore fisheries of British North America and to use Canada's canal system and the St. Lawrence River. With all parties supporting the measure—and with plenty of money and liquor to lubricate its passage—the treaty slipped through Congress without a recorded vote and began its uncertain life. It was to exist for at least ten years and indefinitely thereafter, unless either country gave the other twelve months' notice.

Not till the great awakening of interest in Rupert's Land in 1858–59 did the people of Minnesota concern themselves with the Reciprocity Treaty. Then to their horror, they discovered that the treaty, whose "free" list included furs and skins, did not extend to the Hudson's Bay territories. "We have no choice in this matter," boomed (24 February 1859) the editor of the *Pioneer and Democrat*, "but reciprocity or conquest." Coming back to earth, he quickly added that since conquest was not practicable, the treaty would have to be re-tailored to fit the state's needs. During the ensuing year, other and more influential figures sided with the editor. Taylor easily induced the St. Paul Chamber of Commerce to join the campaign, passing resolutions and printing brochures; and soon political action succeeded public pressure. Governor Sibley urged the legislature to petition Congress for the expansion of the Reciprocity Treaty and thus secure "unrestricted commercial facilities" with Rupert's Land.[54] And once again, Taylor added his voice, addressing a standing-room-only crowd in the chamber of the lower house and pursuing his subject, "A Reciprocity Treaty and a National Policy for the Northwest," with—as one reporter remarked— all "the ardor of a special mission."[55] Soon afterwards, the House unanimously passed the Senate's memorial, asking Congress for "a free trade between the United States and the Hudson's Bay Territory, north of the boundary of Minnesota."[56]

It was difficult enough to keep the treaty alive, let alone expand it. Even in the peaceful, pre-Civil War period of Anglo-American relations, dissatisfaction with reciprocity existed here and there in the United States. Just one month after Minnesota's memorial, Congress published a report written by Israel T. Hatch, a Treasury agent and

[54]Minnesota, *Journal of the House, 1859–1860*, pp. 30–1.
[55]St. Paul *Pioneer and Democrat*, 20 Dec. 1859.
[56]Minnesota, *Journal of the House, 1859–1860*, p. 146.

ex-New York congressman.[57] Hatch was unsparingly critical of the treaty, claiming that Canada was violating its terms both in substance and in spirit. Particularly reprehensible to him were Canada's newly imposed import duties upon American manufactures. So far as he was concerned, the Canadians were enjoying "most of the benefits of annexation to this country, without any of the taxes. . . ," and the only "proper, radical and sufficient remedy . . . [was] the speedy abrogation of the treaty itself."

However the Hatch report had a strange companion-piece—a contradictory statement by Taylor. Since Hatch's sentiments regarding reciprocity had become known before publication, Senator Rice of Minnesota learned of them and consequently "represented to the President . . . a strong distrust of the soundness and impartiality of Mr. Hatch's views. . . ."[58] As a result, the President appointed another man with a different point of view. Taylor was the choice—and he produced the desired document. He maintained that everyone west of Buffalo liked the treaty and hinted that Hatch was opposed simply because he was a partisan of New York's railroad and shipping interests. Moreover Taylor showed that Canada's import duties were much less protective than America's and that, despite their imposition, Canada's importation of American manufactured goods had risen steadily. If there were to be a revision in the treaty, he believed it should "be in the direction of the principle which the United States has always advanced, freedom, not restriction, of commercial intercourse."

Had not the Civil War broken out, dissatisfaction with the treaty might never have gone beyond the sporadic criticisms of men like Hatch. Most Americans, like their own Treasury Department, seemed quite unconcerned about it. However indifference vanished with the coming of war and the installing of a protectionist, Republican administration in Washington. If the war made some men more critical of the Reciprocity Treaty, it made Minnesotans more appreciative than ever of its benefits and much more concerned about its future. Like so many of her sister states in the Middle West, Minnesota felt the pinch of wartime transportation. The war closed the Mississippi River; government shipping jammed east-west rail lines; and freight charges

[57]"Reports of Hatch and Taylor in reference to the operations of the reciprocity treaty," *House Executive Document No. 96*, 36th Cong., 1st Sess., Serial 1057, pp. 1–60.
[58]Letter of Lord Lyons (copy), 21 Jan. 1860, quoted in Canada, *Sessional Papers*, 1860, vol. XVIII, no. 4, Section 30, p. 13. Lyons also enclosed the memorial from the Minnesota legislature praying for the extension of reciprocity.

consequently rose while transportation facilities shrank. To accommodate their ever waxing wheat harvests, Minnesota and other Mid-
western states wanted to retain the St. Lawrence River as a permanent
highway to the world's markets.

The distemper of war doomed the treaty and all its provisions,
however. Americans became angry at Britain's haste in issuing a
neutrality proclamation which they regarded as an unseemly and premature recognition of the South as a nation; and thereafter they
anxiously awaited and expected complete recognition. There was ample
evidence of pro-Southern sentiment in Britain. Her middle and upper
classes—the voting classes—openly favoured the Confederacy; and
though Whitehall's position was usually correct, it too left no doubt
as to its sympathies. In contrast to the mother country's changeless
temper, Canadian public opinion was exuberantly pro-Northern when
war was first declared. It only began to change once it became clear
that Lincoln was fighting to save the Union and not to free the slaves.[59]
And needless to say, Canada's change of heart was quickened and confirmed by Anglophobic editorials in the American press.

Into this atmosphere of international ill will intruded those incidents
(the *Trent* affair and others) inevitable in any great conflict. In the
United States Anglophobia was soon synonymous with anti-Canadianism. It was merely a matter of time before Congress looked at the
Reciprocity Treaty; when it did, the ultimate examination would be
made with a hostile eye—and a pressing need for revenue.

The first excuse for an inquiry came in the winter of 1861–62, when
New York asked Congress to investigate certain Canadian practices
which seemed to contravene the spirit of reciprocity. The memorial
was referred to the House Committee on Commerce, of which Elijah
Ward (New York) was chairman. His committee examined the whole
treaty and emerged with a curious report[60]—a literary smorgasbord,
offering tantalizing tidbits for almost everyone. On behalf of reciprocity's friends, Ward claimed that all the major ports and cities in
the Great Lakes region liked the treaty because of the commercial
favours it bestowed. Indeed he presented St. Paul's peculiar position
with such feeling that he sounded like a Taylor-tutored prophet of
Minnesota's manifest destiny. After stating that "the various parts of

[59]Helen G. Macdonald, *Canadian Public Opinion in the American Civil War*
(New York, 1926), chaps. 3 and 4.

[60]*Reports of Committees of the House of Representatives* No. 22, 37th Cong.,
2nd Sess., Serial 1144, pp. 1–35.

the American continent, like those of the human body, are wonderfully adapted to each other," he drew attention to the British Northwest and remarked that it was vast enough to comprise "twenty-five states equal in size to Illinois." On the other hand, he submitted data pleasing to the foes of reciprocity, evidence illustrating that Canada seemed to be violating the spirit of the Reciprocity Treaty. Despite this general and unfair indictment of Canada, Ward did not want to abrogate the treaty. He hoped instead to transform it from a commercial pact into a continental customs union. However the House of Representatives was not interested in reciprocity and even less in a common market. Though it printed the Ward Report, it took no action upon it or its recommendations in this or in the next session of 1862–63.

The session of 1863–64 had scarcely started, however, when Justin S. Morrill announced that he would introduce a resolution terminating the treaty. At once Ward responded by offering one of his own, authorizing the appointment of a commission to negotiate a new treaty; and he, in turn, was followed by a man from Maine whose resolution required the President to end the treaty. Observing these and other manoeuvres, Taylor became uneasy and gravely commented to a Canadian friend that the tide was "running heavily against the Treaty."[61] With a presidential election coming up, the present congressional session—as Taylor well knew—would not be remembered for its "dispassionate discussion." Though he thought that Secretary of the Treasury Chase was favourably disposed towards the treaty, "Still," he warned, "*revenue* has now become the vital question with the American Government...."

The House referred the treaty to Ward's committee and thereby gave Taylor two more months to lobby on behalf of Minnesota, Canada, and reciprocity. During those anxious weeks he was in constant communication with the committee, giving it information upon request and advice without solicitation. So closely did his views resemble Ward's that he must have been shocked when the latter subsequently introduced a resolution empowering the President to give notice in the manner prescribed by the treaty. Perhaps Taylor's spirits rose a bit

[61]Taylor to Brydges, 2 Feb. [1864], Taylor Papers. Taylor and Brydges were in constant correspondence that winter, as each sought to revitalize the Reciprocity Treaty. In addition to his work with the Grand Trunk, Brydges served the Hudson's Bay Company as agent, and it seems more than likely that he employed Taylor as a lobbyist in Washington. Dual, even triple, employment never seemed to trouble Taylor's code of ethics, so long as his employers all sought the same end.

when Ward also moved that the President be given authority "to negotiate a new treaty . . . based upon the true principles of reciprocity, and for the removal of existing difficulties."[62] By "true principles," he meant a customs union, and by "existing difficulties," he was referring to Canada's duties upon American manufactures.

Although Ward introduced his resolution on 1 April, it was not until 18 May that the House began to consider the treaty and all its implications. Ultimately there were three resolutions before it: Ward's (also known as the Arnold amendment); Morrill's, which gave the President discretionary power to terminate the treaty; and joint resolution number 56, which required the President to do so. Number 56 had already received two readings, while the other resolutions were in the nature of amendments to it; and the ensuing debate regarding all three generated more heat than light.

As an issue, reciprocity cut across party and sectional lines. Its most rational supporter was Elijah Ward, who touched off the ten-day debate. In a long but closely reasoned speech, he showed how the United States had benefited from the current treaty: a favourable and mounting trade with Canada, the rewarding exploitation of the inshore fisheries, and the use of the St. Lawrence. Finding only one defect—Canada's restrictive tariff policy—he pleaded with the House to seek the renegotiation of reciprocity upon its true principles before ending the existing agreement. On the following day, Frederick Pike of Maine replied. He began by saying that he wanted the treaty "to draw its last breath as soon as possible."[63] He stated that Maine's fishermen derived little profit from the inshore fisheries, plucked the protectionist strings and sang out the old refrain about America's loss of markets and revenue, and then ended with a long-winded recitation of British wrongdoing: the recognition of the South as a belligerent and so forth. "Why, then," he asked, "should we go about begging for a new treaty?" Isaac Arnold of Illinois answered him, speaking for the commercial and agricultural interests of the Northwest. He argued that reciprocity's fate should not be determined by British actions. His people, with their grain-growing economy, sorely needed the St. Lawrence River— the "one great avenue the West has to the Ocean. . . ."[64] "God made the St. Lawrence river," he went on. "For what purpose? Was it for the use of the small Canadian provinces, or did he make it for floating upon its waters the products of our great western empire?" The answer

[62]*Congressional Globe*, 38th Cong., 1st Sess., 1 April 1864, p. 1387.
[63]*Ibid.*, 19 May 1864, pp. 2364 *et seq.*
[64]*Ibid.*, 19 May 1864, pp. 2368–2371.

was obvious to Arnold, and he concluded: "as a means of obtaining it we wish to continue this reciprocity treaty."

Beyond the slim support tendered by some representatives of the commercial East and the commercial-agricultural West, Arnold got little sympathy. The treaty's foes were too consumed with Anglophobia and too concerned with protectionism to listen to arguments based upon economic facts or inspired by expansionism. One of them mercilessly twitted Arnold and Ward: "If this commission is to be provided for, I want the name changed to 'A commission to arrange terms for continuing, in a dignified position, the wet-nurse of the sick British colonies.' (Laughter) I have done."[65] "Done" also was the Ward-Arnold amendment. Morrill's amending resolution was likewise defeated, if by the scantest of margins. Fortunately for reciprocity's friends, the original resolution (number 56) never got to the floor. By a very close vote, they deferred its consideration until December.

Taylor spent the early part of the summer trying to convince the governments of Canada and the United States of the merits of a compromise scheme which theoretically looked after America's need for revenue and yet kept Canada's affection for the free list in mind. In a mid-winter conversation with Secretary Chase, he had learned— or so he thought—that the latter would support a treaty which placed a permanent duty upon all goods now on the free list. But to insure the unimpeded flow of trade, it could not be too high. Taylor accordingly came up with the extraordinary suggestion that both the United States and Canada establish a 5 per cent *ad valorem* duty upon all articles within the free list. It was this scheme that he pressed upon Secretary Chase during the summer, while his Canadian friend and confidant, Charles J. Brydges, informally brought it to the attention of Canada's Finance Minister, Alexander T. Galt.

This unlikely scheme never got beyond the exploratory stage. Chase's reaction to it remains unknown but, given his general disregard for the Reciprocity Treaty and Canadian-American trade, it can scarcely be imagined that he would have lent his support. On the other hand, Galt's response was clearly and instantly unsympathetic. He would never agree to a 5 per cent duty, because he claimed it "would in all probability divert from us the great part of the imports which we now have from the western states."[66] In addition, he simply did not believe it was in Canada's interests to put any duty on the

---

[65]*Ibid.*, 26 May 1864, p. 2503.

[66]Galt to [Brydges], 9 June 1864, enclosed in Brydges to Taylor, 11 June 1864, Taylor Papers.

free list. At this point, Taylor's scheme collapsed, carrying with it reciprocity's last chance for survival.

In all his visions of a broader reciprocal relationship, Taylor had been following a false gleam. Five per cent reciprocity had been doomed long before he conceived of it. A customs union was equally impossible. To it, Galt was unalterably opposed, knowing that it would weaken Canada's British connection while it strengthened American industry at Canada's expense. As for the extension of reciprocity to Rupert's Land, this was the most chimerical of all Taylor's dreams. For only the briefest moment in time had the Hudson's Bay Company wondered about extending the Reciprocity Treaty to its chartered and licensed holdings—and then only to Vancouver Island and the adjacent coastal region. Following Simpson's sage advice, however, the Company had done nothing about it. Simpson saw no purpose in permitting a Pacific reciprocity treaty which "would lead to the extinction of the Indian trade, and in every way prove highly injurious to the Company's interest in that quarter."[67] No one in the Company ever considered the possibility of reciprocity for Rupert's Land.

In the fall, events conspired to make Congress more opposed than ever to the Reciprocity Treaty. Though the treaty was already in a moribund state, St. Albans Raid and Canada's subsequent release of the Confederate raiders provided the death blow. The House passed H.R. No. 56 by a large majority on 13 December and transmitted it to the Senate on the following day—the day before the liberation of the Confederates in Montreal. Immediate action was forestalled by John Hale of New Hampshire, who feared the "excited state of feeling" and successfully moved for a postponement until mid-January.[68] At best, the treaty gained only a reprieve. For though the friends of reciprocity had all the logical arguments, they failed to persuade their jingoist-protectionist brethren. In a long speech probably written for him by Taylor, Senator Ramsey of Minnesota carefully explained how important the St. Lawrence was in the carriage of all the Northwest's produce. In fact—he went on—Minnesota wanted the provisions of the treaty expanded to include Rupert's Land. "Why," he plaintively asked, "multiply barriers and restrictions against our commercial intercourse in that direction?"[69]

On 12 January 1865, the day of reckoning, the Senate was not in a

[67]Simpson's report, enclosed in Shepherd to Labouchere, 8 May 1856, H.B.C., Series A.8/7.

[68]*Congressional Globe*, 38th Cong., 2nd Sess., 21 Dec. 1864, p. 95.

[69]*Ibid.*, 11 Jan. 1865, p. 209.

deliberate mood. Many of its members from the Northwest turned away from their true course of economic imperialism to the delusive one of expansionism. Other senators wanted to protect the economy of their own state or region;[70] still others were primarily interested in bolstering the federal revenue;[71] and through it all the administration remained indifferent and inactive. Thus the joint resolution passed by a vote of thirty-three to eight,[72] and in March, as directed, President Lincoln signed it. Reciprocity came to an end twelve months later.

Canadian-American relations had suffered because of the Civil War and as a result the immediate post-war relationship would be neither easy nor happy. Embittered by Canada's alleged inattention to Confederate border raids and aglow with the spirit of victorious nationalism, many Northerners began to think and talk in terms of a new Manifest Destiny. In this post-war atmosphere, there was no hope of reviving reciprocity. Indeed when expansionist-minded men reappraised number 56, they wondered whether abrogation might not force Canada into the Union. The formula became: economic pressure equals political absorption. It was simple but exciting; and to Minnesotans no one explained it better and more forcefully than a Canadian apostate and ex-editor of the Toronto *Globe* named George Sheppard:

Renew reciprocity, & you postpone annexation indefinitely. Refuse reciprocity —or insist upon conditions with w^h a colony cannot comply—& you ensure annexation within a brief period. On this point I am positive.

To you in the North-West the matter has a significance apart frm commercial considerations. For reciprocity will help the Confederation scheme; and that involves the erection of a British province at yr very doors. Defeat reciprocity, & the Red River country will drop like a ripe plum into your hands.[73]

---

[70]For example, Michigan lumbermen joined hands with the men of Maine to exclude Canadian competition. See Robert C. Johnson, "Logs for Saginaw: An Episode in Canadian-American Tariff Relations," *Michigan History*, XXXIV (Sept., 1950), 213–14.

[71]Although John Sherman (Ohio) admitted that he had not studied either the Reciprocity Treaty or its operations, he opposed it because of the loss in revenue and the wholly unfounded suspicion that Great Britain had somehow hoodwinked the United States in the first place. *Congressional Globe*, 38th Cong., 2nd Sess., 11 Jan. 1865, p. 209.

[72]*Ibid.*, 12 Jan. 1865, p. 234. Of the Northwest's senators, only Ramsey, Timothy O. Howe (Wisconsin), and Thomas A. Hendricks (Indiana) voted against the resolution.

[73]Sheppard to George L. Becker (of the St. Paul and Pacific Railroad), 30 June 1865, Taylor Papers.

Chapter *7*. *Minnesota's Post-War Expansionism*

THE IMMEDIATE POST-WAR YEARS WERE, FOR MINNESOTA, A TIME OF GREAT material growth. Railroads, held back so long by scandals, wars, and depressions, were finally given free rein and began their race for the Red River Valley. The whole frontier was revitalized. By stage and by rail, pioneers pushed west and north, threatening to take up all the state's free land within a decade. With improved transportation systems and larger markets, trade with the Red River Settlement thrived and seemed to foreshadow the eventual creation of a common market.

Materialism and expansionism accompanied one another. A striking change could be seen in the attitude of Minnesota towards Rupert's Land. Greed displaced good fellowship when the continued failure to secure and enlarge reciprocity demolished the prospects of a commercial hinterland beyond the 49th parallel. To the state and her leaders it became more and more evident that if the British Northwest were not annexed, it would soon be lost. The blooming of Canadian transcontinentalism in the late 'sixties gave further stimulus to Minnesota's expansionism. This was an era of militant manifest destiny, 1865–1869/70, and Minnesota used all her talents and seized all her chances to detach Rupert's Land from British North America.

I

On 8 April 1865 citizens of St. Paul gathered in great excitement. The roar of cannon and chiming of church bells announced the fall of

Richmond, and the Civil War, save for Appomattox, had ended. Immersed in self-pity, St. Paul believed that her destiny had been cut short by a company of unkindly fates—"when the Great Rebellion, swiftly followed by a disastrous Indian war on our own frontier, inter- posed to retard, though not wholly to arrest, the rapid march of its development."[1] But on this particular day, St. Paul's citizenry heard more than one speaker tell them that, with all wars behind them, theirs would be a most prosperous future. James Taylor stood on the platform that day, pleading with the President of the United States to return Minnesota's manhood. Then, said he, "Let us storm the Rocky Moun- tains with all their mineral treasures—let the nation consolidate, [and] organize the wilderness. . . ."[2]

Soon after the war was over, Minnesota's long-awaited tide of settle- ment reached flood stage. Swedes and Norwegians swept into the state, following after the Germans and rushing towards the Red River Valley. It was a mass invasion that permanently altered Minnesota's ethnic character. It also subjected the state's transportation system to considerable strain. Although daily coaches were installed on the route between St. Cloud and Sauk Center, they "rarely accommodated the daily rush adequately."[3] The Scandinavians were numerous and land- hungry pioneers. The federal land offices at St. Cloud and Alexandria were the state's busiest; their annual sales from 1865 to 1871 were nearly half of Minnesota's total volume.[4] Towns that had slumbered since 1861 awoke. St. Cloud, Sauk Center, Alexandria, Osakis, and Ottertail City—all were flourishing little frontier cities, but big stepping- stones to the Northwest. Minnesota's frontier salient had scarcely reached Sauk Center by 1865, but by 1869 it had enveloped Alexandria. In that year, a passenger on a stage line en route to the Red River Valley travelled over country he had not seen in four years. The changes that had taken place astounded him.[5] He found the land between St. Cloud and Sauk Center almost entirely fenced in, with wheat fields stretching to the horizon. On every hand he could see the signs of an advancing civilization: stores, houses, and churches; and in the Red River Valley itself he discovered farms as far north as George- town. Given another decade, the whole valley would be settled.

In the post-war era, Minnesota's railroads finally began to grow. It

[1]St. Paul *Press*, 26 April 1866. Cf. *ibid.*, 11 April and 2 Nov. 1865.
[2]Quoted in *ibid.*, 9 April 1865.
[3]Arthur J. Larsen, "The Northwestern Express and Transportation Company," *North Dakota Historical Quarterly*, VI (Oct., 1931), 53.
[4]See the records of Minnesota's land sales in the official reports of the United States Land Office.
[5]St. Paul *Press*, 13 July 1869. Cf. the St. Paul *Pioneer*, 26 Dec. 1869.

was late, for they had lain virtually dormant for more than twenty years. Like other trans-Mississippi states and territories during the 'fifties, Minnesota had cherished its railroad dreams, but despite a widespread interest, many charters, and considerable promotional activity, not one foot of track was laid down till 1861 and very little until 1865. There had been too many forces conspiring against construction. When it was discovered that the first (1854) Congressional land grant given to a Minnesota railroad had been conceived by a sinful promoter and brought into the world by a venal representative, Congress revoked it and would not issue another to the state until 1857.[6] Among the four railroads allowed to share in the second grant was the Minnesota and Pacific Railroad Company. According to its charter, it was to proceed from "Stillwater, by way of St. Paul and St. Anthony, to a point below the foot of Big Stone Lake and the mouth of the Sioux Wood River . . . , with a branch via St. Cloud and Crow Wing, to the navigable waters of the Red River of the North. . . ."[7]

Edmund Rice, president of the Minnesota and Pacific, spoke and wrote in the most glowing terms about his line. He claimed it would perform any number of Herculean tasks. It would transport goods into the Red River Valley, Dakota Territory, and Rupert's Land. It would develop northwestern Minnesota and open up the Hudson's Bay territories. And merely by selling land at the rate of $57,600 per mile, it would not only finance its own growth but finish up with a handsome surplus. Thus did Rice list and linger over his company's eventual accomplishments when he made a statement to a St. Paul newspaper in the fall of 1857.[8] If the historian were curious enough to turn over the page of that paper, he would find the reverse side shingled with notices of mortgage foreclosures. Though the Minnesota and Pacific had been chartered in May, Rice had trouble just getting it under way. Early in the summer engineers surveyed as far as Big Stone Lake and Crow Wing, and the contractor began his preliminary work. But the latter had only thirty days on the job before the Panic of 1857 intervened and ended his labours. Not a spike was driven that summer.

Although the Panic ended all railroad construction in the territory, it did not frustrate the inventive mind of Edmund Rice. He and the other railroad men soon talked the legislature and the people of the new State of Minnesota into underwriting them with the now infamous

[6]See Rasmus S. Saby, "Railroad Legislation in Minnesota, 1849 to 1875," *Minnesota Historical Society Collections*, XV, 1–188.

[7]Quoted in Wilson P. Shortridge, *The Transition of a Typical Frontier* (Menasha, Wisconsin, 1922), pp. 133–4.

[8]Undated newspaper clipping in James Taylor's Scrapbooks, Taylor Papers, M.H.S.

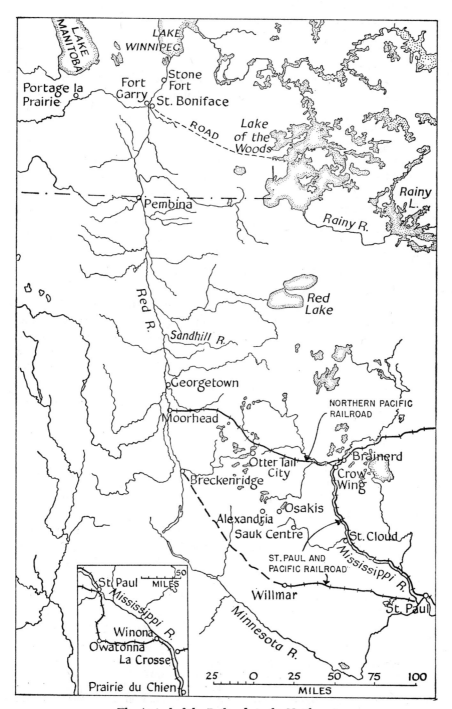

The Arrival of the Railroads in the Northwest

Five Million Dollar Loan. Under the odd illusion that they were not guaranteeing a loan, the people ratified a constitutional amendment authorizing their governor to subsidize railroad construction with a $5,000,000 bond issue. He was to distribute the bonds in return for rather vague collateral as the work itself progressed. However by December, 1859, when the governor had handed over more than $2,000,000, the railroads had only graded about 240 miles and had been unable to build anything. For the Panic made it impossible for them to find a decent market for the bonds. As late as 1860, the bonds were only getting twenty-five to thirty cents on the dollar.[9] Believing themselves duped, Minnesota's legislators re-amended the constitution. They tossed out the old amendment and further provided that, unless a popular referendum decided otherwise, the state would not be responsible for any of the bonds already floated. Then in June, 1860, the state foreclosed the Minnesota and Pacific.

Revived in the following year, the railroad laboured all summer and brought forth one locomotive, one car, and a half mile of track.[10] Despite a September celebration commemorating Minnesota's "first" railroad, the Minnesota and Pacific was again foreclosed because it had failed to build a stipulated ten-mile strip between St. Paul and St. Anthony. Reopened again in 1862, but on this occasion as the St. Paul and Pacific, it managed to finish the section and keep its franchise; but further progress was painfully slow. Only fifty miles had been completed by 1865.

Just before the close of the Civil War, the St. Paul and Pacific was again reorganized. Rice was replaced by George L. Becker and Edward H. Litchfield, two clever promoters who straightway created a company within a company—the First Division of the St. Paul and Pacific Railroad Company. By this opaque manoeuvre, they hoped to achieve a more rapid rate of growth, build individual sections, and make their whole enterprise more attractive to foreign investors. It was an effective scheme. Dutch bankers poured money into the new company; and with capital in hand and their credit established, Becker and Litchfield pushed ahead, spending without restraint or sensible economy. The results were slow, costly, but sure. The branch line or First Division headed for Brainerd in the north central part of the state at the alleged cost of $61,500 per mile.[11] The main line inched its way towards Breckenridge and the Red River for $68,100 per mile. The former was

[9]Shortridge, *The Transition of a Typical Frontier*, p. 143.
[10]Ramsey's Diary, 19 Sept. 1861, Ramsey Papers, M.H.S.
[11]Saby, "Railroad Legislation in Minnesota, 1849 to 1875," pp. 55–6. See W. W. Folwell, *A History of Minnesota* (4 vols., St. Paul, Minnesota Historical Society, 1921–30), III, 442.

completed by 1866–67, the latter by 1871; and by then, both were so heavily mortgaged that the Panic of 1873 knocked them over like tenpins.

For all the troubles of the St. Paul and Pacific, the Northern Pacific —Minnesota's transcontinental—had not fared nearly as well. Its incorporators had received lavish land grants in their federal charter of 1864, twenty alternate sections through the states and forty in the territories— a gigantic checkerboard from Lake Superior to Puget Sound. Yet unlike the promoters of the Union and the Central Pacific railways, they had neglected to get Washington's guarantee for their bonds. For the next five years they sought this aid which they regarded as the *sine qua non* of any capitalization scheme.

Minnesota gave the Northern Pacific all the support it could muster. With legislative memorials and popular petitions, it importuned Congress to give this line the same generosity accorded the Union Pacific. It was urged that the Northern Pacific would make magnificent returns not only for its backers but also for the state and the nation as well. Indeed the commercial wealth of the American and the British Northwests would be theirs. And if the railroad were completed before a Canadian or a British rival, it might bring about the annexation of Rupert's Land. But no argument, expansionist or otherwise, loosened Washington's purse strings.

It remained for Jay Cooke, Philadelphia banker and Civil War financier, to breathe life into the railroad. Even so, the road's promoters had to approach him three times before he tentatively agreed in 1869 to underwrite the venture. By then Cooke had reached a crossroads in his career. His banking house had either to begin a distasteful course of retrenchment or uncover new investment opportunities.[12] On the one hand, Europe's appetite for federal bonds seemed to have been met, while, on the other, its desire for American railroad securities appeared to be growing. Indeed the post-war era marked a tremendous boom in American railroading. Mileage doubled; systems such as Vanderbilt's New York Central emerged; and banking firms like the House of Morgan began to peddle railway securities to their overseas customers. Under the circumstances, it undoubtedly seemed to Cooke as if his banking future lay in America's railroads.

Before the tentative agreement became firm, Cooke carefully looked into the subject of western railroads in general and the Northern Pacific in particular. During the summer of 1869 he dispatched parties to explore and report upon the railroad and its proposed route.

[12]Henrietta M. Larson, *Jay Cooke Private Banker* (Cambridge, Mass., 1936), pp. 254–8.

Although the reports ranged from unrestrained exuberance to considered optimism, all were agreed that the Northern Pacific could be built and then run at a profit. Cooke was impressed; and after James W. Taylor had gained his ear, his interest mounted. On a visit to Philadelphia, Taylor poured out his dreams of a vast commercial empire in the Northwest; and in later correspondence, he added the spice of annexation to this commercial brew.[13] Taylor's optimism seemed well founded and had an undoubted effect upon the financier. That fall the Riel Rebellion broke out, fashioning what appeared to be the perfect milieu for the annexation of Rupert's Land. Cooke signed the final contract to underwrite the railroad on 1 January 1870. Actual construction started the following summer, and by 1873, the year of the panic and of Cooke's own downfall, the railroad reached from Lake Superior to the Missouri River.

Thus by 1870–71, Minnesota possessed a promising if elementary transportation system. The branch line of the St. Paul and Pacific went almost straight north to Brainerd; its main line wandered in a westerly direction from St. Paul to Breckenridge; and the Northern Pacific cut an undeviating course due west from Duluth to Moorhead. Underlying this basic pattern and furnishing it with feeders were the various stage and freight companies, most of which were very profitable ventures in the post-war period. At least three such lines operated out of St. Cloud, competing for the "heavy contracts for carrying goods to the Hudson's Bay Company."[14] And when the St. Paul and Pacific puffed into St. Cloud in the fall of 1866, it automatically made that little city into a central point of transshipment, where rail cargoes were transferred either to Yankee freighters whose wagons joined together the railway and the Red River steamboat, or to Red River carters for the long, overland passage to Rupert's Land. In the final event the railroad would displace first the cart and wagon and then the steamboat, but during the late 'sixties all three means of transportation were still in use, harmoniously complementing each other and building a broad bridge between the Twin Cities and the Red River Settlement.

An improved transportation system inevitably stimulated the growth of trade. Its measurement can be quite accurately determined by an examination of the customs reports emanating from the port of Pembina.[15] In the fiscal year ending 30 June 1865 the collector Joseph

13Taylor to Cooke, 5 May 1869, Taylor Papers.
14Larsen, "The Northwestern Express and Transportation Company," p. 54.
15Enos Stutsman to the Treasury Department, 10 Aug. 1866 and 23 Oct. 1868, Reports and Correspondence from Special Agent Enos Stutsman, 1866–1869, N.A.

Lemay exacted $7,678.56 in duties on the furs, buffalo robes, hides, and whatnot that were imported into Minnesota from Rupert's Land. Two years later he collected almost three times as much. During this same period the total value of all imports and exports passing through Pembina, foreign as well as domestic, rose from $314,366.06 to $487,448.81. And Lemay reported that in some years more than $500,000 in bonded goods "pass[ed] inspection at this point."[16] By 1870 the grand total of all trade, including both bonded and smuggled goods, must have exceeded a million or more dollars.

In its general characteristics, the post-war trade resembled that of the early 'sixties. Though the means of transportation changed, the trade routes remained substantially the same. Greater reliance was placed upon railroads, however, and they, in turn, somewhat altered the old trading patterns. For example, the coming of the St. Paul and Pacific to St. Cloud transformed that city not only into a vital point of transshipment but also into an important market place. After 1866 Red River merchants often shopped there rather than at St. Paul, although the large fur sales continued to take place at the latter site. In addition, more and more of the general trade between St. Paul and the Red River Settlement was conducted by specialists, the commission and forwarding merchants. The only difference between them and their predecessors in the 'fifties lay in names and numbers. James J. Hill now made his debut as a commission and forwarding merchant. He was soon handling the accounts of such Red River notables as the Bishop of St. Boniface and the merchant and journalist, Alexander Begg; and he even aspired to gain the Hudson's Bay Company's freighting contract from New York to Fort Garry. In this auspicious way, Hill—a Canadian-American—gained the knowledge, capital, friends, and experience that would make his later railroad ventures such a success.

II

According to the editors of the St. Paul *Press* (16 March 1866), their city was striding militantly forward "like the Dorian Thebes through her hundred gates, to the commercial empire of the new Northwest." Despite many moments of Anglo-American bitterness during the Civil War, Minnesota had coveted the trade of the British Northwest, only

[16]Lemay to the Deputy Commissioner in charge of the Bureau of Statistics, 10 May 1869, Letters from Collectors to the Treasury Department, 1869, N.A.

rarely her landed possessions; and for some time after the war, the spirit of neighbourliness, be it ever so materialist-minded, remained. But with the death of reciprocity in 1866 and the repeated failures to resurrect it, Minnesota's mood changed. Political annexation of Rupert's Land seemed the only way by which the state could realize its commercial destiny.

And yet in 1865 citizens of Minnesota were still pleading the cause of reciprocal trade with British North America. Speaking before the St. Paul Board of Trade in late April, James W. Taylor stated his disbelief in any policy seeking political union. He claimed, without elaboration, that both Minnesota and the United States would benefit more from a confederated than an annexed Canada. Reciprocity was the only policy to pursue. The Board agreed and sent him to Detroit to represent his state's views at a commercial convention to be held there, 11–14 July.

The Detroit Convention brought together representatives from commercial organizations throughout the United States and Canada. Like many other western groups, Taylor's Minnesota delegation wanted a reciprocal trading agreement with Canada in order to get cheaper means of transportation as well as freer trade. Unfortunately for them, the convention had more foes than friends. There were the protectionists and there were the annexationists—those who argued that if Canada were denied reciprocity, she would be forced into the United States. In support of this position, Consul General John Potter (Montreal) championed the "ripe-plum" argument of Manifest Destiny. "Now we are ready to give you in Canada the most perfect reciprocity," he gratuitously informed the Canadian visitors, "but we ask you to come and share with us the responsibilities of our own government. . . ."[17]

For the friends of reciprocity, Detroit was a frustrating experience. Although Taylor was chosen as a member of a committee to investigate reciprocity and report its findings back to the convention, he was unable to give the treaty the kind of support he would have liked. The committee was composed of too many men with an implacable hostility towards greater freedom of trade, and the resulting report was a meaningless compromise, presented in the form of two incompatible resolutions. The first sanctioned the Congressional order to abrogate

[17]J. Lawrence Laughlin and H. Parker Wellis, *Reciprocity* (New York, [1903]), quoted by Theodore L. Blegen, "A Plan for the Union of British North America and the United States, 1866," *Mississippi Valley Historical Review*, IV (March, 1918), 477.

the existing treaty; the second suggested another treaty, built upon "equitable principles" and encompassing British Columbia, Vancouver Island, and Rupert's Land as well as the other British North American provinces. It was also to provide for the free navigation of the St. Lawrence—and here the hand of Taylor was seen—upon principles "as shall render them adequate for the requirements of the West in communicating with the ocean."[18]

The first resolution was unanimously endorsed by the convention but the second was suspiciously received. Only after Joseph Howe of Nova Scotia had delivered a frank and flowery speech replying to reciprocity's critics and reiterating the benefits that each party had enjoyed under the treaty did the convention reluctantly approve the second resolution. Yet the Detroit Convention really accomplished nothing. Opposing interests cancelled each other out and only the bitterness remained. To Canadians, Potter's plums became rotten fruit, and editorials such as the St. Paul *Press*'s crude effort of 27 July could scarcely have been reassuring:

If the Canadians imagine that they are of so much importance that the United States are watching them with longing eyes, it is time they were undeceived. There is not the least anxiety on that point. Ultimately the Canadas will undoubtedly form a portion of the United States, but unless the event is hastened by a war with England, it will be at the earnest solicitation of the provinces themselves.

Before too long, it was Minnesota, not Canada, which grew solicitous.

Both Canada and Minnesota wanted reciprocity renewed and each fought to get it, but there was no room for reciprocity in post-war Washington. A Canadian delegation seeking to re-negotiate in late July, 1865, was disappointed by the administration; and when the same delegates returned in the following winter to confer with the House Committee on Ways and Means, they not only re-encountered disappointment but also the indelicately annexationist temper of Representative Justin S. Morrill. After expressing his views on the inevitability of political union, Morrill, who also was an inveterate protectionist, made an outrageous proposal. In return for America's use of Canada's inshore fisheries and the St. Lawrence, he offered a free list that included nothing but millstones, rags, firewood, grindstones, and plaster.[19]

Canada was justly indignant. "I need hardly say," wrote Charles

[18]St. Paul *Press*, 14 July 1865. Both the *Press* and the *Pioneer* followed closely and reported fully upon the convention and its proceedings.
[19]L. B. Shippee, *Canadian-American Relations* (New Haven, 1939), pp. 294–5.

Brydges, general manager of the Grand Trunk Railway, to James W. Taylor, "that so far as this country is concerned any such terms are simply the close of all possible negotiations as I am perfectly certain that I am only speaking the entire sentiment of the country when I say that we should be prepared to submit to any possible difficulties rather than even consider terms which on the face of them we look upon simply as insult."[20] The prose was complicated but the meaning was clear: Canada would not be dragooned into accepting reciprocity upon Morrill's terms, and annexation was out of the question. Brydges pessimistically added that when the seventeenth of March rolled around, the treaty would be terminated forever. That day would surely come, but that it should signalize the end of reciprocity was the wish of neither Taylor nor his state.

A month earlier, in January, 1866, Taylor had addressed the citizens of St. Paul on the subject of "The Mississippi and St. Lawrence Rivers as Commercial Highways."[21] While he had little to say about the former, he asserted that free navigation of the St. Lawrence, if improved by enlarged canals en route, promised Minnesota a 50 per cent reduction in freight rates to the Atlantic Ocean. The state's true need was reciprocity; there was no logical place for protectionism in North America. Moreover annexation of Canada was an uncertain policy to pursue and could never be gained by unneighbourly actions. The only way to political union—an assertion that betrayed Taylor's turn of mind, from supporting reciprocity to suggesting annexation—lay along the path of commercial unity. Once again the St. Paul Board of Trade accepted Taylor's lead and sent a memorial to Congress representing his views and theirs on North American trade and reciprocity. The memorial urged that a joint Canadian-American commission be created and instructed to expand and improve the old Reciprocity Treaty along the following lines. Inshore fisheries were to be given the same freedom granted them in 1854. On the one hand, Americans would be allowed the use of Canada's border canals, enlarged to accommodate vessels up to 1,000 tons, and on the other, Canadian ships could freely ply the waters of Lake Michigan. The free list, for both parties, was to be extended, although all goods would be subjected to a standard 5 per cent duty imposed for the purposes of revenue. In addition, both countries would adopt common patent and copyright laws, and the treaty in its operation would apply to all British North America.

Most of the memorial's suggestions were only chaff to Minnesotans.

[20]Charles J. Brydges to Taylor, 26 Feb. 1866, Taylor Papers.
[21]St. Paul *Press*, 9 Jan. 1866.

They were primarily concerned with the "great need of the West," inexpensive transportation, and with the extension of reciprocity to Rupert's Land. Their wheat production was destined to climb during the decade, 1860–70, from 5,101,432 bushels to 18,789,188.[22] In 1865 alone, slightly more than 6,000,000 bushels were exported from the state[23]—startling evidence that her post-war economy was fast becoming dependent upon wheat. To realize the maximum profits from their staple, however, Minnesota farmers had to possess an inexpensive but adequate transportation system to the world market. Unfortunately for them the Civil War had turned their old system upside down. The war closed the Mississippi River to downriver traffic and directed western trade along an east-west railroad axis. Not only was trade diverted but freight costs soared without the competition of steamboats. In the immediate post-war era, anti-monopoly groups arose throughout the entire Northwest, protesting high freight rates and preluding with their actions and attitudes the Granger movement of the 'seventies. Farmers and merchants alike wanted a cheap water route either to supplant or offset the railroads. The Mississippi River could no longer be considered, for Minnesotans regarded New Orleans, with its "tropical climate and humid atmosphere," as an *entrepôt* unfit for their wheat.[24] The only practicable course lay through the Great Lakes and down the St. Lawrence and the only way to get it was to renew the reciprocity treaty.

Moreover the merchants of St. Paul professedly believed that God and Nature had decreed an economic marriage between Minnesota and the British Northwest. "The commercial interests of the Red River country and St. Paul are very closely identified," a special agent of the United States Treasury reported, "the trade of the Dakota, and British American Red River Settlements, and of the Hudson's Bay Co. of that district, is exclusively with, or passes through St. Paul."[25] In an editorial upon "The Commerce of St. Paul—Wonderful Growth of its Wholesale Trade," the St. Paul *Press* (26 January 1867) explained the growth in geographic terms. Nature, it asserted, had bestowed upon St. Paul a trading area that extended from the St. Croix Valley to the Sauk River and reached northwestward to the flourishing settlements of Rupert's Land.

[22]United States, Ninth Census, 1870, *Industry and Wealth*, 42nd Cong., 1st Sess., Serial 1475.
[23]St. Paul *Press*, 19 Dec. 1865.
[24]*Ibid.*, 25 Feb. and 8 April 1869.
[25]Enos Stutsman to the Treasury Department, 31 July 1867, Reports and Correspondence from Special Agent Enos Stutsman, 1866–1869.

Tomorrow's empire seemed almost boundless. Surely St. Paul's hinterland would arc westward to the Rockies and northwestward to encompass all the Hudson's Bay Company's territories. Equally inevitable were the settlement and colonization of the British Northwest. With reciprocity that region's economy would be dependent upon Minnesota; but without reciprocity, St. Paul's key to a commercial kingdom, the whole hinterland might be lost. After the second failure of the Canadian commissioners to re-open negotiations with Washington in the winter of 1866, reciprocity was doomed. Spring and St. Patrick's Day marked its official demise, but in Minnesota, only the Irish of St. Paul celebrated.

III

With the passing of reciprocity, Minnesota became openly and positively annexationist. Led by its press, politicians, and publicists, the state eagerly pursued a policy designed to annex any part or all of British North America. Though the philosophy underlying this policy may well have been irrational, based as it was upon quasi-divine and natural tenets, it promised very practical ends. Political union would guarantee the merchants and shippers of St. Paul a vast commercial empire and, for the farmers, it promised assurance of the free navigation of the St. Lawrence.

Minnesota's annexationism was not a stratagem adopted by self-seeking politicians. It is true that Senator Alexander Ramsey collaborated with other radical Republicans in Congress, men like Nathaniel Banks and Zachariah Chandler who apparently used expansionism to appease their constituents, to wrest control of foreign affairs away from the President, or to perpetuate the confusion created by the Civil War.[26] Ramsey worked with these men, cheek by jowl, but he always pursued expansionism for its own sake, believing that only through annexation could his state achieve its commercial destiny. Similarly, Taylor also turned to annexation in the belief that, even if Canada acquired the Northwest, her limited finances would preclude the internal improvements necessary to exploit—for St. Paul's sake—the region's natural resources. Together, Taylor and Ramsey shaped Minnesota's expansionist policy regarding the British Northwest.

[26]See Joe Patterson Smith, *The Radical Expansionists of the Early Reconstruction Era* (Chicago, 1930), pp. 117–18.

Elsewhere in the United States, expansion might be employed by such men as General Banks of Massachusetts in order to coddle his Irish constituents; but of Minnesota's Congressmen, only Ignatius Donnelly, whose ancestors were obviously "exiles" from the green isle, publicly championed the cause of Irish nationalism. It was not that there were no Irish in Minnesota. They constituted (1869–70) between 5 and 10 per cent of the total population,[27] and like Irishmen everywhere, they made up an independent, clannish, and vocal bloc, with their Irish American Club, Irish Immigration Society, and even (1865) their own political party. Despite the Irish—who congregated in St. Paul—and their anti-English sentiments, Fenianism was never a strong force in municipal or state politics. Neither St. Paul's Democratic *Pioneer* nor its Republican *Press* sympathized with or supported Fenian ideals. In the opinion of the *Press* (29 November 1865), Fenianism cherished "no principles which commend it to the sympathy of Americans"; it was "simply an assertion of clannish antipathy to the Anglo-Saxon." Its intended invasion of Canada was (7 March 1866) a senseless venture, and, in fact, the whole movement resembled (10 March 1866) a "ghost story."

The Protestant press was not alone in its opposition. Minnesota's Catholic hierarchy, like that of Ireland, denounced Fenianism in unmistakable terms. It was, said Bishop Thomas L. Grace, speaking on St. Patrick's Day, 1866, "the laughing-stock of the world" and could only end in disaster.[28] When J. F. McCormick, an Inspector General of the Fenian Brotherhood, pleaded before a large audience in St. Paul's Ingersoll Hall to establish a local "circle," the eloquent Father John Ireland—born in County Kilkenny—took the floor to oppose him. The priest's sharp tongue quickly routed McCormick. The meeting closed in tumult—and without a circle.

After the ill-fated Fenian invasion of Canada in June, 1866, St. Paul's newspapers criticized both Fenianism and the lax federal administration that had permitted its growth. The *Press* (3 June 1866) called the Fenians "wretched victims of an insane delusion" whose raids were "an insulting travesty of the Government of the United States." The *Pioneer* (5 June 1866) fully agreed: "However much we may delight

---

[27]Minnesota, Assistant Secretary of State, *Statistics of Minnesota . . . for 1869* (St. Paul, 1870), p. 66. Cf. *ibid.*, *Statistics of Minnesota . . . for 1870* (St. Paul, 1871), p. 125. These statistics differed. The first work gave the Irish a percentage of nearly ten; the second gave them only about five.

[28]St. Paul *Press*, 18 March 1866. Not till 1867 was a Fenian circle formed in St. Paul, but neither then nor thereafter was the movement a dangerous or a powerful force within the state.

to see the English ox gored in return for recent kindness (?), justice demands that the United States authorities shall prevent further movements in our borders to attack a nation with whom we are at peace." Moreover the *Press* already (25 March 1866) suspected that Canadian politicians used Fenianism to foster patriotism and guessed, with greater insight than its editors usually possessed, that "the only result Fenians are likely to accomplish . . . is the consolidation of British power on this continent." When it later became known that a bill was to be introduced into Congress altering the neutrality laws in order to protect the Irish nationalists, Minnesota's newspapers were unequivocally opposed. There was, in sum, no evidence to show that the state urged an expansionist policy out of sympathy for the Irish or any other nationalist group. Minnesota's leaders pursued expansionism because of the practical ends it promised.

In the spring of 1866 Minnesota was suddenly and unexpectedly given a chance to publicize its expansionist programme. On 28 March the House of Representatives asked the Secretary of the Treasury for a statement of the trade between the United States and the British North American provinces, 1854–65. Secretary Hugh McCulloch acceded to the request and assigned the task to Taylor, as Special Agent of the Treasury. The latter knew an opportunity when he saw one. Interpreting his instructions according to Minnesota's interests, he drew up a sensational report entitled, "Commercial Relations with British America" and presented it to the House on 12 June.[29] Although all the commercial statistics sought by Congress were included, they made up a small portion of the whole paper. The heart of the report was an elaborate scheme for the annexation and development of British North America.

Taylor's report paid particular attention to the British Northwest or Central British America, to use his own descriptive title for the region. It was extravagantly portrayed as a land whose soil was eminently suited to the production of grain and livestock, a well-watered region blessed with a salubrious climate, and an area well adapted by nature to transportation routes by steam or rail. He pointed out that present trade lines in the Northwest ran north and south, carrying goods between Rupert's Land and Minnesota whose annual value amounted to nearly $2,000,000, and he prophesied that this trade would expand, once pioneers had moved into and settled the Northwest. "For the production of wheat, barley, rye, oats, peas, potatoes, vegetables, grass—whatever is grown in Minnesota, except

[29]*House Executive Document No. 128*, 39th Cong., 1st Sess., Serial 1263.

maize—the region in question will," he claimed, "be unsurpassed by any other area of similar extent on the continent." Rich though the land was, he maintained that Canada would be unable to profit from it, since she herself could not provide it with sufficient transportation, whether by a "seaway" to the Atlantic or a transcontinental railroad. The United States, on the other hand, could install transportation lines and immediately exploit the resources of the region.

For this unfortunate state of affairs, there seemed only one solution—annexation to the United States of British North America. "I cannot resist the conclusion," declared Taylor, "that events have presented to the people and government of the United States the opportunity—of interposing by an overture to the people of the English colonies on this continent, of course upon the fullest consultation with the government of Great Britain, to unite their fortunes with the people and government of the United States." He went boldly on to outline a plan for political union. Four provinces (Nova Scotia, New Brunswick, Canada East, and Canada West—but not Prince Edward Island) would enter as states, and three territories would be created from the Northwest: Selkirk, Saskatchewan, and Columbia. The new states would be equal in every way to the existing states within the union, and the territories would be organized and governed after the fashion of Montana, that is, in the usual manner. The American land system would prevail, with its rectangular surveys and provisions for school aid. Provincial debts would be assumed and federal grants extended to offset the loss in revenue from customs. A "St. Lawrence Seaway" would be straightway constructed and a land-grant, stock-guaranteed railroad built across the continent.

If only the British Northwest wished to be annexed—and here Taylor came to the inner heart of his report—the United States would accept the part and not the whole, organize it into territories, and facilitate the construction of a railroad from the western shore of Lake Superior to the Pacific Slope. But whether in whole or in part, Taylor summed up his plan for a continental union in ringing terms:

I will not extend this paper by any presentation of what I regard as the great preponderance of benefit to the people of the provinces. I only reiterate that they have a right to demand of their present rulers two great objects, a Mediterranean to Superior, and a railway to the Pacific ocean, and these before 1880; and I cannot believe these objects will be assured to this generation by a provincial confederation, or by the intervention of England. The United States may interpose, with the requisite guarantees; and if so, why shall we not combine to extend an American Union to the Arctic circle?

"Why not?" the average Minnesotan would have echoed, for Taylor had cleverly if erroneously equated his wishes with those of all Canadians.

Taylor's plan of union gained considerable notoriety when General Banks introduced it as a bill (the Taylor-Banks bill) into the House on 3 July 1866. If the plan itself was manifestly Taylor's articulation of Minnesota's policy, Bank's bill was just as obviously introduced in order to catch the eye of the discontented Irish in his constituency and the disenchanted friends of reciprocity everywhere.

The bill received a varied response from the American press.[30] The Detroit *Free Press* called it an intelligent plan, since "nature itself has decreed that the provinces and the Northern and Western States of the United States *must* be governed by the same laws and controlled by the same powers." The Troy *Whig* likened the bill to a "handle of the basket" held out to capture ripe Canadian fruit, but the Chicago *Tribune* thought the whole plan much too generous and rhetorically asked its authors if they had forgotten the Civil War. The Detroit *Post* also objected, but on different grounds. The Canadians were "not quite ready"; they needed a broad social and political education before they could graduate from provincial status into statehood. The Chicago *Times* agreed. Annexation seemed premature, and its terms, too liberal. Why accept a peanut vendor as a full partner? The Buffalo *Advertiser* caustically referred to Taylor as a wild, impractical genius who would annex Europe if there were not an Atlantic Ocean to block him.

No cheers from the Canadian press greeted the Taylor-Banks bill. Though the Toronto *Globe* faintly praised Taylor's report, it belittled his plan for a continental union. "The only thing to be said in his favour," it pronounced, "is that the absurdity of his proposal does something to relieve its insolence. . . . Mr. Taylor might next try his hand on a plan for the annexation of the moon." On the other hand, the Hamilton *Spectator* professed to find the many examples of American generosity to Canadians—the Fenian raids, the throttling of reciprocity, the Taylor-Banks bill—somewhat inexplicable to the mind of mortal man. "The Americans," it commented, "draw their inspirations from very high sources; and remembering that it is said of the Great Father of us all, that, whom He loveth He chasteneth."

The St. Paul *Press* (7 July 1866) thought the Taylor-Banks bill "an

[30]Clippings from the Detroit *Free Press* and other American and Canadian papers were found in Taylor's Scrapbooks, Taylor Papers.

able and comprehensive measure" which the Canadians ought quickly
to accept. And what if they rejected it? The *Press* assured its readers
that "eventually they . . . [would] fall like a ripe apple into the lap of
the American Union." The *Pioneer* reacted in a strangely disinterested
way. It reprinted the bill, without commenting upon it then or thereafter. As for the bill, it was read twice in the House and then referred
to the Committee on Foreign Affairs, headed by Banks himself. Here
it perished, acknowledging with its death the real intentions of its
stepfather.

All the politicking of General Banks could not still Minnesota's
expansionist spirit. During the next two years, the state bombarded
Congress with memorials and petitions praying for various measures
that would stimulate the growth of her commercial empire. Congress was
asked to encourage the Red River trade by altering the customs laws.
It was urged to develop transportation routes within the state's commercial orbit—to improve the state road from St. Cloud to Fort Abercrombie, to better the highway between the fort and Pembina, and
to build a new wagon road to Montana. And with the enthusiastic
support of Dakota Territory, Minnesota pleaded with Congress to
hasten the settlement of the Red River Valley by creating more land
offices, conducting additional surveys, and removing all the remaining
Indians.

If Minnesotans could accurately have foreseen the future, they
would have realized that it would be easier to remove Indians from the
Red River Valley than Canadians from the British Northwest. However they interpreted events in 1866–67 to suit their interests and
complement their own wishes. Like many other Americans, they
had no faith, for example, in the future of the new Dominion of
Canada. In the belief that Canadians themselves took only "a passive
interest" in confederation, St. Paul's newspapers accorded Canada's
first birthday a slight, almost scornful recognition.[31] Moreover the
myth was soon cultivated that although Canada longed for political
union with the Northwest, the citizens of Red River did not share that
feeling. Would not the Taylor-Banks bill resolve all problems north
of the line? The St. Paul *Press* held that Canada could never give to
the Northwest all the material advantages enumerated in the bill.
With annexation to the United States of British North America, not only
would the Northwest be quickly and efficiently settled, but—claimed
James W. Taylor—Canadians could also cease "dragging out a

[31]St. Paul *Pioneer*, 6 July 1867. Cf. the *Press*, 6 July 1867.

dependent and precarious political life under Confederation. . . ."[32]
He gloated over evidences of anti-confederationist sentiment that he
found in the Maritimes and concluded that the moment for America's
manifest continental destiny was almost at hand. "We have only to
place an 'open basket' (to use an illustration of the N.Y. Evening
Post applied to this [Taylor-Banks] bill) under the tree," wrote
Taylor, first to the Treasury, then to the State Department, "and the
ripe fruit will speedily fall." Deluded by their own dreams, Taylor
and his fellow expansionists began to put basket after basket under
the Canadian tree.

IV

The expansionist pace quickened in 1867, when it became apparent
that the Dominion of Canada, with the blessings of the British North
America Act, was actively moving to incorporate the Northwest.
For the B.N.A. Act specifically allowed Canada to annex and provide
government for Rupert's Land. Not to be outdone, Minnesota matched
the Canadian cadence and began to speak somewhat grandly of
another, a second Louisiana Purchase. Five days after William
McDougall (4 December 1867) introduced a resolution into the
Canadian House of Commons petitioning the Queen to transfer the
Northwest, Alexander Ramsey brought a similar resolution to the floor
of the United States Senate.[33]

Ramsey directed his resolution to the attention of the Senate's
Committee on Foreign Relations, asking its members "to inquire into
the expediency of a treaty between the United States and the
Dominion of Canada." For the guidance of the committee, he enclosed
a treaty whose provisions were carefully outlined. The whole measure
was obviously Taylor's handiwork and represented an amalgamation
of ideas that he had already advanced in advocating both reciprocity
and political union with Canada. In the field of Canadian-American
trade, the measure again proposed that an *ad valorem* 5 per cent duty
be placed on the produce and manufactures indigenous to either
country. Otherwise, there would be free trade. Excise duties would
be assimilated. Similarly, a common system of copyrights, patent

---

[32]Taylor to Edward Cooper, Assistant Secretary of the Treasury, 23 Nov. 1867,
Consular Dispatches, Winnipeg, Special Agent, Red River Affairs, 1867–1870,
N.A. Taylor sent the same letter to Secretary of State Seward.

[33]*Senate Miscellaneous Document No. 4,* 40th Cong., 2nd Sess., Serial 1319.

rights, and postal rates would prevail in both nations. The Great Lakes and the St. Lawrence would be open to navigation by Canadians and Americans alike, and there were to be no restrictions on either the coastal trade or the inshore fisheries. Such were the details contained in the treaty's first six provisions.

The seventh and final provision contained the heart of the measure:

That Canada, with the consent of Great Britain, shall cede to the United States the districts of North America west of longitude 90°, on conditions following, to wit: 1st. The United States will pay $6,000,000 to the Hudson [sic] Bay Company in full discharge of all claims to territory or jurisdiction in North America, whether founded on the charter of the company, or any treaty, law, or usage. 2d. The United States will assume the public debt of British Columbia, no[t] exceeding the sum of $2,000,000. 3d. To aid the construction of the Northern Pacific railroad from the western extremity of Lake Superior to Puget Sound, the United States, in addition to the grant of land heretofore made, will guarantee dividends of five per cent. upon the stock of said company: *Provided*, That the amount of stock shall not exceed $20,000 per mile, and Congress shall regulate the securities for advances on account thereof. 4th. The northwest territory shall be divided and organized into Territories of the United States, not less than three in number, with all the rights and privileges of the citizens and government of Montana Territory, so far as the same can be made applicable.

Here was a scheme as meticulously and skilfully drawn as a lawyer's brief, which, if successful, might guarantee Minnesota's commercial greatness: $8,000,000 in return for a quitclaim deed to all the British Northwest.

On the day he introduced his resolution, Ramsey offered his colleagues a brief apologia in its support.[34] He told the Senate that Canada was preparing a bill that would permit her to expand to the Pacific, and since British Columbia had already applied for admission into the dominion, he claimed that "the passage of such an act by the Parliament at Ottawa, with the assent of the queen in council, will consummate the annexation of northwest British America to Canada." At this point, it apparently slipped his mind that a considerable portion of the continent was known as British America. Or perhaps his enthusiasm simply outran his source material, for he subsequently maintained—without tendering any statistical support—that the "people" of British Columbia and Rupert's Land would rather become citizens of the United States than subjects of the Queen in Canada. To deny these "people" a choice would be unpardonable!

[34]*Congressional Globe*, 40th Cong., 2nd Sess., 9 Dec. 1867, p. 79.

"I believe," he pontificated, "it has become the duty of the American Congress to indicate openly and distinctly the terms and conditions which we are willing to offer as an alternative to the Canadian venture." As for the odd inclusion within the resolution of an enlarged reciprocity treaty, he asserted that it "might not only result in a desirable extension of our institutions in northwest America, but would go far to remove all grounds of offense and antagonism of interests between the communities planted in the valley of the St. Lawrence." Stripped of its vague and evangelical verbiage, Ramsey's little speech had a simple message: expansionism might be a profitable policy for the United States to pursue.

His legislative pot-pourri neither intrigued nor impressed the Senate. "It struck me," commented Grimes of Iowa, " . . . that it embraced several incongruous subjects."[35] When a colleague said that he would get the drift of the measure with a second reading of certain key paragraphs, Grimes called for it and then remarked that he was absolutely opposed to another reciprocity treaty. Without further debate or comment, Ramsey's resolution was tabled and ordered to be printed.

In composing the above resolution, Ramsey and Taylor had collaborated very closely.[36] The senator had drawn upon the latter's voluminous though partisan knowledge of the British Northwest and had freely sampled from his store of journalistic talents; and together they had designed a document calculated to catch the eye of expansionists and appease the temper of protectionists throughout the nation. The final product of their labours was a creature of crooked logic. They hoped that the 5 per cent duty would separate Canada from Great Britain and eventually lead towards annexation, but they knew that, in itself, the proposition was "free trade." They also believed that "Canada would cheerfully agree to the cession proposed of Northwest America, if the privilege of buying and selling in the United States was assured." Here was a double-edged sword that would cut to Minnesota's advantage no matter how it was wielded. The policy regarding the Northwest seemed to have the same qualities. If the terms of the resolution's seventh provision failed to entice British Columbia and Rupert's Land into the United States, then surely Great

[35]*Ibid.*

[36]Taylor to Ramsey, 6 Dec. 1867, Ramsey Papers. In this letter, Taylor fully explained the resolution's rationale, giving both his and Ramsey's reasoning for the inclusion of every provision. Enclosed in the above was a revised copy of the 9 December resolution, with certain amendments written in the margin in Taylor's hand.

Britain and Canada would have to promise a similar programme of internal improvements in order to retain the loyalty of the two regions. In either event, Minnesota would profit. Ramsey and Taylor, with more guile than good sense, were betting on annexation and then hedging.

They placed a good many wagers upon the race for annexation. On 31 January 1868 the senator introduced a second resolution, much like the first but slightly re-worded to meet certain contingencies initially overlooked. It too was tabled and printed;[37] but on this occasion, Ramsey put off his explanatory remarks until later. At an earlier date, Taylor had suggested to President Andrew Johnson that he noncommittally call the attention of Congress to the Taylor-Banks plan of union. And in his last annual message, the President responded in a surprisingly expansionist vein: "Comprehensive national policy would seem to sanction the acquisition and incorporation into our Federal Union of the several adjacent continental and insular communities as speedily as it can be done peacefully, lawfully, and without any violation of national justice, faith or honor."[38] Taylor also preached the gospel of Minnesota's expansionism into Secretary of State Seward's open ears, having for some time received the latter's permission "to advise the Department of State, of the progress of American interests and institutions, northwest of Lake Superior."[39] It was no trouble at all for Taylor to work with a man of Seward's Anglophobic, jingoist temper, and he cleverly knew how to cater to the Secretary's interest, particularly when Alaska was concerned.

To gain greater support for his and Ramsey's expansionist programme, Taylor returned to Minnesota and enlisted the aid of the state legislature and St. Paul's newspapers. As a publicist and as a lobbyist, he was never more effective. He had, however, been more objective. For the propaganda campaign he waged was a combination of truth, half-truth, and falsehood, all contrived to fit the expansionist spirit of his state. He told Minnesotans of Britain's underhanded "scheme" to annex the Northwest to Canada by order in council, and he added that the people of the Northwest would thus be transferred, without either advance notice or consultation, "to a government with

[37]*Senate Miscellaneous Document No. 22*, 40th Cong., 2nd Sess., Serial 1319.

[38]Fourth Annual Message, 9 Dec. 1868, James D. Richardson, ed., *A Compilation of the Messages and Papers of the Presidents 1789–1897* (10 vols., Washington, D.C., 1897–99), VI, 688.

[39]Taylor to Seward, 14 March 1868, Consular Dispatches, Winnipeg, Special Agent, Red River Affairs, 1867–1870. Cf. Seward to Ramsey, 11 April 1868, Ramsey Papers.

which they have no affinity or tastes, interests, or business."[40] Though the newspapers gave Taylor enthusiastic support, the legislature was even more receptive. It was with some pride that he later informed Seward that he had secured a resolution "requesting Congress to confirm . . . the annexation of Alaska, and presenting other views of national policy in respect to Northwest British America. . . ."[41] The resolution was entirely his own. He wrote it, handed it over to a member of the state's "Senate Committee on Foreign Affairs," banqueted with some of the Solons, and was rewarded for his efforts by seeing the legislature act favourably and with fantastic speed. Within ten days after its introduction in the upper house, the resolution received its final approval, was signed by the governor, and sent on to Congress.

It is to be doubted whether any other state legislatures possessed committees on foreign affairs, a field of government constitutionally confined to Washington; and even if they did, it would be difficult to find one less diplomatic than Minnesota's. The resolution, which Ramsey brought to the floor of the United States Senate on 31 March, was brief but bellicose.[42] It called upon Congress to confirm the treaty with Russia and thus annex Alaska, and it urged both Congress and the President to protest Canada's pending annexation of the British Northwest. Such a move, "without a vote of the people of Selkirk and the settlers upon the sources of the Saskatchewan river, who largely consist of emigrants from the United States . . . will be an unwarrantable interference with the principle of self-government, and cannot be regarded with indifference by the people of the United States." If, on the other hand, the region were ceded to the United States, all friction—the vexatious legacies from the Civil War—between Great Britain, Canada, and the United States would be removed. The self-righteous tone of resolution, as well as its patently false references to numerous American emigrants, needs little comment. The historian is reminded of the War Hawks of 1812 who were sure that all their international ills would be quickly settled if Britain would only hand over Canada to the United States.

In 1867, the year of the purchase of Russian Alaska, Minnesota's press had not been too enthusiastic about the acquisition. Alaska seemed to possess the advantages of an over-priced icebox. But it was not long before the state began to see certain geopolitical advantages

[40]*St. Paul Press*, 27 Feb. 1868.

[41]13 March 1868, Consular Dispatches, Winnipeg, Special Agent, Red River Affairs, 1867–1870.

[42]*Senate Miscellaneous Document No. 68*, 40th Cong., 2nd Sess., Serial 1319.

that had been instantly apparent to Senator Charles Sumner (Massachusetts), chairman of the Senate's Foreign Relations Committee. The latter candidly thought that the annexation of Alaska would be "a visible step in the occupation of the whole North American continent."[43] The St. Paul *Press*, the more expansionist of that city's papers, had to concede the point. Though it still thought the price too high, nevertheless, after the treaty's ratification, it admitted (10 April 1867) that Alaska "affords a new anchorage for that policy of northward expansion by which Mr. Seward hopes, before long, to absorb the intermediate British possessions, and a new base for the extension of our commerce and power in the Pacific." Between the Senate's ratification in April, 1867, and the House's passage of the necessary appropriations in July of the following year, Minnesota's attitude towards Alaska—as revealed by its press, politicians, and its publicists—changed from guarded approval to open approbation. Alaska and the British Northwest had been tied together as a unit in the strategy of continental expansion.

The July debates in the House of Representatives, and particularly Minnesota's contributions thereto, were remarkably, blatantly expansionist. By accepting the treaty, according to one congressman, the United States would cage the British lion on the Pacific coast and cripple "that great and grasping monopoly, the Hudson's Bay Company. . . ."[44] He and others too expressed the hope that, with the Alaskan addition, Canada would finally fall like ripe fruit—some men preferred pears to apples—into American hands.

Ignatius Donnelly of Minnesota differed from his imperialist colleagues only in language. "I shall vote for this bill," he declared, " . . . because I consider it one of the necessary steps in the expansion of our institutions and nationality over the entire domain of the North American continent." "But," he went on:

the great significance this purchase possesses is found in the fact that it points the way to the acquisition by the United States of that great and valuable region, Western British America. . . . With our great nation on the south of this region, and our new acquisition of Alaska resting upon its northern boundary, British dominion will be inevitably pressed out of western British America. It will disappear between the upper and the nether mill-stones. These jaws of the nation will swallow it up.

The United States needed all western North America. Donnelly said that "nothing less than a continent can suffice as the basis and foundation for that nation in whose destiny is involved the destiny of mankind."

43Smith, *The Radical Expansionists*, p. 113.
44*Congressional Globe*, 40th Cong., 2nd Sess., pp. 3659–62, 3808 *et seq.*

The Lord had intended the United States to enjoy it all. One congressman mildly rebuked the Minnesotan, suggesting that as grinders of others the United States had not been too successful, but most men concurred with Donnelly. Rufus Spalding (Ohio), carried away by the doctrine of a God-given destiny, asserted that the United States "will not culminate until she rules the whole American continent, and all the isles contiguous thereto." When Frederick Pike (Maine) interjected: "Including South America [?]," Spalding replied, "Including South America, by all means." And here the geography exercise ended, for no one thought to mention Europe, Africa, or Asia.

Four weeks later, Ramsey echoed the raucous notes of Donnelly's expansionism when he took the floor of the Senate and spoke to his resolutions of the past winter.[45] It was a long and rambling speech, tramping over the same ground and uncovering the same old landmarks, and it must have been tedious to all present. Once again Ramsey recited the material glories of the British Northwest—its wheat production would one day equal Russia's—and once again he sadly noted that this potential would never be realized without annexation to the United States. He claimed that the moment for action had arrived. Canada would soon possess the region, and once railroads were on the land, it would be forever British. Would it not be better to acquire the Northwest by granting Canada a new reciprocity treaty? That would be "a perfect and adequate arrangement." But the Senate was not interested. A bill (S 578) that Ramsey had brought forward earlier, regulating the trade between the United States and British North America, was read twice, referred to the Foreign Relations Committee, ordered printed—and then it perished.

Senatorial indifference could not dampen Minnesota's expansionism. Taylor never stopped trying to influence Seward until the latter had left office. He advised him that, without reciprocity, Nova Scotia would not join the confederation. "In this stress," he asked, "will not the Ottawa politicians be willing to transfer the Northwest Territory in exchange for a Reciprocity Treaty?"[46] And would not Britain give its approval, if the United States forgot its *Alabama* claims? To Taylor's questions, there could only be negative answers. For all its post-war imperialism and muscular nationalism, the United States would not lower its protective tariff walls in order to gain new territories. It was always more protectionist than expansionist. Furthermore,

45*Ibid.*, 27 July 1868, pp. 4503–6.
46Taylor to Seward, 18 Nov. 1868, Consular Dispatches, Winnipeg, Special Agent, Red River Affairs, 1867–1870.

no Ottawa politician would dare suggest exchanging the Northwest territory for reciprocity. Though Taylor and Ramsey spoke time and again of moments of action, the moments, if they ever had existed, disappeared with the coming of Canadian confederation and Canada's subsequent negotiations for the Hudson's Bay Company's territories. None the less, ideas of cession, reciprocity, the *Alabama* claims, and intriguing combinations of all three, lingered within the state long after Canada had completed negotiations with Britain and the Company in the spring of 1869.

V

The news of the transfer of the British Northwest, when first made known to Minnesota, made very little impact. It was as if the full significance were not grasped. But when realization finally overcame incredulity, it brought a sense of embittered frustration in its train. In an editorial, "Our Commercial Empire," the St. Paul *Press* (1 May 1869) acidly commented upon the change in Rupert's Land: "If politically it belongs to Canada, geographically and commercially it belongs not to Canada but to Minnesota. Shut off and walled out from Canada by the wild and rugged uplift of primary rocks which divides the Hudson and Superior basins . . . nothing but an imaginary line . . . separates it from Minnesota." It added, with a proprietary and epigrammatic air, that "Canadian policy may propose, but American enterprise will dispose." Taylor, disappointed, fired off critical articles to various newspapers carefully pointing out that the people of Rupert's Land had had no voice in the transfer of their land and were apparently to have none in the new government. In one sent to the Chicago *Tribune*, he referred to the administrative plans of Canada as "a mere transcript of the Star Chamber hitherto organized by . . . the Hudson [*sic*] Bay Company."[47] To Ramsey in Washington, he wrote that the proposed Canadian government was "a complete proconsulship" that "must be obnoxious to the people of Selkirk."[48] These were the bitter sentiments of a man who had proudly borne the sobriquet, "Saskatchewan" Taylor. Now his career seemed to be teetering on the rim of disaster. With the change in the federal government, he had forfeited his position with the State Department. With changed events in Rupert's Land, he seemed about to lose his expansionist dreams as

[47]Copy, dated 8 June 1869, Taylor Papers.
[48]14 June 1869, *ibid.*

well. For if Canada gained and held Rupert's Land, might not "Saskatchewan" Taylor lose the subject that had sustained him for so many years?

These were discouraging times. Reciprocity was defunct and there appeared to be no hope for its revival. Plans to bolster the financial position of the Northern Pacific, through federal guarantees, had been unsuccessful. Taylor's pet scheme for an international, Canadian-American railroad to the Pacific had been upset. Canada, new owner of the Hudson's Bay territories, apparently possessed neither the design nor the funds to develop the Northwest. Taylor himself, for all his unseemly and unprincipled scrambling for employment—from the Northern Pacific Railroad, the Chicago and Northwestern, and the Grand Trunk, as well as the Hudson's Bay Company and the State Department—could find nothing of permanence. Both his career and the commercial destiny of his patron city, St. Paul, seemed to have ended—cut short by an order in council.

But in Washington, Senator Ramsey had just embarked on another expansionist course without regard for the State Department. Like his fellow senators of a radical Republican stamp, he had long believed that the Senate was constitutionally competent to advise the President on foreign affairs, and "as a Minnesota senator, [he was] determined to rouse the country from its attitude of passivity in regard to . . . [Minnesota's] developement [sic] Northward. . . ."[49] With bland disregard for the Secretary of State, he introduced (3 February 1869) an amendment to the consular and diplomatic appropriations bill to establish a consulate at Winnipeg in the Red River Settlement. After demonstrating the need for the post because of trade, he added opaquely: "For this reason, and for political reasons which every Senator can very well appreciate, it has been thought advisable by our people to have a consul there."[50] When Morrill of Vermont inquired if the State Department had recommended the consulate, Ramsey boldly replied: "I suppose the Department know nothing about it. I imagine we can inform the Department quite as well as they can inform us on such a subject as this. I doubt if the Department know anything about it." The amendment passed Congress, and the Department, ignorant or not, accepted the decision and filled the post.

Thus did Ramsey create his own listening post in the British Northwest. The first consul was Oscar Malmros, a loyal working friend of the Republican party and an intimate of Ramsey's. If in theory he was

[49]Taylor to Ramsey, 6 Dec. 1867, Ramsey Papers.
[50]*Congressional Globe,* 40th Cong., 3rd Sess., p. 821.

appointed by the Department of State on 20 April 1869, in fact he was the appointee of Alexander Ramsey, to whom he subsequently reported with a greater candour and completeness than he ever accorded the Secretary of State. On 13 August Malmros opened his consulate in Emmerling's Hotel in Winnipeg, the locus then and thereafter of the Red River Settlement's American party. The stage was set for intrigue!

Chapter 8. *Canada, the Company, and Rupert's Land, 1857–1869*

WHEN THE NORTH WEST COMPANY AND THE HUDSON'S BAY COMPANY merged in 1821, Canada's stake in the commercial empire of the great Northwest came to an end. At last the Hudson's Bay Company was master in its own house; and to protect itself from the chance Canadian interloper, it had kept open only those portages lying west of Rat Portage at the far end of Lake of the Woods. As a result, the eastern trails grew annually more obscure as the forest reasserted its ancient sovereignty. No longer did the wilderness resound to the songs of the voyageurs from the St. Lawrence. Now its silence was rarely broken, save by the occasional Hudson's Bay express or by the swiftly moving canoe of Sir George Simpson, hastening westward on one of his many tours of inspection.

In the 'forties Canadians began to dream again of the Northwest; in the 'fifties the dreams assumed recognizable form; and in the next decade, Canada reached out for her prize. Here, as in the United States, westward expansion was powered by many forces. In Canada West, the Precambrian Shield restricted agricultural progress and squeezed many a land-hungry farmer into the Middle West. Merchants of Toronto wanted to share in the fur trade of Rupert's Land. Other men, of a broader vision, were caught up by the prospect of a transcontinental nationhood; fear of the advancing American frontier spurred on still others in their pursuit of a nation from sea to sea. Whatever man's motivation might have been, it was very clear by the late 'fifties that Canada's moment of decision would soon be at hand. Driven into the apex of an awkward triangle sided by the Shield and the States, she either had to escape over the Shield and move into the Northwest or face the future as a petty state in the East—overshadowed and perhaps overpowered by the United States.

I

In 1857 the various forces working out Canada's northwestern destiny were brought into sharp focus when the Select Committee of the British House of Commons made its inquiry into the affairs of the Hudson's Bay Company. As early as December, 1856, Henry Labouchere, Secretary of State for the Colonies, had informed Canada of the impending investigation and suggested that she send witnesses to attend it and watch over her interests. With some reservations, Canada accepted the invitation and appointed Chief Justice William H. Draper as her representative before the Select Committee. The instructions given him were most imprecise. He was told to look after his country's interests and put forth her claims. These territorial claims sprang somewhat mystically out of the eighteenth century, for Canada had resurrected—as part of her legacy of 1763—all the territorial rights and pretensions of New France. She laid claim to the lion's share of the Northwest as the property of La Vérendrye and his successors and restricted the holdings of the Hudson's Bay Company to the shoreline. Draper was directed to inform the committee of this title. In regard to the menace from the United States, his instructions were more explicit:

. . . to urge the expediency of marking out the limits, and so protecting the frontier of the lands above Lake Superior, about Red River, and from thence to the Pacific, as effectually to secure them against violent seizure or irregular settlement until the advancing tide of emigrants from Canada and the United Kingdom may fairly flow into them, and occupy them as subjects of the Queen, on behalf of the British empire.[1]

The land, in other words, was Canada's, and Britain should hold it in escrow until Canadian and British pioneers could possess it.

[1]E. A. Meredith to Draper, 20 Feb. 1857, cited in Great Britain, House of Commons, *Report from the Select Committee on the Hudson's Bay Company; Together with the Proceedings of the Committee, Minutes of Evidence, Appendix and Index* (London, 1857), p. 436. See also the report of the Executive Council, 16 Feb. 1857, enclosed in the Governor General to the Colonial Secretary, 17 Feb. 1857, Canada, *Sessional Papers*, 1857, vol. XV, no. 4, section 17.

The judge carried out his instructions to the letter. He carefully explained his mission to the Select Committee and accounted for his country's interests in the inquiry:

First, very materially with regard to what I conceive to be the true boundary of Canada. I may say, secondly, with regard to the deep interest that the people of Canada have, that that territory should be maintained as a British possession. I may say, thirdly, because the people of Canada look to it as a country into which they ought to be permitted to extend their settlements. Those three points I think would involve all that I could say upon that subject.[2]

Canada's case was well presented. The committee's recommendations— "that it is essential to meet the just and reasonable wishes of Canada to be enabled to annex to her territory such portion of the land in her neighbourhood as may be available to her for the purposes of settlement, with which lands she is willing to open and maintain communications, and for which she will provide the means of local administration"[3] —must have been extremely gratifying both to Draper and to his government.

The attractions drawing Canadian eyes westward were disclosed over and again in the evidence given to the Select Committee in 1857 and demonstrated by events in the succeeding years. Of primary significance was the testimony of Alfred R. Roche, aide to Draper and a clerk in the provincial secretary's office. He claimed that Canada needed *lebensraum*, maintaining that "a great many of the available lands are taken up in Canada; most of the lands for disposal are far back; they are up the Ottawa."[4] And to him, one conclusion seemed most clear: Canada had to have Rupert's Land.

Roche might have overstated his case, but within a few years it was very apparent that Canada had a land problem. By 1859, although the Commissioner of Crown Lands offered evidence to prove "the increasing demand for and settlement of our wild lands," a close inspection of his report reveals that much of the land sold was rather poor and found only in scattered, virtually inaccessible tracts.[5] Three years later, the commissioner's report could hardly have been blacker. Land sales had fallen off almost 40 per cent. Seeking some explanation, the commissioner lumped together three likely causes: the distractions of the

---

[2]*Report from the Select Committee on the Hudson's Bay Company*, pp. 211–12.
[3]*Ibid.*, pp. iii–iv.
[4]*Ibid.*, p. 251.
[5]*Sessional Papers*, 1860, vol. XVIII, no. 2, section 12.

American Civil War, the decline in immigration, and the deficiency in agricultural production. Then he added one more:

Another cause may be mentioned, which, in an official view, is more important . . . because its influence is not accidental or temporary. It is the fact that the best lands of the Crown, in both sections of the Province have already been sold. The quantity of really good land now open for sale, is, notwithstanding recent surveys, much less than formerly, and is rapidly diminishing. . . . it may be doubted if there are today as many acres of wild land of the first quality at the disposal of the Department, as there were in 1857.⁶

Good and bountiful farm land, the backbone of any nation, was fast disappearing—and with it vanished many pioneer farmers who were seeking out more available and arable lands in the American Midwest.

Canada's agricultural problems did not end here, for even her old acreage was declining. The farm economy of Canada was in the throes of an illness that beset most eastern states and provinces in mid-nineteenth–century North America: its over-cropped, disease-prone, and costly lands could not compete with the West. Small wonder it was that Canadians looked westward, coveting the prairie land of the Hudson's Bay Company and "longing for the privilege of planting it with grain . . . without the labour of clearing it from timber or the cost of manuring it."⁷

Businessmen as well as farmers eyed the British Northwest. When the Select Committee asked Draper what Canadians wanted the territory, he answered that a "very large portion" of his fellow subjects were interested in it "from a desire to share in the commercial profits of the fur trade."⁸ Another witness, John Ross of the Grand Trunk Railway, added that "certain gentlemen at Toronto [were] anxious to get up a second North-west Company. . . ."⁹ In fact, there were quite a number of both anxious and aggressive Torontonians—fur traders, transporters, merchants, and the like—who wanted to re-open the old border-lake route to Red River, displace the Hudson's Bay Company, and convert Rupert's Land into a commercial hinterland.

This economic interest in the Northwest flared up so suddenly that the historian is tempted to blame it on spontaneous combustion. In

⁶*Ibid.*, 1863, vol. XXI, no. 3, section 5.

⁷Anon. [Colonel Garnet Wolseley], "Narrative of the Red River Expedition," *Blackwood's Edinburgh Magazine*, CVIII (Dec., 1870), p. 706.

⁸*Report from the Select Committee on the Hudson's Bay Company*, pp. 216–17.

⁹*Ibid.*, p. 7. Cf. James W. Taylor, "Central British America," *Atlantic Monthly*, V (Jan., 1860), 104.

the hearings of the Select Committee, John Ross was asked whether questions regarding Canada, the Company, and Rupert's Land had been receiving public attention for some time or only recently. His reply was most revealing: "I think it was during the very last summer that the discussions first commenced upon the subject. The question of the opening up of the territory has often for years been incidentally mooted, but a regular discussion has never arisen until the course of the last summer, that I am aware of."[10] He might have added that the "regular discussion" was centred in Toronto and that the chief discussants were—as Simpson unkindly characterized them—politicians and adventurers raising a hue and cry against the Company and conjuring up fanciful claims to Rupert's Land in order to gain their own electioneering and commercial ends.

The sudden interest in Rupert's Land was touched off by the completion in January, 1855, of the Northern Railway. Its little, wood-burning locomotives chugged through ninety-four miles of wilderness between Toronto and Collingwood. Its proprietors hoped that the Northern would serve as a portage railway, tying traffic of the Upper Lakes to Lake Ontario. Stimulated by the railway's commercial possibilities and inspired by the prosperity engrossing all North America in the 'fifties, a number of Toronto businessmen began to consider and then to push plans for reviving the old river-and-lake route to the Red River Settlement. In mid-August, 1856, a vital second step was taken when the North Western Steamboat Company was formed.[11] It would build and operate vessels on Huron and Superior; and now all that remained was to re-conquer the "canoe country" between Fort William and Fort Garry—and then Toronto could create a second, stronger, and more diversified North West Company.

As these schemes took shape, the politicians naturally took notice. George Brown, Liberal chieftain of Canada West, started a campaign in the *Globe*, educating his readers about the wonders of Rupert's Land and the vices of its overlord, the Hudson's Bay Company. In January, 1857, he called a convention of the Liberal leaders and journalists of Canada West. One of their proposals was "the incorporation of the Hudson's Bay territories as Canadian soil." It was pressure like this that forced the government to assume that stand, modest though it was, before the Select Committee. The same pressure

[10]*Report from the Select Committee on the Hudson's Bay Company*, p. 3.
[11]J. M. S. Careless, *Brown of the Globe*. I. *The Voice of Upper Canada 1818–1859* (Toronto, 1959), 227–33.

eventually prompted the Canadian parliament to conduct its inquiry into the affairs of the Company and subsequently to launch its own exploratory expeditions into the Northwest.

Once under way, the promotors from Toronto remained afloat till 1860–61. In December, 1856, Toronto's Board of Trade listened to Allan Macdonell and William Kennedy. They talked of Rupert's Land and its people and asserted that the one should—and the other wanted to—belong to Canada. In January the North West Trading and Colonization Company was established, a charterless concern backed by wealthy Torontonians (including George Brown's brother Gordon) and spearheaded by "Captain" Kennedy. The latter was given two tasks. The first was to re-open the Lake Superior route and re-direct the furs of Rupert's Land to Toronto, and in this, he inevitably failed. The second task was more feasible—to encourage the people of Red River to petition Canada for annexation—here, as we have seen, he succeeded, if in a limited way.[12]

Although Kennedy's North West Company collapsed, Macdonell was on hand to build another. And even if Kennedy's petition did not mirror the mind of Red River, the hand that had held the glass still remained. Like St. Paul, Toronto was a city filled with prophets who used statistics and petitions to portray Rupert's Land as they would like it to be and not as it really was. Perhaps the master of all Toronto's prophets was Allan Macdonell. He was one of three witnesses examined by Canada's own select committee in June, 1857, and his testimony bespoke his hopes and ambitions. "If the route was opened [to Red River] from Lake Superior," he maintained, "I have no doubt but the whole trade of that country would come down Lake Superior."[13] He claimed that St. Paul would not be able to compete with Toronto because its route was slower and longer. Thus with a wave of the hand he dismissed the Precambrian Shield; and he did not even consider

[12]The petition printed in the Toronto *Globe* (12 June 1857) was signed by Roderick Kennedy and 372 others. Another copy, printed in the *Report from the Select Committee on the Hudson's Bay Company* (p. 439) was signed by Roderick Kennedy and 574 others. Thus though the petition was long on words, it was decidedly short on signatures, for there were about 6,000 people in Red River. Roderick was the "Captain's" brother. There can be little doubt that this undated petition was contrived by William Kennedy and quite probably written by the Toronto Board of Trade, whose own petition (20 April 1857) to the Legislative Council for Red River's annexation was suspiciously similar in tone and terminology.

[13]"Report of the Canadian Select Committee," *Sessional Papers*, 1857, vol. XV, no. 4, section 17.

the York Factory route as a possible rival to his envisioned highway. A quarter-century of history had hidden well the reasons for the failure of the original North West Company.

But the rest of the witnesses agreed with Macdonell; and so too did a great many other Torontonians. In May and June they could read the *Globe*'s glowing reports of Rupert's Land. George Brown printed Kennedy's Red River letters and supplied articles and editorials for supplementary reading. In the last week of August a meeting was held in Toronto's St. Lawrence Hall to protest the Hudson's Bay Company's control over half the continent. The audience was treated to a rich and expansionist diet, served up by Macdonell and his fellow evangelists. After recounting the many wonders of Rupert's Land, Macdonell moved a resolution to throw the whole region open to trade so that it could be developed by the other British North American provinces—to which it manifestly belonged. Though he was followed by other speakers, his basic theme was unaltered; only the expressions varied, as one man would seek verbally to outdo the other. But no one topped Ogle R. Gowan, who informed the audience that he wanted a "specific and pacific" boundary for Canada.[14] Then, lest his play on words come to nought, he added: "I go for the territory, and the whole territory."

What followed was hardly unexpected. The Select Committee of the British House of Commons had recommended that Canada be permitted to annex those portions of the Northwest to which it could—among other things—extend communications; Toronto's expansionists were now exerting like pressures; and consequently Macdonell got (1858) a charter for his North-West Transportation, Navigation and Railway Company after the Canadian legislature had refused him three times in the past seven years.[15] He and his associates planned to combine rail, steamer, wagon, and almost anything else that could be floated or rolled in order to tie Toronto and the Red River Settlement together.

The story of the North-West Transportation Company could well have been created by Gilbert and Sullivan. When the company's steamer, *Rescue*, made its maiden voyage from Collingwood to Fort William in June, 1858, it brought out William Kennedy and some mail from Canada. Poor Kennedy acted as if he were a *métis* in Sioux country. As the officer in charge of the mail party, he came fully armed

[14]Undated clippings from the Toronto *Globe* in James W. Taylor's Scrapbooks, Taylor Papers, M.H.S. Cf. St. Paul *Pioneer and Democrat*, 11 Sept. 1857.

[15]G. P. de T. Glazebrook, *A History of Transportation in Canada* (Toronto, 1938), p. 236.

for an invasion of the Hudson's Bay Company's domain. Instead of opposing him, the Company lent its aid, and for this the captain of the *Rescue* later gave public thanks. Throughout that season and the first part of the next, the North-West Transportation Company continued to receive the Company's assistance. Mail bags left hanging on trees were picked up and delivered to Red River. All this was done without the knowledge or approval of Sir George Simpson, however. As soon as he heard that his men were delivering Macdonell's mail, he took immediate steps to "guard against such mistakes occurring in the future."[16] Without the Company's support, Macdonell's enterprise failed. A government contract reckoned at £200 per year was not enough to make ends meet, particularly when Macdonell's complex of steamboats, canoes, and dog teams could not compete on even terms with Minnesota's Burbank line. In June, 1860, only six letters from Red River went eastward over the Canadian route, while 208 letters and 532 newspapers used the southern or Minnesota route.[17] Fewer and fewer Toronto merchants put notices in the advertising columns of the *Nor'-Wester*. And by the end of the year Macdonell's dream had been shattered. The obstacles facing him had been too great to overcome. He could not conquer the rugged "canoe country" between Lake Superior and the Red River Settlement. Canada's triumph over nature and the Minnesota route would have to await the coming of the Canadian Pacific Railway.

If Rupert's Land held out visions of fertile farm land and commercial fortunes to some Canadians, to others it bore the promise of a glorious sea-to-sea nationhood. Incipient nationalists were quick to see the geopolitical significance of the Red River colony. "All who have any regard for the future of Canada," the *Globe* intoned, "who desire to see her rise into real greatness and become a power in the world, regard her union with the neighboring colony as an indispensible [*sic*] step towards the attainment of that end."[18] Though there were a good many people crusading for the annexation of the Northwest, none was more zealous than the *Globe*'s owner, George Brown. In 1858 he addressed a political meeting at Belleville:

Who cannot see that Providence has entrusted to us the building up of a great northern people, fit to cope with our neighbours of the United States, and to advance step by step with them in the march of civilization? Sir, it is my fervent aspiration and belief that some here to-night may live to see

---

[16]Simpson to the Governor and Committee, 21 June 1859, H.B.C., Series A.12/10.

[17]*Nor'-Wester*, 14 June 1860.   [18]Quoted in *ibid.*, 30 Aug. 1862.

the day when the British American flag shall proudly wave from Labrador to Vancouver Island and from our own Niagara to the shores of Hudson Bay.[19]

The speech is justly famous, but it should be remembered for its expansionist sentiment as well as its accurate forecast. Here was the same sort of providential nationalism that had impelled John L. O'Sullivan, editor of the New York *Morning News* to coin the expression, "Manifest Destiny," in 1845. And it was not confined to Canada West. Speaking at a public dinner at Halifax in 1864, Joseph Howe con-vivially confessed that he too "looked across the broad continent as the great territory which the Almighty has given us for an in-heritance. . . ."[20]

If God meant Canada to be a transcontinental nation, how could mere man prevent it? Clearly enough, it was Canada's duty to colonize Rupert's Land as a territorial way station en route to the Pacific. Here was a manifest destiny with all the characteristics of the American type; the only difference was that the Canadian variety bloomed a decade or so later in history. Both however busily planted their flags over North America regardless of the private or public rights of others.

Moreover as fears of Britain had stimulated America's Manifest Destiny, so too did fears of the United States intensify and sustain Canadianism during the 'fifties and 'sixties. Time and again the state-ment was made that Americans were a greater threat to Canadian interests in Rupert's Land than the Hudson's Bay Company. Even the *métis*, Alexander K. Isbister, had urged the Select Committee to press for the annexation of Rupert's Land to Canada. He warned them that "the United States have their eye upon this [Red River] settlement, and I believe are fomenting the discontents which are going on there."[21] This was an extraordinary statement from an artful political agent with more than ten years' experience in his chosen field and would normally be put down as an incredible, tongue-in-cheek utter-ance were it not that so many other witnesses corroborated him. Canada always kept the northwestward movement of Minnesota's frontier under uneasy surveillance. When Colonel Smith and his cavalry detachment reconnoitred the border country, it was a disquiet-ing event for Canadian observers. George Gladman, leader of Canada's exploratory expedition in 1857, was sure that "the time . . . [had]

[19]John Lewis, *George Brown* (Toronto, 1911), p. 219.
[20]Joseph A. Chisholm, ed., *The Speeches and Public Letters of Joseph Howe* (2 vols., Halifax, 1909), II, 433.
[21]*Report from the Select Committee on the Hudson's Bay Company*, p. 135. Cf. *ibid.*, pp. 4, 23, and 212.

arrived for the occupation, in strong agricultural force at least, of that portion of the British Dominions, If we would save it from the rapacious talons of the American eagle."[22] Canada was concerned whenever any Americans drew near the 49th parallel. Even the chance of their coming was somewhat unnerving. Gold discoveries on the Saskatchewan River in 1862 caused the Provincial Secretary's office to figure the odds for or against a tidal wave of Yankee miners, whose culture and numbers would possibly lead to Americanization and perhaps to annexation. As late as 1864 a report from the Executive Council pointed out that the need for Canadian government in Rupert's Land was "doubly expedient" because of the intimate relationship between St. Paul and Red River and also because of "the removal of many Americans into the Territory."[23]

As the hearings of the Select Committee had progressed, two facts became increasingly evident. Neither Canada nor Britain knew much about the Northwest; and the men of the Hudson's Bay Company, if the most knowledgeable of all people, were the most reluctant teachers. As a result, both Britain and Canada had to find out for themselves about the region and its resources. In 1857, and again in 1858, Canada sent out small compact parties who travelled as far as the Rockies, making ubiquitous observations and compiling voluminous reports. The first expedition (1857) was headed by George Gladman, a disgruntled ex-chief factor in the Hudson's Bay Company, and its purpose was to ascertain the best route for both trade and immigration, on British soil, from Lake Superior "to the Red River Settlements, and ultimately to the great tracts of cultivable land beyond them."[24] Among its complement, the expedition included Professor Henry Y. Hind, a geologist and naturalist from Trinity College, Toronto, and the surveyor Samuel J. Dawson; and in the following year, they continued the explorations begun by Gladman. Dawson went over much the same ground covered in 1857 between Fort William and Fort Garry, while Hind, nominal leader of both parties, explored the area west of Red River and south of the Assiniboine and Saskatchewan rivers. Throughout their summer-long surveys, the Canadians received considerable aid from the Hudson's Bay Company. It was freely extended and

[22]Gladman to Vankoughnet, 29 Dec. 1856, Governor General's Numbered Files, No. 50, vol. 1(a), P.A.C.

[23]11 Nov. 1864, enclosed in the Governor General to the Colonial Secretary, 12 Nov. 1864, Governor General's Numbered Files, No. 50, vol. 1(b).

[24]See Henry Y. Hind, *Report of the Exploration of the Country between Lake Superior and the Red River Settlement* (Toronto, 1858), pp. 5–6. See also the report of Samuel Dawson, in *Sessional Papers*, 1859, vol. XVII, no. 4, section 36.

gratefully received. However the Company rarely if ever acted without self-interested motivation, and, in this particular case, it apparently hoped that the explorers would "open the eyes of the public to the false statements which have been made in reference to the facilities of opening up the communication between Lake Superior and Red River."[25] It was never more mistaken.

The surveyors of the Lake Superior route, Gladman and Dawson, were highly optimistic about it, whether it took the line of the Pigeon or the Kaministiquia River. Gladman personally favoured the former. Though realizing that it presented its share of problems, he did not think they were "insuperable to Canadian energy and enterprise."[26] Not only was the route a good deal shorter than any of the Red River trails but it terminated at Fort William, which possessed a good harbour where transshipments could be easily made to Canadian carriers.

Gladman's measured optimism was overwhelmed by Dawson's rosy dreams. He preferred the Kaministiquia because it could transport larger vessels, and in his exhaustive report of 1859, he stated that it would be from one-third to one-half shorter than all the St. Paul highways and, when finished, would surpass any means of transportation from Minnesota to Red River, with the exception of railways. As a Canadian competitor to the Minnesota route, he suggested two possibilities: either a rail-and-water or a road-and-water combination. In the first case, two railroads and two locks would have to be built; in the second, four lengths of road. In either case, as soon as the road was completed, Dawson was positive that the fur trade of Rupert's Land would instantly seek the more convenient Canadian channel, while countless immigrants would immediately make their way into the Northwest.

Both he and Hind championed the agricultural potential of the region. They correctly regarded the Red River Settlement as its heartland, but their estimate of its worth was (for the 'fifties) grossly overstated. To them, it seemed like a Garden of Eden capable of growing every crop seen in Canada. Hind scouted the tales told of Red River's late spring and early fall frosts, referring to them as rumours conceived and circulated by the Hudson's Bay Company. He became ecstatic about the soil—ten to twenty inches of "rich black mould"— and claimed that the Red River Valley could provide mankind with all life's necessities, save for iron. It was only because of the Company that Red River's growth had been stunted. "That agriculture and all

25The Secretary to Simpson, 30 Oct. 1857, H.B.C., Series A.6/33.
26Gladman to the President of the Council, 24 March 1858. in Hind, *Report*, pp. 164–6.

the simpler arts have been discouraged," he maintained, "is but too apparent"; and, he added, "it is difficult to resist the impression that these failures were designed by some in authority."[27] Thus began the fantasy about Canada and the Northwest. It had been blighted by the Company and needed only the touch of Canada to bloom.

Concurrently with Canada, the Crown conducted its own exploration of the Northwest. Heading the royal expedition was Captain John Palliser, a plains hunter of the 'forties and a vigorous gentleman with a scientific bent. His surveys carried him from the present Prairie Provinces to the Pacific slope. He and his associates wrote a long and detailed report of their observations—observations made by eyes much less sanguine than those of Hind and his fellow Canadians. The British were not, for example, overly optimistic about a Lake Superior route to the Red River Settlement, contending that it would be an extremely laborious undertaking, very expensive, and of a dubious all-weather nature. "In addition," one of them opined, "the difficulty of direct communication between Canada and the Saskatchewan country, as compared with the comparatively easy route through the United States by St. Paul's [*sic*], renders it very unlikely that the great work of constructing a road across the continent can be solely the work of British enterprise."[28]

None the less, Palliser and his colleagues strongly urged that some sort of Canadian road be built. Without it, they argued, a political union of all British North America seemed impossible; even with it, union was "somewhat speculative" and a "work of time." But before any union could be brought about, some physical connection had to be made and the sooner it was done the better. For the explorers saw, virtually on every hand, evidence of danger to British sovereignty—land speculators just below the 49th parallel, Yankee merchants in the Red River Settlement, and the many and multiplying ties of trade that stretched south to St. Paul. To them, the intimate relationship between Minnesota and Rupert's Land was, in itself, a very real danger:

This connexion, which is year by year increasing will, if some steps are not taken for the opening of a practicable route with Canada, monopolize the whole traffic of the interior, and thus drawing those strong ties of commerce

---

[27]*Ibid.*, pp. 143–4.

[28]Palliser to Her Majesty's Principal Secretary of State for the Colonies, 8 July 1860, in Captain John Palliser, *Further Papers relative to the Exploration by the Expedition under Captain Palliser of that Portion of British North America which Lies between the Northern Branch of the River Saskatchewan and the Frontier of the United States; and between the Red River and the Rocky Mountains, and thence to the Pacific Ocean* (London, 1860), p. 22.

and mutual interest tighter, may yet cost England a province, and offer an impassable barrier to the contemplated connexion of her Atlantic and Pacific Colonies.[29]

If the Red River Settlement were ever brought into the United States, Britain's hold upon the Far West would be immeasurably weakened and Canada's chances for a sea-to-sea dominion, incalculably slim.

II

Expansionist pressures in Canada West and the spate of publicity regarding the Northwest had their own rewards. During the late 'fifties and early 'sixties, small numbers of Canadians began to migrate to Rupert's Land. For the most part, they were men with a purpose, pioneers on the make, self-seeking folk of the sort seen everywhere on the North American frontier. They formed the cutting edge of Canadian civilization; they and their paper, the *Nor'-Wester*, exercised a dynamic effect upon the Arcadian society and government of the Red River Settlement; and without them, it would be hard to account for the Riel Rebellion.

History is determined by events as well as people; and the events of a dozen years, 1857–69, created the right atmosphere in which the Canadians, their party, and their press could work at the task of undermining the Hudson's Bay Company. Ever since the parliamentary inquiry of 1857, the Company had declined in power as well as prestige. In 1858 British Columbia was created a Crown colony, carved out of Indian Country controlled by the Company through its licences of exclusive trade since 1821 and 1838. Also in 1858 Vancouver Island, over which the Company had ruled as royal trustee for almost a decade, was handed back to the Crown. And in May, 1859, the licence to the rest of the Indian Country, that oddly shaped wedge of land between the Rockies and Rupert's Land, expired. Thus, less than two years after the Select Committee had made its recommendations, the once proud "lords and owners of the soil" were confined to Rupert's Land, the last stronghold of a majestic, continental empire.

Even here the Company's position was none too secure. From 1858 until 1864 it had to defend itself against the Colonial Office, which tried to remove the Company and either make a Crown colony out of Rupert's Land or annex it to Canada. But removal by any means required the purchase of the Company's property and title—a costly

[29]Palliser, *Further Papers*, p. 57. Cf. Hind, *Report*, pp. 394 and 397–8.

step which the Crown for financial reasons, and Canada for political reasons, could not take. The results resembled a square dance. The colonial secretary did all the calling, sporadic though it was; Canada and the Company came together at odd intervals but never for any length of time; and eventually the Company found another partner, a new group of proprietors to whom the old stockholders sold out in 1863. At this point, the dance began all over again—and lasted till 1869, when Canada finally bought Rupert's Land.

Under the circumstances, in the confusion of imperial policy and Company ownership, is it any wonder that the Canadian party flourished in Red River while the Company floundered? An ugly uncertainty characterized life within the settlement and anarchy flowered amidst it all. It had never been easy to govern the little colony and it now became virtually impossible. "With an emphasis transcending profanity," William Mactavish, the last governor of Rupert's Land, once remarked "that a stoker in hell was to be envied compared with his position. . . ."[30]

Two of the most energetic Canadian pioneers who came out to Red River in the 'fifties were William Coldwell and William Buckingham. Talented and enterprising young men, they exchanged Canada and Toronto's newsrooms in 1859 for the Northwest and their own newspaper. Like so many other Canadians, they travelled westward *via* St. Paul, where they paused just long enough to pick up the tools of their trade. In the last week of September, armed with presses and paper, they set out for Red River. On 28 December 1859 Buckingham and Coldwell published the first edition of the *Nor'-Wester* and set forth their working credo: "We came persuaded that the time has arrived when this fertile and magnificent country, thrown open to the people of all lands, needs an exponent of its opinion, its feeling, its varied and yet common interests, through the medium of the Press." Despite its high-sounding purpose, the paper proved in the long run to be little more than the exponent of its editors and the small circle of Canadians living in Red River; even though it changed hands several times, its opinion varied but the slightest. None the less, the *Nor'-Wester*'s editorials—a confusion of truth, half-truth, and deliberate misrepresentation—became to Canadians back East a mirror with which to view Rupert's Land and the Hudson's Bay Company. It never mattered that the glass gave back a distorted image; the paper wrote what most Canadians wanted to read.

[30]Quoted in the fragment of an article written—but then deleted—by James W. Taylor, Taylor Papers.

Throughout its existence, the *Nor'-Wester* warned Canada of the dangers of Americanization in Rupert's Land.[31] It anxiously charted Minnesota's growth in various ways—vanishing prairie land, the extension of postal services, military movements, new developments in transportation, and changes in trade and government—and concluded that her progress, northwestward and across the 49th parallel, was predestined. It was continually illustrating the intimate commercial relation between Minnesota and Rupert's Land and pointing out the perils therein. St. Paul was Red River's emporium, providing its citizens with all the goods and services they wanted. For years the people of Red River had made annual pilgrimages to the south, but with the advent of the Burbank line, and its regular, year-around shipments, goods came directly up from St. Paul. "Thus it is," warned (15 August 1861) the *Nor'-Wester*, "that Minnesota stretches out her arms to embrace the little colony of British subjects in the far north"; and asked: "Is it a matter of wonder, then, that the Minnesotians [*sic*] consider annexation to their state as the 'manifest destiny of Red River?'" Out of Red River's close commercial attachment to Minnesota —or so the *Nor'-Wester* alleged—had grown a strong sentimental attraction towards the United States. It maintained that the people of Red River were only slightly interested in the British connection and not at all in the Canadian. It was the Minnesota kinship that counted. To many of them, it seemed as if Minnesota had played the Promethean role in their development, providing swift and reliable mail service, an assured all-weather trading route to the outside world, the only decent pathway for immigrants, and many other bountiful gifts. In contrast, what had Great Britain done to improve Red River's lot? "Annexation to the United States," answered the *Nor'-Wester* (28 May 1862), "is the universal demand of the people of this country, seeing that the Home Government will do nothing."

To all this editorial chanting, there was usually an antiphonal response from the Canadian press. One particularly excited editorial, "American Proclivities in Red River," was widely reprinted by Canadian papers and apparently accepted as a true account of the American "connection." After Buckingham sold out and returned to the East, he bought the Norfolk *Reformer* and faithfully echoed the ministerial voice from Red River. But always, George Brown's *Globe* was the most accurate sounding board. It reprinted "American Proclivities . . ." in full, merely adding the rhetorical comment: ". . . how can we wonder

---

[31]See the *Nor'-Wester*, 14 April 1860, 1 June and 1 Oct. 1861, and 31 May 1864.

that the [Red River] people allow their sympathies to follow their business interests."[32]

Although editors and owners came and went, the policy of the *Nor'-Wester* regarding the Hudson's Bay Company was always the same. The Company was attacked year in and year out. It mattered not that the Company generously supported the paper—directly, by purchasing all its offerings; indirectly, by allotting it certain printing jobs.[33] The Company remained the cause of all Red River's evil, and in the end the *Nor'-Wester* created the unfortunate illusion that the Company was only a despotic overlord, ruling Red River by means of its hirelings, the councillors of Assiniboia. As for the settlement, it was "the handmaid of a Hudson's Bay Company Post, administering to the wants and conveniences of that Company and receiving in return treatment which only an unfeeling stepmother can bestow."[34]

However there was a sound basis for the paper's hostility. It wanted to rid Rupert's Land of Company rule and join it to Canada; to that end, the editors worked without regard for means or morality, supporting the lawless elements of Red River, campaigning for an all-Canadian route to the East, working for Crown colonial status and then confederation, delivering diatribes against the Company, and exaggerating the menace from Minnesota. In all its editorializing the *Nor'-Wester* was more responsible to heart than to head, for it dearly wanted Rupert's Land and Red River to be united with Canada.

For all the confusion in the Company's career, the Red River Settlement remained remarkably tranquil from 1859 to 1862. Of course, London received the usual reports about "designing persons" trying to stir up discontent within the settlement; but, as the Company's Secretary admitted, "in the present uncertainty as to the intentions of the Government, it was to be expected."[35] The presence till 1861 of the Royal Canadian Rifles may have been a restraining influence upon any would-be demagogues; and perhaps the public peace that continued for almost another year could be explained by the absence of any real issue or of any contentious circumstances which a political agitator could shape to the Company's disadvantage.

[32]Quoted in *ibid.*, 14 May 1862.
[33]The Company regretted the ill will but came to accept it philosophically, realizing "as the paper was started for Canadian purposes and the articles written for Canadian readers [,] it is not easy to see how that hostility can be counteracted, as it is the principal Capital of the concern." The Secretary to William Mactavish, 9 May 1860, H.B.C., Series A.6/35.
[34]*Nor'-Wester*, 22 Oct. 1862.
[35]Fraser to Mactavish, 20 July 1860, H.B.C., Series A.6/35.

Life in Red River went on much as it always had. The Council of Assiniboia was concerned with the same time-worn problems: trying to patch up the customs in order to prevent smuggling and derive some revenue; worrying about the whisky, good and bad, that was being imported from Minnesota; considering public works, both large and small; and making the limited number of public appointments available in the little colony. The free traders went along their old competitive course, becoming a bit more numerous and certainly more injurious to the Company's welfare. A few more Americans joined their lists and some Canadians too, notably Dr. John Christian Schultz, whose later career as chief of the Canadian party would do so much to wreck the well-being of the settlement. Together, these free traders worked the whole line, from Fort Garry to York Factory, using the same strategy and tactics as their predecessors and making money despite London's instructions to the wintering partners to oppose them "at whatever cost to the Company."[36]

In 1862, the Company took steps to relieve some of Red River's political uncertainty when it filled the two posts, long vacant, of Governor-in-Chief of Rupert's Land and Recorder of Assiniboia.[37] Alexander G. Dallas was appointed governor; and in May he came to Red River, accompanied by the new recorder, John Black, whose primary responsibility was to preside over the courts.

Despite its good intentions, the Company probably did more to aggravate than to relieve an uneasy situation. Neither appointee was suited to his post, Black least of all. As a chief trader, he had managed the Lower Red River District, 1850–52, where his record was scarcely exemplary, and though he had also aided in the administration of justice, the Governor of Rupert's Land, acid-tongued Eden Colvile, had called him "as stupid as an owl." Black's retirement from the Company and subsequent service in New South Wales as Minister of Lands did little to alter that judgment. He never lent dignity or strength to the bench.

---

[36]The Secretary to Mactavish, 13 June 1861, H.B.C., Series A.6/36.

[37]The gubernatorial office had been officially vacant since the death of Sir George Simpson in 1860. William Mactavish had only been the acting governor, combining that post with his existing office as governor of Assiniboia. The recordership had been untended since 1858 and the resignation of Francis G. Johnson. On an informal basis, Dr. John Bunn, whose portfolio of local offices bulged, had assumed that position and held it till his death in 1861. Throughout the years and despite pleas from both Simpson and Mactavish for a replacement, the Company had left the recordership unfilled. Thus with deliberate inaction, which the Company frankly accredited to its own vacillating state of affairs, it unwittingly promoted the growth of political uncertainty in Red River.

Dallas also proved a feckless public servant. With the brashness of a young executive of indifferent ability following in the steps of a gifted man, he found nothing but fault with Simpson's administration. Though there was some truth in his complaints, he seems in retrospect to have been a better blaster than a builder. Shocked to find that free traders were selling goods for Company notes and using them to make their remittances, Dallas stopped the issuance of notes, adopted the policy of giving goods for agricultural produce, and paid out cash or notes only when he had to. In so doing, he may have hindered free-trade operations, but he also severely contracted the currency upon which everyone in Red River depended. Whatever popularity had attended his initial entrance into office soon disappeared; and quick to seize an advantage, the *Nor'-Wester* (9 July 1862) denounced him for his "petty and ungenerous course."

In the fall, the paper went on to take an advantage where none seemed to exist. When the Sioux wars broke out in Minnesota and pushed so many savages into Rupert's Land, the people of Red River became alarmed, for they had no military protection. As a result, the Council of Assiniboia directed the recorder to draw up a petition to the Crown praying for troops. Black acted accordingly and presented the finished document to the *Nor'-Wester*'s office for printing. The paper had known of the council's intentions and already expressed its approval (22 October 1862) in a strange manner. It claimed that the Company could get troops whether the people wanted them or not and warned its readers to beware any scheme which asked them to share in the costs of sustaining the soldiers. This would be taxation without representation. After Black had delivered his petition, the *Nor'-Wester*'s editors pigeon-holed it and printed another instead. Like the council's, their petition sought military aid; unlike it, it also asked for representative government in Rupert's Land. In commenting (17 November 1862) upon this "switch" the paper blandly remarked: "The official document is spurned as a suspicious concern, while the other is everywhere welcomed with enthusiasm."

Although the original petition was ultimately printed, signed, and sent on to London, the Governor and Council could not ignore the *Nor'-Wester*'s conduct, and for once in its life, the paper was peculiarly vulnerable. James Ross, co-editor and co-owner since 1860, held a number of public offices; he was the postmaster, sheriff, and governor of the jail.[38] How he managed to compartmentalize his loyalties is

[38]Buckingham and Coldwell were co-owners until 1860, when the latter sold his share to James Ross, son of the historian Alexander Ross. This partnership

somewhat of a mystery. However the Governor and Council soon provided a solution by divesting him of all his offices for conduct "incompatible with his position as an Officer of Government."[39] The motion to oust him had been made by Mactavish, seconded by Bishop Taché, and secured the unanimous approval of the council. Once again the Catholic hierarchy had put itself on the side of the Company and in direct opposition to the *Nor'-Wester* and the Canadian party.

But neither church nor Company nor government could check the course of the *Nor'-Wester* and its political associates. In the winter, the *Nor'-Wester* took a sordid case being tried by the General Quarterly Court and made of it a *cause célèbre.* The defendant was an Anglican cleric and he was accused of most outrageous behaviour. He was the Reverend Griffith O. Corbett, an active member of the Canadian party and a witness hostile to the Company's interests when he had appeared before the Select Committee in 1857. He had been arrested in December and confined without bail on the charge that he had, with attendant injury, repeatedly attempted an abortion upon a young girl in his employ. Like other ministers in rural surroundings, he had often performed minor medical services, but till now he had never done this particular operation. The reason was simple: he had seduced the girl. But when the justice of the peace permitted him no bail, the *Nor'-Wester* (12 December 1862) drew attention to the Company's known dislike of the prisoner and concluded that it was "a very petty way to persecute an opponent. . . ." Then and thereafter, the paper claimed that Corbett was being crucified for his past conduct; the enormity of his present crime was of little or no consequence.

Evidently the jury thought otherwise; in February, 1863, Corbett was sentenced to six months' imprisonment. Dallas was surprised that so mild a sentence was imposed for a crime "which in England would have consigned him to penal servitude for life" and believed that the recorder had been unduly influenced by "a small but loud talking mob. . . ."[40] He was right about the mob but wrong about the sentence,

lasted until 1864, when Ross sold out to John C. Schultz, medical doctor and free trader. A year later, Coldwell left the settlement, disposing of his share to Schultz. In 1868 Schultz sold out to Walter R. Bown, dentist and free trader. With the exception of Ross, all the proprietors were Canadians; and Ross had received his collegiate training from the University of Toronto. Thus throughout the paper's career, there existed editorial continuity. However, it is to be doubted that the *Nor'-Wester* ever made any man's fortune.

[39]Minutes of the Council of Assiniboia, 25 Nov. 1862, in E. H. Oliver, ed., *The Canadian North-West: Its Early Development and Legislative Records* (2 vols., Ottawa, 1914–15), I, 514.

[40]Dallas to Ellice, 10 March 1863, Ellice Papers, P.A.C.

for justice in Red River had never been harsh.[41] But benign though it was, Corbett's sentence seemed too severe to his friends. In April, after the minister had served scarcely two months, they petitioned the Governor and Council of Assiniboia for his release. Lacking authority to act, the council directed the petition to Governor Dallas, who denied its prayers. By so doing Dallas stirred up a hornets' nest. Eleven days after the petition's presentation a small party of Corbett's supporters broke into jail and released the prisoner. Warrants were quickly issued to apprehend them and a ringleader was seized on the next day. But on the day following that another and larger mob liberated him too. In his feeble efforts to control a worsening situation, Dallas resembled the "Old Major," Governor Caldwell. As the latter had surrendered to the free trading mob in 1849, so did Dallas capitulate to the Canadian party in 1863. Caught in similar circumstances, Caldwell had done nothing because he was outnumbered, but in Dallas's case, caution approached cowardice. Sitting later in the ruins of his government, he pleaded with London to bring about the changes necessary to insure peace and order in Red River.

The four magistrates who made up the Quarterly Court were deeply disturbed. One of them, François Bruneau, a representative of the French-speaking half-breeds, said that "he would never sign another warrant. . . ."[42] And though he was eventually persuaded to stay in office, he and his colleagues on the bench were constrained to express their dissatisfaction in a long letter to Dallas.[43] It was clear to them that they could not administer justice so long as their decisions were so easily and violently overthrown. Even more evident was Red River's need for "a Military Force under the Queen's authority. . . . as much required to keep down internal tumult, as to guard against Indian disturbances." The Governor and Council, not Dallas, replied to the magistrates. They published a notice to the people of Red River, expressing their abhorrence of the lawlessness and their gratitude to those who had volunteered to suppress it. Then they tried to explain away Dallas's reluctance to use force "by motives of humanity; by the desire to avoid bloodshed; by a wish to prevent deadly exasperation

[41]In 1861 a man convicted of manslaughter received only ten months' imprisonment and was subsequently freed after serving but six months, on the grounds that his family was suffering for want of material support and the prisoner himself seemed in danger of going out of his mind. Minutes of the Council of Assiniboia, 13 March 1862, in Oliver, ed., *The Canadian North-West*, I, 481 *et seq.*
[42]Dallas to the Secretary, 6 May 1863, H.B.C., Series A.12/43.
[43]Minutes of the Council of Assiniboia, 28 April 1863, in Oliver, ed., *The Canadian North-West*, I, 525–6.

of feeling among the Settlers, and above all, by a consideration of the dangerous consequences . . . that would have arisen from the Indian Tribes witnessing the spectacle of open warfare between sections of the people."[44] Such was the explanation tendered the people; to the historian, it seems weak and unfounded. The lawless members of Red River's society were too few to be feared. The disturbance should have been put down; had it been, men like John C. Schultz might have acquired a greater respect for law and order.

As a result, the *Nor'-Wester*'s attitude toward Corbett and his lawless friends remained defiantly sympathetic. Stretching its principles to the breaking point, it referred (27 April 1863) to the unsavoury episode "as one of many solemn protests against the rule and policy of the Hudson's Bay Company in this country." One wonders how the affair would have turned out if Ross had still been sheriff and governor of the jail. Out of office and out of sorts, Ross and his co-editor gave Corbett the status of a martyr whose downfall had resulted from the Company's misgovernment.

To an outsider incautiously reading the *Nor'-Wester*, it probably seemed as if there were only two parties playing politics in Red River, the people and the Company. But if in appearance the paper made the people synonymous with the Canadian party, in reality that party made up only a fraction of the whole populace. The discriminating reader could have found that out for himself. On 24 January 1863 the paper described meetings held to memorialize Canada for a Lake Superior route as "a large attendance," and so forth. Given a closer view, our reader could easily have discerned the nature and numbers of the *Nor'-Wester*'s "people." For the paper later (9 February 1863) reported an illuminating exchange which had taken place at the January meeting between two members of the Canadian party, Archdeacon Henry Cochrane and John McLean. "Mr. M'Lean, I think," said the archdeacon, "is convinced that we should have nothing to do with the Red River people in the matter. (hear and laughter) Let them help themselves. We will make the road before they will hear about it. (laughter)." The archdeacon then quipped: "Could there not be a great many subscribers to that Journal amongst us?"

Certainly there were few or no French-speaking half-breeds who subscribed to the paper. The *Nor'-Wester* and the Canadian party never represented them or their interests, although they were the most numerous group in the settlement. A "French" section was run but briefly and then only in the paper's formative months and it never

[44]*Ibid.*, I, 527.

contained other than the most general world news. The Church opposed the Canadian party and its press; and if one can judge anything by the conduct of Louis Riel's father, the *métis* were equally hostile. In the fall of 1862, at a meeting to consider the *Nor'-Wester's* petition to the Queen for both troops and representative government, the elder Riel crudely yet effectively denounced James Ross. "I wish to show and prove that Mr. Ross is a deceiver, misleading the people," he cried, "for he says that the dissatisfaction with the Company and the Council is 'universal'; whereas the truth is, that among my people, the French Halfbreeds, there is no such dissatisfaction. Thus I have proved that he is imposing upon you, and is therefore, an imposter."[45] The audience's only recorded comment was an "oh! oh!" of surprise.

Despite its numerical weakness and manifest unpopularity, the Canadian party and its press always exercised an influence that exceeded mere numbers. "Between James Ross and Corbitt [*sic*]," as a middle-roader in Red River politics wrote a London friend, "they have managed to make the place too hot to live in."[46]

III

The political temper soon cooled and many months passed serenely by before the settlement entered its final and most disruptive phase. As late as the winter of 1865–66 the colony was still quiet, although by then, William Mactavish, Dallas's successor as Governor of Rupert's Land, was vaguely uneasy about the future. There was some talk about representative government and some muttering about taxation without representation; but "this," he gloomily forecast, "will pass over till some question turns up, when some designing demagogue may aspire to the glory of martyrdom."[47] Before the year was out, the prediction came to pass: two men, Thomas Spence and John C. Schultz, revealed themselves as "designing" demagogues.

Spence began his revolutionary career in Rupert's Land as the— to use Mactavish's own expression—"coadjutor" of the *Nor'-Wester* and terminated it as editor of Riel's journal, the *New Nation*. He and "several other Canadian gentlemen of capital" had started out for Red River, or so they claimed, "with a view to settlement there, and

[45]Quoted in the *Nor'-Wester*, 29 Nov. 1862.
[46]Bannatyne to Ellice, 1 July 1863, quoted in G. F. G. Stanley, *The Birth of Western Canada* (London, New York, Toronto, 1936), p. 52.
[47]Mactavish to the Secretary, 13 Feb. 1866, H.B.C., Series A.12/44.

[to] induce a system of immigration. . . ."[48] But when he arrived on the scene in the late summer or early fall of 1866, he bore little resemblance to a man of capital. On the contrary, he appeared to be exactly what he was: an indigent adventurer from Montreal whose mission would be pursued with words instead of money. He had barely arrived when he and four others convened as a popular assembly and composed a memorial to the Queen, urging Her Majesty to make Rupert's Land into a Crown colony complete with a transcontinental communications system, a postal service, and military protection.

Soon after this farce had ended, Spence moved further west and took up residence in Portage la Prairie, a small settlement popular with the new Canadian immigrants. The location suited his ambitions and his talents, for it lay just beyond the municipal district of Assiniboia. Beyond the pale, he could safely embarrass Assiniboia's authorities and, as a member of an almost exclusively Canadian circle, he could work without fear or restraint for Canada's annexation of the Northwest. He could also labour in his own vineyard; and though the motives driving men like him are often difficult to separate from the welter of patriotic prose that they write, it seems clear that Spence was primarily interested in his own welfare. For his labours at Portage la Prairie, he expected political preferment as soon as Ottawa had acquired the region and established a governmental hold over it.[49]

Unfortunately Spence's patience could not keep up with his ambition, and in January, 1868, he and other Portage residents turned to the time-honoured frontier practice of state-making, creating the "Government and Council of Manitoba" and electing Spence as president. With this bold manoeuvre they hoped to hurry along Canada's annexation of Rupert's Land. Indeed Spence himself threatened to get recognition from the United States, if either Canada or Britain did not take "immediate steps to grant . . . [his] people civil rights and representation in the Parliament of Canada."[50] But soon he overshot the mark. For when he appealed to the Colonial Office to recognize Manitoba, the secretary informed him that his government had no legal standing whatsoever. One letter from London

---

[48]Spence to the Earl of Carnarvon, 13 Aug. 1866, enclosed in Carnarvon to Monck, 29 Sept. 1866, *Sessional Papers*, 1867–68, vol. I, no. 7, section 19.

[49]See Angus Morrison to Spence, 17 Sept. and 30 Nov. 1867, Spence, Thomas: Red River Troubles, 1869–70, P.A.C. Cf. Mactavish to the Secretary, 27 Nov. 1866, H.B.C., Series A.12/44.

[50]Morrison to Spence, 4 April 1868, Spence, Thomas, Red River Troubles, 1869–70.

was enough to do the trick. As a provisional government, Manitoba disappeared; and Spence went into the business of salt- instead of state-making.

He had been a fool and foredoomed. But what of the circumstances that had fostered his growth? "This Portage La Prairie business would be simply ridiculous," Mactavish commented to the Company, "were it not for the ignorance of the people who are always ready . . . to follow the lead of any one who chooses to tell them how much they have been oppressed and promises that this will be rectified by the course they are invited to follow."[51] He must have had Dr. Schultz in mind—the incubus of Assiniboia and bane of the Hudson's Bay Company.

Schultz's career in Red River probably started shortly after he received his medical degree in 1860. Though then a young man of only twenty years, he found age to be no barrier to success in a frontier community. And here, despite all his detractors, was a man of many talents. He successfully combined the occupations of medicine, trade, and journalism. He sparked the creation of the Institute of Rupert's Land, a scientific body dedicated to the promotion and development of the region's natural resources.[52] He was the moving spirit behind Freemasonry in the settlement, starting and heading its first lodge in November, 1864. Such a record should have brought recognition, prestige, and even affection; and in the first stage of his career, he apparently gained all these rewards. He was associated with A. G. B. Bannatyne, in Freemasonry; he served with Mactavish as co-secretary in the institute; and he seemingly won the gratitude of the *métis* and their clergy for his medical services. Yet in the end he alienated nearly every ethnic and economic group in Red River, save his own Canadian party.

The turning point in his career came when he entered politics. Not as a free trader did he forfeit Mactavish's friendship; the Company had long tolerated competition and continued to do so. Not as a Mason did he forego the sympathy of the *métis* and their church; other Masons like Bannatyne kept their friendship. It was as a highly injudicious partisan of Canadian rule over Rupert's Land that Schultz lost whatever goodwill he had built up in Red River. What were his motivations for so strenuously championing Canadianism? Perhaps it was patriotism, pure and simple; or maybe frustration, for he

[51]Mactavish to the Secretary, 24 Feb. 1868, H.B.C., Series A.12/45.
[52]See the correspondence of the Institute of Rupert's Land, H.B.C., Series D.10/1.

never won from Rupert's Land the political preferment that he hungered for. Whatever the reasons, there emerged in the man after 1866 certain traits that do not win friends or influence people. As a citizen, he put himself above the law. As a businessman, he behaved unethically.[53] And as the owner and editor (after 1864) of the *Nor'- Wester*, he was unscrupulous and irresponsible. Under his and his partner's (Walter R. Bown) leadership, the newspaper was precisely what the diarist Alexander Begg called it: "A one sided, unpopular, mismanaged sheet [cast] in the interests of the [Canadian] clique . . . [which] endeavoured to mislead the minds of the people abroad regarding the true state of affairs in the settlement. . . ."[54]

Schultz and the people of Red River first collided in the spring of 1866. In May he appeared before the Quarterly Court to answer charges brought against him and his ex-partner, Henry McKenney, for non-payment of a note. The two were tried separately. McKenney found the judgment against him and had to pay part of the debt, but it was not, in Schultz's opinion, a fair share. When he got his day in court, he asked the recorder to quash the suit against him on the grounds that McKenney had bullied the bench and that the court would accordingly not do him justice. Recorder Black was quick to take offence. He demanded a retraction, and when the latter refused, Black ruled that he could not appear in court again until he had apologized.

As the recorder later explained, he intended "to check an offender in a course of obstinate and deliberate insolence, which was directly fitted to bring the Magistracy into general contempt. . . ."[55] But the means he used were inept. They were also unique, probably illegal, and set off an explosive train of events. Silenced in the court, Schultz became a martyr in the columns of his newspaper. He insinuated that the Company was using the Quarterly Court in order to ruin him as a business competitor. Unfortunately, Black's ruling seemed to bear out the ridiculous charge. When the case came up again in 1867, the impenitent Schultz was tried *in absentia* and ordered to pay his share of the debt.

Now it was up to the sheriff, Henry McKenney, to enforce the

[53]Evidence exists to show that, in one instance, Schultz tried to blackmail a competitor and, in another, to cheat a creditor. See Mactavish to the Secretary, 12 March 1867, H.B.C., Series A.12/44.

[54]William L. Morton, ed., *Alexander Begg's Red River Journal and Other Papers Relative to the Red River Resistance of 1869–1870* (Toronto, 1956), pp. 158–9. (Cited hereafter as *Begg's Journal and Other Papers.*)

[55]Black to the Secretary, 17 Dec. 1866, H.B.C., Series A.11/98.

decision. When Schultz refused to pay, the court sent McKenney and his bailiffs to levy upon his goods. By forcibly resisting the sheriff and his men, Schultz managed to keep his property; but for his pains, he was arrested, bound, and borne off to jail. That night his wife and several other known individuals broke into the jail, overpowered the constable, and freed the prisoner. Safe again in his editor's chair, Schultz referred to the recorder as Red River's Judge Jeffrey, blasted the government as "the Red River Star Chamber Council," and then blandly asserted that public opinion was right behind him.

Overnight, Schultz *vs.* a London creditor became Schultz *vs.* the people. The whole affair was handed over to Governor Mactavish, to whom it seemed a nasty dilemma. If he failed to act, the power of the court would be jeopardized and his government discredited. And yet if he carried out the sentence, regardless of the risks involved, the prestige of his government would not be enhanced because its real authority would still rest upon popular sufferance instead of police power. Therefore he brought the whole matter to the council for advice. The councillors, none of whom was Canadian or sympathetic to Schultz, urged him to swear in "special constables" and forthrightly carry out the court's decision.

It was worthless advice, for not enough men were willing to serve. Though Mactavish reconvened the council a fortnight later, nothing new was suggested except the silly scheme that everybody be sworn in as constables. But once again those who responded were disquietingly few in number. Mactavish now sensed a strong if unexpressed desire on the part of the people to have a greater voice in government and a governor unconnected with the Company. "So strong is this feeling," he wrote London, "that any one inclined to take advantage of it for his own purposes can make trouble under the present circumstances."[56] Not one to take unnecessary chances, he wisely induced the recorder to re-try Doctor Schultz.

In May, 1868, Schultz appeared in court for the final time. In the trial, one of his former clerks, James Stewart—a ringleader in Corbett's liberation of 1863—testified that he had seen the defendant hand over a large amount of money to the plaintiff. His testimony convinced the jury and it directed Schultz to pay only the paltry sum that remained.[57]

[56]To the Secretary, 16 Feb. 1868, H.B.C., Series A.12/45.
[57]A good many people, including Mactavish, thought that Stewart had perjured himself. And their suspicions were strongly reinforced when Schultz swiftly re-hired him. See extracts from a private letter, Mactavish to the Secretary, 2 June 1868, enclosed in Mactavish to the Secretary of the same date, H.B.C., Series A.12/45.

The farce was over at last. Who had won? The doctor claimed the honour. Who had lost? Every citizen in Red River had, for the Quarterly Court never regained that semblance of strength and dignity it had possessed on the eve of the trial.

The Quarterly Court was not Schultz's only target. He and his *Nor'-Wester* assailed the Council of Assiniboia more often and more viciously than the court. None the less, when a councillor died in 1867, Schultz had several petitions directed to the council in support of his own candidacy. He must have known that petitions would not win him a seat and the suspicion flashes to mind that he meant only to embarrass the Council. Certainly he knew that councillors were commissioned by the Governor and Committee, not the Council of Assiniboia. Thus to all his petition—and to a counter-petition calling him "not an eligible person"—the council replied that it could do nothing but forward them to London.

Though London theoretically made all the appointments, it actually followed Mactavish's lead. The relationship between the governor of Rupert's Land and the Governor and Committee had changed since the day of Sir George Simpson. It was not that Mactavish was stronger or more persuasive; the difference lay not in the man nor in the office, but in the attitude of the Company itself. After 1863, if not before, London lost interest in Red River's local problems. In that field, the Company had become a kind of constitutional monarch content to register the will of William Mactavish. It was Mactavish who dealt with the doctor. Which would be worse, Schultz in or out of the Council? Although the governor thought several other men had better claims, "still," he told London, "I am doubtful if the evils arising from his exclusion would not exceed those which could be caused by his admission."[58] In the end, the doctor made up Mactavish's mind for him by writing a scurrilous article in the *Nor'-Wester* denigrating the Council and urging everybody to disregard its laws. As a result, he never got a seat.

However Mactavish believed that the empty seat should not only be filled but that several others should also be created. He was aware of a "pretty general feeling" in the settlement that some changes ought to be made in Red River's government. Most of the councillors had grown old in office and some were not suited for dealing with the

[58]Mactavish to the Secretary, 12 March 1867, H.B.C., Series A.12/44. The Bishop of St. Boniface, also a councillor, later maintained that if Schultz had been added to the Council, "many members would have resigned. . . ." A. A. Taché, *Sketch of the North-West of America*, translated by D. R. Cameron (Montreal, 1870), pp. 67–8.

people "as have for some years past been coming into the Settlement. . . ."[59] Therefore he asked the Governor and Committee to
appoint eleven new councillors, and from this list, London eventually
selected eight men. In January, 1868, when they were all sworn into
office, the Council of Assiniboia had doubled in size. Not since Johnson's administration had the Council been so quickly and greatly
enlarged. His admission of half-breeds and free traders had made the
government virtually impervious to Captain Kennedy's attacks.
Mactavish's manoeuvre had not the same success. Though his nominees
were also influential men, they were all from groups long established
in Red River and already represented on the Council: the English
half-breeds, French half-breeds, the Scots, and the English settlers.
From the fastest growing and most articulate body in the settlement,
the Canadians, not a man was named.

Mactavish still regarded the Canadians as tourists instead of settlers.
For their omission from the Council, he alone must be blamed; and
because of it, he and his government suffered. When, without a
broadly based council, he tried to support Black's judgment against
Schultz, he failed in the attempt and shamefully had to accommodate
his government to the culprit. If he had been a more astute politician,
he would have included a Canadian in his council. Though Schultz's
inclusion would either have split the government or ruined its reputation, there were other men of more moderate views. Their representation might have muffled the *Nor'-Wester*—might even have silenced
Schultz. Constituted as it was, Mactavish's new council failed in its
first effort at a strong government. Schultz went on his way, and the
pressure for more popular government in Red River merely mounted.

To Mactavish's credit, it must be said that he realized the need
for an organic change in Red River's government. He was not precisely sure what form it should take, but of certain guiding principles
he was positive. It should be a strong and just government, based upon
the popular will and deriving its constitutional authority from some
body other than the Company. He recognized the incompatible relationship between managing a fur-trading company and governing a
colony. "For my part," he lamented to London, "I feel my position
perfectly intolerable and I most sincerely hope that I may be soon
relieved from duties which have always been disagreeable and are
becoming perfectly disgusting."[60] The responses he received must
have been disheartening. Now that there seemed some hope of

[59]Mactavish to the Secretary, 18 April 1867, H.B.C., Series A.12/44.
[60]Mactavish to the Secretary, 28 April 1868, H.B.C., Series A.12/45.

negotiating with Canada for Rupert's Land, the Company was indifferent to Red River's problems. There would be no change in government; until Rupert's Land had been transferred, nothing could be done. This was a tiresome old tune that the Governor and Committee had been playing since 1858 and it scarcely soothed the breast of Dr. Schultz. He could defy law and order because Mactavish lacked the wisdom to make the Council of Assiniboia genuinely representative and because the Company carelessly failed to alter its constitutional makeup.

If the Schultz affair illustrated the weakness of the Company's rule over Red River, it also gave evidence of Red River's dislike for the doctor and his party. After the *Nor'-Wester* had fatuously claimed that a majority of the people approved of the jail-breaking escapade, a large group of them drew up a petition protesting the action and gave it to the paper to be printed. Bown, however, would have none of it. Incensed by his refusal and convinced that the paper had been as responsible as anyone for the recent disorders, a mob of *métis* gathered in front of his office and threatened to destroy the presses and run him out of town. Had not Mactavish intervened and secured the editor's promise to print the petition, the *Nor'-Wester's* career might have ended right then and there. The Canadian party was not popular in a settlement that had come to appreciate law and order, and the association of this group with governmental officials and agents from Canada shifted the hostility from the party to the Dominion. When reports reached Red River in 1868 of the impending consignment of Rupert's Land, there was little rejoicing save in the camp of Dr. Schultz. So far as Mactavish could see, "the Settlers here [,] I mean those who belong to the Settlement [,] look with little favour on the transfer of the Colony to Canada."[61]

The unfortunate union of interests between Canada and the Canadian party became particularly evident in 1868—the year of Red River's great calamity. In July locusts descended upon the fields and devoured the crops; disaster struck again, when the plains provisions also failed. Despite the efforts of the Governor and Council to stave off famine, there were not enough funds for relief and an appeal had to be made for outside help. The response was generous and widespread. St. Paul's Chamber of Commerce formed a "Red River Relief Committee" and raised more than $4,000 to buy wheat and flour. A bill providing cash for Red River flew through Minnesota's legislature and

---

[61]Extract from a private letter of Mactavish's dated 9 June 1868 and enclosed in Mactavish to the Secretary, 2 June 1868, *ibid.*

received the governor's signature in ten days. Citizens of Ottawa donated $1,200, and in London a public appeal by the Hudson's Bay Company brought in over £2,000, of which the Company itself gave £500.

Instead of a dole, Canada decided upon a relief project—the immediate construction of the westernmost end of the Dawson road. This was the dream of Simon J. Dawson, who hoped to combine sections of land road with waterways and build a highway from Thunder Bay (Fort William) to Fort Garry. Work was first begun in 1867 and a few miles of the eastern end were actually completed. Then in September, 1868, the Minister of Public Works suddenly determined to start the section between Fort Garry and Lake of the Woods, using labourers from Red River and paying them about $18 per month. It seemed such a wise thing to do, for here was charity with a purpose.

Early in November a Canadian surveyor, John A. Snow, and his party arrived in the settlement. They were not wholly unexpected. From the Toronto *Globe*, the *Nor'-Wester* had learned of the relief project and duly informed its readers. As for Mactavish, he first heard about it from a local merchant. Until Snow's appearance, all the governor's knowledge was secondhand and even afterwards he heard nothing of an official nature. Consequently when Snow actually arrived and showed his instructions, Mactavish was more than a little nonplussed—and well he might have been. Viewed from any angle, the whole scheme seems most presumptuous. Without permission from the Crown or the Company, Snow was about to start road-building on someone else's property. However Mactavish did not protest. Indeed, as he confessed to the Governor and Committee, he could not have done so without antagonizing the people, many of whom regarded Snow as a "God-send" when he first arrived.[62]

Before too long, he seemed more like a "Schultz-send", and his work resembled a relief project for the benefit of Canada and the Canadian party. The Canadian poet, Charles Mair, was paymaster; Thomas Spence acted in a subordinate role; Schultz himself served as general agent, forwarding, handling, and dispensing food and supplies. The total number of men working on the road was never large, but most of these seem to have been recent Canadian immigrants. The

[62]Extract of a letter from Mactavish, 11 Nov. 1868, H.B.C., Series A.11/98. Snow suggested to Mactavish that the question of permission be left in the hands of Her Majesty's Government until Mactavish had heard from the Company regarding its own position in the matter. In February, 1869, the Company finally notified Mactavish that it approved of Snow's application (forwarded *via* Mactavish) to build the road.

Red River settlers were not eager to work, particularly after they discovered that they would be paid "chiefly in provisions at cost price.[63] Furthermore the price was set at Schultz's new store some thirty miles east of Red River, where rates exceeded those of the settlement.[64] To all appearances, it seemed as if the charity of Canada's Minister of Public Works began in his own home. Under these circumstances, how could Snow and his project have avoided unpopularity in Red River? Unpopularity soon turned to hostility when members of the road-building crew committed a series of unpardonable indiscretions. Some bought land from the Indians. Snow himself sold liquor to them. Deeds like these vexed the people of Red River, and their anger grew hotter when Mair, in a letter to his brother, lampooned them and their settlement. In Mair's defence it must be said that he never meant the letter to be published, but the damage was done. As Alexander Begg stated in the preface to his journal: "These . . . are minor matters but they are pointed out to show the gradual feeling those actions of a few individuals caused of dislike to the government who would send out such men as examples of their employees."

In the following summer Ottawa made a worse blunder when it decided to survey Rupert's Land so that Canadian pioneers could take up land as soon as the transfer had been completed. Though the scheme was both foolish and presumptuous, the Company agreed to it. Even Mactavish concurred, if reluctantly, knowing well that "the whole land question . . . [was] fruitful of future troubles which it will take time and great labor to settle."[65] "I expect," he predicted, "that as soon as the survey commences the Half breeds and Indians will at once come forward and assert their right to the land and possibly stop the work till their claim is satisfied." On 20 August the chief surveyor, Lieutenant-Colonel John S. Dennis, arrived in Red River. Like Snow he unwisely associated with the Canadian party; yet unlike him, he attempted to explain his mission. To Father Lestanc, who headed the diocese in Taché's absence, and to Louis Riel, self-appointed leader of the French-speaking half-breeds, he carefully pointed out

[63]Snow to McDougall, 4 May 1869, *Sessional Papers*, 1869, vol. II, no. 5. In writing the Company's Secretary, Mactavish (24 Nov. 1868) reported that the people of Red River were not very "desirous" to work for Snow, because of the nature and size of the wages given; and in a subsequent letter (12 Oct. 1869), in which he related the difficulties that Snow was experiencing with his labourers, Mactavish referred to the men in Snow's crew, "the most of whom . . . are strangers." H.B.C., Series A.12/45.

[64]Morton, ed., *Begg's Journal and Other Papers*, p. 155.

[65]Mactavish to the Secretary, 10 Aug. 1869, H.B.C., Series A.12/45.

that he intended to lay out only two or three townships and that no man's title would be jeopardized in the process. With much the same care, the *Nor'-Wester* (31 August 1869) also described the colonel's plans, stating that he would be surveying occupied land only in order to give proper deeds to the owners. "This course on the part of the Dominion Government," continued the paper, "shews a determination to respect fully the rights hitherto acquired by Settlers under the rule of the Company and is a guarantee of a sound and just policy in the future. . . ."

No explanation could have saved Dennis's mission. In the first place, few *métis* read the *Nor'-Wester*; and in the second, they simply did not want any surveying because most of them were squatters. Giving in to their grumbling, audible even before his arrival, Dennis turned first to fixing the international line. Then he began laying off a principal meridian proceeding straight north from the 49th parallel and passing through the settlement. On 11 October, as the surveyors were running a base line out from the meridian, Riel and a few other *métis* stopped the survey by stepping on the chains. Straight to Mactavish went the colonel, but the pleas of neither man could change Riel's course. Though he and his compatriots readily admitted that the survey was harmless, they still wished Canada to know that they did not want it—"that they consider, if the Canadians wished to come here, the terms on which they were to enter should have been arranged with the local government here. . . ."[66]

Canada was not finally in a position to annex Rupert's Land and the Northwest until Dominion Day, 1 July 1867. In the involved arrangements which were made, the Colonial Office acted as real estate agent, transferring the Northwest Territory from the Crown to Canada and negotiating the sale to Canada of the Hudson's Bay Company's properties. The deed to Rupert's Land was finally signed in the fall of 1869 and the date of possession was tentatively set for 1 December. For the sake of expediency, the Canadian parliament passed "An Act for the temporary Government of Rupert's Land and the North-Western Territory when united with Canada."[67] According to it, the Lieutenant Governor of the North-West Territories was to administer justice and, together with a small appointed council, legislate for peace, order, and good government. However all existing laws would remain in effect except for those repugnant to the British North America Act, and all public officers, save for the head administrator,

[66]Mactavish to the Secretary, 12 Oct. 1869, *ibid.*
[67]Oliver, ed., *The Canadian North-West*, II, 972–3.

would continue to hold their posts. Though somewhat vague, it was on the whole a well-conceived statute; and Sir John A. Macdonald meant to execute it in such a way as to avoid giving offence to the people of Red River.

Despite the merits of the act and his own good intentions, Macdonald made a serious mistake when he appointed William McDougall as lieutenant governor. The choice probably seemed logical. No one in the cabinet knew more about Rupert's Land than the Minister of Public Works and few had shown a greater interest in it. None the less, McDougall was the wrong man. His knowledge of the Northwest was statistical rather than sentimental; he knew its resources but not its inhabitants. As an expansionist-minded politician and journalist, he would inevitably be marked down by the men of Red River as a friend of the Canadian party and as a sounding board for the *Nor'-Wester*. As Minister of Public Works, he had been directly or indirectly responsible for building the Dawson Road and surveying the settlement—two deeds which won him little popularity in Red River. McDougall was the wrong man.

On 28 September he left Ottawa in high spirits, but when he reached Pembina on the evening of 30 October, he was handed a message from the "National Committee of the Métis of Red River" ordering him not to cross the border without their permission. Disheartened but not dissuaded, he rode on to the Hudson's Bay post just over the line. Here he had barely settled down when a large and well-armed troop of *métis* confronted him and forcibly escorted him back into the United States. Canada had been locked out of her new addition. A long-lived climate of political uncertainty, complicated by religious and cultural problems and pressures and rendered more anxious by Canada's mistaken policies, had fashioned the Riel Rebellion.

IV

It was the *métis* and their leader, Louis Riel, who planned and carried out the rebellion. They were a proud people who had lived on the Red River plain for nearly one hundred years, long enough to attain a racial, cultural, and even national identity. So far as they were concerned, Canada's connection with them and their land lay buried in the past. As Bishop Taché so cogently put it: the name of the North West Company did not prove that Canada had any possessory rights to Rupert's Land.[68] Broken were all historical bonds; gone too were any sentimental ties.

Canada ought to have been aware of these facts. Moreover, intelligent observers had often pointed out to her "that in the event of an organic change occurring in the Government of the country, the 'native' or half-breed population should not be neglected, or thrust to one side."[69] Now, despite the warning voices of men like Hind, Mactavish, Taché, and others, Canada was attempting to annex Rupert's Land without consulting its inhabitants and impose a government that seemed somewhat like a proconsulship. "It is not Canada we object to," wrote the editor of Riel's paper, the *New Nation* (29 April 1870), "but the means used, by which we were to be ushered into a connection with it." He then added: ". . . we certainly had no idea of concurring in measures that had apparently in view, the extinction of ourselves." If McDougall had been able to enter Red River and explain the workings of his government, he might have been able to brush away some of these fears. He might even have been able to educate the *métis* in the mysteries of British institutions in general and Canadian democracy in particular—subjects about which they knew little or nothing. But he never entered Red River, and the government he offered seemed, from a distance, to be less popular and less independent than the old Council of Assiniboia. For it must be remembered that by 1869 the *métis* were filling many public offices in Assiniboia, serving as councillors, magistrates, and customs collectors. They were not wild people living in some uncivilized backwater.

What sort of role could they have hoped to play in the new political order? Up to the moment of McDougall's arrival, only three men— all from the East—had been named to his council. What of the rest? Since McDougall's range of Red River acquaintances was limited to the Canadian party, surely some of them would have been selected. But would he ever have added a half-breed or two? It seems unlikely so long as men like Schultz, Snow, Dennis, and Mair held his ear. And it should be borne in mind that even Sir John A. Macdonald did not advise him to add any *métis*—and then but two—until the unpleasant facts of a revolution had been brought back to Ottawa.[70] In October then, the half-breeds needed no soothsayer to predict their political subservience in the new North-West Territories.

[68]Taché, *Sketch of the North-West*, p. 62.
[69]Hind, *Report*, p. 305.
[70]Macdonald to McDougall, 20 Nov. 1869, Macdonald Papers, P.A.C.

They also feared that "their interests would be overlooked [by Canada] and their religion interfered with."[71] They knew that most of the Canadian immigrants would come from Orange-minded Ontario and concluded that their own Catholicism would suffer. It might not have been the most logical conclusion, but, logical or not, it came from the practice of equating Masons and Orangemen of the known Canadian party with every unknown Canadian. More rational was their concern for their way of life. Perhaps, as the Anglican bishop suggested, the root of the rebellion was very simple—"a feeling in the French section that the French Half-breeds . . . [would] not stand the new state of things to be developed by a considerable Emigration [*sic*]. . . ."[72] Some of the Catholic clergy confided to the American consul that, with the majority of the *métis* still living by the chase, it would be years before they could be permanently placed on farms. Indeed they feared that a Canadian invasion, coupled with a rise in taxes, would force the farming minority off their lands "by voluntary sale or otherwise."[73]

What of the English-speaking settlers? Surely they did not share in all the fears and fantasies of the *métis*. Yet, as a most perceptive British observer remarked, they might have been "thoroughly loyal and anxious for annexation to Canada"; but they disliked the terms of annexation because they had not been consulted in the first place and, in the second, Ottawa had kept an unbecoming silence about the nature of their future government.[74] Consequently, if they did not aid the *métis* in any overtly revolutionary acts, neither did they energetically oppose them. Instead of neutrality, the English-speaking settlers opted for co-operation—helping to work out the terms for Red River's admission into the Dominion and collaborating in the establishment and operation of Riel's Provisional Government.

Both the French and English settlers spurned the Canadian party, suspected Canada's past and present policies, and worried about their future within the Dominion. The chain of incredible indiscretions that McDougall forged that fall merely bolstered their prejudgments and

[71]Mactavish to the Secretary, 2 Nov. 1869, H.B.C., Series A.12/45.

[72]Bishop Robert Machray to Young, 18 March 1870, Document XXI, in Morton, ed., *Begg's Journal and Other Papers*, p. 506.

[73]Malmros to J. C. B. Davis, 6 Jan. 1870, Consular Dispatches, from Winnipeg, 11 June 1869 to 19 December 1871, N.A. See also Taché, *Sketch of the North-West*, p. 69; and William F. Butler, *The Great Lone Land* (10th ed.; London, 1881), p. 38.

[74][Wolseley], "Narrative of the Red River Expedition," p. 708. Cf. Machray to Young, 18 March 1870, Document XXI, in Morton ed., *Begg's Journal and Other Papers*, p. 505.

confirmed their solidarity. Though the historian may conveniently group Red River's people into this or that racial or linguistic category, he often forgets that they had been living together in comparative harmony for many, many years. Among the "old settlers" there existed, by 1869, a spiritual unity that bridged most of their differences, and it would have been very strange if this same spirit had not been quickened by the various pressures that Canada exerted upon the settlement after 1867. When the first of many moments of decision was at hand—when the *métis* stopped McDougall from crossing the line— the English settlers "had no interest in opposing their [French-speaking] neighbours with whom they had lived so long in amity especially in support of a cause that intended apparently to reduce their rights as British subjects to nothing and in fact when the thing was canvassed . . . there could not be found 50 men amongst the settlers themselves to offer their assistance in bringing the new governor as far as Fort Garry."[75]

In the preface to his journal, Alexander Begg wondered whether it would not have been wiser for Canada to have sent agents to Red River "for the purpose of feeling the pulse of the settlers." The men dispatched by Ottawa to manage her affairs in Rupert's Land were second-rate and not the least of their errors was to form an intimate association with Dr. Schultz and his colleagues. So consistently critical were Macdonald's analyses of Dennis ("he has got no head"), Snow ("injudicious conduct"), Schultz ("exceedingly cantankerous & ill-conditioned"), and Bown ("rather an ill-conditioned fellow"), that although one may appreciate the premier's good judgment, one cannot help wondering why the appointments were made and the damaging associations allowed to develop.

Canada blundered; and it is of no consequence whether the blunders were the result of ignorance, indifference, or both. There was an unseemly haste and an unbecoming acquisitiveness about her acts and attitudes towards Rupert's Land. The road-building project, if not the actual construction, was launched before either the Company or the Council of Assiniboia had been advised. To survey the Red River Settlement before gaining legal possession of it could hardly have failed to irritate the people living there; it was not an empty tract to be measured and platted at will. To plan a government for people who already possessed one was equally exasperating, and it should be remembered that Ottawa's "temporary government" was apparently less liberal and more subservient than the old Council of Assiniboia—

[75]Morton, ed., *Begg's Journal and Other Papers*, pp. 160–1.

and "temporary" only in the sense that most governments mean.[76] And finally, to send a lieutenant governor to Red River before the territorial transfer was an act as presumptuous as it was premature. How could these ill-considered acts have failed not to arouse the belief that Canada's policy towards Red River was conceived in, and dedicated to, her own self-interest.

From the blunders of Canada and out of the fears of his countrymen, Louis Riel created a rebellion that achieved its purpose of safe-guarding the rights of his people (and all Red River) and led ultimately to the formation of Manitoba as an equal province within the Dominion. Riel was the rebellion's mainspring. Though only one-eighth Indian, he was a *métis* and passionately proud of his race. He was also a young man whose twenty-fifth birthday occurred as his men were throwing up barricades on the road to Pembina. He was well educated, the product of several years at the College of Montreal; he was also ambitious, perspicacious, and driven by an extraordinary nervous energy. Such were the signs of political leadership that he manifested. Less evident but still discernible was a fatal defect of character: he was "excessively suspicious of others." Indeed so suspicious was his nature, so erratic and violent his temper, and so strange his behaviour that the historian is tempted to describe him as a paranoid. But if it was paranoia that eventually twisted his mind, there was not much evidence of it in the fall of 1869, when he methodically planned and put forward the rebellion that would bear his name.

Throughout 1869 there had been rumours of mysterious meetings among the *métis*. Soon after Dennis's arrival, the gatherings gained in substance and grew into assemblies. It was an un-named body of men that halted the surveys on 11 October; but a week or so later the same men had formed the National Committee, a representative group drawn from French-speaking parishes and headed by John Bruce and Louis Riel. Bruce was a quiet, persevering man in his middle years and he was given the title of president, but from the beginning it was obvious that he was only a figurehead and that Riel was the real leader.

As McDougall drew near the border, Riel and the National Committee moved with assurance and dispatch. They sent out a call for recruits and enrolled about 200 men. Though these men served thereafter without pay, they served remarkably well. For they were experi-

[76]Ottawa did not anticipate a fast and easy transition to self-government. See Howe to Thibault, 4 Dec. 1869, quoted in Alexander Begg, *History of the North-West* (3 vols., Toronto, 1894), I, 431–3.

enced, well armed, and disciplined frontiersmen capable of dealing with the Sioux Indians on more equal terms than Custer's cavalry. His army in hand, Riel acted with extraordinary decision. He set up headquarters south of Fort Garry, built and manned barricades on the road to Pembina, and notified McDougall not to cross the 49th parallel without permission. Everything went smoothly. On 30 October the *métis* pushed McDougall south of the line; on 1 November they turned back two of his would-be councillors; and on the following day they seized Fort Garry itself. It was a bloodless coup, skilfully and efficiently executed. By holding the fort—with its cannon, its guns and ammunition, its provisions, and its governmental records—Riel effectively commanded the whole Red River Settlement. By blocking off the Pembina road, he had isolated the settlement from the outside world. Unless some internal force overthrew him, he was master of the situation until spring.

A few days later, he invited the English-speaking settlers to elect delegates to join with him and the National Committee "to consider the present political state of this Country and to adopt such measures as may be deemed best for the future welfare of the same."[77] The invitation smacked of state-building but the English accepted it anyway, and both groups convened in mid-November according to schedule. Unanimity did not follow. From first till last, the convention was split on ethnic lines, the divisions arising from means to be used and not ends to be sought. As one of the English delegates candidly explained it to a friend, "the difficulty we . . . felt was that the French wanted us to do what was unlawful, and as law-abiding subjects we could not consent."[78] About all that either party gained from the convention's early sessions was an awareness of each other's point of view. On the afternoon of the twenty-third this philosophic log jam was broken up. Riel made the explosive suggestion that the convention establish a provisional government to deal with Canada. At first the English instinctively recoiled from what seemed to be a treasonous step. Then they wisely decided to mark time, replying that they could do nothing without consulting their own parish-constituencies. On this indecisive note, the convention adjourned until 1 December.

In the week's noisy and nervous passing, perhaps the least disturbance was caused by consultation. Most of the politicking was of the boisterous backstage variety. Almost every party in Red River

[77]Morton, ed., *Begg's Journal and Other Papers*, p. 164.
[78]James Ross's notebook on events in Red River, 1 Dec. to 14 Dec. 1869, Document X, in Morton, ed., *Begg's Journal and Other Papers*, p. 438.

elbowed for position and searched for allies. Of them all, none was busier than Schultz's Canadian party. It was their last chance to divide the French and English, uproot Riel, and bring McDougall safely into port. All their efforts were in vain. As Schultz had failed earlier to coalesce with the English, so now he found the Americans similarly unwilling to join with him. He was a political pariah, untrusted and unwanted; and the final proof of his unpopularity came during the week. By failing to pack the consultative meetings in his own parish-constituency of Winnipeg, he lost all possible control over its delegates to the convention—and the convention itself. From that moment, his thoughts must have turned to counter-revolution.

Elsewhere in the settlement, more moderate men were trying to heal the split that was growing between the French and English parties. In their search for a compromise, they hit upon a novel idea: to retain the old Council of Assiniboia (refashioned "in the shape of a legislative council") and elect an executive council whose primary function would be to treat with Ottawa regarding annexation.[79] The scheme won the support of several men of stature within the English party. Moreover Oscar Malmros, the American consul—and by now self-appointed adviser to Louis Riel—urged the *métis* to accept the compromise. Even William B. O'Donoghue, an Irish-American who had recently shed his *soutane* and donned revolutionary garb as one of Riel's lieutenants, favoured the measure. But all Red River's support was useless unless Riel himself could be convinced—and he blew hot and cold.

By the thirtieth time was running out and the settlement was in a desperate mood. That night, writing London of the situation, Mactavish was positive that he would wake in the morning and find that Red River had become a battlefield.

McDougall, however, had already set in motion certain events which would lead to the fusing of the French and English parties and to his own withdrawal from the Northwest. Viewed from this historical vantage point, his conduct seems incredible; yet such a judgment reckons without the character of the man. For here was an imperturbable egotist who was forever standing on ceremony and acting without common sense. Not till the eve of his departure for Ottawa in mid-December did he venture to suggest to Riel that they discuss grievances and consider compromises. He ignored all the good advice given him and listened instead to Schultz, Snow, Mair, and Dennis. Without figuring the odds against him or even considering the consequences

[79]Morton, ed., *Begg's Journal and Other Papers*, p. 185.

of failure, McDougall decided upon coercion rather than diplomacy. On the night of 29 November, he crossed the 49th parallel and—going against all instructions—took possession of Rupert's Land. To make matters worse, he sent Colonel Dennis on a mission to "inspire all the inhabitants of the [Northwest] Territory with respect . . . [for their lieutenant-governor], and compel the traitors and conspirators to cry 'God save the Queen', or beat a hasty retreat."[80]

Though Dennis's plans were secret and still remain vague, a close reading of his correspondence reveals them in outline. Upon entering Rupert's Land, he was to determine whether or not the English settlers would support a counter-revolution or rising. If they would, he was to arm and organize them and then proceed to recover the Northwest. More specifically, he planned to unite his forces at the Stone Fort (his headquarters), declare martial law, descend upon Fort Garry, and disperse the rebels. If the colonel's first few days seemed promising, it was mainly because he wanted it that way. He sampled public opinion and found it misleadingly positive and he took the Stone Fort without resistance. Then he divided Red River's parishes into company-districts, selected his officers, and started drilling.[81] By 4 December he estimated that his little army needed only ten or twelve more days of training until it would be ready. But by that very day, opposing pressures had already built up so fast and furiously that, within another three days, the counter-revolution would be smashed.

The eye of the storm that destroyed it was the house and store of Dr. Schultz. The doctor's Winnipeg establishment, long a Canadian rendezvous, had recently become a supply depot, housing a large quantity of food originally intended for the ill-fated surveying party. Since it now held enough food for a Red River "army," it became strategically important. Armed Canadians began to gather there; simultaneously at Fort Garry, scarcely a cannon shot away, Riel congregated more and more *métis*. The tension mounted and it was merely a question of time before the two forces collided. Needing time more than anything else, Dennis ordered and re-ordered Schultz to withdraw. Thinking himself secure, the doctor refused to budge until the seventh of December, when he belatedly sent word that he and some forty others were beseiged without food, wood, or water and desperately needed help. At once Dennis scurried about for the man-

[80]McDougall to Howe, 6 Dec. 1869, *Sessional Papers*, 1870, vol. III, no. 5, section 12, p. 76.
[81]Dennis kept a daily journal of events, 1–10 Dec. 1869, *ibid.*, pp. 106–14.

power to relieve the Canadians, but when he asked for volunteers from the company recently organized in the Scottish parish of St. Andrew's, only a few of the men and none of their leaders stepped forward. Under the circumstances, all he could do was to abort the relief expedition and tell Schultz to get the best possible surrender terms. Before the end of that momentous day, the doctor and his men were imprisoned in Fort Garry.

Fortunately for all concerned, McDougall's counter-revolution never regained its original momentum. Merely to think of the consequences that might have otherwise occurred sends a shiver up one's back— whether a bloody civil war or another Seven Oaks "massacre." McDougall and Dennis were playing with the lives of Red River's people and the fate of their own country. And one is relieved to learn that the sensible men of St. Andrew's made their position very clear to Dennis on 7 December: ". . . the only condition on which the Scotch people would now arm and drill, would be to act strictly on the defensive."[82]

Before that day was finally done, Dennis received a copy of Riel's "Declaration of Independence." The colonel's attitude, ordinarily un- yielding, now bent with the circumstances, and he tried to set up a personal meeting with Riel. But this deathbed repentance, though uttered with undoubted sincerity, meant nothing to the *métis*. On 9 December Dennis ordered all the loyalists to return to their homes and, in the same breath, pleaded with the French to send a deputation to McDougall. The loyalists did as they were told, but there was no response from the French, save the symbolic one of hoisting their own flag over Fort Garry. Later that day (10 December), Dennis learned that "there was no prospect of getting the French leaders to agree to a meeting."[83]

It was all over. Neither a counter-revolution nor conciliation would make Canadians out of *métis* that season. On the eleventh Colonel Dennis left the Stone Fort, bound for Pembina *via* Portage, and reached his destination four days later.

On 8 December Louis Riel published the Declaration of the People of Rupert's Land and the North West.[84] This was the document to which both McDougall and Dennis referred as Riel's "Declaration of Independence." Though the similarity between it and Jefferson's prose

[82]Dennis's Journal, 7 Dec. 1869, *ibid.*, p. 112.
[83]Dennis to McDougall, 17 Dec. 1869, *ibid.*, pp. 123–4.
[84]Enclosed in Malmros to Davis, 11 Dec. 1869, *Senate Executive Document No. 33*, 41st Cong., 2nd Sess., Serial 1405. See also *Sessional Papers.* 1870, vol. III, no. 5, section 12, pp. 99–100.

is superficial, there was enough resemblance to horrify Canadians and intrigue Americans. The declaration justified the establishment of a provisional government—"the only and lawful authority in Rupert's Land and the North West"—on the grounds "that a people, when it has no Government, is free to adopt one form of Government in preference to another, to give or refuse allegiance to that which is proposed." However, that this government was meant to be truly provisional and not sovereign was shown by the concluding statement: "That . . . we hold ourselves in readiness to enter into negotiations with the Canadian Government as may be favourable for the good government and prosperity of this people."

On 10 December the *métis* exultantly raised the flag of the new government. A year that had begun with CANADA flying from Schultz's flag staff came to an end with the unlikely combination of fleur-de-lis, a harp, and a shamrock fluttering over Fort Garry. Riel and the Provisional Government controlled Rupert's Land. Though—as William Mactavish well knew—"the great majority of the inhabitants . . . [had] not authorized either Bruce or Riel to act for them, and . . . the great bulk of them object[ed] to the means used to enforce their rights,"[85] nevertheless it appeared to a more mobile observer by the seventeenth "as if the whole people would have to go in for the Provisional Government not only as a means of protection but also to be in a position to claim their rights."[86]

McDougall's counter-revolution had collapsed. Some of the Canadian party had been jailed; the rest were subdued or scattered over the countryside. On 16 December, McDougall wrote Mactavish that he was returning to Canada, "having no force at . . . [his] command to re-establish the supremacy of law. . . ."[87] Riel was left victorious and virtually alone on the stage. In the wings, waiting expectantly, was the American party.

[85]Mactavish to the Secretary, 11 Dec. 1869, H.B.C., Series A.12/45.
[86]Morton, ed., *Begg's Journal and Other Papers*, p. 232.
[87]*Sessional Papers*, 1870, vol. III, no. 5, section 12, pp. 97–9.

Chapter 9 End of the Line: Minnesota and the Riel Rebellion

I

WITH MCDOUGALL AND THE CANADIAN PARTY DRIVEN FROM THE FIELD, IT seemed to many Americans as if the long-awaited moment to acquire Rupert's Land had arrived. Certainly Minnesota's expansionists were quick to see an advantage. "The Red River revolution," crowed (8 February 1870) Joseph Wheelock in the editorial column of his St. Paul *Press*, "is a trump card in the hands of American diplomacy, if there is statesmanship equal to the opportunity, by which, if rightly played, every vestige of British power may be swept from the Western half of the continent."[1] The Minnesota expansionists strove sanctimoniously and unscrupulously to fulfil their state's manifest destiny. In the United States Senate, Alexander Ramsey struggled to win support for a programme of intervention and/or annexation. In the newspapers, James W. Taylor and Wheelock tirelessly disseminated their doctrine of Minnesota's destiny north of the 49th parallel—to which Wheelock referred (St. Paul *Press*, 7 February 1870) as "the irresistible doctrine of Nature." And all three men urged annexation upon the President of the United States, Ulysses S. Grant, and his Secretary of State, Hamilton Fish.

Although both Grant and Fish were receptive to Minnesota's pleadings and more than willing to accept any part or all of British North

---

[1]With some changes, this chapter was originally published as "The Riel Rebellion and Canadian-American Relations," *Canadian Historical Review*, XXXVI (Sept., 1955), 199–221.

America, the "short-of-war" policy which they followed, 1869–70, failed to win the prize. Nothing less than armed intervention could have secured Rupert's Land for the United States. Whenever Riel flirted with American expansionists, he probably did so only to gain security for his people and provincial status for Red River. Moreover, in the diplomatic contest for the affections of Riel and Red River, Grant and Fish were sadly outmatched. Sir John A. Macdonald, the Canadian prime minister, was too skilful for them. He recognized the limits of Fish's foreign policy regarding Rupert's Land, quieted the rebellious *métis* with a rare blending of force and diplomacy, and finally brought the Northwest into the Dominion. But for all Macdonald's talents, the fate of the region was uncertain until imperial troops had reached and overawed Red River in the summer of 1870. Till then, Americans were free to scheme and intrigue for the possession of Rupert's Land.

The first cards in Minnesota's expansionist game were played in the Red River Settlement. The dealer there was General Oscar Malmros, the United States consul and leader of what (for want of a better term) must be called the American party. He had arrived in Winnipeg barely two months before the October outbreak and, with Mactavish's permission, opened his consulate in George Emmerling's hotel. Here was an unscrupulous but perceptive diplomat of the von Papen school. Less than a month after a flag-waving entrance into Emmerling's establishment, he was not only able to communicate to the State Department details of the coming insurrection but also to suggest ways in which the United States might insure its success. One serious defect of character, however, reduced his efficiency as a consular officer: he was unreservedly optimistic, seeing everything and everybody in Rupert's Land through the eyes of a Minnesota expansionist. Therefore his image of Riel and the rebellion was usually shortsighted and often distorted.

The fantastic dispatch that Malmros wrote to the State Department on 11 September 1869 illustrates the false optimism of the man as an expansionist and his ungoverned zeal as a political agent.[2] "The entire French and over one half of the other inhabitants," he unequivocally asserted, "are strongly opposed to annexation to Canada; the rest, with the exception of perhaps a couple of dozen Canadian partisans, are politically indifferent." The Roman Catholic Church and the Hudson's Bay Company—he claimed—"are decided in their expression to me of dislike to Canadian rule," and though he felt that the Company's servants might possibly be won over by the Dominion, he was positive

2Malmros to Davis, Consular Dispatches, Winnipeg, N.A.

that "the Catholic Clergy . . . [could] be relied on in any feasible scheme to sever the connection of this country with Canada." "The mass of the settlers," he continued, "are strongly inclined to get up a riot to expel the new Governor. . . ." And if there were a riot or a rebellion, he maintained that, counting both Indians and half-breeds, the rebels could raise a force of from 2,000 to 2,500 men—". . . a nucleus around which volunteers from the North Western States might collect." He added that Rupert's Land could be easily defended; and if by chance the United States acquired it, he reminded the State Department that "a great confederation north of the United States [would be] an impossibility."

Malmros consistently denied to Washington that he ever left his proper position of disinterested observation. He merely "on proper occasions, by conversing on the causes of success or failure of revolutions in other countries . . . indirectly endeavoured to prevent mistakes and ill considered movements. . . ."[3] And oddly enough, his political activities long escaped the notice of Red River's most inquisitive citizen, Alexander Begg. But despite the consul's protests to the State Department that he maintained a perfect political neutrality, his superiors obviously knew he was acting as an *agent provocateur*. Certainly Alexander Ramsey, Malmros's political patron and confidant, knew of his Red River activities. To him, Malmros fully confessed his role in the rebellion when he wrote (6 January 1870) that ". . . instructions or no instructions [from Washington] I felt it my duty to act and have the satisfaction of knowing that I without committing the Administration in the least degree & without having by outsiders my real position suspected [,] materially assisted in producing the present situation & of having prevented many mistakes on the part of the popular leaders. . . ."[4] From early September to mid-March of the following year, Oscar Malmros worked, each day somewhat more openly, to guide Riel, his people, and his country into the American fold.

After McDougall's withdrawal, the *métis* issued their declaration and raised the Provisional Government's bizarre flag. To celebrate the occasion, the cathedral band from St. Boniface serenaded the crowd at Fort Garry and then moved on to play before the American consulate. At last the mystery that had attended the consul's movements was gone, and the moment had arrived when he could openly bid for Riel's hand—and for annexation. Until Canada made amends and

[3]*Ibid.*
[4]Ramsey Papers, M.H.S.

tendered acceptable proposals to the French, he could help shape
policy for the Provisional Government. And, in the interim, it was only
good sense for Riel to accept the American as an adviser. For the
United States served him as an ace-in-the-hole, if Canada should ever
refuse to bargain with his government.

As December slipped by, it became increasingly apparent to the
English party that the Americans were associating themselves and
their political schemes with Louis Riel. "The American residents in
the Town of Winnipeg and those at Pembina," Begg noted with alarm
on the twenty-seventh, "have of late greatly interested themselves in
the movements of the French and are evidently trying to mislead Riel
in favor of annexation to the States. H. [Hugh] S. Donaldson, Major
[Henry M.] Robinson, Oscar Malmoras [*sic*], and [Enos] Stutsman at
Pembina are all admitted to the secret councils of Riel."[5]

Though clandestinely given, the nature of the advice offered by the
Americans to Riel can hardly be doubted. Their other actions betray
them. They tried to discredit Canada and exalt the United States.
Would-be filibusters like the cripple, Stutsman, bent in body and
mind, broadcast rumours that McDougall had spoken contemptuously
of the *métis*. And he urged Riel not to admit the vanguard of Canada's
conciliators, Colonel Charles de Salaberry and Father Jean-Baptiste
Thibault. McDougall had been barred from Rupert's Land—Stutsman
argued—why not do likewise with these men? He warned Riel that if
they came to Red River they would surely turn the *métis* against the
Provisional Government.

The greatest organ of all Yankee propaganda was not a man, however, but a newspaper, the *New Nation*. In the course of the rebellion,
it usurped the monopoly held by the *Nor'-Wester* and, for the first
three weeks of its life, was as partisan in its political philosophy and
as scurrilously written as its predecessor. There has always been an air
of mystery about the paper. Its masthead listed the publisher simply
as H. M. Robinson & Co. Though Robinson was well known in Red
River as a prominent American merchant, most of his contemporaries,
including Alexander Begg, could only guess at the identity of the
"Company." Yet from this vantage point in time, it is evident that
Louis Riel was the "Company."[6] He contributed most of the capital

[5]William L. Morton, ed., *Alexander Begg's Red River Journal and Other
Papers Relative to the Red River Resistance of 1869–1870* (Toronto, 1956), p.
242. (Cited hereafter as *Begg's Journal and Other Papers*.)

[6]On 28 December, Robinson acquired William Coldwell's *Red River Pioneer*
—type, fixtures, and all—for approximately £550. He paid Coldwell in "parcels
of money . . . marked in the handwriting of J. H. Mctavish," in Morton, ed.,

supporting the paper; he controlled its editorial policy; and so long as it suited his purpose, he permitted it to take a pro-American position.

If the ownership of the *New Nation* was somewhat mysterious, its editorial policy was unmistakable. In tone and in content, the first issue (7 January 1870) was offensively annexationist. On the one hand the editorial ("Our Policy") regarded government by the Hudson's Bay Company "as obsolete, and never to be resuscitated," and on the other it scorned the prospect of political union with Canada. The Dominion "by its criminal blunders and gross injustice to this people . . . [has] forever alienated them; and by . . . [its] forfeiture of all right to our respect, will prevent us in future from either seeking or permitting its protection." "The Imperial Government," the editor added, was "too far distant to intelligently administer our affairs." To this sort of crooked logic, there could be only two political conclusions: either independence or annexation to the United States. Though the *New Nation* advocated independence "as a present cure for public ills," it maintained that annexation would eventually follow "and bring with it the advantages this land so much requires."

Also in the *New Nation*'s first edition was an unsigned article entitled "Annexation our Manifest Destiny." Though none in the Red River Settlement suspected, the article had been secretly dictated by Oscar Malmros.[7] It was the classical expression, couched in geopolitical terms, of Minnesota's expansionist "party line." Malmros argued that nature had separated Canada from the British Northwest by "one dismal waste of rocks and water." "In fact," he wrote, "we form a separate colony and people with different views of life, distinct habits, and different interests and necessities; we have nothing in common

---

Begg's Journal and Other Papers, p. 244. There can be no doubt that this money represented part of a forced loan extracted by Riel from the Hudson's Bay Company on the twenty-second. On that day, Riel carried out a threat—intimated to William Mactavish on the fourteenth and then openly re-stated on the twentieth—when he seized the Company's accountant, John H. McTavish, took his key to the Fort Garry safe, opened the depository, and removed over £1000 in specie and notes. (Mactavish to the Secretary, 25 Dec. 1869, H.B.C., Series A.12/45.) For the "loan," W. B. O'Donoghue gave a receipt, carefully listing all the bills and notes that were taken. (H.B.C., Series D.10/1.) This money was apparently not used by Riel either to pay his troops or buy supplies for them. The troops remained unpaid, and provisions and goods were simply confiscated, when needed, from the Company's stores. Under the circumstances, how can we doubt James W. Taylor, when he wrote the State Department that "the first instalment of a loan forced from the Hudson [*sic*] Bay Company by Riel—about £600—was applied to the purchase. . ." of the *New Nation?* Taylor to Hamilton Fish, 27 Jan. 1870, Consular Dispatches, Winnipeg, Special Agent, Red River Affairs, N.A.

[7]Malmros to Ramsey, 6 Jan. 1870, Ramsey Papers.

with that country [Canada] or its government." But if nature had split British North America asunder, it had joined together Minnesota and Rupert's Land in a union that was at once economic, geographic, and permanent.

The next two issues of the *New Nation* followed this theme with undeviating fidelity. In the second issue, 14 January 1870, Canada was upbraided for the "blundering" and "gross mismanagement" that had brought about the October uprising. And in the third, 21 January 1870, annexation to the United States was urged in front-page headlines and bold type:

Consolidation!

The Future
of the
American Continent.

One Flag! One Empire!!

Natural Lines must Prevail.

The editorial beneath conjured up the magnificent sight of a truly continental nation, "a vision of a grand consolidation of peoples and interests, such as can be paralleled nowhere else among all the Kingdoms of the earth." It was fantastic journalism. At the same time that H. M. Robinson & Co. warned its readers against "Canadian Carpet-Baggers," the *New Nation* was uninhibitedly planting the Stars and Stripes all over the North American continent.

The American party did not confine its propaganda to the Red River Settlement. Some Yankees like Stutsman wrote "anonymous" letters to St. Paul's newspapers, proclaiming the righteousness of Riel's cause and denigrating Canada and the Canadians.[8] But Malmros, as chief of the party, had his eye on bigger game. Soon after the rebellion's outbreak, he was suggesting policy to the State Department. With undisguised pleasure, he reported (6 November 1869) to Washington that "the prospect now is that in a short time the country will be a unit in favor of independence, i.e., annexation to the U.S. although some favor the formation of a separate British Crown Colony. . . . Should this revolution be successfull [*sic*] it may, I think, be safely predicted that in less than 2 years time all the British Colonies on this Continent will apply for admission into the Union."[9] Two months later, when the Hudson's Bay Company was secretly trying to blunt Riel's military strength by hiring away his *métis* as boatmen, Malmros

---

[8]See the St. Paul *Press*, 14 Nov. 1869.
[9]Malmros to Davis, Consular Dispatches, Winnipeg.

urged the State Department to underwrite Riel. "The sum of about $25000 promptly sent would materially aid and I think secure the success of the independence movement."[10] And later, when he had begun to doubt the success of his political machinations, he sought permission to extend a *de facto* recognition to the Provisional Government.

Subvention and recognition were the eleventh-hour suggestions of a desperate man. Indeed Malmros's whole expansionist philosophy had always been grounded upon false premises. He believed, without knowing of Bishop Taché's true position, that the Catholic clergy in the Northwest were irreconcilably opposed to confederation. He thought that Canada and Rupert's Land were by nature so dissimilar that they would be politically incompatible—"their historical life is unconnected with that of Canada and all intercourse, social or commercial between the respective communities, at least direct intercourse has been prevented through natural obstacles."[11] Moreover he contended, in ignorance of Macdonald's political talents, that Ottawa could never work its way out of McDougall's morass. And finally he reasoned that, if all the above were true, Rupert's Land would inevitably ally itself to the United States. No political agent ever charted his course by more delusive stars. No party was ever founded on more uncertain grounds. Far from achieving their ends, Malmros and his American party, through their subversive propaganda and political intrigue, only succeeded in discrediting the United States and in arousing a needless hostility in Canada towards the American government. The high-water mark of American influence upon Riel's Provisional Government was reached in December; by mid-January, the tide was visibly, swiftly ebbing.

As soon as Donald A. Smith, the third Canadian commissioner to come to Red River, extended Ottawa's "olive branch" to the people, the American party was doomed. When Smith addressed the people for the second time, on 20 January, Alexander Begg noted "that only one or two of the Americans made their appearance amongst the crowd" that so cordially received the commissioner.[12] On the following day, the third edition of the *New Nation* came out, but despite the fact that Robinson handed out free copies throughout the settlement, his office was soon inundated with rejects—"and many of the returned papers . . . [had] some pretty hard writings on them such as 'The

[10]Malmros to Davis, 15 Jan. 1870, *ibid.*
[11]Malmros to Davis, 6 Jan. 1870, *ibid.*
[12]Morton, ed., *Begg's Journal and Other Papers*, p. 277.

New Damnation'—&c. &c."[13] The fourth edition gave evidence of Riel's censorship; and, in March, the paper was entrusted by him to a new editor. Of the first edition of the reconstructed *New Nation*, Begg laconically commented: "Annexation is knocked on the head."

The power and prestige of the American party vanished as if touched by a magician's wand. On 12 January Bob O'Lone's saloon resounded with the jubilant noise of Americans drinking toasts to annexation, and on the very same day, the American flag was raised over Emmerling's hotel. On the twenty-sixth, the flag was lowered never to fly again and, on Washington's birthday, a scheduled ball had to be cancelled because there were no funds available to support it. In early January, Malmros wrote Ramsey that he would stay on as consul, because the rebels wanted him and would not confide so intimately in a successor—and if his salary were "materially raised."[14] Two months later, hurriedly and without a raise, he departed for the United States, murmuring something about an urgent need to tend to some Chicago real estate. Though no one in Red River knew the exact reason for his departure, few were fooled by his story. Malmros left because he had to. When the United States government unwittingly published certain of his consular dispatches without adequate pruning, his position in Red River, already precarious, became—as he himself admitted to Ramsey—"entirely untenable, impracticable and in fact intolerable."[15]

Quite unnecessarily, Malmros added that the American consulate was, as an office, "really not worth having." But before leaving Winnipeg for the last time, he named H. M. Robinson, editor of the *New Nation*, as the American vice-consul. It was a gesture as ineffectual as it was informal. Within a fortnight, Robinson's authority had been completely destroyed, for he was arrested by Riel and forced to give up his keys to the editorial offices. By the end of March the American party had been permanently silenced—quieted by threats or driven into exile across the border.

[13]*Ibid.*, p. 288.
[14]6 Jan. 1870, Ramsey Papers.
[15]15 March 1870, *ibid.* In February, in response to a Senate resolution of 8 January, the State Department transmitted to that chamber a bundle of papers and documents dealing with McDougall's presence on American soil and the opposition in Rupert's Land to him as lieutenant governor. The papers were read, referred to the Committee on Foreign Relations, and printed as *Senate Executive Document No. 33*, 41st Cong., 2nd Sess., Serial 1405. Malmros's dispatches had not been sufficiently censored. They revealed, for example, certain conversations between himself and either the Church or the Company which, when published, destroyed his usefulness in Red River.

The Yankee expansionists in Red River had overplayed their hand. It had always been a difficult political situation for them to exploit. Though the people of Red River admired many things about the United States, they were emotionally anti-American; and, to their way of thinking, anything that was socially or culturally unattractive in Rupert's Land usually came from the United States. Many of them disliked the "typical" American. His philosophy of materialism, his chauvinism, his apparent disregard for law and order, and his social crudities had never appealed to the observant and sensitive citizen of Red River.[16] "I suppose," intoned a *Nor'-Wester* correspondent (9 July 1862) with unrestrained acrimony, "that there are some fine families [in Minnesota], there must be; but, generally speaking, the population is of that hard unsympathetic kind that instinctively repels you." And now, 1870, when the annexation of Rupert's Land seemed almost within Minnesota's reach, Malmros and his American party failed to grasp it. Perhaps they had been too acquisitive, too eager for political union; whatever the reason, they repelled rather than attracted the people of Red River.

Canada was now the favoured suitor and perhaps had always been so. It may be that Riel always intended to confederate with Canada, provided the grievances of his countrymen could be redressed and their security in the dominion assured. As it was stated by Riel and understood by Bannatyne and others, the primary object of the Provisional Government "was to treat if possible with Canada for a just union with that country or England—failing these two to look elsewhere."[17] At best, annexation to the United States was a policy to be pursued when all other political alternatives had failed. It therefore seems clear that when Riel dallied with Malmros and the American party, he did so either to induce Ottawa to accept confederation on his terms or to hedge an almost certain political bet. If these were his tactics, they succeeded. By the middle of March Sir John A. Macdonald had given positive assurances that he would meet the fundamental ends sought by the rebels. Donald A. Smith and Bishop Taché, with their promises and persuasions, turned Rupert's Land into the Canadian fold and unalterably away from the United States.

When William R. Marshall, ex-governor of Minnesota, came to the Red River Settlement on a mission of intrigue, the flag of the Pro-

16See Morton, ed., *Begg's Journal and Other Papers*, pp. 254, 259, and 291; Alexander Ross, *The Red River Settlement* (London, 1856), pp. 338–9; and Mactavish to the Secretary, 11 Dec. 1869, H.B.C., Series A.12/45.

17Morton, ed., *Begg's Journal and Other Papers* (6 Jan. 1870), p. 253.

visional Government was no longer flying over Fort Garry. A few days before his arrival on 24 April 1870 Louis Riel had raised the Union Jack in a dramatic ceremony symbolizing his allegiance to the Queen. Marshall came as the agent of Jay Cooke and the unofficial representative of Minnesota's expansionist junto, and he meant to guide Riel towards political independence and eventual union with the United States.[18] Of the recent change in the climate of opinion, he apparently knew nothing. Otherwise he would never have taken the trip, for by the time he got to Red River there were probably not more than fifty men in the entire settlement who backed the annexation movement.[19] Marshall carried on conversations with both Riel and his adviser, W. B. O'Donoghue. The *métis* was scrupulously circumspect and the Irishman was an outspoken annexationist. And yet O'Donoghue candidly informed Marshall that, if Canada agreed to the demands of the Provisional Government, Riel would bring Rupert's Land into the Dominion; but if Canada demurred, he would seek American aid. At this point in Marshall's talk with O'Donoghue, Riel joined them and said emphatically that his and O'Donoghue's views "were in perfect harmony and accord."[20] Thus it should have been clear to all members of the Marshall party that Riel would consider American aid only if Canada failed to accept his terms for confederation.

II

Marshall's mission was but one example of the efforts of Minnesota's expansionists to detach the British Northwest. Though few in numbers, they were forceful and articulate men who could, as the occasion demanded, make their presence and their wishes felt and heard. They collaborated closely with one another, despite the fact that their activities nearly spanned the continent. Here were those "Yankee wire pullers" whom Ottawa feared: Alexander Ramsey, Joseph A. Wheelock, James W. Taylor, Oscar Malmros, and the railroad men, George Becker of the St. Paul and Pacific and Jay Cooke of the

[18]Joseph A. Wheelock to Ramsey, 7 April 1870, Ramsey Papers.
[19]Nathaniel P. Langford to J. W. Taylor, 10 July 1870, Taylor Papers, M.H.S. Langford accompanied Marshall and, while in Red River, conversed with Donaldson, Robinson, and other members of the discredited American party. They were bitter men, claiming that Riel "had led them to believe that he favored annexation, and in this respect had deceived them."
[20]*Ibid.* Langford was either a witness to, or heard directly of, Marshall's conversations with both O'Donoghue and Riel.

Northern Pacific. Though conservative in matters of business and politics, they were ultra-radical on the subject of Rupert's Land and British North America. Moreover most of these men occupied positions of peculiar strength. Wheelock's paper, the St. Paul *Press*, undoubtedly had a greater circulation and more influence than any other newspaper in the state. Ramsey, a political prophet forever enchanted with his state's northern destiny, had held a seat in the United States Senate since 1863. He was the leader of the Republican party in Minnesota, and to him, Malmros and Taylor owed their jobs. They were, in fact, the State Department's only official sources of information regarding Rupert's Land and the Riel Rebellion.

In common, these Minnesotans worked out a policy designed to cut off Rupert's Land from its British connection and annex it to the United States. And in their pursuit of another man's property, they were often indifferent about the means to be employed. They intervened in internal matters across the 49th parallel. Through the press and other means of publicity, they strove to justify Riel's course and to awaken American interest in and sympathy for Minnesota's manifest destiny. They tried to block Canada's efforts to regain her lost heritage and they exhorted Grant's administration to adopt their expansionist views.

For a brief moment in time, Minnesotans had assumed a kindly and cautious attitude towards William McDougall and his problems. When he passed through St. Paul in October en route to Red River, Wheelock's *Press* (13 October 1869) bade him Godspeed in his mission to create a sea-to-sea confederation. Though the disorder that attended his arrival at the border shocked the *Press*, it was blissfully sure that he would soon talk the *métis* into dismantling the barricades. But when he failed to do so—when an uprising turned into a rebellion—the general attitude of Minnesota changed. Sympathy for Canada vanished. McDougall was straightway translated into a despotic villain; Riel just as quickly became a freedom-fighter. The *Press* (16 November 1869) now described the insurrection not as a "contemptible movement" but as a popular protest against Canada's effort to make a "satrapy" out of Rupert's Land. The St. Paul *Pioneer*, a Democratic organ, concurred (17 November 1869) with its Republican rival, and both papers began hesitantly to speak of annexation.

In late November, James W. Taylor had an audience in Washington with the Secretary of State, Hamilton Fish.[21] The meeting had been

[21]Hamilton Fish's diary, 28 Nov. 1869, typewritten copy in the Manuscript Division of the Library of Congress. (Cited hereafter as Fish's Diary.)

arranged by Senator Ramsey and other influential Minnesotans, and their purpose was soon made evident. Taylor revealed to Fish all the Canadian blunders that had, in his opinion, produced the Riel Rebellion. Though he then advised Fish against any American interference, shortly afterwards he was appointed a secret agent of the State Department and consistently thereafter used his position to promote the idea of intervention. Taylor knew more about Rupert's Land than any other living American and his appointment seems fitting, but it was as contrived as the initial meeting with Fish. Beyond any doubt, he owed his appointment to the interposition of his Minnesota friends, the G.O.P. chieftains: Governor Marshall and Senators Ramsey and Wilkinson; and in all probability, he composed his own instructions.[22] Taylor's official role was that of a confidential agent for the State Department. He was directed not only to write detailed reports on the Riel Rebellion but also to present Fish with a full account of the British Northwest and its political and economic relations with both Canada and the United States. When he received his instructions late in December, Malmros and the American party were just reaching the peak of their influence in Red River affairs. To Taylor—to all Minnesota expansionists—it seemed as if the moment had arrived when the United States might act affirmatively to acquire the British Northwest. They immediately sloughed off their neutralist garb and began campaigning for annexation.

Taylor and his friends found a receptive audience. To Americans, and especially the expansionist-minded, Canada was a loosely knit confederation with a dubious future. The Canadian dream of sea-to-sea dominion was fantastic. Had not geography sliced British North America into sections that inhibited political union north of the international line? Did not this same sectionalism encourage economic alliances to the south? In fact, the Maritime Provinces seemed more akin to New England than to Quebec. Quebec and Ontario were geographically separated by the Precambrian Shield from the British Northwest, which was, in turn, bound by nature to Minnesota. Even farther to the west lay British Columbia, removed from Central Canada in

---

[22]Among the Taylor papers, there is an undated draft of instructions—in Taylor's hand—from the State Department to himself. It was written in 1859, when Taylor vainly sought a post like that secured in 1869, and it duplicates almost word for word the instrument that appointed and instructed him as a special agent of the State Department. See Fish to Taylor, 30 Dec. 1869, Instructions to Special Missions, 1852–86, Department of State. Quoted in its entirety by G. F. G. Stanley, *The Birth of Western Canada* (London, New York, Toronto, 1936), pp. 59–60.

time and in space by the Rockies, the Great Plains, and the Shield. Rupert's Land was in a state of rebellion; certain citizens of British Columbia were soon to petition President Grant for admission into the union; and there were signs of disaffection in the Maritimes. Glancing northward, seeing events through imperialist eyes, the unthinking and insensitive American could easily conclude that all British North America was breaking up into its natural, geographical components—and that to Minnesota would fall Rupert's Land.

The Minnesota expansionists broadcast their propaganda high and low, seeking to influence public opinion everywhere, stimulate action in the State Department, and—not incidentally—catch the eye of Louis Riel. In a long report to the Secretary of State, Taylor described (20 January 1870) the British Northwest in enthusiastic, extravagant phrases. It was, he claimed, a rich territorial prize with resources sufficient "to constitute four states equal to Minnesota."[23] In the Senate, Ramsey reiterated Taylor's words and nostalgically retold his own impressions of the Winnipeg Basin that he had visited nearly twenty years ago. In the St. Paul *Press* Wheelock sounded his antiphonal response. Together all three men played the song of Nature, Minnesota, and Manifest Destiny. Nature, Taylor contended, had united Minnesota with Rupert's Land. The two regions were tied together by the Red River and further entwined by the trade that travelled along the valley. Wheelock's *Press* (16 January 1870) maintained that, even if Canada met all Riel's demands, Rupert's Land could never remain a permanent part of the Dominion: "The attempt to plant a Canadian colony across the track of American domination and expansion on the Northwestern areas of this continent—is the vainest and most futile of chimeras." Canada was walled off from Rupert's Land by an impenetrable barrier of forests, granite-ridged lakes, and swift rivers which could accommodate nothing but canoes upon their waters. The Shield had barred Canadian merchants from Red River; it could keep out British soldiers just as well.

The cession of Rupert's Land to the United States was the obvious solution to Canada's ills in Red River. Furthermore, why should she seek a Northwest that could never be held? Or—as the *Press* (23 December 1869) put it, with Wheelock editorially mixing metaphors, providence, and the marriage rites—Great Britain ought to avail herself of a grand opportunity "to settle the Alabama claims with the

[23]Consular Dispatches, Winnipeg, Special Agent, Red River Affairs. A good many of Taylor's reports to Fish may also be found in *Senate Executive Document No. 33*, 41st Cong., 2nd Sess., Serial 1405.

cession to the United States of a country whose destinies God has indissolubly wedded to ours by geographical affinities which no human power can sunder, as He has divorced it from Canada by physical barriers which no human power can overcome." In a more restrained but equally presumptuous way, Taylor described Washington's climate of opinion to a prominent Canadian friend: " . . . the situation in the Northwest—at Selkirk and in British Columbia—suggests to almost every one I meet the possibility of a treaty with England and Canada for the cession to the United States of the territory beyond the Lakes simultaneously with the settlement of the Alabama controversy and the adjustment of commercial relations with the Dominion."[24] Cession of a province precariously held would insure Canada of reciprocity with the United States and promise, for England, the settlement of the troublesome *Alabama* claims.

Taylor and Wheelock described the Riel Rebellion in terms designed to attract the sympathy of Americans. Wheelock likened the rebellious *métis* to the patriots of Lexington and Concord. In an article written for the Washington *Chronicle* (11 February 1870),[25] Taylor claimed that Canada never intended to give representative government to the half-breeds but, like George III, would try to beat them into submission with armed troops. To Fish, he made the ridiculous assertion, late in May, that Riel's Provisional Government was the *de jure* as well as *de facto* government of Rupert's Land. In justifying this position, he followed Riel's line of reasoning: The Hudson's Bay Company had abdicated; Canada had vainly tried to take over land that was not legally nor morally hers—"Thus the Red River people were instinctively logical in all their resistance to Canadian authority."[26]

Every move made by the *métis* leader, whether heroic or brutal, was extolled. When Dr. Schultz surrendered on 7 December and McDougall's counter-revolution collapsed, Wheelock's *Press* (21 December 1869) heralded the event as "the signal for a popular uprising against Canadian authority. . . ." Riel's execution of the Orangeman, Thomas Scott—whose death was regarded by Protestant Ontario as murder—was reported by the *Press* (27 March 1870) with a ready understanding and an easy forgiveness. Only Riel could know whether or not such a terrible example of his authority was "necessary to crush

[24]Taylor to Charles J. Brydges, 5 Jan. 1870, draft letter in the Taylor Papers. Brydges was managing director of the Grand Trunk Railway and a close friend of Sir John A. Macdonald.
[25]Enclosed in Taylor to Fish, 12 Feb. 1870, Consular Dispatches, Winnipeg, Special Agent, Red River Affairs.
[26]24 May 1870, *ibid.*

the treasonable machinations of the Canadians." In a report (24 May 1870) to Fish, Taylor attempted to vindicate Riel by stating that the taking of Scott's life had been a dreadful measure meant to prevent any further uprisings in the settlement.

As they tried to aid Riel, so too did the Minnesota expansionists endeavour to obstruct Canada's course of action in the Northwest. The presence of McDougall on American soil was questioned by Ramsey in the Senate. Almost to a man, Ramsey and the others claimed that the lieutenant governor and his Canadian party were ingratiating themselves with the Sioux murderers of 1862 and that another and bloodier Indian war might be the result. Neither McDougall nor official Ottawa were to be trusted. Wheelock's *Press* (18 May 1870) warned Riel time and again—and assured him that, without an amnesty, he and his followers would meet a hangman's noose.

The Minnesotans consistently tried to prevent or impede a Canadian military expedition against Rupert's Land. So far as they were concerned, to give Canada the right to transit over American soil would be unthinkable, and permission to use the locks at Sault Sainte Marie ought never to be considered. In fact the United States should not even countenance such an expedition, regardless of its route, unless Canada and Great Britain first agreed to grant a general amnesty to all the rebels. There also ought to be assurances given that the Canadian expedition would be peaceful and not punitive or coercive in nature. The columns of the *Press* frequently threatened that if one Canadian rifle were discharged in Rupert's Land, it would immediately be answered by a volley from volunteer American frontiersmen. Indeed, if the belligerent Wheelock had had his way, Washington would have provided Riel with "one or two batteries and men to work them."[27]

The Minnesota expansionists wanted the State Department to follow a policy of unsubtle intervention, not mere diplomatic pressure. In mid-January, Ramsey made his position clear to Hamilton Fish, when he suggested that the secretary heavily subsidize Riel's government. Failing in this venture, Ramsey offered a resolution in the Senate on 1 February 1870:

That the Committee on Foreign Relations be instructed to consider the expediency of recommending to the President of the United States that this Government shall tender its mediation between the Dominion of Canada

---

[27]Wheelock to Ramsey, 7 April 1870, Ramsey Papers. On 30 April Wheelock editorialized in the *Press* that "if the Fenians really desire to strike an effective blow against British power on this continent, the place, and the only place to strike is in Western British America."

and the people of the Red River district for the adjustment of existing difficulties and the establishment of responsible government in the territory included in the charter of the Hudson [*sic*] Bay Company.[28]

So far as the Minnesota senator was concerned, justice demanded that the United States intervene in Rupert's Land. "Let me ask, is there no other alternative for the people of northwest British America than to be cajoled or dragooned into this unnatural union with Canada? I say 'unnatural', for the fact of the continent, the course of trade, postal relations, the immediate future of railroad communications, all point to close commercial relations with Minnesota, Wisconsin, and Illinois. . . ." "Why should not the way be found or made," he asked his fellow senators, "for a submission to the people of Selkirk whether they desire to join their political destiny with the United States or with Canada?" He felt that Great Britain would not stand in the way of Selkirk's annexation to the United States and hoped that Canada's loss of real estate could be repaid with a reciprocal trade agreement.

Ramsey's resolution was sent off to the Committee on Foreign Relations and nothing further was said about it until 19 April 1870. On that day Michigan's Zachariah Chandler offered a second resolution, bolder, blunter, and more ridiculous than Ramsey's: "That the President of the United States be, and he hereby is, directed to appoint two or more commissioners, or other diplomatic agents, to open negotiations with the people of Winnipeg, with a view to the annexation of that district of country to the United States as a Territory or as a State."[29] Three days later (22 April 1870), Chandler spoke to his resolution; or, in the less reverent words of the Boston *Daily Advertiser* (25 April 1870), "put on his cap and bells and performed one of his periodical war dances." After making an introductory statement that his resolution was offered "in the interest of peace, of good neighborhood, and of good-fellowship as between Great Britain and the United States of America," Senator Chandler turned to the task of dismembering the Dominion of Canada.[30] Though Canada was then "a mere speck upon the map," it was "an intolerable nuisance," and if it ever reached the Pacific, it would become "a standing menace . . . that we ought not to tolerate and will not tolerate." He therefore suggested that Great Britain give the United States "a quit-claim deed" to all British North America; in return, the United States would forgive Britain's debts arising from the *Alabama* claims, which he reckoned at the absurd figure of $2,220,000,000, a sum about equal

[28]*Congressional Globe*, 41st Cong., 2nd Sess., pp. 931–3.
[29]*Ibid.*, p. 2808. Chandler's seat in the Senate was next to Ramsey's.
[30]*Ibid.*, pp. 2888–90.

to half the costs of the Civil War. He warned Canada against sending a military expedition into Rupert's Land. Both Fenians and frontiersmen were marching northward—and behind them was "the strongest military Power on earth." "Mr. President," Chandler concluded, "this continent is ours."

Though the speech was—as the New York *Herald* (23 April 1870) unkindly called it—"a new dish of 'hash' from the famous Chandler," it looked somewhat palatable to Alexander Ramsey. As soon as the senior Senator from Michigan had finished, Ramsey hastened to gain the floor in order to ask whether Charles Sumner's Committee on Foreign Relations had taken any action regarding his own resolution of 1 February. When Sumner replied that the resolution was still "pending," for the reason that his committee lacked authentic facts about the situation in Red River, Ramsey gratuitously provided an assortment of facts, rumours, and half-truths. He assured the Senate that Canada was calling out the Lake Superior Indians for aid in putting down the half-breed rebellion. Hearing this, Timothy O. Howe (Wisconsin) asked if Ramsey's information were authentic. In reply, the Minnesota senator said that the press was full of information—and Howe asked no more questions—and quickly went on to state that Canada meant to slip some regular troops through the canal at Sault Ste. Marie and dispatch others, disguised as civilians, through the border states in order to cut off any possible retreat into the United States by Riel. At this point, Justin S. Morrill (Vermont) interrupted. "Will the Chairman of the Post Office Committee," he jocularly inquired, "inform us whether he cannot introduce a bill for carrying the mails and extending our commerce to Winnipeg?" His remark evoked laughter from his fellows and a retort from Ramsey: "That will be the next step if the Committee on Foreign Relations do not take some action on the subject." Again the Senate laughed, but on this occasion, Jacob M. Howard (Michigan) did not share in the merriment. He bluntly told his colleagues that the canal at the Sault belonged to Michigan and British troops would never be allowed to use it.

III

Grant's administration did not require the rumours of Ramsey to goad it into adopting a foreign policy designed to acquire all or any part of British North America. The President and his Secretary of

State were almost as expansionist as the Minnesota junto. There is no doubt that both men wanted Canada. However their expansionism was tempered by the responsibilities of high office and assumed a more subtle form. While Joseph Wheelock's St. Paul *Press* exhorted the Fenians to cross the 49th parallel, Hamilton Fish employed detectives to watch them and faithfully reported their movements to the British minister. Wiser than Wheelock, he did not want needlessly to offend either Canada or Great Britain.

Nevertheless, Fish magnified all the signs of pro-annexationist sentiment that he saw in Canada. Upon such false premises did he reason that, if Great Britain withdrew from the continent, leaving Canada as a separate and independent country, the Dominion and all the other segments of British North America would gravitate towards the United States and eventually be absorbed within it. In repeated conversations with Sir Edward Thornton, the British minister, Fish argued in behalf of Canadian independence.[31] He artfully asserted that if Britain withdrew from North America, the causes of Anglo-American enmity—"Indians, Fenians, disorderly soldiers &c"—would be removed, and the *Alabama* claims could be settled immediately. He claimed "that with the exception of the Government Officials, and the Bankers, and some few wealthy families, there was a preponderance of sentiment in favor of separation from Great Britain." He pointed out to Thornton the evidences of political unrest in British North America and drew his attention to the geographical forces that stunted Canada's transcontinental growth and encouraged regional relationships on a north-south axis.

To these overtures, Thornton generally made the same reply. He himself could find no evidence of annexationist sentiment in Canada. His country was "willing and even desirous" to bring about Canada's political separation and yet his hands were tied. "The Canadians," he confessed, "find fault with me for saying so openly as I do that we are ready to let them go whenever they wish, but they do not desire it."[32] Nevertheless, on one occasion, Thornton indiscreetly intimated to Fish that the United States probably could, by continuing its restrictions upon Canadian-American trade, subject Canada to great financial strain, induce political unrest, and thus alter Ottawa's attitude toward separation."[33] An unwise slip of Thornton's tongue,

[31]Fish's Diary, 23 Dec. 1869, 6 Jan. and 24 March 1870.
[32]*Ibid.*, 23 Dec. 1869.
[33]Fish reported this secret and confidential conversation with Thornton at a cabinet meeting. *Ibid.*, 1 April 1870.

a change within the British cabinet, the start of the Franco-Prussian War—events like these were erroneously interpreted by the State Department as signs prophesying Britain's withdrawal from North America, Canada's independence, and her annexation to the United States.

President Grant coveted Canada. He informed his cabinet in November that he wanted to delay diplomatic negotiations over the *Alabama* claims until Britain was ready to settle them by ceding Canada to the United States. It was the sort of policy that appealed to his expansionist, Anglophobic turn of mind, but it possessed two flaws which Fish immediately pointed out: Great Britain would never yield up an unwilling Canada, and Canada did not wish to be annexed. Grant's policy soon appeared more promising, however, when William McDougall and Canada were locked out of Rupert's Land—and when, less than a month after that event, some residents of British Columbia memorialized the President for admission into the United States. Here were civil disorders and expressions of pro-Americanism which might be utilized to gain at least a slice of British North America.

Fish sensed the expansionist opportunities presented by circumstances but refused to adopt Machiavellian tactics. Perhaps he feared that intervention in the Pacific Northwest would forever alienate Canada—a far richer prize than Rupert's Land. Whatever the reason, he never replied to the petition from British Columbia. Both he and the President were convinced that their "proper course . . . [was] to abstain from action [,] to keep our eyes fixedly on the movement, & to keep our hands off."[34]

And at first, Fish followed the same policy regarding Rupert's Land. When Senator Ramsey asked Grant and his Secretary of State in mid-January whether or not $25,000 could be sent up to Winnipeg in order to sustain the revolutionaries, Fish said there were no funds available. He piously added that "we should not use money in this way."[35] To a similar request from Oscar Malmros, he gave no reply at all; and when the consul brashly inquired if he might tender *de jure* recognition to Riel's Provisional Government, the State Department instantly reprimanded him. If Ramsey was annoyed by Fish's morality, Malmros—a diplomat of easy virtue—was shocked. "I must conclude," he wrote in disgust to Ramsey, "that our administration has no foreign policy."[36]

For all his protestations, Fish sloughed off his moralistic garb as

[34]*Ibid.*, 4 Jan. 1870.
[35]*Ibid.*, 15 Jan. 1870.   [36]6 Jan. 1870, Ramsey Papers.

soon as he learned of an amazing conversation allegedly held between Malmros and Mactavish. On 23 December 1869 the Hudson's Bay man had confidentially told the consul "that he intended to submit to their House in London . . . whether it might not be in the interest of the Company to favor annexation of this Country [Rupert's Land] to the United States."[37] Malmros's dispatch reached the State Department on 12 January and spurred Fish into action. He immediately apprised John L. Motley, the American minister to England, of the dispatch and instructed him to find out whether Mactavish had really written the Company regarding annexation and "also to learn their views or feelings on the subject."[38] If Motley detected any evidence of willingness by the Company or the British Government to part with Rupert's Land, he was "discreetly" to encourage it—"without however compromitting [*sic*] the Government in any respect."

With equal speed, Fish directed James W. Taylor to give the State Department his interpretation of the Malmros-Mactavish conversation. Within a fortnight, Taylor had complied, handing in a lengthy report which may be summarized as follows:[39] It was his opinion that Mactavish and the Company's other wintering partners "have been embittered against political connexion with Canada . . ." for a long time. Although Dr. Schultz and his party were the principal reasons for this enmity, there were other reasons too. Given a choice in the matter, the wintering partners would probably prefer the United States to Canada. They had long enjoyed a felicitous and far-reaching relationship with Minnesota. In the Canadian sale, they would get no share of the receipts. In an American sale, the Company and perhaps the wintering partners would undoubtedly receive more money, and fur trading—and continued profits for the wintering partners who shared with the stockholders in the trade—would go on much as before.

Motley's responses were more realistic than Taylor's.[40] In his first reply, Motley asserted that Mactavish had never submitted any such proposal to the Hudson's Bay Company in London. Although he did not name the source of his information, which had apparently been given him in confidence, he was certain of its credibility. And, to date,

[37]Malmros to Davis, 24 Dec. 1869, Consular Dispatches, Winnipeg.

[38]Fish to Motley, 14 Jan. 1870, Records of the Foreign Service Posts of the United States, Instructions, Great Britain, 1870, N.A.

[39]Taylor to Fish, 25 Jan. 1870, Consular Dispatches, Winnipeg, Special Agent, Red River Affairs.

[40]Motley to Fish, 2 and 17 Feb. 1870, Diplomatic Dispatches, Great Britain, Vols. 101 and 102, Nos. 232 and 248, N.A.

no research in the Company's archives has turned up a letter from Mactavish on the subject. In his second reply, Motley stated that he had been unable to express his nation's views regarding Rupert's Land to any members of the British government. However he doubted whether it would serve any purpose and underscored his pessimism by enclosing a clipping from the *Pall Mall Gazette* (16 February 1870) in which the Home Secretary had been quoted to the effect that his government was "most anxious to preserve intact the existing relations" between the colonies and the mother country.

There the matter might have ended, had not an unusual opportunity been presented to the State Department for direct negotiation with the Hudson's Bay Company itself. On 17 February 1870, Sir Curtis M. Lampson, Deputy Governor of the Company and an American expatriate, wrote a personal letter to J. C. Bancroft Davis, Fish's Assistant Secretary of State.[41] Lampson had met Davis while the latter was in London during the Civil War but this letter was not meant to revive an old friendship. In writing Davis, Sir Curtis was acting for the British Foreign Office, though in an unofficial capacity, and seeking a new departure for the settlement of the *Alabama* claims.

The American State Department seized upon this unexpected diplomatic invitation and Davis replied (12 March 1870) at great length, giving Lampson a very frank statement of his country's views and wishes.[42]

There is one way in which this matter can be adjusted, and I see but one way that is absolutely certain to succeed—I mean a territorial adjustment. . . . It may be that Great Britain is not prepared to consent to the direct transfer of any part of her American empire to the United States. I do not think that that would make it more difficult to settle the Alabama claims, provided Great Britain is willing to use her influence in favor of independence. That policy carried to a successful result would, in my judgement make the simultaneous settlement of the questions growing out [of] the piracies of the rebel [Alabama] cruisers . . . [more certain]. I believe that a large portion of the British empire on this continent would be glad today to come to the United States, and that Great Britain would be richer & stronger for having them do so.

Davis claimed that British Columbia wanted to join the union; it realized that only through annexation could it get railway connections to the Atlantic seaboard. The rebellion in the Red River Settlement had progressed to the point where it would be foolish for Canada to force Rupert's Land and its rebels into the Dominion. The Maritime

41Davis Papers, Manuscript Division, Library of Congress.
42*Ibid.*

Provinces were dissatisfied with confederation; indeed Newfound-
land and Prince Edward Island had summarily rejected the very
principle of confederation. "Why should not all these provinces be
permitted to become independent as they desire to be even if they are
not allowed to transfer their allegiance to the United States? And
why could not this change be accompanied by a settlement of differences on which we now appear to be too far apart to adjust in any
other way?"

Lampson never replied. Despite the silence that followed the
above correspondence, the State Department remained strangely
optimistic. As late as May the London legation was sure that—"with
tact and caution"—the United States could get both Rupert's Land
and British Columbia. Fish was in complete agreement. He wrote the
legation's secretary, Benjamin Moran: "Our Canadian friends seem to
think that they have adjusted the Red River troubles—*For a time* they
probably have—Existing relations there cannot be permanent—nor even
of long continuance."[43] Such unreasonable optimism could not endure.
On the twenty-seventh Moran informed Davis that, although the
British government would permit the cession of Rupert's Land, public
opinion was decidedly against it. Then he added, in a way that indicated the approach of despair, that if "we could use a little money
on the press here, I think we could create a public sentiment in
favor of a fair settlement of the Alabama Claims which settlement might
give us British Columbia and Red River."[44] In conclusion he said that
he had neither seen Lampson nor heard from him and now doubted
whether anything could be accomplished through the Hudson's Bay
Company.

With the coming of summer, the policy-makers in the State Department knew they had been victimized by their own wishful thinking.
When Moran finally saw Lampson in mid-June, all his doubts were
confirmed. The Hudson's Bay Company had completed the sale of
Rupert's Land; the bargain with Canada was sealed. He now lamely
suggested that Washington turn its attention back to Canada and seek
to manipulate public opinion there to favour annexation. Thus had
diplomacy failed to dislodge Rupert's Land from its Canadian orbit.
However there still remained one last ounce of optimism in the State
Department, and long before diplomacy's failure it had come about
on another tack in its quest for Rupert's Land.

[43]13 May 1870, Letterbook No. 2, p. 443, Fish Papers, Manuscript Division,
Library of Congress.
[44]Davis Papers.

IV

In the spring, when it became known that Canada intended to send a military expedition to Red River, Grant's administration adopted a policy designed to obstruct that course of action. Underlying it was the belief that the odds on the British Northwest's annexation to the United States would grow in proportion to the months of Riel's isolation from Canada. In addition, geography seemed to favour the scheme. Though Canada's easiest access to Red River was through Minnesota, that door was effectively locked by public opinion, and while Hudson Bay offered a second avenue of approach, it would be both precarious and time-consuming. The only feasible route for an expedition was *via* the Great Lakes and overland from Lake Superior, paddling and portaging over the Precambrian Shield. With one vital exception—the American locks at Sault Ste. Marie—this route lay wholly within Canadian territory. But if the United States should ever close the Sault, Canadian transports could not get into Lake Superior and the expedition might be dangerously delayed. As early as November, 1869, Grant's administration tentatively decided that, if the demand were ever made, Canada should not be allowed to send troops through or over American territory. On 12 April 1870, when rumours of an impending military expedition to Red River reached Washington, the earlier decision was reconfirmed. With the full backing of his cabinet, Grant directed "that orders be given . . . to refuse permission to pass the Canal until the question be referred here for further instruction."[45] More than any other man in the cabinet, Fish was responsible for this decision, although he personally believed that Canada would never request permission to use the Sault. For, in all their intimate conversations, Edward Thornton had always denied the possibility.

Friends though Fish and Thornton were, one feels sure that the Englishman got most of the non-spiritual benefits to be derived from that relationship. Only on 14 April, when Canada's plans for a military expedition had nearly reached maturity, did Thornton reveal that troops would be dispatched to Red River in order to—so he claimed—"keep the Indians quiet."[46] However, at the same time, he voiced his doubts about American willingness to let Canadian transports through the Sault; Fish was quick to confirm them, adding that Thornton "had better not ask for" permission. A fortnight later, the British minister

[45]Fish's Diary.   [46]*Ibid.*, 14 and 28 April 1870.

announced that troops had been sent and diplomatically suggested that the United States open the Sault—as Canada had opened the Welland during the Civil War—to vessels "in mercantile or commercial service." He promised that all the troops would get off the vessels and cross overland, on Canadian soil, before re-embarking on the other (Lake Superior) side. Fish was still unconvinced. He told Thornton that the canal would be closed whether troops were on board or not.

Five days later, the State Department instructed the Governor of Michigan to close the Sault. Shortly thereafter, Canada managed to send a "trial" steamer with a "purely mercantile cargo" through the canal, but when the *Chicora* arrived, similarly laden, she was not given clearance and had to turn about and steam back to Canada.[47] Thornton complained bitterly, claiming that the ship had carried no contraband, and re-asserted that the expedition's purpose was wholly peaceful. Fish then tried to bargain, hinting that if both a British and a Canadian amnesty were given the rebels, the canal might be opened. Thornton merely countered that, if the Sault were not opened, the Welland might be closed.

President Grant called (16 May 1870) a special meeting of his cabinet to consider the *Chicora* case. The meeting opened in a jocular way. Grant said "he regarded the refusal to let the vessel go through as unfriendly to England"—and then remarked: "I guess we all feel so too."[48] His sarcasm evoked appreciative laughter from all the cabinet members. But at this point, frivolity came to an end. In the discussion that followed, the cabinet was unanimous in deciding that the Sault should be opened to vessels carrying provisions, lest Canada retaliate by closing the Welland to American shipping. However the opening was made contingent upon a British promise of amnesty to Riel and his rebellious cohorts, before Canada actually assumed Rupert's Land.[49]

The *Chicora* steamed uneventfully through the locks, carrying only general supplies and provisions. The actual implements of war were

[47]Anon. [Col. Garnet Wolseley] "Narrative of the Red River Expedition," *Blackwood's Edinburgh Magazine*, CIX (Jan., 1871), 48.

[48]Davis to Fish, 16 May 1870, Davis Papers.

[49]In response, Thornton agreed that the *Chicora* would carry an "ordinary commercial cargo and no war stores." He also stated that all difficulties between the *métis* and Canada had been "amicably arranged" and that the troops were being sent to Red River only to maintain order and insure the harmonious establishment of the new government. Upon reception of a note from Thornton, containing the above information—but no promise of an imperial amnesty—the State Department instructed the Governor of Michigan to let the *Chicora* pass through the Sault. See R. S. Chew to Fish, 17 May 1870, Fish Papers.

put ashore, portaged across the narrow neck of Canadian soil, and re-shipped on the Lake Superior side of the Sault. From the moment of initial failure to final success, the ship had not been delayed more than a fortnight. Grant's obstructionism had never jeopardized Canada's military expedition. In fact, the only tangible result of his policy had been to revitalize Canada's anti-American sentiment. Moreover the condition of amnesty which had been attached to the canal's use proved to be of greater benefit to Ottawa than to Washington. For Thornton's diplomatic half-promises of a forthcoming imperial amnesty prevented the United States from interfering with the military expedition after it had passed through the Sault.

Not till mid-September, almost a month after British soldiers had marched into Fort Garry, did Thornton admit that Riel would not receive an amnesty. By then, Thornton could triumphantly tell Fish that British Columbia was "nearly unanimous for annexation to the Dominion, & that the feeling through Canada, . . . [was] entirely opposed to annexation & that Independence . . . [meant] Annexation, they . . . [were] one and the same thing."[50] And thus in a quiet, friendly conversation, he damaged, if he did not destroy, all Fish's dreams of a territorial adjustment of the *Alabama* claims. "I do not find much in the tone and style of . . . [Thornton's] conversation today," reflected the American in his diary, "to encourage the idea either of a settlement of the Alabama question or the Canadian or the Fisheries question. . . ."

The United States had failed in its quest for Rupert's Land. Within the Red River Settlement the intrigues of Malmros and the American party had borne nothing but bitter fruit. Minnesota's expansionists had not fared much better. At best, they managed to reinforce an annexationist policy in the State Department, but that policy had then been muffled in soft, diplomatic garments by an artless President and a moralistic Secretary of State. For success, Manifest Destiny demands as its maker a disingenuous man whose actions are not governed by moral precepts. Grant's hands-off, short-of-war policy was predestined to fail. But even if James K. Polk had been in the White House, no mere sleight of the presidential hand could have changed Rupert's Land into another Oregon. For there was not and there never had been a strong annexationist sentiment in the Red River Settlement. Pro-Americanism, such as it was, enjoyed only a fleeting existence in 1869–70, before Riel's devotion to the Crown and Sir John A. Macdonald's political powers knocked it on the head.

[50]Fish's Diary, 18 Sept. 1870.

Active intervention by the United States would probably have led to war—and a war involving Great Britain as well as Canada. Despite President Grant's intense dislike of Britain, his belligerence was always tempered by a realistic awareness of America's massive Civil War debts.[51] Despite great military strength and a navy whose iron-clad warships dominated the entire western hemisphere "from Buenos Ayres to Quebec,"[52] he and his administration never considered the possibility of fighting to get any part of British North America. Indeed, with the exception of the State of Minnesota, it seems evident that the Midwest, the section that would have benefited most from the annexation of Rupert's Land, was more interested in achieving reciprocity with Canada than in annexing any part of the Northwest.

None the less, the Riel Rebellion was—as Joseph Wheelock so aptly termed it—"a trump card in the hands of American diplomacy . . . by which, if rightly played, every vestige of British power may be swept from the Western half of the continent." Had Canada been unable to hold Rupert's Land, she would probably have lost British Columbia too; and then all her dreams of a sea-to-sea nationhood would have vanished. But if Wheelock remembered his cards, he forgot his players. In the game for the British Northwest, the wily Canadian premier, John A. Macdonald, outdealt and outplayed his American opponents.

V

Sir John was a superb politician and statesman whose skills were graphically demonstrated in his dealing with Louis Riel. At first, he had not taken the uprising too seriously, but once aware of the situation, he moved quickly to accommodate the *métis* and bring them peacefully into the Dominion.

He selected Donald A. Smith, then a chief factor in charge of the Company's Montreal District, to "carry the olive branch" to Red River. Smith was given broad, discretionary powers; and he made the most of them, for he was clever, quite capable of manipulating men in a delightfully vague but effectual way. Long after he had left Red River and even after Manitoba had been annexed, the memoirs of the *métis* leaders reveal that they were still not exactly sure how the

[51]See *ibid.*, 22 March 1870.
[52]"Our Naval Defences: Where are We?" *Blackwood's*, X (Jan., 1867), 10–11. Cf. "The American Navy in the late War," *Edinburgh Review*, CXXIV (July, 1866), 94–116.

man had succeeded in his mission. As one of them later recalled, "Donald Smith was not only an old trickster, he was also a Hudson's Bay Company man. . . ."[53] It was a combination that worked wonders. With prestige, a full purse, and a persuasive tongue, Smith achieved his fondest hopes: he convinced the people of Red River that they ought "to appoint delegates . . . to give expression to their views, and to treat for the transfer of the territory to Canada."[54]

If Smith carried the "olive branch" to Red River, it was Bishop Taché who was chiefly responsible for bearing it back to Ottawa. Macdonald had recalled the bishop from the Ecumenical Conference in Rome and sent him to Red River as a messenger from his ministry in order to reassure the people that Canada intended "to grant . . . [them] the same free institutions which they themselves enjoy."[55] Taché was the best ambassador that Macdonald could have sent and his influence was felt almost immediately. He spoke from the pulpit; he conversed privately with individuals, French and English alike; and he addressed the Provisional Government. To all men, his message was one of goodwill. To them and to Red River, his presence was a blessing. For he persuaded the settlement's wavering delegates to put their fears aside and go to Ottawa with their list of rights.

For his part, Sir John had never doubted that he could "make satisfactory arrangements" with any delegates sent from the Northwest.[56] Though he rejected some of Riel's terms and modified others, he accepted most and swiftly translated them into statute form. The result was the Manitoba Act, which was introduced on 3 May and became law nine days later. Final arrangements for installing the new province were delayed when Macdonald was suddenly and most seriously taken ill. However his lieutenant, Sir George-Etienne Cartier, finished the negotiations without faltering. The £300,000 was handed over to the Hudson's Bay Company, and by order in council Great Britain transferred Rupert's Land and the Northwest Territory to Canada. To prevent any power vacuum between the transfer (scheduled for 15 July) and Canada's actual assumption of the Northwest, the Hudson's Bay Company appointed Canada's Governor General as

[53]Memoirs of Louis Schmidt, Document XV, in Morton, ed., *Begg's Journal and Other Papers*, p. 469.

[54]Smith to Macdonald, 18 Jan. 1870, Sir Joseph Pope, ed., *Correspondence of Sir John A. Macdonald* (Toronto [c. 1921]), p. 120.

[55]Macdonald to Taché, 16 Feb. 1870, Macdonald Papers, P.A.C.

[56]Macdonald to Smith, 21 Jan. 1870, in Pope, ed., *Correspondence of Macdonald*, pp. 122–3.

Governor of Rupert's Land, and Canada then temporarily commissioned him as Lieutenant Governor of Manitoba.

By the time the temporary commission expired in mid-August, Ottawa hoped that a "permanent" lieutenant governor would be seated in Fort Garry. The man selected for the post was Adams G. Archibald, an excellent choice. He was a much more kindly, cordial, and conciliatory man than his predecessor. He was also a neutral, French-speaking Nova Scotian; there was every reason to believe he would please the people of Manitoba.

For all Archibald's charms, it would have been foolish to send him to Red River without a military force to clear the way—it was such a small premium to pay for success. Furthermore Macdonald dared not trust Riel. He could not even accept the Red River delegation as evidence of the man's good faith, suspecting that he might be stalling "until the approach of Summer enables him to get material support from the United States."[57] And certainly Washington's expansionist climate of opinion could not be ignored. Therefore Macdonald determined upon an expedition long before Riel's delegation had reached Ottawa. His decision to man it with British regulars as well as Canadian militia was a stroke of genius. The Queen's soldiers would overawe the *métis* much as they had done before, and—as Macdonald revealed to an intimate friend—"the sending of some of Her Majesty's troops there will show the United States Government and people that England is resolved not to abandon her Colonies, or is indifferent to the future of the Great West."[58] As commanding officer, Macdonald chose Colonel Garnet J. Wolseley, another of those Anglo-Irish soldiers who have brought honour to "West Britain" and glory to the empire. Of all the colonel's talents, none was more brilliantly displayed than that of managing an army. Only someone like him, with the experience of canoeing in the Canadian bush, could have unified this mixed force and led it from Port Arthur to Fort Garry—600 miles through the wilderness—without injuring a single man.

Few military expeditions in North America have ever matched

[57]Macdonald to Rose, 11 March 1870, Macdonald Papers.
[58]Macdonald to Rose, 26 Jan. 1870. Quoted in C. P. Stacey, *Canada and the British Army 1846–1871* (London, 1936), 234. Macdonald was always aware of Hamilton Fish's desire to secure Canada's independence from Great Britain and its eventual annexation to the United States. That particular American dream would not vanish till the Treaty of Washington, 1871—if then. Evidence to illustrate Fish's misguided expansionism is scattered throughout the Fish and Davis Papers in the Manuscript Collection of the Library of Congress.

Wolseley's. Like a giant sea serpent, it wound westward from Lake Superior, struggling across Lake of the Woods, shooting the wild waters of the Winnipeg River—where "the pace . . . [was] too quick to admit of self-examination"[59]—and still making about fifteen miles a day. On 23 August, barely three weeks after the last boat's launching, Wolseley's men rowed around Lake Winnipeg's southern shore and ascended the Red River. As they drew near the Stone Fort, "the people turned out from every house on both banks—the men cheered, the women waved handkerchiefs, and the bells of the churches . . . were rung. . . ."[60] That night, Wolseley made his last camp just six miles below Fort Garry and looked forward to the morning when he could advance "upon the Fort in all the pride, pomp, and circumstances of war" and rid the world of that "cowardly murderer," Louis Riel.[61] But when Wolseley and the 60th Rifles marched up to the fort, they found the gates open and no rebels within. Canada and the colonel entered the front of Fort Garry almost as Riel and the last of his supporters galloped out the rear; and thus the expedition had to settle for ceremony instead of bloodshed. "The Union Jack was . . . hoisted over the Fort [,] a Royal Salute fired and three cheers given for the Queen which were quickly caught up and heartily repeated by numbers of the inhabitants who had followed the troops from the village."[62]

Now that the rebellion had collapsed, the old order in Rupert's Land changed quickly and forever. Wolseley handed over all governmental responsibilities to Donald A. Smith, and he, in turn, passed them hurriedly on to Archibald shortly after the latter's arrival in the settlement on 2 September. So swiftly did Wolseley complete his mission that the last of his regulars departed on the next day. He himself resigned his command into the hands of the senior officer of the Canadian militia, left Red River on the tenth, and was on board a vessel in Montreal harbour by the end of the month. By 1 October, he was bound for Britain and the much-deserved honour of Knight Commander of the Most Distinguished Order of St. Michael and St. George.

By annexing the Northwest, Sir John A. Macdonald made two of

[59]Field-Marshal Viscount Wolseley, *The Story of a Soldier's Life* (2 vols., Westminster, 1903), II, 212.

[60][Wolseley], "Narrative of the Red River Expedition," *Blackwood's Edinburgh Magazine*, CIX (Feb., 1871), 174.

[61]Sir George Arthur, ed., *The Letters of Lord and Lady Wolseley, 1870–1911* (London, 1923), pp. 5–6.

[62]Wolseley to Lindsay, Fort Garry, 24 Aug. 1870, enclosed in William Earle to the Military Secretary of the Governor-General, 9 Sept. 1870, Record Group 9, Red River Expedition, Series A3, P.A.C. Earle was Lindsay's military secretary.

the most momentous decisions in the history of Canadian-American relations. He assured Canada of its destiny as a continental nation, and he damped down the expansionist fires in Minnesota and elsewhere in the United States.

When Riel memorialized President Grant in October, 1870, to investigate certain injustices allegedly dealt out to him and his people, he made it very clear that he now wanted the Northwest to be independent of Canada and that he looked forward to its eventual absorption within the United States. But there was no response from Washington. In answering a sympathetic letter upon the subject by James W. Taylor, Senator Ramsey could only apologize for his tardy reply. But, said he, "there is absolutely no interest at all here just now in Red River matters—at least in their politics & it would be entirely *mal appropos* to introduce these remarks without some little excuse or provocation, if some such offers I will yet call the attention of the *Senate* to the matter."[63] No excuse ever presented itself; and as soon as the Treaty of Washington had been signed in the spring of 1871, cleaning the slate of Anglo-Canadian-American ills, "Saskatchewan" Taylor and his expansionist schemes were no longer of interest to the Grant administration.[64] By then, it should have been apparent even to the most expansionist-minded Minnesotan that his state's quest for the British Northwest had reached the end of the line.

It had been a long quest, marked by many minor victories along the way. Norman W. Kittson had ended Red River's economic isolation by providing a market for the free traders and thereby relieving them from the overlordship of the Hudson's Bay Company. In the process, he and his fellow Americans had converted the primitive Red River trails into an intricate transportation system built upon stage lines, steamboats, and railroads; and though it was not without faults, almost straightway, it outmoded the ancient system of the Hudson's Bay Company. Indeed, for a moment, it seemed as if the Minnesota route would displace the Bay just as the Bay itself had thrust aside

[63][winter, 1870–71], Taylor Papers.

[64]For Taylor, there were to be no honours at the nation's capital. Instead, the man to whom the Assistant Secretary of State referred in the winter of 1870–71 as "the best man we have got in all the Canadian provinces," was called a "blunderhead" by the Secretary himself, barely two and a half years later. And when Taylor foolishly sought permission from the State Department in 1874 to report to Ottawa upon the question of amnesty for Louis Riel, the Assistant Secretary bluntly and finally told him that Washington "didn't care a continental . . . about Riel which shut him up." Ramsey to Taylor [winter, 1870–71], Taylor Papers; Fish to Davis, I Aug. 1873, Fish Papers; and Davis to Fish, 4 April 1874, *ibid.*

the old river-and-lake line of the Nor'Westers. For a moment, it was the standard and accepted highway into the Northwest, conveying people, trade goods, and mail. When the Royal Canadian Rifles were stationed at Fort Garry, 1857–61, their lieutenant colonel in Montreal issued the following memorandum: "Any letter going to *Pembina* is certain to come on to Fort Garry. The words via *St. Paul* & *Pembina*, it appears are necessary or letters, as many have done, take a very long time to reach their destination."[65] Then to underscore his meaning, he added: "The words 'Red River Settlement & Hudson's Bay Territory' I am informed are superfluous and incumber the address."

Concomitant with the rise and development of the Minnesota route had come an inevitable growth and extension of the north-south trade. The freight of the 'forties—simple goods to suit the requirements of the fur trade—was changed; more numerous and sophisticated cargoes followed until it seemed as if most of Red River's imports came either *via* or from St. Paul. Together with the growth of trade and transportation were to be seen the harbingers of the American civilization to come: speculators frenetically staking out choice townsites; lonely frontiersmen squatting down in Indian country; federal agents bargaining with the Indians for the last of the aboriginal land within the state; and finally the surveyors platting cessions for future sale at various government land offices. The activities of the land office were geared to a real need; settlers poured into the state during the 'fifties and the post-war period, pushed up the Mississippi River and out along the valley of the Sauk, to strike the Red and then to extend their homesteads down the valley. But long before the march of American civilization had reached the 49th parallel, the British Northwest had been consigned to Canada and all Minnesota's expansionist dreams had vanished.

Why had the state failed to realize the destiny that so many of its prophets had forecast? In the first place, its frontier thrust had been repeatedly checked. The Panic of 1857 severely blunted its edge. The Sioux and Civil wars, acting in concert, 1861–65, held back, even retarded Minnesota's northwestward movement by draining off many settlers and terrorizing others. And in the second place, the Hudson's Bay Company itself acted as a brake. When it brought troops to Fort Garry in 1846–48 and again in 1857–61, it thwarted the free trade upon which the American traders depended and temporarily regained its control over trade and government in the Red River Settlement.

[65]Memorandum of correct address to Red River, Montreal, 17 April 1858, Military Series C, Vol. 364, p. 128.

Furthermore, when it began to use the Minnesota route in 1858, it turned the American revolution in transportation to its own advantage and beat Kittson and the other American traders at their own game. In fact, maturation of the Minnesota route probably owed more to the contributions of the Hudson's Bay Company than to any other agency. By protecting itself, its property, and its trade, the Company helped preserve the Northwest for Canada.

There can also be little doubt that Canada lent greater and more meaningful support to its expansionists than did the United States. Federal aid given Minnesota's promoters was frequently late, often niggardly. Insufficient grants were given to various transportation schemes; plans to acquire the Red River Valley from the Indians were frustrated until late in the day; and military aid, whether rendered by dispatching expeditions or establishing posts, was either given reluctantly or without purpose. As a rule of history, military posts have played a significant role in furthering the American frontier; there was none planted in the Red River Valley until Fort Abercrombie was ineffectually located at its base and no "permanent" fort established at its head (Pembina) until 1870. In contrast, as soon as confederation had been achieved, Canada moved energetically and skilfully to secure the Northwest. Moreover, hers was the purposeful, moralist, and aggressive position; and once the Riel Rebellion had occurred, Washington assumed only a defensive attitude, conscious of the weakness of her moral position, unwilling to risk war by intervention, and contenting herself by acting as a nuisance in such matters as closing the Sault Ste. Marie to the *Chicora*.

Not the least of the determinant factors in the failure of Minnesota's quest for the Northwest was the undoubted preference of its people to be confederated with Canada rather than be annexed to the United States. Canada could afford to blunder in her dealings with the inhabitants of the Northwest. This was British territory, legally acquired; and after its people had discovered that Ottawa would meet their wishes, they willingly entered the Dominion.

Once the Northwest was safely installed, most Minnesotans seem to have accepted the fact. Their spirit, if still materialist, changed from militant expansionism to co-operative exploitation. A new era was at hand, exemplified by the business careers of Kittson, James J. Hill, Donald A. Smith, and George Stephen of the Bank of Montreal. In 1878, these four, acting as a Canadian-American syndicate, bought the St. Paul and Pacific, renamed it the St. Paul, Minneapolis and Manitoba Railway, and soon ran it all the way to Winnipeg. In the next decade, they used their skills, capital, and influence to construct the Canadian Pacific Railroad, a swift and sure means of internal communication welding Canada's provinces into a sea-to-sea nation. By then, no man in North America would have dreamed of addressing a letter to Red River or Winnipeg with "the words via *St. Paul & Pembina.*"

Index

300 *Index*

59–71, 72, 123, 292; costs of expeditions to Northwest, 68–69, 127, 237; expedition to Northwest (1857–61), 112, 121, 124, 125, 127; expedition of, requested (1862), 173–74, 177–79, 237; expedition of, requested (1866), 242; expedition (1870), 259–61, 263, 274–78, 289

Colonial Office, 129, 174, 251; and troops for Red River, 62, 66, 70, 72n, 128

Foreign Office, 40, 122, 282

House of Commons, Select Committee on the Hudson's Bay Company (1857), 129–30, 130–32, 221–24, 226, 228, 229, 238

War Office, 66, 122, 123, 127, 128

Great Lakes, 27, 124, 186, 275; as access route, 3, 165, 203, 211, 284

Great Northern Railroad, 98n

Grey, Sir Henry George, third Earl Grey, 69, 70, 71

Groseilliers, Médard Chouart, sieur des. *See* Chouart, Médard

HALE, SENATOR JOHN, 190

Half-breed. *See Métis*

Hamelin, Salomon, 125n

Hatch, Major Edwin A. C., 175–80

Hatch, Israel T., 184, 185

Hayes River, 93

Henry, Professor Joseph, 131–32

Hill, James J., 153, 199, 293

Hind, Professor Henry Yule, 154, 229–31, 253

House of Representatives, United States. *See* United States

Howard, Senator Jacob, 182n, 278

Howe, Joseph, 201, 228

Howe, Senator Timothy O., 191n, 278

Hudson Bay, 3, 4, 94, 105, 115, 173, 228

Hudson's Bay Company, 46, 59, 106, 118, 121, 126, 142, 145, 146, 173, 181, 199, 229, 252; charter, 3, 56, 58, 61, 73, 74, 75, 86, 120–21, 190, 211; and North West Company, 4, 5, 6, 8, 93, 220; and Selkirk grant, 5, 25; and St. Lawrence access route, 6, 220; trading monopoly of, 8, 12, 13, 30, 54, 60, 73, 120, 126, 129, 137, 215, 220, 291; policy in Northwest, 9, 10, 21, 62, 122, 128,

232–33, 236–40, 243–45, 246–48, 249; and Clarke-Bulger rivalry, 12–13; stores in Red River, 14, 16, 86, 91, 127, 140, 146; *versus* free traders, 17, 38, 40, 48, 50–52, 54, 58, 71, 72–77, 81–83, 85, 86, 87–92, 100, 220, 293; and Minnesota route, 28, 30, 137, 146, 152, 158, 164, 198, 203, 292–93; at Pembina, 31–33, 63n, 72, 78, 104; *versus* Renville, 31, 35; *versus* Columbia Fur Company, 33, 36; profits, 36, 41, 80, 86, 91, 92, 120, 138; licensing, 36, 37–38; and Aitkin, 39, 43; *versus* American Fur Company, 42, 44; London headquarters, 43, 76, 90, 145, 146, 147, 235, 236, 237, 239, 245, 246–47, 258, 281; and shipping, 54, 142–43, 145; currency, 54, 56, 167, 237; and Sioux, 63n, 107, 161, 162–63, 172–75, 177, 180; and defence of Rupert's Land, 67, 69, 70, 71, 120–21, 121–22, 126, 127–28, 292; and Sayer, 74, 75, 76; employees, 85, 89, 90, 229, 281, 287, 288; districts, 87–88, 236, 287; transportation dilemma, 91, 102, 140, 165; and transportation, 93–95, 103; brigades, 94, 95, 102, 103, 142, 165, 267; and Minnesota, 104, 118, 123, 128, 134, 135, 147; and *métis*, 120, 125, 126; and Canadian party in Red River, 124, 235–40; licence, 129–30; and Burbanks, 139, 146–48, 163–64, 167; and *Anson Northup*, 144–45; Kittson joins, 153; and Wisconsin route, 165–66; and sale of Rupert's Land, 180, 217, 218, 221, 223–26, 228, 233, 248, 251, 281, 283, 288; and reciprocity, 184, 190; and United States manifest destiny, 211, 263–64, 266–67, 269n, 277, 282; and Taylor, 217, 218; and Select Committee of 1857, 221; land policy, 223, 230–31; and North-West Transportation Company, 227–28; and Canadian survey (1858), 229–30, 250, 251; and *Nor'-Wester*, 233, 235, 237, 238, 240; and Dawson road, 249, 255; and Riel, 266n, 275; and *New Nation*, 266; archives, 282